A Very Social Time

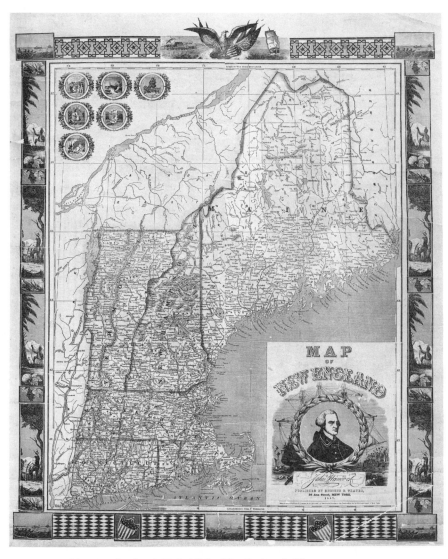

New England, 1847. Published by Ensign & Thayer.
Courtesy of the Harvard Map Collection, Harvard University,
Cambridge, Massachusetts.

A Very Social Time

Crafting Community in
Antebellum New England

Karen V. Hansen

UNIVERSITY OF CALIFORNIA PRESS
Berkeley · Los Angeles · London

University of California Press
Berkeley and Los Angeles, California

University of California Press, Ltd.
London, England

Library of Congress Cataloging-in-Publication Data

Hansen, Karen V.
  A very social time : crafting community in antebellum New England / Karen V.
Hansen.
      p.   cm.
  Includes bibliographical references and index.
  ISBN 0-520-08474-8 (alk. paper)
  1. New England—Social life and customs.   2. Women—New England—History—
19th century.   I. Title.
F8.H34   1994
974.04—dc20   93-39611
                                                                          CIP

Printed in the United States of America
9 8 7 6 5 4 3 2 1

Passages from Karen V. Hansen, " 'Helped Put In a Quilt': Male Intimacy and Men's
Work in Nineteenth-Century New England," *Gender & Society* 3, no. 3 (September
1989): 334–54; and from Karen V. Hansen, " 'Our Eyes Behold Each Other':
Masculinity and Intimate Friendship in Antebellum New England," in *Men's
Friendships*, edited by Peter Nardi (Newbury Park, Calif.: Sage, 1992), reprinted by
permission of Sage Publications.

Material from Karen V. Hansen, "The Power of Talk in Antebellum New England,"
Agricultural History 67, no. 2 (Spring 1993): 43–63, is used by permission.

The engraving of Bethany Veney from *Collected Black Women's Narratives* (New York:
Oxford University Press, 1988) is reprinted by permission.

The photograph of Harriet A. Jacobs from *Incidents in the Life of a Slave Girl, Written
by Herself*, by Harriet A. Jacobs, edited by Jean Fagan Yellin (Cambridge, Mass.:
Harvard University Press, copyright 1987 by the President and Fellows of Harvard
College), is reprinted by permission of the publisher and owner of the photograph.

The photograph of Isaac Mason from *Life of Isaac Mason as a Slave* (Coral Gables,
Fla.: Mnemosyne Publishing, 1969) is used by permission.

For Andrew

Contents

Illustrations and Tables

MAP

TABLES

Acknowledgments

This book's cover illustration, the "Pic Nick" at Camden, Maine, captures several of the many compelling dimensions of life in antebellum New England. It is bursting with people of all ages and both genders who are celebrating, entertaining, teasing, courting, eating, and drinking. Like the diaries, letters, and autobiographies of working people that contain the rich material upon which this book is based, it depicts an everyday life that contains surprises and merriment as well as hardship and drudgery. In much the same way that these archival materials offer glimpses and suggest possibilities of a different way of life, the painting overflows with personalities and faces—blending and clashing, illuminating and obscuring, affirming and transforming. One is drawn in, irresistibly, as curious about what is absent as what is revealed, and eager for more.

The eloquent voices and intriguing faces of these people and the challenge of unraveling their mysteries moved me to write this book. The ways that working people thought, their critiques of their society and culture, and the dignity with which they lived their lives astounded me, challenged my sociological and theoretical training, and offered a new perspective on American history.

The pages between these bindings reflect the collective endeavors of many people who have supported and assisted me in my research and writing over the past several years. Cameron Macdonald provided indispensable research assistance by scouring the archives for additional diaries of working women and documents about African Americans in antebellum New England. She pursued census data and genealogical information like a true historical detective and helped to transform the project into a shared rather than solitary endeavor. Christianna Nelson, my Junior Partner in the innovative Radcliffe Research Partnership Program, constructed her first footnotes working on this project and a year later has become an amiable expert on the *Chicago Manual of Style*. Julie Goldsmith turned Philadelphia upside down to discover what she could about Addie Brown and the circumstances of her death.

Some of my friends and colleagues willingly took on the task of reading the manuscript in its virtual entirety. My heartfelt thanks go to the following people for providing critical feedback: Paula Aymer, Carol Brown, Andrew Bundy, McGeorge Bundy, Mary Anne Clawson, Anita Garey, Susan Ostrander, JoAnne Preston, Naomi Schneider, Carmen Sirianni, and Andrea Walsh. Many others brought their clear thinking and invaluable expertise to bear on individual chapters: Sarah Allen, Egon Bittner, Marion Abbott Bundy, Stephen Bundy, John Corrigan, Alice Friedman, Gila Hayim, Arlie Hochschild, Cameron Macdonald, Calvin Morrill, Christianna Nelson, Mary Odem, Nancy Grey Osterud, Katy Park, Shula Reinharz, Richie Salmi, Susan Sibbet, Kate Stearns, Jeff Weintraub, Lisa Wilson, and Marcia Yudkin. I want to extend a special thanks to the able editors at the University of California Press who skillfully guided this manuscript through its various transformations: Dore Brown, Naomi Schneider, and Ellen Stein.

Several institutions provided generous financial support that enabled me to finish the book. The Andrew W. Mellon Faculty Fellowship in the Humanities at Harvard University financed a year's leave from teaching and offered a congenial environment for exchanging ideas as well as movie tips. I spent my unforgettable year in the stimulating company of sister fellows at the Bunting Institute at Radcliffe College, a creative haven for women where constructive feedback and impassioned support could be assumed. The supportive environment of the Biography, Culture, and History study group at the Bunting spurred intellectual leaps and spiritual bounds. A grant from the Presidential Discretionary Fund for Research at Radcliffe College enabled me to hire a research assistant while at the Bunting. I also received assistance in the form of a summer stipend from the National Endowment for the Humanities, and a Mazer Grant for Faculty Research in the Humanities, Arts and Social Sciences from Brandeis University. These resources would not have been so accessible were it not for the staunch support of Arlie Hochschild, George Ross, Mary Ryan, Neil Smelser, and Ronald Zboray.

The images and the primary documents quoted at length in the text come from the following archives, which have generously granted me permission to publish: the American Antiquarian Society, the Beverly Historical Society and Museum, the Boston Public Library, the Connecticut Historical Society, the Connecticut State Library, the Historical Society of Cheshire County in Keene, N.H., the James Duncan Phillips Library at the Peabody & Essex Museum, the Lynn Historical Society, the Museum of American Textile History, the Museum of Fine Arts in Boston, the Massachusetts Historical Society, the New Hampshire Historical Society, the New Hampshire State Archives, the Old Sturbridge Village Library, the Peabody Historical Society, the Pocumtuck Valley Memorial Association Library, the Schlesinger Library at Radcliffe College, the Society for the Preservation of New England Antiquities, the Sophia Smith Collection at Smith College Library, and the Vermont Historical Society. The New England Historic Genealogical Society has proven fertile ground for fundamental but otherwise elusive information about all of my ordinary yet remarkable subjects. The staffs of these archives have been extremely helpful in locating documents and researching the backgrounds of individual subjects. I especially want to thank Barbara Doucette at the Peabody Historical Society, who found invaluable fragments about Martha Osborne Barrett's life and unearthed the only known surviving photograph of her.

JoAnne Preston has beneficently shared her remarkable private collection of letters with me in an act of true collegiality and sisterhood. Both she and Alice Friedman dug through their tintypes and daguerreotypes to lend me visual images of working people, which add immeasurably to the book.

I have been sustained throughout the process of researching and writing the book by the humor and good will of the staff at Brandeis University, in particular Judy Hanley, who resourcefully finds ways to make the bureaucracy work. Sarah Allen and Kate Moriarty have been faithful companions to and caretakers of Benjamin Hansen-Bundy, helping him cheerfully write his own books when I had to work. Luckily, Benjy kept a hefty supply of "poison that makes you play," so I was regularly liberated from the everyday social life of antebellum New England and catapulted into the fantasy world of pirates and knights. Playing has also been part of the process of regeneration with my life partner, Andrew Bundy. His nurturance, generosity of spirit, and commitment to creating a better world for children have sustained and inspired me, in countless ways making this project possible.

Author's Note

To facilitate interpreting the written words of the subjects, I have modernized the capitalization and punctuation of excerpts from diaries and letters. The spelling, however, has been left as it appears in the original documents. Where the subjects' handwriting is illegible, or nearly so, I present my best guess as to the text; such guesses are enclosed in brackets.

Map 1. Primary residences of subjects.

CHAPTER ONE

Making the Social Central

An Introduction

In the autumn of 1851, farmer Elizabeth Metcalf participated in a neighborhood quilting party held to help prepare her friends Lizzie and Frank for their upcoming wedding. "We had a very social time," she wrote in a letter to her mother-in-law, Chloe Metcalf, invoking a consuming dimension of her life and the lives of her contemporaries. In their letters, journals, and family records, antebellum working men and women speak of an intricate web of social exchange and interaction, a *social* sphere of life that has been largely ignored in studies of New England society. Historians and sociologists debate the roles of the "public" and the "private" spheres in structuring antebellum society; such a focus loses sight of the richness and depth of the social dimension. This social sphere, which working people so elaborately detail in their narratives, provided a meeting ground for men and women that enabled them to mingle with greater equality of circumstance and to act with greater freedom than in either their public or private worlds. These vital accounts not only challenge the way contemporary scholars frame social structure but also call into question the general acceptance of a broad, dominant middle-class culture and the supposition that nineteenth-century women led lives entirely separate from men.[1]

When we test the public/private frame's ability to account for the events and preoccupations in the lives of working people, we quickly recognize the need to add the social sphere. In the process, we rethink the meaning and importance of the other spheres and their relationship to one another. Many activities previously ignored become visible and

1

legitimate objects of study. Incorporating the social sphere into an overarching framework of nineteenth-century society requires us to acknowledge that distinct, socially sanctioned rules governed behavior within a context of known people—a neighborhood, a village, a domestic network—in contrast to the laws of an organized state, or the customs of an intimate household of people related by blood or marriage. Like the public and private, the idea of the social is a powerful one that illuminates the everyday lives of working people, and invites questions about the ways that men and women exercise power, authority, and control. If we mark social relations as distinct from those of the market, the state, and the family, we bring them to center stage.

First-person accounts by Elizabeth Metcalf and dozens of others—European American and African American—afford us a rare opportunity to consider what working people actually thought and did. A great deal of scholarship on the nineteenth-century United States relies on prescriptive literature—the advice of ministers, social reformers, and authors of self-help books much like those which flood the modern American marketplace. In contrast, this book turns to the very people to whom these numerous messages about proper behavior and moral standards were addressed.

To uncover an important and largely untapped history, this book investigates the first-person narratives—in the form of diaries, letters, and autobiographies—of textile workers, sailors, domestic servants, day laborers, and other working people of New England. These documents dismantle the mythology produced by advice literature and middle-class accounts and uniquely offer a view of everyday life that helps to fill a gaping hole in American history and sociology. In language that differed from that of the middle class—marked by greater directness in addressing others, frequent grammatical idiosyncracies, and a terse style—the personal writings of these working people articulate a rich and complex set of stories and experiences in considerable detail, frequently challenging traditional analyses of their experience. Some of the diarists themselves understood how rare and potentially illuminating a description of the world from their vantage point might be. In 1820, Minerva Mayo, a seventeen-year-old woman living in the village of Orange, Massachusetts, wrote:

> My writings will not be very correspondent, as it is but seldom that I am favoured with the privileges of writing. Was I a minister, or some rich gentleman's daughter, and had nothing to do but [write], doubtless I could write more sensibly and correct. But as all who have hitherto wrote are

mostly of such honoured and learned persons, perhaps it will be something new. To see the writings of one who has but little or no learning, and who writes altogether by chance.[2]

In searching for the history that eluded historians with a middle-class focus, I have sought those people who had to work for a living, those who did not enjoy the leisure and learning that Minerva Mayo ascribes to privileged Americans. Although none of my subjects were wealthy, their complex personal circumstances cannot be readily adapted into traditional categories of class. They constitute an analytically distinct group, one which created a cultural practice that gets lost in the broad formulations of the "middling classes" or the narrow definitions of the working class. The documents of this research—diaries of 56 men and women, 20 collections of letters, and 19 autobiographies—were written by the likes of shoe-binders, farmers, seamstresses, and carpenters— approximately 170 individuals in all (see Appendix A). Most toiled at some kind of manual labor, skilled or unskilled, and none had attended college. They lived in households that owned an average of $978 worth of real estate and personal property in 1850. By no stretch of the imagination can they be characterized as professionals or elites. As one anonymous author put it, "the winds of circumstance" buffeted them about, leaving them "stranded on the shore of disappointment." These subjects almost certainly do not represent the New England working population as a whole, but at a minimum their narratives clearly illustrate a broad range of life experiences and cultural practices. The subjects and their stories give us a sense of what was *possible*. And, as the reader will soon see, they speak with extraordinary power.[3]

Contemporary scholars have viewed working people and antebellum U.S. history largely through the prism of the public and private spheres. Although some women's historians have challenged the framework, the public/private and their gender associations—male and female—stand as the dominant paradigm against which competing perspectives must still be compared.

Early in my investigation, I was struck by the glaring inaccuracy of the idea that women occupied the private sphere and men the public. "Public" was far too vague and inclusive, and "private" was too narrow and stultifying. How could these households, the hubs of community activity, come to be defined as private? Antebellum working women dashed about daily in the city and on the farm, unself-consciously disregarding the boundaries set by the household structure or by middle-class cultural standards. They visited neighbors, attended lectures, joined temperance and anti-slavery movements, and generally behaved in a manner that could hardly be characterized as private. Moreover, men did not exempt themselves from so-called private sphere activities such as child care and household work.

Scrutiny of everyday life can transform a traditional conception of the structure of society and debunk assumptions about gender roles. A single entry from Martha Barrett's diary challenges the orthodox perspective. Like Minerva Mayo, Martha (see Figure 1), a one-time machine-shop worker and later a millinery clerk, lamented her limited material resources: "Oh! The want of means! How it does cramp and crush one." On Saturday, the eighth of January, 1853, Martha logged her busy day in her diary:

> To-day the Quarterly Meeting of the Essex Co. Anti-Slavery Society commenced . . . I have not been. We have had a great many callers today. Before I had cleared away the dinner dishes, Pease Page called. Before she left, Cousin Hannah Grant came, before she went, Sophia [Robts] and little Mary. While chatting with the latter, a rap on the front door. Opened it, and who should be there but our friend Parker Pillsbury. I was delighted to see him. He made but a short call however. Was on his way to the evening meeting. At the usual time commenced getting supper. Was interrupted by a call from Lucy A.C. Went again to my work but soon heard Mother calling me . . .

Martha Barrett was an ordinary woman, living and working in the small town of South Danvers (now Peabody), Massachusetts, remarkable mainly in that she kept a diary for thirty-one years, writing in it at least weekly. She joined political movements but did not rise to positions of leadership. She attended lectures but did not give them. She never married; she lived with her mother, a widow of limited means, and had to support herself. Martha Barrett matters to us precisely because of her ordinariness and because the life she diligently recorded gives us a window into another century and the roots of modern American culture. Indeed, this seemingly inconsequential fragment of Martha Barrett's diary deeply challenges the way recent social theorists, political thinkers, and historians conceptualize social structure of the nineteenth century. Specifically, the Barrett diary, like many of these texts, aggressively asserts the centrality of one dimension of antebellum experience—the social.[4]

TESTING THE LIMITS OF
THE PUBLIC/PRIVATE DICHOTOMY

Sociological conceptions of American society often rest on the division between "public" and "private." Discussions of the family, for example, often rely on the public and private as an analytic axis. Feminist theorists have used the public/private dichotomy as a way to understand the universal subordination of women. In the last twenty years in particular, scholars in the humanities and social sciences have rediscovered the widespread usefulness of these concepts and amassed a literature analyzing them. Because of the volume and variety of this literature, and despite the common use of the categories, a widespread diversity of assumptions and definitions has clouded these debates. As omnipresent as the categories are in contemporary academic discourse and the popular imagination, and as powerful as they appear to be, by themselves, they prove highly inadequate for conceptualizing human behavior in antebellum New England.[5]

Using the public/private dichotomy, how do we think about Martha Barrett's activities? Was hers a private life? "Private" implies seclusion and withdrawal from the world; a lack of involvement outside of a small, familial circle—none of which apply to Martha Barrett's day. Though her visiting took place in a private home, it was a household of adults, involving many women and men, extended family members, neighbors, and a colleague from a political organization. Martha's diary entry for that day continued:

> Went into the parlor and whom should I find but 'Uncle Thomas and Aunt Hetty Haskell.' From Glocester. Two of the best elderly people I know. Uncle T. went back to the [port]. Aunt Hetty tarried with us. How happy her visit is making Mother. She is an excentric, but noble-hearted woman, largely gifted with intellect. I love her very much and prize her acquaintance very much. Called on Mrs. Lind (Aunt H.'s neice) for an hour. Left Uncle Joshua and Aunt Mary at home. And James Wilkins called during the evening. We sat conversing till eleven o'clock. Aunt H., Mother and I, or rather Mother lay upon the bed, and we sat by the stove. Had a right pleasant evening.

If these activities were not private, can we think of them as *public*? After all, the Barrett household certainly held its doors open to the community and some of its conversations were clearly of a political nature. Still, the word *public* evokes images of power, authority, law and justice, and male leadership. On the surface, these characteristics bear little relation to the Saturday bustle of the Barrett home.[6]

A vast literature contests the meaning of the public/private framework, analyzes its adequacy, and illustrates its historical fluctuation. Feminists in particular have explored the public and the private as a means to understand the status of women in society. Because of the widespread association of the public sphere with men and the private sphere with women, feminists have been particularly interested in the kinds of power that these gender-linked associations enable or frustrate, and in the related possibilities for liberation and change that might result from a breakdown of the associations. So feminists attempting to better understand the condition of women have tried to turn what once were prescriptive terms into analytic ones—and in so doing, they have redefined the terms, changed the terms, accepted the terms only as ideology, or rejected the terms altogether. While I find this critical scrutiny helpful, I do not reject the public/private axis out of hand. I find the dichotomy continues to shed light on gender ideology and on the way society is structured, *if* it is broadened to include a category for the *social*.[7]

Despite the intensity of the debate on the subject, "public" and "private" are not simply ideas or ideology; to borrow from W. I. Thomas: "Categories are real because they are real in their consequences." My subjects and their contemporaries formed their individual conceptions of the division of society, and through their behavior they variously faced up to limited options, acknowledged invisible boundaries, challenged convention, and exploited new opportunities. For example, although they could not vote or hold public office, a significant number of women in this study recorded town meetings, which were public events. The male caretakers of the political order probably assiduously enforced women's exclusion. To the best of my knowledge, none of the women in my study actually participated in town-meeting debates. For the most part, they recognized and accepted many of the limits to their citizenship, those points in the public sphere beyond which they could not venture. At the same time, many women did not observe the tacit and explicit boundaries intended to "guard" the public from women. Instead, they routinely breached social etiquette and tested legal boundaries in the effort to expand their role in the public domain. They engaged in the political process by signing petitions and lobbying for temperance, abolition, and the ten hour day, and by exerting political influence when possible. Men were also quite capable of overlooking the prescribed constraints on the role in the private sphere. The example of Brigham Nims, who "helped put in a quilt," very quickly shatters stereotypes of the boundaries of male behavior. Even the quilting party, a social activity that has come to be seen as one of the most exclusive rituals of female culture, was something Nims and his contemporaries could participate in.[8]

In spite of the debate, or perhaps, in part, because of it, the public/private dichotomy continues to hold an unyielding grip on both the popular imagination and academic discourse. Many scholars continue to use the concepts—critically or not—from a conviction that they establish fruitful distinctions. Perhaps the endurance of the framework results from the fact that the division continues to order society, by separating production from reproduction and men's experience from women's. Also, its conceptual simplicity reassures people of a "natural" order to the social world in times of great change, such as the pre–Civil War period and the late twentieth century. Each of these periods witnessed dramatic changes in the condition of women—in particular, a large influx of women into the paid labor force and a protracted national discussion about the nature of women and their "proper" role in society. For better or for worse, the public/private paradigm locates a place for women.

REINTRODUCING THE SOCIAL

The public and private are useful categories for historical sociological analysis if used in conjunction with the social. My work uses the critiques of the public/private dichotomy as a way of reconceptualizing rather than totally abandoning this approach. Based on the accounts of everyday life provided by my subjects, I advance a more encompassing framework: the public, the private, and a third, mediating category, the social. While I recognize the importance of the economy, in this book I address it only insofar as it overlaps with other spheres. These spheres are historically drawn and situationally rooted. At their core, each has a meaning in antebellum New England, a meaning that is historically contingent, shaped by race, class, and gender. In contrast, the dichotomy of public and private blurs the distinctiveness of social activities; social behavior is rendered subsidiary, if not wholly invisible or irrelevant, on the basis of theoretical presuppositions underlying scholars' definitions of the terms. From the vantage point of working people's everyday lives, this is a terrible mistake. The voices of these people enable us to reframe the traditional public/private duality.

In considering this period and these subjects, my starting point is behavior and action. A great deal of working people's action in the antebellum period fell outside the narrow categories of public and private. Rather than compress their activities into an inappropriate framework or dismiss them as subsidiary, I make them the center of my attention and study.

For the purpose of this inquiry, the *social* includes that range of behaviors that mediates public and private activities, linking households to neighbors and individuals to institutions. The social operates via informal rules and emotional and economic interdependence. It encompasses a variety of activities that are not simply public or private. So, for example, Parker Pillsbury, a leading anti-slavery activist and feminist, called on Martha Barrett on his way to an abolitionist meeting. He paid his respects to Martha and may have inquired about her attendance at the meeting. In effect, although he was socializing, he was simultaneously organizing for a political movement. While it transpired in a household, this brief encounter was not simply a private one. Further, although at least part of its substance was political, it was also clearly not a public exchange. The visit was simultaneously private, political, and social. In this and other circumstances, the spheres expand and contract, and their boundaries become more or less fluid in different contexts, altering the meaning of the spheres, as well as actors' interpretations of their own behavior. Spheres were not mutually exclusive; as the above example illustrates, they often overlapped. It was possible for public activities to be social, private activities to be public, and so on. Behavior could be interpreted in different ways, depending on the context. The physical setting combined with the situation to create the meaning of an action.

The definition and boundaries of the social sphere have been as embattled as those of the public and the private. In assessing the modern dilemmas of moral obligation, sociologist Alan Wolfe develops a synthetic definition of civil society that embraces "families, communities, friendship networks, solidaristic workplace ties, voluntarism, spontaneous groups and movements." Wolfe sees a vibrant civil society as essential to a democracy because it is, among other things, a forum for political debate and action.[9]

While my conception of the social is consonant with civil society, I define the social more narrowly than Wolfe, who includes the family in civil society. Analytically, I find it more useful to consider the private domain a distinct sphere of action rooted in the activities of the household and nuclear family. I do so because of its veneration of emotion, blood ties, and bodily needs, aspects I see as authentically "private." My conceptualization of the social grows out of my interpretation of everyday life in antebellum New England. It embraces activities that transcend individual households and operate independent of the state, such as visiting, gossiping, churchgoing, attending lectures, joining political movements, baby-sitting a neighbor's child, and shopping. In addition, it encompasses institutions such as churches, schools, and lyceums. In antebellum New England, the social was characterized by rules and negotiation, as compared to the laws and litigation of the public, and in contrast to the motivating forces of emotion and need in the private. The social's unique values included mutuality, reciprocity, voluntarism, and localism.

I prefer the term "the social" to Wolfe's "civil society" because of the way it descriptively captures the everyday activities and communal relations detailed in the diaries, letters, and autobiographies of my subjects. Analytically, the social distinguishes between activities that engage family members only and those that transcend household barriers. The category also illuminates action in the public sphere. Because social activities constituted a common meeting ground where interactions were rooted in largely shared assumptions, it proved a fertile ground for politicization. In the social sphere, citizens could be roused by their neighbors and kin to fight the "sloth of intemperance" or the "evil kingdom" of slavery. It was precisely through their knowledge of each other that political action was possible. In addition, by highlighting the activities of everyday life, the "social" turns the spotlight on women, who regularly get lost or ignored in other formulations of civil society.[10]

Private in my proposed scheme includes the household and activities related to the individual, family members who live together, and other household members. In the private sphere, individuals attend to bodily needs, sexuality, identity, intense emotion, and domestic concerns. Privacy in antebellum New England was not coincident with the individual. As Mary P. Ryan attests, "The doctrine of privacy venerated not the isolated individual but rather a set of intense and intimate social relations, essentially those of the conjugal family. Privacy was a social construction, in other words, and as a consequence, a product of concrete historical actions."[11]

Public encompasses the state and all state-related activities, such as the law, the party system, and local, state, and national government.

The antebellum manifestation of the public included exclusively male activities such as jury service, muster training, leadership of town meetings, and voting. The laws allowed women to petition the government, but otherwise they had access to the state only through political mobilization or indirect influence on male citizens.[12]

It is essential to emphasize the distinction between the *political* and the *public*, because the two are not equivalent. Paula Baker broadly defines politics as "any action, formal or informal, taken to affect the course or behavior of government or the community." In her conception, political activity is confined neither to the state nor to public space but can take place in social or private spheres as well. All talk and action—from convening a family gathering to recruiting someone to attend an abolitionist church—have the *potential* to be politicized, as the participants may or may not realize. Conversely, the state performs many functions, such as feeding the poor, that are not purely political. Virtually nothing is ever purely public or private or social, as is suggested by the commonplace occurrence of people conducting business through old-boy networks or pursuing politics "in the back room" rather than in the capitol.[13]

A separate but overlapping and interconnected entity, existing both outside and within this framework, is the market. It operates with its own cultural assumptions, values, and principles of inclusion and exclusion. Economic relations pervade social activities, overlapping and intertwining with social relations. It was not unusual for social exchanges to be assigned economic value and for economic exchange to be embedded in a social context. In fact, I argue in Chapter 4 that the economy and society were inextricable in antebellum New England; for example, as unlikely as it may seem, brothers were known to pay their sisters for their caretaking services. However, because of the scope and complexity of the economic issues, I will leave their elaboration to another time.

The incorporation of the social sphere as distinct from, yet comparable to, the other realms draws attention to otherwise invisible or marginalized activities—such as visiting, exchanging labor, informally debating politics. The social confers on these processes and on the people who engage in them a far greater value than does the dichotomy. This careful refocusing recognizes these behaviors as central to the creation and sustenance of communities. And it separates them from other aspects of a broadly defined civil society. In the social sphere, individuals circulated among neighbors and kin and became both participants in and the focus of a community audience which observed individuals and held them accountable for their behavior. The social sphere embraces life lived among people beyond the household, with consequences that could be positive (such as the exchange of goods and services, the dissemination of information and ideas, and political mobilization) or negative (community sanctions such as racial slurs or slanderous gossip). As the thread mediating public and private activities, the social serves as the nexus of communal interaction.

In terms of these definitions, Martha Barrett's activities were decidedly social. Her enthusiastic involvement in the lives of friends and relatives enriched her own life, reinforced the ties between her and her friends, and engaged her in a flurry of communal ventures. Her experience in the social dimension affected both her private and her public activities. Because Martha and her mother did not close their doors to those outside their household, their extended kin and neighbors entered their "private" home and in the process shaped Martha's relationship with her mother. On the public side, her personal friendship with Parker Pillsbury connected her to a wide circle of political activists and abolitionist organizers, linking individuals in kitchens, general stores, and other "nonpolitical" settings.[14]

REDRAWING THE BOUNDARIES

The boundaries of the public, private, and social realms are not absolute; they shift and blur depending on the historical period and the situational context. Citing the work of other feminist writers, Susan Ostrander points out that "what have been defined as 'natural' public and private spheres of social life are in fact socially and historically constructed, and are representations of socially enforced patterns of gender." For example, the reorganization of production under industrial capitalism altered the parameters and purpose of the private sphere. The factory absorbed production, expanded the economy, and correspondingly shrunk the private sphere. Ryan, in her study of middle-class white women's associations, demonstrates convincingly that boundaries between public and private changed with the fundamental structural, economic, and ideological upheavals of the antebellum period. By the mid-nineteenth century, however, the ideological boundaries grew rigid and altered white middle-class women's behavior. Thus we witness a shift in the prescriptive limits of the private sphere and a contraction of women's access to activities outside the household.[15]

Boundaries between the spheres were also deliberately targeted: people sometimes mobilized purposely to shift the frame within which a particular activity was perceived and executed. For example, from the 1830s through 1860, many middle-class white women in New York City joined the militant Female Moral Reform Society in a campaign "against sexual transgression." The cultural prescriptions of the cult of true womanhood did not categorically circumscribe the activities of these women. Ironically, in an ardent effort to defend the sanctity of their role as keepers of the familial domain and its cherished, symbol-laden way of life, women stepped beyond that role and entered political life.[16]

As bold crusaders and agents of God, women in the Female Moral Reform Society strategized to expose and ostracize licentious men and to reform "fallen" women. They published a weekly newspaper, spoke at public gatherings, and encouraged women to take justice into their own hands by identifying those men who were "seducers" within their communities and by shunning "all social contact with men suspected of improper behavior." To curb men's patronage of prostitutes, they surreptitiously monitored the traffic in and out of brothels, publishing the names of Saturday night customers in their newspaper, *The Advocate of Moral Reform*. While men found their anti-male sentiment and activism strident and extreme, the women themselves saw their position as wholly in keeping with Protestant evangelism and the cult of true womanhood.[17]

In this situation, boundary-shifting reached a crescendo. Women repeatedly challenged the barriers confining them in the private sphere by taking action in the public and social worlds. At the same time, they justified their violation of convention in the social and public spheres through their privately cultivated ideological beliefs. They debated what constituted appropriate behavior, when and where a boundary should be observed between public and private spheres, and indeed, whether such a boundary should exist at all. In the process, their positions and practices were frequently in conflict with one another, as well as with the conventions of the day.

Similarly, abolitionist sentiment in antebellum New England remained largely a social concern until activists and organizations struggled to make it a political issue by bringing it forcefully into the public sphere. They did so by sponsoring lecture tours exposing the conditions of slavery and by petitioning the government to criminalize the buying and selling of human beings. Their alternative strategy, no less modest, proposed an amendment to the United States Constitution. Their attempt to shift the abolition issue from the social to the public realm met with great resistance. Even some who were sympathetic to the anti-slavery position believed the U.S. government had no business meddling in the economic affairs of the southern states. The fight in the North over slavery was in part a dispute about where to draw boundaries between concerns of the state, the community, and the individual.

SOCIAL INCLUSION AND EXCLUSION

Social activities conducted in a spirit of mutuality often disguised deeply divisive outcomes, especially with regard to race. The experience of free blacks and ex-slaves in the antebellum North illuminates the ominous side of the social in a racially stratified society.

Community networks created hierarchies of inclusion in the social sphere. They defined some people as members and others as outsiders. Native-born white working-class and agrarian communities often purposely shunned African Americans, Native Americans, and Irish immigrants. And people of color often built their own institutions, many of which orbited around the church and served to minimize contact with white society.

The social sphere was rife with conflict as well as cooperation. In discussing the post–Civil War South, Leon Litwack contrasts "social equality" to "public equality" for African Americans: the federal government legislated *public* equality, but *social* equality remained elusive as bigotry and racism raged unchecked. In antebellum New England, too, a social racism targeted free blacks, circumscribing the areas in which they could comfortably travel. Using verbal abuse and sometimes violence, some white working people expressed this racism in their private households, and others did so out in the community. Throughout the antebellum North, race riots erupted in the 1830s and 1840s as European Americans vented their rage against African Americans. The distinctions between privately held opinions, publicly legislated laws, and the social consequences of racism vividly surface when we juxtapose the everyday lives of whites and blacks. "Colored people had little or no protection from the law at those times," recalled William J. Brown, a free black man born and raised in Providence, Rhode Island, "unless they resided with some white gentleman that would take up their case for them. If you were well dressed they would insult you for that, and if you were ragged you would surely be insulted for being so; be as peaceable as you could there was no shield for you." This ugly and foreboding dimension of community life underlies the sunny side of the social sphere.[18]

CULTURAL MESSAGES CLASH WITH THE SPIRIT OF INDEPENDENCE

These contrasting themes of mutuality and conflict must be understood in the context of economic and cultural forces that were shaping antebellum New England. Industrial development, urbanization, and western expansion fundamentally reordered American society in the postcolonial period. Each of these three developments caused massive shifts in population, as marginal farm workers sought jobs in newly established shoe or textile factories, moved to the city to learn a trade, or migrated west to homestead cheap land or pan for gold. Industrialization in particular had a tremendous impact on the organization of social and economic life. It moved production out of the household, creating a separation between "home life" and "work life." Throughout the nineteenth century, however, a majority of Americans lived in rural areas, and it was not uncommon for men and women to go back and forth between factory and farm employment or between city and country. On the farm, the proto-industrial economy organized a division of labor and social life different from that of the city, even after industrialization and commercial agriculture entered the countryside. Furthermore, while engaged in various "employments," working women and men had little conception of a lifelong career. With the industrial organization of textile production, workers moved between farm and factory; and to the extent possible, they manipulated their work experience within the factory to suit their needs and habits.[19]

In villages and small towns, people largely knew one another, and business transactions intermingled with community ones. Conversely, while on social visits, men and women often exchanged labor, helping with domestic chores or farm labor. The daily close contact made anonymity impossible and seemed to grant a license to the community to judge informally the behavior of its members. In rural areas, many women became "hired girls" on neighboring farms, entered the developing network of textile factories in the New England hinterland, or contracted piecework in the "outwork" system, binding shoes, sewing buttons on cards, or making straw hats. As many as one in four women taught school at some point in her life. Still other women, bound to the farm and responsible for household chores, produced and sold dairy products. While men had more employment options out of the home and exercised greater geographical mobility, we know little about what work they did *in* the home. The assumption of historians—based on accessible evidence—has been that men had little to do with the domestic sphere and its activities. In essence, they have been viewed as primarily public beings, shaped by the instrumentalism of economic exchange and formal political bargaining.[20]

The rise of industrial textile production in New England threatened to undo local mechanisms of social control, particularly over young women. The new organization of work granted women temporary economic independence and unprecedented freedom from family and community surveillance (see Figure 2). In the industrializing towns, such as Lowell, Massachusetts, and Nashua, New Hampshire, textile manufacturers attempted to replicate mechanisms for social control in response to the threat of social disorganization. In larger cities such as Lynn, Massachusetts, and Concord, New Hampshire, these controls were less effective but nonetheless continued to operate through kin networks, friendship and neighborhood circles, and religious organizations. In the cities, when men left the home to work in industry, commerce, and government, some women stayed at home to care for children and attend to family needs exclusively, while other urban women attempted to stave off poverty by joining the ranks of domestic servants or workers in the needle trades.[21]

Legally, white men had the power to vote, own property, and hold public office. Black men in the North could vote in some states if they owned property. However, after passage of the Fugitive Slave Act in 1850, free blacks were in effect denied citizenship, and they did "not fail to recognize that they had no reasonable protection under the Constitution." Neither black nor white women could vote or hold political office; in the words of Elizabeth Cady Stanton, women were "civilly dead." Married women could not own property and had no right to the wages they earned until the Married Women's Property Acts were passed in the 1840s and 1850s. Economically, white men controlled nearly all of the country's wealth, earned more than twice the wages of working women, and dominated skilled positions in the labor market.[22]

MIDDLE-CLASS IDEOLOGY AND SEPARATE SPHERES

The 1820s and 1830s gave birth to a new dictum regarding the place of middle-class white women that dovetailed neatly with the separation of work from family life, and public from private space. The shift of production of household goods from home to factory meant that women's work at home, textile manufacturing in particular, was being usurped by industry. What were women to do? The advice literature encouraged wives and mothers to focus their energies on caring for their families and uplifting the morals of society. Women were to guard their sphere and rightful place—the home—with all the virtues imbued in a proper wife-mother: "piety, purity, submissiveness and domesticity." Cultural arbiters such as ministers and advice writers propagated this "cult of true womanhood," in what began as simple advice to uncertain readers and culminated decades later in a crusade to save the older social order from change.[23]

The middle-class male companions to true women were to be "the movers, the doers, the actors," those who provided for and protected the family. By 1852 *The Ladies Counsellor* had delineated this "beau ideal": a man who was energetic, self-denying, benevolent, cultivated, economical, and religious. In his study of self-made men, Ronald Byars describes the fashionable middle-class man as someone who exhibited ambition, courage, and strength, and was "almost ascetically devoted to the work-related virtues." Male virtue required concerted effort because the new man was vulnerable to the lure of vice and evil, particularly under the influence of corrupt women. E. Anthony Rotundo points to the critical transition from youth to manhood that involved a strong commitment to a career, marriage, and a house of one's own: "The identity of a middle-class man was founded on independent action, cool detachment, and sober responsibility." The home, according to the advice manuals studied by Byars, was "an appendage to a man's life. It had sentimental significance, but was not a major factor in his life. It did not contribute much to his sense of personal identity." Rotundo finds middle-class men even fearful of the "cage of domesticity" that women represented, prompting some men to reject those aspects of life that held feminine associations—religion, culture, the home, and women themselves.[24] Men, as breadwinners, theoretically had the public world to themselves and reigned over the household only as distant patriarchs.

This ideology of the cult of true womanhood fit neatly with the developing separation of work and family life. Gerda Lerner draws our attention to the cult's attempt to construct a mythic past with a "natural" gendered order by making "claims to tradition, universality, and a history dating back to antiquity, or at least to the Mayflower." But instead of resurrecting a perfect order, in her view, the cult constricted work opportunities for women and diminished their social status: "It is no accident that the slogan 'woman's place is in the home' took on a certain aggressiveness and shrillness at the time when increasing numbers of poorer women *left* their homes to become factory workers." The ideology had a clear class message: impoverished domesticity was preferable to an unwomanly economic independence outside the home.[25]

Concomitant with the growing separation of work and family, the cult of true womanhood developed a companion ideology of gendered spheres. Beginning in the 1820s, a body of advice literature developed that addressed concerns of domestic life. It advocated construction of a metaphorical wall between public and private life in middle-class families and, in effect, recommended a new gendered division of labor. It relegated women to domestic life and men to the marketplace and world of politics. The advice literature admonished women not to leave the safety of the home—"the empire of Mother"—to enter into the dangerous outside world. Women's place was by the hearth fires, tending the education of their children, guarding the morals of society, and mitigating the ill effects of calculating, harsh market relations. In essence, women's confinement to the home was to be rewarded with security and power, or at least influence, in the domestic sphere. Men, as providers, theoretically had the public world to themselves and reigned over the household only as distant patriarchs. In part, this advice literature attempted to address the tension created by the separation of work from family life. It posited gendered spheres of influence in which the sphere of instrumental rationality is countered by the realm of intimacy and emotion.[26]

Scholars of women's history and the sociology of gender have attempted to explain the status of women in society by using a corresponding theory, originating in the nineteenth century, that divides society into male and female realms of influence and power. One school of thought claims that the division of labor into paid production and unpaid reproduction created physically, emotionally, and culturally separate spheres of influence and activity for men and women. Some historians, drawing largely from research on the middle class, retrospectively interpret the divide as absolute. For example, Karen Halttunen writes, "By definition the domestic sphere was closed off, hermetically sealed from the poisonous air of the world outside."[27] While subjecting the paradigm to scrutiny, much influential feminist research has accepted the assumption that a separate sphere encouraged a distinct women's culture to flourish.[28]

Contemporary scholars who criticize the notion of separate spheres as a central nineteenth-century cultural practice do so for three reasons. First, recent scholarship that investigates the practices of rural communities has raised significant questions about the degree to which men and women absolutely cordoned off their lives from each other. In addition to evidence of strictly gender-specific realms of labor and influence, historian Nancy Grey Osterud finds extensive mingling of men and women—economically, socially, and emotionally—in rural upstate New York. Men were routinely involved in household chores, women labored in the fields, and they socialized side by side: "The degree to which they shared farm and household labor was exceeded only by the commonality of their social activities." Women constructed female networks of support, but they did not necessarily prefer them to relationships with men; "rather," Osterud concludes, men and women "strove to create mutuality in their marriages, reciprocity in their performance of labor, and integration in their patterns of sociability."[29]

Second, even for white antebellum middle-class women, the ideological and practical divisions between the sexes were less extreme than domestic ideology purported. C. Dallett Hemphill's recent reassessment of the period's conduct literature suggests that in focusing only on women, the nineteenth-century historiography conducted in the 1960s and 1970s missed the symmetry between cultural portraits of men's and women's roles. In the realm of behavior, Ryan finds that women's labors in the home contributed to the local economy, and significant numbers of women found gainful employment outside of the household. In addition, women actively joined churches, voluntary associations, and charitable organizations. These studies call into question the legitimacy of the separate-spheres framework for conceptualizing the experience even of middle-class women.[30]

Third, some feminists have more recently argued that "the metaphor of separate spheres has been stretched too far." Linda Kerber suggests that it is best understood as a means to enforce cultural norms for women. Similarly, Nancy Cott finds that separate spheres remain useful "only in reference to ideology." Kerber and Cott assert that separate spheres can only be used in specific, restricted ways.[31]

Although I agree that a concept of separate spheres is a useful tool for analyzing ideology, I also challenge the class-based assumptions that inform the separate-spheres perspective. The evidence in this book reveals a practice of gender mixing in social situations, not the extreme separation of men and women that was culturally prescribed. Nonetheless, a deeply gendered division of labor underlay their practice. To the degree that manufacturing moved into factories, the separation between work and the household profoundly transformed production and social relations. The gendered division of labor in the home and in the workforce therefore remains at the center of my structural framework.

WOMEN'S CONCEPTIONS OF SELF AND WORK

Given the pervasiveness of these cultural messages, one question inevitably emerges: How did they actually affect people's attitudes and behavior? While the ideology of domesticity and true womanhood found a resonant audience within a segment of the urban white middle class, the extent to which it affected others—poor, working-class, black, or rural peoples—remains a disputed question. What did ordinary working people think of these ideas?[32]

For economic, cultural, and geographic reasons, the cult of true womanhood failed to influence many women. Literary historian Hazel Carby points to the dialectical relationship between standards of white womanhood and black female sexuality which helped to specify the essence of the true woman in the nineteenth century. She writes that black womanhood existed outside these newly constructed standards, beyond boundaries defined by a distorted image of black female sexuality: "The contradictions at a material and ideological level can clearly be seen in the dichotomy between repressed and overt representations of sexuality and in the simultaneous existence of two definitions of motherhood: the glorified and the breeder." African American autobiographies and other literature demonstrate that in the antebellum period and after, black women constructed their own ideal of black womanhood. Their ideal included an ability to make a living, cleverness, tenacity, and a strong commitment to the family.[33]

The messages about "ladies" also created dissonance in the minds of young white farm girls, many of whom worked in the first textile factories in New England. Neither farm girls nor factory girls could fulfill the prescriptions of the cult of true womanhood. As Lerner points out, in northern white society, which was presumed to be egalitarian, "the cult of the lady . . . serve[d] as a means of preserving class distinctions." The cult of true womanhood notwithstanding, it was the young women of New England, not their farming fathers, who left the household for factory work. Many others earned income through the putting-out system, by weaving palm-leaf hats, sewing shirt collars, doing leather piecework, and covering cloth buttons. Within this system, some women actively pursued the goals of middle-class domesticity. Others, recognizing the profound "limitations and the possibilities of their situation," collectively rejected new cultural demands and constructed an ideal woman in their own image.[34]

Millgirls consciously countered dominant images of the "true woman" by "extolling the virtues of wage-earning women." Judged unfeminine by a newer, more exacting standard, millgirls constructed a countervailing definition that included the virtues of self-improvement, intelligence, spiritedness, financial independence, and productivity. Adaline Shaw, working at a mill in Providence, Rhode Island, attempted to dissuade her father from calling her home to Bangor, Maine:

> When you ask me to leave my work, and return to Maine you ask me to make myself unhappy indeed; for I think that I can never again be contented there. We have been earning but a very little ever since we came from home till we came here, and now we are doing quite well, and I do not wish to leave so soon. I do not know as I am in the habit of disobeying you, but dear father, if you knew my feelings you could not, would not blame me.
>
> While I know that I am supporting myself independent of the assistance of my friends, I feel much happier than to be dependent upon them for every cent that I have. Besides, I think that I am as well able to maintain myself as they are to do it. You think that I had better leave the factory and work at my trade in that it would be more for my health. But I must be allowed to differ from you in that respect. I know by experience that it is very injurious to my health to confine myself to sewing. I am confident that the exercise of a factory life is much more conducive to health and truely I like it far better. I do not know why it is that our friends have such an aversion to a factory. Is it wholly because it tends to injure health? . . . Or is it because they consider it disgraceful? If I never bring any more disgrace upon our family than that, I think that I shall be entirely free from that charge. A factory life is not looked upon in such light here. I cannot think that it is any disparagement to a girl to get an honest living. Do you think it is?[35]

Through the vehicle of *The Lowell Offering*, a newspaper printed by mill operatives in cooperation with mill owners, millgirls put forth an alternative vision of an American factory worker that incorporated a new female ideal: an upstanding, moral, literate, white woman who aspired to improve herself through education and spiritual growth. Thus one Lowell millgirl published a poem called "A Cultivated Intellect Superior to Beauty." As the conditions of work in the mills harshened and wages dropped in the 1830s and 1840s, millgirls created a less sanitized version of the factory worker. A more militant picture emerged, developed in their independent newspaper, *The Voice of Industry*, which recognized the plight of women workers as an exploited group and focused on the oppression of workers and the profits of the mill owners. This more contentious self-portrait clashed strikingly with that of the middle-class true woman.[36]

Similarly, in another female-dominated and poorly paid occupation, schoolteachers shaped an image that contradicted the ideal of the female teacher promoted by education reformers of the 1830s and 1840s. Consonant with true womanhood, the reformers' ideal teacher nurtured students, drew on her womanly skills, and "mothered" the children as only a woman could. But the teachers, most of whom were young and single, and who received wages comparable to those of textile workers—worse, actually, since teaching work was seasonal—often found the factory a work environment superior to the disorderly and demanding classroom. Female teachers pursued intellectual self-improvement and prioritized their search for good wages. Unlike other female workers, such as seamstresses and domestic servants, teachers and mill operatives had the opportunity to define their womanhood in concert with one another through their writings, meetings, and publications.[37]

Although many of the working women in my study did not have the same collective opportunities, they too expressed objections to the middle-class conception of true womanhood. Sarah Trask, a Beverly, Massachusetts, shoebinder and the diarist in my research most drawn to domesticity, believed that a wife must think for herself. Of a neighbor, the bride of a drunkard, Sarah wrote: "I pity her. Yet, I don't know as she needs my pity, for she knew what he was before she married him. *Why did she not have a mind of her own?*" Martha Barrett, while selectively seizing upon cultural messages with which to judge herself, took pride in her strength of character, her active brain, her industrious work habits, her tenacity, her sound judgment, and her reason, which rose above the influence of romance and love. But she did struggle with cultural messages. When attempting to contact her deceased friends at a séance, she reprimanded herself for being unable to achieve the calm, passive, meditative state necessary to contact the spirits herself (and essential to the ideal middle-class woman), qualities antithetical to her very being. In a stanza from one of her untitled poems of 1854, Martha described the effusive energy that women could not and should not bridle:

> Yet I'll not curb my spirit down
> Nor bow to fashion's iron will.
> And through my brain my thoughts shall course
> In freedom still!

Four years later, at the age of thirty-one, Martha continued to grapple with the cult of domesticity, to acknowledge and value her animated vigor, and to come to terms with the path laid before her:

> I do not usually feel older than I did a dozen years ago. Here I am 31 years old, really quite *an old maid*. May I grow old gracefully! If I am to be an old maid may I be an honor to the sisterhood. And help to redeem it from the stigma that is so often cast upon it. May I feel the glory and dignity of *true* womanhood and live it.

So, like the millgirls and teachers, this woman, living in "single blessedness," struggled to define her own version of womanhood, one that accounted for her independent spirit and recognized the honor of autonomy and economic self-sufficiency.[38]

In an equally feminist vein, the Adams sisters of Manchester, New Hampshire—Hannah, Mary, and Margaret—all independent wage-earners, were profoundly swayed by the abolitionist and temperance critiques of the American legal system, and in particular the laws concerning slavery and marriage. In a letter to their mother in 1842 they jointly articulated the parallel between the condition of slaves and that of women, a minority position heard consistently in abolitionist circles before the Civil War:

> My dear Mother, we are not wanting in affection for you, but do you, can you as one so kind & tender-hearted to your children, believe this dreadful doctrine that your daughters were born slaves to serve you until they are married & afterwards it may be to serve drunken husbands? It were better that they had never been born than to be born slaves. But Mother you do not believe it, I feel that you do not believe it. Are we not as good & free to act for ourselves as your sons? If we are not, pray tell us, for we are yet to learn that daughters of freeborn citizens are not as free as sons according to the laws of our country.[39]

These few examples illustrate working women's knowledge of the cultural messages promulgated by and for the antebellum middle class. Their awareness, far from guaranteeing that they adopted or even aspired to the prescriptive ideals, strengthened their skepticism as often as it encouraged their conformity. Subjects actively evaluated messages, consciously assessing their rationality, value, worthiness, appropriateness, and desirability, before making decisions about how to proceed in their own lives. The extensive historical evidence presented in this book refutes the view that all women participated in the cult of domesticity or accepted a place in the private sphere.

MEN AND THE DIVISION OF HOUSEHOLD LABOR

The working men of my research did not consistently follow the rigid division of labor prescribed by the culture of separate spheres. The theory of separate spheres posits that the division of labor became rigid in the nineteenth century, and that men and women faithfully observed it. Although there were indeed traditions regarding the division of labor, they lacked a consistent principle and varied dramatically by region. In fact, the men in my study broke many gender "rules" casually and routinely.[40]

Fully thirty percent of the male diarists under study commonly recorded doing household chores, shopping for food, washing clothes, and caring for children. Washing clothes, unquestionably a labor-intensive chore, required heating water, scrubbing layers of dirt, moving wet, heavy clothes from one tub to another, and wringing many yards of fabric free of excess water. Two or more people often did the wash, a task that would be difficult for one individual. Elizabeth Metcalf wrote to her mother-in-law that when visitors arrived on the morning of June 15, 1857, her husband "Charles had just finished *his washing*." In what sounds very much like a late-twentieth-century negotiated division of labor, Elizabeth reported that Charles "has washed twice, does not make any fuss about it." An anonymous farm woman in Newburyport, Massachusetts recorded matter-of-factly, "Husband & I washed." Farmer Horatio Chandler recorded that he "assisted wife about washing a.m." On an extremely cold morning in January, 1859, John Plummer Foster "washed the clothes for the family, with the machine." Brigham Nims ironed clothes in addition to helping with the wash: "Helped Mother iron then mowed the oats," he wrote, and on another occasion, "Fixt my cloths. Cleaned. Ironed & mended &c." Most indicators point to the fact that men who did laundry regarded their work as *assistance* as opposed to responsibility.[41]

These examples contradict the notion that a culture of strictly separated spheres pervaded the lives of working men or, as we will see, circumscribed the activities of women. Definitions of men's and women's work were hardly absolute, and nineteenth-century culture had sufficient flexibility to accommodate divergent work practices. The matter-of-fact way that all of these men recorded their activities indicates that their practices were probably typical. If their behavior was unusual to others, it was not to them.[42]

Why were men and women able to mingle extensively and to engage in work deemed appropriate for the opposite sex, while living in separate spheres defined by the cult of true womanhood? The most obvious explanation is that advice books did not successfully dictate the way people lived. They might have set standards for debate, but they did not always exert substantial influence on how people lived their lives. Reliance on prescriptive literature has distorted twentieth-century perceptions of behavior in the nineteenth century. Diaries, letters, and autobiographies indicate that cultural prescriptions were neither as pervasive nor as inflexible as twentieth-century scholars have inferred.

Another possible explanation lies in the mode of production. Self-employment as an artisan or farmer enabled involvement in the various kinds of activities—producing, maintaining, renewing—that took place in the household. When production was in the home, boundaries between paid and unpaid labor and between men's and women's work were more fluid, even while gender-based areas of responsibility existed. The solidification of separate spheres for men and women occurred only in the urban middle class, if it occurred anywhere, where the distinction between work and home life was more pronounced because industrialization had taken greater hold over the organization of work.[43]

A third, less persuasive, explanation concerns material resources. One could argue that poor people actually aspired to the ideal of domesticity but because of their economic circumstances were unable to observe its precepts. I find this argument unconvincing. The diaries, letters, and autobiographies reveal that subjects rarely aspired to middle-class standards and repeatedly rejected them in practice. Furthermore, working women constructed their own vision of womanhood. Most women liked to work and enjoyed the freedom made possible by even limited economic autonomy.

The ideologies of true womanhood and separate spheres may have pervaded antebellum culture in sermons, advice books, literature, and the like, but the everyday practices of the working people of this study made the ideologies largely irrelevant. In their letters, diaries, and autobiographies, the working-class and farm men and women were not receptive to these ideals. They constructed their own, which grew out of their own experience and culture.

SHIFTING THE DEBATE

Despite challenges, the public/private categories remain ubiquitous in social science and are fundamental to nineteenth- and twentieth-century American historiography. This dichotomy, however, insufficiently addresses the complexity of working people's behavior and cultural practices. In particular, the transfer of production outside the home and the emergence of the nation-state transformed the texture of family life and complicated the public arena. The addition of the social dimension provides a framework for representing that sphere of interactive relations which built and transformed nineteenth-century communities.

With working people's daily lives as our starting point, the "social" emerges as a central realm of activity ordering economic, political, and family life. Several advantages stem from examining the world through the prism of the public/private/social rather than simply the public/private. First, the historical evidence presented in this book reveals "private" to be a misnomer when applied to nineteenth-century working women's lives. In contrast to the assertion that women were primarily private beings, working-class and farm women in this study did not exist in isolation, nor were they concerned exclusively with "particular interests." Their everyday lives charted territory far from the confines of the home, diminishing its importance in their social universe. Schoolteacher Mary Mudge, for example, involved herself in the community in Lynn, Massachusetts; she nurtured multiple work and friend relationships and understandably cared about her reputation. Like Martha Barrett and many others, she frequently went out to church meetings, to care for sick friends, to visit, to sew, to teach school, and to attend temperance lectures.

Second, feminist scholars accurately criticize the public/private framework when they emphasize the interconnectedness of the public and private, elevate the importance of work done in the private sphere, and highlight the inaccuracy of this simplistic "separate but equal" formulation. However, acknowledging the permeability of private life stops short of the conceptual transformation needed.

Third, rejecting the terms *public* and *private* altogether fails as a solution for at least two reasons, one theoretical, one political. Theoretically, the framework of public and private continues to order popular and academic thinking about women. The call to banish the terms has fallen on largely unresponsive ears, and therefore it makes sense to modify and redefine them in a way that disentangles their gender associations and makes them historically specific and class sensitive. It remains useful for us to understand what the terms mean to individual actors and how, as ideology, they help to structure the world. Politically, the gendered associations of public and private prompt people to use them interchangeably with men and women. They then quickly turn into prescriptions for behavior and geographic mobility. "Private" comes to be what women *should have been* because it is natural, normal, and inevitable. The political overtones are not subtle. These stereotypical associations need to be continually challenged and decoded. Their historical malleability and legacy must be uncovered, told, and retold.

And finally, the common corollary to public and private—the idea of separate spheres—must be replaced by an acknowledgment of the extensive mingling of the sexes in daily life and the understanding that the interaction occurred in the context of a division of labor based on sex. In their letters, diaries, and autobiographies, antebellum working men and women refuted the idea that their worlds were ideologically and materially separate from one another. Women's lives intertwined with men's through work, visiting, and involvement in the church. Men performed domestic work and interacted with women as friends, as fathers, and as partners. However, underneath the mingling of the sexes lay a deeply gendered division of labor, in the household and in the world of work. Women continued to retain major responsibility for household work and child rearing. The culture continued to expect men to be the primary breadwinners. Because of this, while the concept of separate spheres should be rejected, the awareness of a *gendered* social and economic division of labor must be retained.

This book takes us on a journey through a time we thought we knew but which we now have occasion to rediscover. In exploring the universe of working people's activities, I have followed the agenda set by my subjects, who, after the inevitable weather reports in their diary entries, wrote most about visitors and religious views. This book maps the realm of friendship for men and women, the ritual practices of visiting, the power of gossip in light of people's concern for their reputations, and individuals' involvement in the social dimensions of the church.

Chapter 2 charts the path I took in seeking out and selecting documents for this study. It raises questions about how to locate an individual within the class structure of the antebellum United States and how to interpret first-person narratives. It then elaborates some of the consequences of constructing a category of "working person" for this historical and sociological analysis. And, in order to bring the subjects of study to life as complete human beings, the chapter introduces a handful of the most absorbing diarists and correspondents, those to whom I repeatedly return throughout the book.

In Chapter 3, I explore the boundaries mapped by men and women in their friendships with one another. As a central feature of community life, friendship laid a foundation of reciprocity and practical support for working women and men. The chapter considers whether friendships of working men and women proved to be as intimate and romantic as those documented in the white middle-class female world of love and ritual.

The number and frequency of visitors to homes astonishes any new reader of antebellum diaries, and raises the question of how to think about these teeming households and the constant comings and goings of guests, relatives, neighbors, coworkers, and friends. In Chapter 4, I posit that the elaborate system of social exchange created through visiting was inextricable from economic exchange. On a daily basis, neighbors and kin actively maintained community networks by performing "social work"—caring for the sick, exchanging labor, and sharing emotional support. They did all of this in largely gender-integrated environments.

The subjects' intense interest in maintaining their good name and in determining the status of their neighbors and kin is the focus of Chapter 5. Women in particular discussed at length the reputations of women and men, the degree to which they met their familial responsibilities, and whether they kept their sexual appetites in check. Gossip provided a medium for monitoring as well as negotiating community opinion. Although nineteenth-century women did not exert as much formal authority in establishing reputations as their colonial foremothers, they wielded considerable influence over the contours of the social sphere and the substance of everyday life.

Chapter 6 explores various ways that the ostensibly private observance of personal faith was in fact a social enterprise. The church sponsored numerous lectures and fairs and provided mutual aid, rendering its social features at least as important in the worlds of antebellum working people as its role as a promulgator of religious ideology. Its social aspects enticed members of villages, towns, and cities to observe a spectacle, to listen to the oratory of a charismatic preacher, to visit, and to gossip with other parishioners. Working men and women often looked beyond the divisive and pedantic dogma emanating from the frothy waters of the Second Great Awakening and took advantage of another of its consequences by engaging in the popular and ecumenical practice of church-visiting. They willingly entertained new theological and ritual approaches to observing and practicing religious beliefs. Most important, religious faith empowered people—women in particular—to act in the social sphere, to leap over cultural barriers, and to make their way into the public domain.

Each chapter, on its own terms, assesses the adequacy of the public and private to frame theoretically the everyday lives of working people. Within each orbit of activity, the social emerges clearly superior in its theoretical power and facility. As the surprising world of antebellum working New Englanders unfolds, their resonant voices tell an insightful tale of toil, fortitude, and spirited resilience that enabled them to shape their everyday lives and rebuff the restrictions of middle-class culture.

CHAPTER TWO

"I Never Forget
What I Remember"

Delving into Antebellum New England

In this book, I bridge some gaps between history and sociology. Although the assumptions of the two disciplines do occasionally clash, I approach this historical material and these theoretical questions believing that on the whole the two disciplines mutually reinforce and inform one another. I use historical sociology, which brings a theoretical framework to bear on historical evidence, to ask how gender, class, and race inequality operated from 1820 to 1865 in the social sphere. Instead of developing causal models, I interpret the meanings of social activities and examine the connections among gender and social practices, ideology and attitudes, and industrialization and social behavior. In addition to mapping the constellation of interpersonal connections that extended beyond the household into social space, I focus on subjects' own evaluation of circumstances and ideas. What did the shoebinder say about what she read? What did the machine-shop worker write about what ministers told her? What priorities ordered her social life? What criteria did a schoolteacher use to determine whether his behavior was acceptable to his community?[1]

Throughout the book my foremost concern is with the broad comparison between men and women. Half of the diarists are women and half men; slightly more than half of the correspondents are women, while men constitute the majority of autobiographers. This comparison insists that men and women be understood in relation to one another and questions some current assumptions about how northern antebellum society worked. What similarities and differences did men and women exhibit in their social activities? Did working men and women inhabit separate social spaces? How did they collectively maneuver within their social circles? In what ways did the division of social labor shape masculinity and femininity?

When possible, I also compare working people to men and women of the middle class. I derive accounts of middle-class life from the extensive historical literature rather than from archival materials. In this comparison, I am interested in the variation in cultural practices and the potential audiences for an urban-initiated culture and the cult of true womanhood. Were working people aware of middle-class ideologies? Did they care about them? What rituals distinguished their social worlds, if any?[2]

Finally, I contrast native-born European Americans to free African Americans, who constituted less than one percent of the antebellum population in New England. Because exceedingly few diaries and letters written by working-class African Americans have survived, autobiographies constitute the primary source of information about free blacks. Differences in structure, focus, and content of autobiographies vis-à-vis letters and diaries prevent systematic comparisons to working-class and farm whites. However, one extraordinarily rich collection of letters—the Primus Family Papers—and one heartfelt diary—that of Charles Benson—together with the free black and ex-slave autobiographies provide sufficient evidence to explore certain aspects of neighborliness, community life, and racial conflict. What criteria did African Americans use to delineate their communities? How similar were their social practices to those of their white counterparts? What role did the church play in creating northern black communities?[3]

LOCATING CLASS

Defining class in early-nineteenth-century America is complicated, for numerous reasons. Most important, prior to the Civil War, the economy had not completed the transition to industrial capitalism. While hierarchies of privilege existed, industrial capitalism and its attendant class structure had not become firmly entrenched. A conception of the working class as an industrial proletariat is too narrow to embody the variation of employments and life circumstances of those who were not privileged. Individual subjects repeatedly challenged sociological wisdom regarding class status: people other than middle-class professionals often owned property; most artisans and factory workers never belonged

to a labor organization; many individuals worked in multiple employments over their life course; and many who struggled to garner sufficient
resources for their everyday needs did not consider themselves poor or
disadvantaged. They were not the laboring poor, nor were they professional elites; they fell somewhere in the middle. This suggests that we
need to re-evaluate class categories.[4]

In my search for subjects, I found working men and women engaged
in a broad range of employments over the course of their diary-keeping
lives. The most common jobs for women included domestic servant/
nurse, teacher, factory worker (usually a weaver in a textile mill), and
needleworker (seamstress or shoebinder) (see Table 1). As with all the
employments, these jobs were not mutually exclusive: a woman might
work in a textile mill in the autumn and winter, teach school in the
summer, and quit her jobs periodically to care for ailing family and
neighbors. Thus, while the categories *semi-skilled* and *unskilled* suggest
a hierarchy of skills, wages, and people, in fact individual women moved
back and forth between these categories. Factory employment paid a
slightly higher wage than teaching if the work was steady and year-
round (which was not guaranteed). Needlework and domestic labor
paid very little. In 1849, Sarah Trask struggled hard to earn $1 per week
at piecework, sewing uppers to the soles of shoes, while factory workers
regularly made $2 per week in addition to room and board.

Men exercised a remarkably similar pattern of making a living via
multiple employments. The most common employment of men was
farming: 59% of the men engaged in farming, although most also
performed day labor and other jobs to bring cash into the household.
Not surprisingly, almost half the men held jobs as skilled artisans—
shoemaker, carpenter, blacksmith—whereas none of the women did.
Men also found jobs as teachers, factory workers, and clerks or peddlers.
Both men and women experienced changes in their job prospects and
fortunes over the course of their lives.[5]

The current practice of lumping together an undifferentiated mass of
people and calling them all the "middling" class is sloppy social science.
An enormous gulf existed between people with abundant economic
resources and those forced to perform manual labor to survive. Although
some would argue that the lack of "fit" between people and categories
is sufficient grounds for rejecting the concept of class, I find that the
principles informing the analytic categories—such as privilege and exploitation—remain too central to ordering the world to abandon them.
Because no study has satisfactorily addressed the analytic issues of class

TABLE I   DIARIST EMPLOYMENTS

	Women		Men		Total	
Artisans	—		13	(46%)	13	(23%)
Shoemaker	—		4		4	
Carpenter	—		3		3	
Potter/cooper	—		2		2	
Surveyor	—		2		2	
Blacksmith	—		2		2	
Semi-Skilled Workers	32	(114%)	19	(68%)	51	(91%)
Teacher	11		5		16	
Factory/millworker (textile/sawmill/gunmill)	8		4		12	
Needleworker (seamstress/tailor)	7		1		8	
Clerk/peddler	1		4		5	
Shoebinder/leather pieceworker/ book folder	4		—		4	
Apprentice (cabinetry/printing)	—		2		2	
Fisherman/mariner/steward	—		3		3	
Spinner (non-factory)	1		—		1	
Unskilled Workers	13	(46%)	3	(11%)	16	(29%)
Day laborer	—		3		3	
Domestic servant/nurse	11		—		11	
Boardinghouse keeper	2		—		2	
Farmers	5	(18%)	17	(61%)	22	(39%)
Missionaries	2	(7%)	—		2	(4%)
Total number of employments	52	(186%)	52	(186%)	104	(186%)
Base number of diarists	28		28		56	

NOTE: Percentages are computed by dividing the number of people in an employment by the number of diarists. Many diarists engaged in two, three, or more employments over the course of their lives.

in the antebellum United States, I have adopted a pragmatic definition of "working people" that comprises people who had to work for a living without the benefit of a college education or plentiful resources. Whether or not this analytic distinction proves to have empirical consequences remains a question of this book. At this juncture, I want to set forth the questions that I asked of the historical documents, and of the categories of class, which clarify the rationale for my principles of selection.

Women pose especially complicated challenges to class categories. Laurel Ulrich describes the intricacies of a colonial New England community in which hierarchy and privilege existed but did not necessarily alleviate the work burden of women nor protect them from the hazards of their time. She reveals the fate of a "pretty gentlewoman":

> Such a woman was distinguished from the common sort by wealth (silver, gold, and pearls), by specialized skills (embroidery silk and fine wrought cushions), and especially by an attitude, an enlarged sense of her own person (fine sleeves, laced petticoats, a tufted cloak). The obvious luxury implied by this assemblage of fabrics and trinkets should not mislead us, however. Mistress Cutt was killed by Indians while haying on her Dover farm.

This type of woman would have fallen outside of the limitations I have set for wealth for this study. But while colonial economic configurations changed in the nineteenth century, some of the same interpretive issues remained. For example, although fine clothes—fashionable gloves, hats, dresses, and other adornments—were no longer the exclusive province of the elite and could be purchased by wage-earning women, it was still common for farm women to produce food and engage in arduous labor regardless of the resources of their husbands or fathers. They labored from dawn to dusk milking, churning, ironing, baking, sewing, spinning, caring for children, hoeing the garden, and also, perhaps, working in the fields. While they were not wage earners, they frequently brought cash and essential services into the household by selling butter and eggs, assisting a nearby household with domestic chores, stitching together leather wallets, or exchanging labor with neighbors. While I reject the notion that all women shared an identical oppression and should be judged as equivalent, there is no question that most wives of comfortable farmers worked as hard cooking, canning, planting, and sewing as their less fortunate sisters. They could more confidently expect to wear warm clothes in winter and to feed their families adequately, but only if they worked constantly. When a married woman, rich or poor, could not vote or own property and did not have control over her own wealth, it is only with caution and great sensitivity to the specific circumstances that we can place her in the same class status as her husband.[6]

In determining the class status of a woman, is her father's occupation most important? Or her husband's? Or her own work history? Is it appropriate to determine a woman's class status on the basis of the wealth owned by her male relatives even if she had no legal right to it? I assume all these factors must be taken into account, because class status was not static; it changed with specific jobs, with the fluctuations of the economy, and over the life course. It was possible for a woman like Mary Grace Holbrook to grow up on a farm in Connecticut, work as a seamstress and a shoebinder for years, and then marry a farmer. Although her specific employments might change—sometimes she earned money and sometimes she did not—she essentially remained a working woman her entire life. In contrast it was also possible for someone like Susan Brown Forbes to be raised the daughter of an average New Hampshire farmer, work in the textile mills, and teach school, the common employments of young women. However, at the age of thirty-five, Susan married a store clerk who later became a department-store magnate, dramatically thrusting her into the upper class. While they were single, the two women shared a class background and similar jobs. However, marriage transformed Susan's circumstances, while it minimally affected Mary's. This life history must be assembled and considered before making a determination about class status. And one must acknowledge that some people's class status changes over the life course—sometimes predictably, as when men inherit the family farm, and other times without any prior indication.

For example, did Brigham Nims, at age thirty-nine, compare in class status with Mary Mudge, age twenty? Both taught school for a low wage at seasonal employment in antebellum New England. In 1850, both remained single and lived with their widowed mothers, Brigham in Roxbury, New Hampshire, and Mary in Lynn, Massachusetts. Brigham, also a farmer, owned $1,800 worth of property according to the 1850 census; Mary owned none, but her mother owned $1,500 of personal property and real estate. In this case, even though the sex/gender system granted Brigham the right to vote and paid him higher wages than Mary, they had more in common with each other than with prosperous farmers. Because their resources fell below the average owned by the general population in 1850, I assume they each had to stretch the fruits of their gardens and place demands on their domestic networks to make ends meet.[7]

Class status is equally murky, if not more so, for African Americans. African Americans were subject to restrictive laws and racist customs which excluded them from much of white society by limiting travel, denying them the right to vote, and restricting them to black churches, restaurants, schools, railway cars, hospitals, and cemeteries. Politically, African Americans were largely disenfranchised, able to vote in only a few states. Most occupations were closed to them, leaving open only such jobs as seaman, day laborer, domestic servant, laundress, barber, teacher, and preacher to other people of color. Unquestionably, some of these occupations had more status in the African-American community than others. But how is this differential in job status to be judged if all wages were inadequate and skin color inevitably rendered African Americans second-class citizens in northern white society? As with women, I included black diarists, correspondents, or autobiographers if they had no significant wealth or faced limited opportunities. I also include black ministers, though no white ministers are to be found in the collection. Typically, African-American congregations had fewer resources to pay their ministers; therefore most black ministers had to practice a trade in addition to preaching. For example, both James Smith and Samuel Harrison made shoes during the week and preached to throngs of parishioners on the weekend. James Smith wrote, "During my whole ministry in the church, I had no regular salary; I worked at my trade to support myself and my family." Obviously, the African-American community placed a premium on piety and schooling, but for black Americans, education did not guarantee a particular type of job, a living wage, or job security.[8]

I decided these questions with an eye to consistency and coherence in the cluster of working people I selected. On principle, I included working men and women who owned little or no property and who did not have a college education in order to test my hypothesis that working people constructed a social life distinct from that of their middle-class counterparts.

READING BACKWARD IN TIME

The primary advantage of first-person narratives—that they are personal testaments of lived behavior, attitudes, and beliefs—offsets what social scientists and historians usually assess as a major disadvantage, the bias of an individual's subjective perspective. Working men and women render the world using their own palette of colors. Their universe revolves around their families, work, and community. Their accounts make few attempts at objectivity, or even balance, in the portraits they paint. They unapologetically record their point of view. Mired in everyday labors, they largely ignore national and global events. In focusing

on the mundane routines of daily life, the letters, diaries, and autobiographies only minimally elaborate feelings, ideas, and opinions about
the political world. While this might create a major problem for another
project, for this book it constitutes a fundamental asset.[9]

Whenever possible, I cross-check an individual's perspective against
alternative accounts of events and people in newspapers, other diaries
and letters, town histories, and other sources. At the same time, the
biases of the historical subject constitute important information. For
example, the circa-1880 memorial volume of Leonard Stockwell (see
Figure 3), a paper-mill worker and farm laborer from Worcester County,
Massachusetts, illustrates some dimensions of historical sensibility that
can be uncovered through cross-examination. The anonymous author
of Stockwell's memorial demonstrates a deep attachment to Stockwell
and an intimate knowledge of his endeavors and disappointments, and
adopts his opinions as her own (the author is very probably female).
This lack of critical distance from the subject occasionally prompts the
reader to imagine that Stockwell dictated parts of the memorial before
his death. The bias of the writer, frequently transparent, reveals the
unachieved aspirations, devastating failures, and bitter resentments of a
Yankee who did not fit the prototype of the financially successful and
comfortable farmer.[10]

Leonard Stockwell's wife of twenty-five years, Orilla, died in 1853.
Immediately following her death, Stockwell hired Hannah Ellis, a forty-
nine-year-old woman who had never married, to care for his house and
his children. Five months later they married. From Leonard's point of
view, Hannah was difficult to live with, willful and contentious. The
memorial describes married life with her as miserable and trying, and
even suggests that she may have been mad:

> The number of years of maiden life had fixed in her nature opinions and
> peculiarities unalterable, becoming more strongly marked and developed as
> the years went on until friends began to think her mind effected. . . . Her
> intense rigid, religious adherence and supreme selfishness narrowed the circle
> of acquaintance and biased her judgement which was confined to the narrow,
> hard and cold line of intolerance.

The recounting of Stockwell's hardships evoked in me a deep sympathy
for the exploitative conditions of his numerous, low-paying employments, for the hardships of his life, and for the twenty-three sorrowful
years of domestic torment he experienced in his second marriage.[11]

Nevertheless, how do we interpret Stockwell's story? Is Stockwell the only aggrieved party in the situation? What exactly was the nature of Hannah's contentiousness? Was she as crazy as the author implied? Was she intolerably antisocial, critical of friends as well as of her husband and his children, an "old maid" who could not make the compromises necessary for married life? Stockwell's memorial reads as a story that he told. Despite his poverty and misfortune, at the time he remarried he was a white, native-born man who held great legal advantage over his new life partner. However, from his perspective, his legal and cultural entitlements provided little leverage in household politics. Hannah was a power broker, a force to be reckoned with.

What about Hannah's perspective? As she is revealed through alternative sources, Hannah emerges as a strikingly different kind of person: prudent, thorough, and decidedly ahead of her time. Before marrying Stockwell, she filed an "ante-nuptial" agreement with the Registry of Deeds that allowed her to retain legal control over the real estate and other property she brought to the marriage. Fourteen years later, after writing her will and leaving only a portion of her property to Leonard (who otherwise owned no real estate), she wrote a letter to the Clerk of Probate in Worcester County stating unequivocally that under *no* circumstances should her husband become executor of her estate, and implying that Stockwell could not be relied upon to be either capable or honest.[12]

While Hannah may have been unreasonable and unpleasant, she wisely and cautiously protected her property and assets at a time when women's legal options were severely limited. Hannah's fragmented, rediscovered story challenges the sympathetic portrait of Leonard—that he was unassuming, kind to a fault, and hardworking. Furthermore, a depiction of him from his own father corroborates Hannah's view: in his will, his father singled out Leonard, specifying that he along with only one of his eight siblings should have no control over his inheritance of $250. The implication of his father's will—that Leonard was, at the very least, imprudent—further calls into question the memorial's characterization of Hannah.[13]

The converging stories agree that conflict lay at the heart of Leonard and Hannah's marriage. It is easy to imagine that Hannah's prudence and independence of mind grated upon a man who was defeated in so many ways by the outside world but who had become accustomed to a congenial wife who let him have his own way at home. Of course, others besides Leonard may have held similar opinions of Hannah, but lacking other sources of information, we cannot know. Nonetheless, my cross-examination of sources exposes Stockwell's biases, and raises fascinating sociological and historical issues: the potential for conflict within marriage; the individual's unbounded capacity for self-deception; the social toll on women who did not conform to male expectations; and the ingenuity of some married women in manipulating a legal system that denied them full citizenship and equal rights.

While one of my major objectives in this book is to retrieve and to publish what working people said about their lives, in their own words, I intend to go beyond telling their stories. In the discussions that follow, I record the extraordinary voices of the subjects, while simultaneously recognizing that alternative truths coexisted with the accounts they offer. Whenever possible, I seek out and present contrasting perspectives. The result is a range of complexity and variation that ultimately defies even the most dedicated attempts at simple resolution. As C. Wright Mills points out, the most insightful sociology focuses on the intersection of biography, history, and society. Individual agency in a historical context created and sustained institutions and social structures. My challenge is to depict each individual as fully as possible, situate the collection of their biographies within the larger social and economic structure, interpret dimensions of the social lives they recorded, and build a composite of American culture from their point of view. To render the diarists and correspondents as complex human actors, I begin by presenting a brief introduction to several principal subjects.[14]

MEET THE SUBJECTS

The lives of ordinary people are not documented in the same way as those of public officials, people of letters, wealthy industrialists, and other elites. Because my subjects of study are common, unprivileged people, piecing together full biographical portraits of them is challenging but necessary for placing them historically where they rightfully belong and for situating them within their family milieus. Here, drawing from genealogies, town histories, local newspapers, and the documents themselves, I present micro-biographies of a handful of the 56 diarists and 100 correspondents. A complete collective biography would fill an entire volume and is therefore impossible in this book. For demographic information about all of the diarists, I refer the reader to Appendix B. I have elected to render more fully only certain subjects—those most colorful and insightful, whose writings I find myself repeatedly returning to throughout the book.

An explorer of antebellum cultural frontiers, *Martha Osborne Barrett* (1827–1905) attended several phrenology lectures and had her head "examined." She painstakingly detailed the "reading" of the phrenologist in her diary:

> Said I have a dense brain. My organs are sharp, and quick, active, lively. Like to see things done up. Am a great care taker! And will prefer to do the work of my family myself. There is nothing lazy about me. Am cautious, ambitious wish to excell, and if I marry and my husband does not do as well as I think he might, or does not come up to my ideas of excellence I shall push him along. Am known for my strong love of my friends . . . When she marrys it will be more from sympathy and friendship than mere love. Will let judgement and reason influence her. For her love is more spiritual than physical.—Is a little [snapp]ish!

Martha seemed generally pleased with this interpretation of her character—ambitious, pushy, reasonable. While she was startled at the phrenologist's description of her as "snappish," she did not take issue.[15]

Martha was born in South Danvers (now Peabody), Massachusetts, and kept a diary for thirty-three years, beginning when she was nineteen. Her father, a farmer and a "trader" (keeper of a country store), died soon after she was born, leaving her mother to raise her and her older brother, Eleazer. She attended Westfield Normal School in 1849 and then moved to Woburn, Massachusetts, to teach. She found teaching extremely trying, and after a few years she experimented with other livelihoods; she worked in a machine shop, took in sewing, and eventually settled into a trade at Mr. Fletcher's millinery shop in Salem. She lived with her mother, brother, and Lydia Buxton (a relative) in 1850. Martha worked hard but resented having to work, being poor, and having insufficient time for reading books and writing poetry. She aspired to achievements beyond her grasp: "Would that I was an artist," she wrote in 1854.[16]

Although she customarily attended the Peabody Unitarian Church (see Figure 4), she did not feel compelled to attend every Sunday: "I have always felt that the religious element is a strong one in my character. Though I think few have been sensible of it." Later in life, however, she engaged more regularly in formal religious observance. A staunch abolitionist, she refused to attend services of pro-slavery ministers because, in her estimation, their beliefs indicated a lack of moral consistency. She acted on her conscience (as abolitionist organizers advocated) by, for example, refusing to participate in Independence Day celebrations because she found them hypocritical. In addition, she expressed her politics through poetry. The last verse of her poem entitled "Appeal to New England Women, written after Reading Uncle Tom's Cabin" read:

> For Slavery now approaches, your loved New England homes,
> Within your own charmed circles there, his baneful influence comes.
> Then stand up in your womanhood, erect and true, and free,
> Give voice, and pen, and earnest prayer, till your sister too is free.[17]

While energetic, Martha suffered from occasional bouts of melancholy. The life she recorded in her diary was full of people and activities, yet she periodically battled loneliness. To help her sustain a sunnier state of mind with greater conviction, one teacher advised her to think of cheerfulness as a duty. For this suggestion she was grateful, yet she admonished herself for not being able to succeed at it constantly. In the space of four months in 1853, her only sibling married and two close young friends unexpectedly died. Martha felt devastated. In her search for psychic peace, she attended séances sponsored by the Harmonial Circle to contact the spirit of her deceased friend Lucy Colby Osborne. She felt acute anguish about her own inability to become a medium. No matter how hard she tried, she found it impossible to attain the calm meditative state necessary to act as a conduit to celestial beings. Once she began working at the millinery, her mood swings stabilized, and she mused that perhaps it was because she no longer had time to dwell on her own troubles.

Martha never married. She sustained her civic and religious involvement primarily through affiliations with the Peabody Unitarian Church. She belonged to the Unity Club, a theatrical group, and was secretary many years for the Ladies' Unitarian Association. In 1892 she read a paper to the Ladies' Unitarian Association in honor of their sixtieth anniversary. She sorted through old minutes and relayed the importance of conversation at meetings: "One report read thus; 'A great deal was *said* but nothing of much importance.' . . . another 'Not much work was accomplished this afternoon, ladies being very much engaged in talking politics.'" The Peabody community continued to count on her good humor and her talent as a poet. She wrote a hymn to be sung at the fiftieth anniversary of the dedication of the First Unitarian Church in 1876 and read her poetry at civic events, such as the dedication of Wilson Square in Peabody in 1903.[18]

Louisa Ann Chapman (1814–1892), thirty-three years old when she began her two-year journal in 1848, was much more sedate in temperament than Martha Barrett. She accepted the world around her, lacking Martha's contentious spark. A pious Baptist, she recorded her own rendition of Sunday church services in her longest diary entries. She thought highly of her pastor, whom others described as a conservative, though an abolitionist, and she taught Sabbath school. She recorded one of her most serious transgressions in 1848 when she attended the Methodist Sewing Society. The meeting "closed with prayer. I laughed during the service. Some one made me but still it was no excuse for me. For all these things I must give account. May I endeavour to be more careful in my deportment and more watchful in every act of life." While not an activist, Louisa was civic-minded. She recorded going to an anti-slavery "Pic-Nic" on Independence Day in 1848. She also attended a temperance picnic, occasionally attended temperance-society meetings, and belonged to a Female Benevolent Society.[19]

The demands of her work as an itinerant seamstress shuttled Louisa frequently between Ipswich, Lawrence, and Danvers, Massachusetts. She periodically sewed in a shop in Lawrence but mostly worked independently. For a short period at the end of 1848 and the beginning of 1849, she taught primary school and supplemented her income with sewing. The Danvers School Committee reported that she taught the children with "zest and energy."[20]

The death of her widowed mother from scarlet fever in March, 1849, left Louisa in the household headed by her younger brother Jeremiah, a shoemaker, which also included her brother Moses and sister Catharine. Soon thereafter, the adult orphaned children, all in their twenties and thirties, were called upon to care for their elderly grandmother because none of their aunts or uncles would assume responsibility. Louisa reluctantly accepted her charge. In the course of the next four years, Louisa and all of her siblings married and began families. In 1853, Louisa married William Perley, a widowed innkeeper and bore two children before he died in 1859.

Shoebinder *Sarah Trask* (1828–1892) began to keep a diary at age twenty-one, when her seaman boyfriend, Luther Woodberry, sailed for Europe (see Figure 5). By her own account, she was the target of community ridicule because of her naive devotion to this elusive man. In spite of the taunting, she remained indignant: "I don't care if I do get laugh at, for looking so soon, something seem to tell me that they will come soon. I rather hope and be disapointed, than have anny one tell me that they will not be here yet, for thats is provoking. I never believe them." While she was not "published" to Luther, and therefore not officially engaged, she waited almost a year for his return, anxiously watching for his ship to sail down the coast on its way to Boston Harbor. Luther's commitment to her was less clear than was hers to him. During his long voyage, she sent him numerous letters while he wrote her but one, and she had to rely on others for news about him. Privately, she poured out her heart to her diary, exploring her longings and confiding her frustration and occasional humiliation.[21]

In 1850, Sarah lived in Beverly, Massachusetts, with her older brother Joshua; her mother; William Lennon, a mariner; and his five-month-old baby. Her father, a common laborer, had died of consumption in 1848. Sarah worked in the regional shoe industry, as did Joshua and numerous friends, binding uppers to soles of shoes. One day she counted the 719 hand-stitches required to sew one upper; for this, she earned two cents. More than once she pledged to earn $1 for the week, a goal she rarely attained. She often sewed in the company of her friends, who also bound shoes, and they would travel together to deliver their work and pick up new assignments.[22]

Sarah despaired over her fate, using her diary as an outlet to express the uncertainty of her love relationship and the pain of her numerous losses of friends to death and marriage. In 1851, during a second voyage, this time to California, Luther died aboard ship. Sarah learned of his demise three months later and plunged into a deep, sorrowful state of mind. She pondered his death and fantasized about romance, pasting an engraving of an elegant lady in her diary and titling it "This was Sarah. Presented by C. H. Lewis" (see Figure 6). Beneath the buxom and bejeweled maiden staring out at her lover in a small rowboat in the bay, Sarah wrote the lines of a poem:

> For never can my soul forget
> The loves of others years
> Their memories fill my spirit yet
> I've kept them green with tears

She stopped keeping a diary shortly thereafter and never married. After 1860 she became a domestic servant, helping her sister and brother-in-law with their boardinghouse.[23]

At age fifty-one, *Pollie Cathcart Tilton* (1805–?) renewed her efforts at journal-keeping, two years after the death of her sister Tryphena and four years after the death of her father. Unmarried and taking care of her eighty-year-old ailing mother in Groshen, Massachusetts, Pollie was robbed of her own time and the certainty of her future. When she visited people, she took her mother along. When she went to church, she arranged to have a friend, usually Wealthy Packard, stay with her mother. In essence, her mother could not be left alone. However taxing this may have been, when Pollie's brother took their mother for a few days, Pollie felt lonely.

Her mother's death in the summer of 1858 thrust Pollie into a world foreign yet familiar. It felt strange to make her way in the world without her mother after fifty-three years. The next summer, she wrote in her diary, "A year tonight in the week since my dear mother died. O how changed now I have no home, but go about from place to place. But it is all right." Pollie used the skills she had developed caring for her mother (and we presume with her father and sister before that) to earn a living. With verve and determination, she became a community nurse and healer, moving into homes for one week to four months at a time to monitor the sick and run the households. Her marginal status changed shortly after Pollie ended her diary. She married farmer William Tilton, a widower twelve years her senior, the man for whom she had been working when the diary ended.[24]

Brigham Nims (1811–1893) was born, lived, and died on the family homestead in Roxbury, New Hampshire (see Figure 7). He was the fourth son in a family of six boys and two girls. He worked seasonally as a teacher over a period of nineteen years. As with most teachers in the 1830s and 1840s, such as his sister, Laura Nims (see Figure 8), teaching kept him busy only sixteen weeks of the year and paid low wages. To supplement his income, he worked intermittently as a clerk in his brother Reuel's store, as an itinerant tailor (living at people's homes while he sewed for them), and as a blacksmith, carpenter, stone splitter, day farm laborer, and most importantly, farmer.

Brigham married in 1853 at age forty-two, shortly after his father died and he inherited the family farm. In a prenuptial letter to Susan Selina Gould, he forthrightly divulged one reason for waiting to marry:

> I know that my owne temper and disposition is not so easily governed as I would wish, and that has been one reason why I waited so long, is to have it grow better before I should attempt to live with annother. But as I grow no better there seemes to be no other alternative than a *gentler hand* to smooth the path of life.[25]

He and Susan raised three children while living with his widowed mother.

The character shortcomings Brigham delineated did not seem to hinder his standing in the community. Very active in civic affairs over the course of his life, he was a town selectman, a representative to the general court, the town treasurer, a member of the school committee, and the school superintendent. His obituary referred to him as a "man of prominence . . . interested in every good work . . . a man of integrity and industry, possessed [of] a vigorous mind and body, and . . . strong in his convictions. In politics he was a staunch Republican."[26]

At the same time, Brigham challenged our stereotypes of nineteenth-century manhood. He emerges as a fascinating figure in part because he does a significant amount of household work, and because of his friendship with *J. Foster Beal* (1810–184?). Foster was from Nelson, New Hampshire, a township neighboring Roxbury. Exactly how they met is not clear. During the early 1830s, the two men worked together in a Boston factory making fish boxes. Brigham wrote home that he "shall work in a few rods of Beal." He then returned to New Hampshire to work and corresponded with Foster. A preserved cache of letters from Foster to Brigham reveals fragmentary evidence of their vital, loving relationship.[27]

Despite Brigham's irascible character, Foster enthusiastically celebrated their friendship. Foster's letters convey a large ("fat" by his own description), jovial soul searching for direction and meaning in his life. He married Sarah Jane Day on May 6, 1838, at the South Boston Broadway Church. Their only child, Foster Ellenborough Lassells Beal was born a year and a half later. After 1840, Foster disappeared from Brigham's life and from official records. From probate records, we can deduce that he died by 1848, but exactly when or where remains unclear.[28]

The letters written by *Adeline Brown* (1841–1870) tell a story about a relationship more than about an individual. Addie wrote dozens of letters to her closest friend, *Rebecca Primus* (1836–1932), five years her senior, revealing the extraordinary bond that sustained them through the economic and political uncertainties of African-American communities in New York City and Hartford, Connecticut, before, during, and after the Civil War. A tall, spirited young woman, Addie made her living as a seamstress and domestic servant, with no evident support or contact from her biological family (with the exception of her brother Ally).

Addie thought of herself as well liked, vitally engaging those around her. She wrote to Rebecca about her popularity, "Dear Rebecca, do not think I'm flattering myself what I'm about to inform you. Well, it's 'tis this. I'm the favorite of this family and also the family leives up stairs. Dear Rebecca I have come to conclusion that I'm human being." Rebecca described Addie's deep involvements as "borrowing trouble." Addie was independent and sure-minded in her opinions about what she had to do in life and how she felt toward people. Her long letters reveal a careful observer and a practical analyzer of the world around her.[29]

Addie created families of fictive kin, sometimes with her employers and sometimes with close friends. For example, in the household where she worked in New York City, she called her employers "Mother" and "Father" (we do not know their last names). Those terms of endearment not withstanding, Addie did not give her heart unconditionally where it was not earned. She made it clear that she did not reciprocate Mother's affectionate feelings for her. "She says I'm just the same to her if I was her own child. All I have to say, I hope she will continue to think so." Addie felt impatient with Mother's irritability and with her new pregnancy that promised to expand an already large family. "I want to leave her. I tell her if I was to go I would make one less. She will not hear to it. Then she think I don't love her. She think right. I like her very well. I treat her according to my feelings, but I cannot help it. As the saying is, I never forget what I remember. My dear do not say anything about it. Mother has not paid me for a month now and I want a great many things."[30]

In contrast, Addie adopted the Primus family without ambivalence. Rebecca's father, Holdridge Primus (see Figure 9), was from a family long established in Hartford. He worked for the Seyms & Co. grocery store for forty-seven years. For several years in the 1850s, he sought his fortune in California. Rebecca's mother, a seamstress, headed the Primus household in his absence. Rebecca's Aunt Emily and, in particular, her mother, served as touchstones for Addie. After one visit in 1859, Addie wrote, "I was treated so rich by all thee Family . . . you Dear Ma, there is no one like her if you was to search all over United States." However, no one could surpass Rebecca in providing sustenance for Addie. The two young women aided one another through the tumultuous 1860s.[31]

According to Addie, Rebecca, a teacher, craved academic stimulation. Addie encouraged her to join the society of intellectuals and teachers in Baltimore after the Civil War. She identified the training and teaching opportunity as "what you soul have been thirsting for." Indeed, Rebecca did go south to Royal Oak, Maryland, to found and teach in a school for ex-slaves. The school, financially supported by the Freedman's Aid Society of Hartford, was later christened the Primus Institute in her honor. It taught seventy-five scholars of various ages—many who began with no familiarity with the alphabet—to read and write. Rebecca's lengthy letters to her family during that time elaborately detailed life in the recently emancipated black community and her commitment to educating people of her race. While in Maryland, Rebecca met and worked with a former slave, Charles H. Thomas, a horse trainer, whom she later married.[32]

Addie approached marriage the way she approached her work. She pragmatically weighed the economic and social advantages of potential marriage against the dangerous prospect of a bad marriage or difficult childbirth. "Dear Rebecca if I should ever see a good chance I will take it for I'm tired roving around this unfriendly world." In 1868, Addie married her suitor of three years, Joseph Tines. They moved to his family home in Philadelphia, and she died two years later of tuberculosis.[33]

An embracing network tied together several generations of the Metcalf-Adams family in the nineteenth century. Of particular interest are the six living children of *Chloe Fales Adams Metcalf* (1797–1897) and *Joseph Metcalf* (1795–1845), four of whom left the farm in Winthrop, Maine, to seek a livelihood in the textile mills of Massachusetts in the 1840s and 1850s. While away, the children—Mary, Sarah, James, and Charles A.—wrote numerous letters home about religion, their work in the mills, and their coworkers, and occasionally (often reluctantly) they sent meager financial contributions to Chloe. When Joseph died in 1845, Chloe, with dependent children—four and seven years old—still at her side, found it necessary to take in boarders, sew for people, and seek other paid employment. Chloe placed financial and emotional demands upon her older children that they sometimes could not or did not want to meet. Their webs of interdependence periodically stretched and contracted, accommodating their individual and collective needs; at times they resided together, cared for each other through illness, or shared responsibility for rearing children. Chloe made alternately futile and successful attempts to fortify the sometimes sagging web. Surviving five of her children, she lived to celebrate her hundredth birthday (see Figure 10).

In April, 1843, the eldest child, *Charles A. Metcalf* (1822–1871), and the eldest daughter, *Sarah Metcalf* (1827–1872), left for Lowell to work in the textile mills. Sarah found work immediately and soon afterward Charles also found employment. Charles stayed just over a year and then quit because "it was too hard for me in the hot weather," found an easier though slightly lower-paying job in a machine shop, and eventually returned to farm in Winthrop, Maine. A regular churchgoer, he was also a patriot. On a trip to Concord, Massachusetts, he spat on the site where the British once battled to maintain their North American colony. He married *Elizabeth Hight* (?–1893) in 1847, who quickly adopted the new family as her own. During Charles's fortune-hunting voyage to the California goldfields from 1850–1852, Elizabeth taught school while Chloe, whom she addressed as "Mother," helped care for their children. They eventually had three children, all named after Charles's siblings. For a while in 1848, Charles's younger sister Sarah lived with the newlyweds. Elizabeth wrote that "in Sarah I find everything desireable in a Sister; indeed we are a happy family."[34]

Between the ages of fifteen and nineteen, Sarah Metcalf went in and out of the mills and exercised a great deal of independence. At eighteen, she rejected her uncle's suggestions that she attend school in South Hadley because "I do not feel as if it would be best." At nineteen, she elaborately defended her decision to remain in the mills rather than go home to help her now-widowed and lonely mother: "I am here *now* and *very pleasantly situated* which is a good deal for factory girls to say." She elaborated other reasons: "I am making three dollars and three and a half, a week," "my health is *good*," and besides, she argued, her younger sister Mary was going home to be with Chloe. In 1849, she prepared to marry *William Mann* (?–1900), a minister, and chastised her mother for not assisting with the wedding:

> I am anxiously writing for you to come home, for in the first place I should like to know whether you are to return or not. And I should like some one to consult. I have to take the whole responsibility of everything relating to myself, and I feel almost ready to give up sometimes. I do not think there are many girls in my circumstances who do not have a mother—or an older sister—or some capable person to consult. But I do not wish to complain— or to underrate my privileges—I have enough to do with, and I desire to be thankful for that.

Sarah and William ultimately had five children.[35]

Whereas Sarah tactfully (although forcefully) made her own decisions, *Mary Metcalf* (1828–1860), a year younger, expressed her independence in a sharper and more impatient manner. Her brother Charles characterized her as self-centered. Her letters to her mother convey a combination of irritability and anger in addition to compassion and concern. Her grating edge visibly surfaced, for example, in response to Chloe's inquiries:

> You ask, have you changed your boarding place? *No*. What could induce me to change my boarding place when I boarded with my brothers? . . . How

could you think, Mother, that I was going to do housework when you heard
me positively say I would not do it?

She earned wages as a textile worker, a hired girl, and a teacher, but
only grudgingly did she send money home. She claimed her wages for
herself to pay for her "necessaries." In 1846 while still in the mills, she
experienced, under the tutelage of a chum in her boardinghouse, a
religious awakening. Ten years later she married *Benjamin Whiting* and
had two children before dying in 1860.[36]

Following a similar family migration, the older sisters of another
Adams family (no relation to Chloe) also forged their way from a farm
to manufacturing centers in New Hampshire and Massachusetts to earn
a living. *Edmund Adams* and *Elizabeth Karr* married and raised eight
children—four boys and four girls, only one of whom ever married—
on a farm in Derry, New Hampshire. The shifts in the agricultural
economy made it impossible for them to continue to support their
unmarried daughters. Initially, the four daughters set out in separate
directions, and all achieved remarkable accomplishments for single, self-
supporting women of their time. *Hannah Thurston Adams* (1809–
1889), the eldest child, attended Atkinson Academy and became a
teacher in 1831. A severe illness confined her to bed for two years, and
upon recuperating, she was urged by her younger sister *Mary Agnes
Adams* (1812–1891) to learn millinery and dressmaking. In 1841,
Hannah wrote a letter to her parents about her undiminished intellectual
endeavors: "As it respects ourselves we live as happy as pigs in the
clover, nothing to do but to work & of that we are overrun. After we
lay our work aside we have a plenty of intellectual enjoyment. Books &
papers, meetings & lectures, & of this kind we also have an abundance."
Mary, the third child and second daughter, attended Adams Female
Academy and thereafter sought to learn the tailoring trade. She worked
as an apprentice in Nashua, determined to learn "to cut" in addition to
other skills of the tailor, so that she could set up her own business rather
than work as a lowly paid wage slave to someone else. Her persistence
and determination paid off; she learned the skills, saved her money, and
in 1838 she and Hannah established a millinery and tailoring business
in Manchester, New Hampshire (see Figure 11). They built a house
together and continued to run their business partnership until the end
of their lives.[37]

All the sisters rotated responsibility for caring for their aging parents,
although they cautiously avoided sacrificing their own livelihoods. To-

gether with their youngest sister, *Margaret Adams* (1817–1880), Hannah and Mary responded pragmatically to their mother's plea for assistance in 1842:

> Perhaps you don't know that it is difficult for either of us to leave & that we are worth $3.00 a week here & that it would not be profitable for you to have one so high priced when one worth a dollar a week would be as good if not better for you. Instead of letting out a girl we should like to hire, we will give you a dollar a week to do our housework & have the rest of your time play. But Mother don't be put out with us for using candor with you. We love you & almost adore you if I may use the expression, & will do any thing for you that reason requires.

So, while reason could elicit a response, the moral persuasion of their mother could not, in spite of the fact that they "almost" adored her.[38]

Eliza Adams (1815–1881), the fourth child, worked in the textile mills in Lowell, Massachusetts, off and on in the late 1830s and early 1840s (see Figure 12). She intermittently worked in Mary and Hannah's shop and saved her money to buy, at the age of forty-two, a farm in South Hadley, Massachusetts. After settling there she adopted two daughters, aged three and seven, and provided a home to several other orphaned girls. She wrote to her brothers and sisters in 1860 about her girls: "Aunt Julia th[ought] I had smart girls, so think my neighbors, but I tell them that my girls have a smart teacher. (You know it helps along to think well of oneself). Indeed when among strangers you must praise yourself to get along." Undoubtedly her hard work and indomitable spirit sustained her ability to stay such an independent and unorthodox course.[39]

The Rhoda Parker Smith Family collection contains numerous letters from the siblings of *Rhoda Parker* (1824–?). The Parker children were orphaned, and Rhoda was sent to West Newbury, Massachusetts, to live with the Lovejoy family, where she became a combmaker's apprentice. The other children remained in North Andover. The letters from her brother *Stephen Parker* (?–1865) constitute the bulk of the collection, but other regular correspondents included Stephen's wife, *Anne Abbott Parker*, their brother *Winthrop Parker* (1812–1845), their sister *Lucy Parker*, and a few cousins and friends. Stephen made a hearty effort to rekindle his relationship with Rhoda, who lived one hour away by stagecoach. He acted the older brother, inquiring about her "dancing school beau" and teasing her about introducing him to her friends. He respectfully accepted her autonomy in making her own romantic deci-

sions but clearly wanted to be consulted, if she was so inclined. She
married her beau *Lewis W. Smith*, a combmaker, in 1848.

What we know about Rhoda comes only from what others say about
her in their letters. In one letter, Anne Abbott Parker described Rhoda's
shyness: "I have a little kitten for company, but then she does not talk
even as much as *you* do." Despite her quiet demeanor, she had many
devoted friends who repeatedly invited her to come visit them and
assured her of their love.[40]

The Holmes Family Papers pose a problem similar to that of the
Rhoda Parker Smith Family Papers. Virtually all of the letters in the
time period relevant to this book were sent by Holmes family members
scattered over the United States, and from a few friends, to *Sarah Carter*
(1827–1913) of Foxcroft, Maine, who, like Rhoda Parker, preserved
the many letters she received. In effect, Sarah remains somewhat of an
enigma, except for the clues about her personality we can reconstruct
from the letters and from local town histories.

Sarah was the eldest of seven daughters and one son, born to farmers
Clark and *Hannah Carter*. She began teaching school at age fourteen
and continued for many years, while also working intermittently as a
milliner and dressmaker. She clerked at Vaughan's store in Foxcroft in
the late 1850s, a job that provided an opportunity to learn the retail
trade. By 1860 she had saved $1,200, which enabled her to purchase a
dry-goods store from D. D. Vaughan. In a local history, Dr. Mary
Chandler Lowell commented that Sarah's "great energy, remarkable
business and commanding intellect" contributed to the store's flourishing
business and profitability. In 1861, she married *Benjamin B. Vaughan,*
a recently widowed man eighteen years her senior, and continued to run
her business independently.[41]

Dr. Lowell, Sarah Carter Vaughan's neighbor, further reflected on
Sarah's character:

> Mrs. Vaughan's strongest characteristic was a well-developed normal strength
> of character, permeated by a well wrought generosity of impulse; a dignified
> and thoughtful expression of feeling . . . she had no patience with those who
> loved pomp and display. Quiet, unostentatious, she lived a simple, normal
> life, this despite the fact that through her own resourcefulness and business
> acumen she became a successful and comfortably situated woman later in
> her life.

"As I grew older," Lowell wrote, "I was better able to appreciate her
steadfastness to high ideals." The remark evokes an image of someone

she admired from across the fence but did not seek as a close friend. However, such was not the case for *Sarah Holmes Clark* (1828–?), who demonstrated her deep attachment to Sarah Carter through proclamations of commitment and love. Several others also sought Sarah as a close friend—*Hephzibah, James Holmes* (1826–?), and later *Marcella Holmes* (1834–1917)—but none quite so confidently and determinedly as Sarah Holmes Clark. In 1858 a kinship link tied them together as well—Sarah Carter's younger sister, Amanda, married Sarah Holmes Clark's brother-in-law, Wallace Clark.[42]

Sarah Holmes Clark also taught school in the 1840s and 1850s. An opinionated person, she typically demonstrated no qualms about speaking her mind. In the early 1850s she became engaged to *John Gilman Clark* (1827–?), a man whom her neighbors considered of no account. Gilman's father, a tailor and real estate speculator whom Lowell described as "a man of superior intellect and well selected vocabulary, but very erratic," lived at an insane asylum in Augusta, Maine, in 1850. Sarah Homes Clark tried to manage the information that circulated about herself and seemed to truly enjoy the torment she caused gossips in her community. After marrying Gilman in 1851, she joined him in Madison, Georgia, where he had begun running a school for boys. Sarah taught a class of younger boys in the school to assist him, but she assured Sarah Carter that she did not receive pay for it (the fact of her teaching was one she did not want circulated back in Foxcroft circles). While it is hard to imagine her curbing her spunky energy and biting her tongue, she wrote in 1855 that "I am not as impudent as I was two years ago, I assure you." This did not stop her, however, from reproaching Sarah Carter for her abolitionist sympathies. She also requested that Sarah Carter not publicize her newly adopted pro-slavery views. Whether Sarah Holmes Clark ceased to write after 1856 or whether some misfortune befell the letters remains unknown.[43]

CHAPTER THREE

"Unbosom Your Heart"

Friendship and the
Construction of Gender

Textile-mill worker Susan Parsons Brown longed for a *true* friend: "Oh that I had one companion in this wide earth that I could call a friend." She defined a true friend as "a companion. One who will share your sorrows, partake of yours, sympathys with, relieve and pity us when sad and distressed. And far [above all] will love us, one to whom each troubled thought, each anxious care may be imparted to a better self." Like other working women, she befriended her neighbors, coworkers, and relatives, sharing secrets with them, exchanging miniature likenesses of themselves or locks of hair, praising each others' virtues, and helping each other find jobs. Through their discussions of health and illness, work and love, marriage, birth, and death, they unveiled the qualities that made for a good friend and revealed the importance of friends to their emotional well-being. Working women's outpourings of love and affection shed light on the question of the class specificity of female friendship left in the wake of research on middle-class white women's relationships with one another. The studies find that middle-class white women shared a common experience based on gender roles, religion, and biological rites of passage, and their relationships functioned as mutual support systems providing security, companionship, and self-esteem in a female "world of love and ritual."[1]

This chapter begins with the sociological proposition that friendship is a central feature of social life. In antebellum New England, friendship was a linchpin of the culture of mutuality, neighborliness, and reciprocity within the social sphere. It provided a bedrock of connection and caring between women and men, men and men, women and women, neighbors and relatives. Friendship was fundamental to building communities, to providing emotional, moral, and practical support, and to sustaining one's sense of identity.[2]

Stacey J. Oliker makes the distinction in contemporary society between intimate and romantic friendship. The contrast usefully distinguishes between the two on a range of emotional intensity varying from casual attachment to committed love. For our purposes, intimacy refers to "a sharing of innermost thoughts and secret emotions." Some friends are intimate without being romantic, while others are companions who share community news but do not bare their souls. In the antebellum period, those female friends who were romantic were also intimate, although not necessarily vice versa. By the twentieth century, romantic marriage supplanted romantic friendship. However, the practice of intimacy, distinct from romance, continued in friendships for women, and the degree to which it continued for men is a matter of debate. Oliker claims that women's romantic friendship declined after the nineteenth century because of greater mixed-gender socializing, increased dating, the spread of psychoanalytic assumptions about pandemic eroticism, the rise of consumer culture and advertising, and the value accorded companionate marriage. And, I would add to her list, the change in the structure of work and occupations. However, despite the reorganization of production, friendship remains staunchly located at the center of women's and men's lives.[3]

This chapter explores the practice of friendship for men and women who were teachers, day laborers, and farmers. How did it differ from friendships of the middle and upper classes? To what degree did the female "world of love and ritual" extend to working women? Was there a *male* "world of love and ritual" that paralleled that of women? Were men's friendships with women different from those with men? What was the relationship between the subjects' construction of masculinity and femininity and their capacity to have intimate friendships?

WORKING WOMEN'S FRIENDSHIPS

Gender separation undergirds the path-breaking work of Smith-Rosenberg and Cott. They build their respective analyses on the extreme cultural divide between men and women. In their estimation, the separation led middle-class women to develop emotional relationships with those who shared their everyday lives and cares: other women. Cott

writes that the romantic ethos of early-nineteenth-century culture and
the prescriptive association between women and the heart "implied that
they would find truly reciprocal interpersonal relationships only with
other women."[4]

In their relationships, women expressed romantic as well as sensual
feelings for their friends. Cott outlines the relationships between Eliza
Chaplin and Laurel Lovell whose friendship stretched over fifty years.
In 1820, Eliza wrote her friend:

> When a letter from you was announced, my dear friend, the letter which I
> had so long, but vainly expected, a tremour pervaded my whole frame. Surely,
> famishing indigence could scarcely hail food with more delight. I loosed the
> seal & read its contents with the same eagerness that we may suppose such
> an individual to partake of a meal.

A year later she wrote that "she would 'have pined like the lover,
doomed to a separation from his mistress' without the letters that filled
in between their visits, apologizing half-seriously, 'if this is romance,
romance imparts the most exquisite delight. And never can I desire to
be divested of that which savors so much of heaven.'" Smith-Rosenberg
also finds that the close bonds between women often became passionate
and sometimes erotic. In their homogeneous world, even at great distances and in the context of heterosexual marriage, middle-class white
women wrote letters professing their great love for each other and
detailing the physical dimension of their relationships. Families and
neighbors accepted explicitly loving relationships between women, as
expressed in a literary form, as normal and natural.[5]

The question remains as to whether this practice of female friendship
was part of working women's culture as well. The extant scholarship's
focus on more privileged women raises the question about generaliz-
ability, as does research on other aspects of middle-class and elite culture.
Did the limits of leisure time imposed by the need to work constrain
working women's opportunities to forge friendships? Was it part of their
culture to share their innermost cares and thoughts, or was that purely
a pastime of the leisured few? Would working women seek the company
as well as solidarity and comfort of other women?

ADDIE AND REBECCA

A tall, spirited woman, Addie Brown made a living as a seamstress and
domestic servant. In 1859, at the age of eighteen, independent and sure-

minded, she had conviction in her opinions about ideas and people. At the same time, she worried about making ends meet and accumulating enough money to buy a warm winter coat, shoes, and a hat so she could go to church.

Addie continually reassessed her current and future prospects, especially about her work. She explored the possibility of going to sea with "Aunt Chatty" (a.k.a. Charity A. Jackson), another domestic employee in the household where she worked in New York City. Aunt Chatty boasted of making $40 a month as a cook on a ship and conjured images of wealth Addie could barely fathom. For a short period in 1865, Addie worked at a Hartford dye factory which paid a salary of $19 per month (an enormous sum relative to the approximately $4 per month she had been making). But soon after beginning her employment, Addie found herself laid off, without a job. She painfully discovered that an industrial job in an unstable economy did not necessarily offer her more than low-paying domestic work and the oscillating demand for sewing skills.

In this environment of scarce resources and uncertain work, no one surpassed her friend, Rebecca Primus, in providing sustenance for Addie. The two young women aided one another through their turbulent lives. In May, 1861, Addie wrote to her "only dear and loving friend" about the nourishment Rebecca's friendship provided for her soul:

> I received a letter from the one that I idolize. . . . Rebecca I want to tell you one thing, that is this: if I went without eating for two or three days and then a person was to bring me something to eat and a letter from you, and they say that I was only to have one or the other, I would take the letter. That would be enough food for me. Now my loving & darling Rebecca, you can imagine how much I think of your letters I recieved from you.

Rebecca's friendship so fundamentally contributed to Addie's emotional well-being, Addie needed it more than food. Addie and Rebecca's relationship endured nine years of intermittent separation, the elation and dispiritedness that accompanies infatuation, the ebb and flow of passion, and male suitors attempting to woo each of them. Embracing the relationship, Addie declared, "as long is *God* is my witness, it pure and true friendship." Addie and Rebecca went for kin: Rebecca invited Addie to address her as "sister" in 1862 and Addie responded enthusiastically.

> My Dearest here is [nise] question. You ask a favor and that is this, too *call* you my *sister*. And then you ask me if it will be agreeable. O My Darling, Darling, you know it would. It has been my wish for sometime I dare not

[vok]. My Dear I cannot find words to express my feelings to you . . . All I can say, I will address you as such.

In several letters, Addie signs her name, "Addie Brown Primus."[6]

Addie's rave review of a novel by Grace Aguilar, *Women's Friendships*, provides another clue as to the importance she placed on friendship. She enthusiastically urged Rebecca to read the book, insisting that it captured the very essence of their friendship. Aguilar affirms and honors friendship between women: "There is always to me a doubt of the warmth, the strength, and purity of her feelings, when a young girl merges into womanhood . . . seeking only the admiration of the other sex." At the same time, it is hard to imagine a novel situated more distantly from the material existence of Addie Brown. A book about two white English aristocrats, it dramatizes the tale of the two women's commitment to one another, which is tested by separation, misfortune, and the uncertain birth origins of one. However, ultimately, they both survive, their friendship restored, and each safely ensconced in a cushion of opulence. Despite the great economic and social gap between Addie's life and the world of these white women, the message of the book resonated deeply for Addie.[7]

Like so many friendships between white women, the relationship between Addie and Rebecca crossed the boundary of intimacy into romance. Addie repeatedly professed her love for her dear friend/sister. "You are the first girl ther I ever *love* so and you are the *last* one. Dear Rebecca, do not say anything against me *loving* you so, for I mean just what I say. O Rebecca, it seem I can see you now, casting those loving eyes at me. If you was a man, what would things come to? They would after come to something very quick. What do you think the matter? Don't laugh at me. I [ant] exactly crazy yet."[8]

Addie found the prospect of loving someone else—male or female—with the same intensity virtually unfathomable: "I cannot be happy if I was to stay a way from you. Rebecca, my *Dearest Love*, could any one love a person as I love you? I cannot, I cannot stay here any longer with out you. I must, I must be near you." In fact, Addie delighted in the fantasy of a marriage to Rebecca. "What a pleasure it would be to me to address you *My Husband*." All evidence indicates that Rebecca reciprocated Addie's love with the same fervent passion, although her return letters to Addie have not survived. The physical dimension of their relationship figured prominently in the letters. Addie often spoke of exchanging caresses, kisses, and hugs. "My Cherish Friend—O my dear dear Rebecca, when you press me to your dear bosom how happy I was. Last night I gave anything if I could only lay my poor aching head on your *bosom*."[9]

In a practical vein, Addie assessed her status as a single woman without kin, engaged in a low-wage occupation. She considered marriage's material advantages in lieu of her feelings of true love for Rebecca. She also evaluated potential marriage in the context of the structural limitations on her relationship with Rebecca in 1861:

> I want to ask you one question. That is, will you not look at my marrying in a diffrent light then you do? Look at this my Darling, I'm here with Mother, perhaps see you about three time in a year. I'm sometime happy, more time unhappy. I will get my money regular for two or three week and then eregular. What would you rather see me do, have one that truly *love* me that would give me a happy home, and or give him up and remain in this home, or part of me? Rebecca, if I could live with you or even be with you some parts of the day, I would never marry.

Both women realized that marriage posed a threat to their relationship.[10]

Addie's loyalty and attachment to Rebecca created obstacles for men. Addie made it clear to her beaus that they had to vie with her love for Rebecca. She explicitly compared her feelings for men to hers for Rebecca. While she lived in New York City, Addie's suitor, Mr. Lee, proposed marriage. Addie relayed the news: "He said it will not be long before he will return and make me his wife. He said that he's met with gr[at] many ladies since he is be gone but none compare with his sweat Addie. He says his love is stronger then ever." Addie undoubtedly imparted this information to inspire jealousy in Rebecca but quickly followed it with a reassuring line to ease the sting: "Dear Rebecca, I never shall love any person as I do you." In another letter that month, an intervention by Aunt Chatty revealed the complexity of the competition. Addie enclosed a short note from Aunt Chat that she dictated *to* Addie (I assume Aunt Chat was not literate). The letter expressed concern about Addie, who had been sick and mournfully pining for Rebecca. Aunt Chat had worried about her:

> Dear Rebecca, I wish that you wear here to see Addie. She look so sad and melencholy. She look as if she lost all her friends. She make me feel very sad. I often [toks] your footstep and Mr. Lee to comfort her. I don't know what she would do without. Addie has been very sick. I to take the best care for your sake and Mr. Lee. She rec two letters from Mr. Lee and I never seen anyone so overjoy as she was. I wish you had of been a witch and been at [its merdow]. You say you do not know what love is. Addie does, I can

assure. I would have written to you before but I did not know [weather] it would be, except it every time Addie rec your letter she said you send your love to me. So I take the pleasure of writing a few lines to you. No more at present. I remain your affectionate friend, Charity A. Jackson.

This letter deeply incriminated Addie. In her own letters, Addie pled her love for Rebecca and consistently reassured her that her love and devotion could not be matched or stolen by any man, certainly not Mr. Lee. And here Aunt Chat recounted Addie's ill health and melancholy, which were buoyed only by Mr. Lee: "I never saw anyone so overjoy as she was." Aunt Chat's description challenged Addie's presentation of self and threatened to unmask Addie's double life with Mr. Lee. Addie responded to the allegations in her own letter that same day:

> Dear Rebecca, Mr. Lee letters. I was very much please to rec his letter, but not in the way that Aunt Chat spoke. I told her that was not what I done and neather was they my feelings. She beg me to pen them to you. I done so. I do not want to make any thing to appear Aunt Chat is a person like to magnify anything. Even Selina think I am very cold and indiffrent with him . . . I want to tell you what I done the evening before. He went, he ask me if I love you better than I did him. I told him, "yes I did."

We can only imagine the conflicted torment Addie must have experienced while writing Aunt Chat's message to Rebecca—with which she so vehemently disagreed—fearful of how Rebecca might interpret it.[11]

Addie did not keep her saucy declarations of love to Rebecca a secret from hers or Rebecca's domestic networks. They openly discussed their relationship with relatives and friends and commiserated over their separation. While Rebecca's kin appeared to harbor no ill feelings about the passion the women felt for each other, several years later her Aunt Emily warned that Addie would be wise not to tell her Hartford beau, Joseph Tines, a waiter, that she loved Rebecca better than anyone. Addie wrote to Rebecca,

> How I have miss you. I have lost all; no more pleasure for me now. Aunt Emily ask me last eve if I was going to carry that [sober] face until you return. She also said if Mr. T. was to see me, think that I care more for you then I did for him. I told, I did love you more then I ever would him. She said I better not tell him so. It would be the truth and most else.

Mr. Tines assured her that best friends must inevitably part.[12]

His prophecy came true, despite the intensity and deep commitment of Addie and Rebecca's relationship. Unlike those lifelong bonds uncovered by Smith-Rosenberg, Addie and Rebecca eventually went their separate ways. While in Maryland after the Civil War, Rebecca met and worked with a former slave, Charles H. Thomas, whom she later married. In 1868, after three years of courtship, Addie married Joseph Tines. Her correspondence to Rebecca stopped shortly before she married. The newlyweds moved to the Tines family home in Philadelphia, and Addie died of tuberculosis two short years later.

WHITE WORKING WOMEN'S FRIENDSHIPS

As in Addie's relationship with Rebecca, trust laid the foundation among white working women for honesty, self-disclosure, and intimacy—the cornerstones of friendship (see Figure 13). In 1841, Lavinia Merrill, a white textile-mill worker, wrote to Rhoda Parker, an apprentice comb-maker, about the importance of openness in a relationship: "I hope you will write soon and tell me just how you feel. Don't keep back one thing but open your heart freely to me with the pen, if we cannot see each other face to face." Similarly, Hephzibah wrote to Sarah Carter, a teacher, that despite the disparity in their educational backgrounds they were friends, because, "as you said, there is enough in this world who profess to be our friends, yet how few amongst that number speak right into our heart & find a responce there." Hephzibah thanked Sarah for the "kind & most welcom letter in which you unbosomed your heart so freely to me." Erlunia, a schoolteacher, in her effort to establish the trust necessary for such openness, prodded Ann Lilley, her schoolteacher friend, about her suitors and reassured her, "Now be canded and I will promise to be a faithful confidant. I will not betray the trust you [repose] in me if you say not; so don't fear but be familiar and tell the whole truth and then we will consult together if you please."[13]

White working women also openly professed their love to one another. Erlunia's relationship with Ann Lilley bristled with the tension between teasing, attraction, and the quest for intimacy. The two attended a teaching academy together, then corresponded after they found jobs. Only letters from Erlunia to Ann exist, so Ann's responses must be inferred. Erlunia forthrightly vaunted her desire to be Ann's friend and confidante. She made it her business to know as much about other people as possible, including Ann. She scorned the lament of others that she was twenty-eight and still unmarried. Her light-hearted letters detailed local gossip. In one letter from Whitins Ville, Massachusetts, in 1841, Erlunia, at Ann's request, sent Ann a poem:

> Look! thy step—oh how elastic,
> and made *with grace* the most exquisit.
> Your voice too! Ah, shall I speak it?
> There is celestial music in it;
> And then they form, ow powers divine!
> *Could I but make this angel mine.*

Defending herself against misinterpretation, even in the context of nineteenth-century romantic friendship, Erlunia qualified her poetry, "Now Ann these few lines are the supposed ideas of some of your Plainfield gallants." She acknowledged the limitations of her own artistic skill: "Now Ann as you value my friendship, do you keep this poetry business to yourself, for I don't profess to be a poetess nor any such thing. I know I don't know enough to be one. I only wrote this trash just to make you laugh a little and make a little variety in the letter." Her disclaimers aside, in adopting the vantage point of men, she exposed some of her own feelings for Ann.[14]

Hephzibah wrote of her joy in hearing from Sarah Carter: "Your letter came and spoke into my heart like a cleer bright sun beam upon the troubled waters after a thunder storm. [A]nd oh, I hope for such sunbeams often." Lavinia wrote of a similar sunny brightness that accompanied her thoughts of Rhoda Parker:

> Dear Friend, It is with the utmost pleasure I now embrace these few fleeting moments and improve them in writing to you, my much loved friend. I suppose you have reason to think I have forgotten you as I have not written to you before, but I assure you I have not. Ah no! Far be it for me to forget a girl lovely and affectionate as you are. I think a great deal of you. There is not a day passes but I think of you and long to see or hear from you.

Diarists and correspondents repeatedly recorded their thoughts of absent friends. If friends could not be close physically, they could at least leave deep impressions on the consciousness of others. Friends regularly exchanged words of love, passion, and longing. Martha Barrett wrote in her diary of her dear friend Lucy:

> Called last eve. on dear Lucy Colby, found her looking extremely well and happy. She seems to have entirely recovered her health. I fear I did her gentle spirit injustice in my lines to her last week. *I do love her.* And I believe my love is sincerely returned. Why should I doubt it.

The following year Martha experienced traumatic emotional dislocation caused by Lucy's marriage, her move to Ohio, and shortly thereafter her death from consumption. Martha traipsed past Lucy's house, retraced familiar walking paths, and requested a picture of Lucy from her family while mourning her death.[15]

While not pitting a suitor directly against her dear friend as did Addie Brown, Sarah Holmes Clark situated her love for Sarah Carter in the context of her recent marriage. She described it first not as competitive, but as complementary to that with her husband:

> But my friend, tho I feel that I love my husband as devotedly and tenderly as woman can love, *I can say truly* that you still hold a warm place in my affections. & if you could know how often I think of you each day, how earnestly I wish you with me again, you would not think that time or absence had lessened my love for you.

She wrote that Sarah Carter "must save some little snug corner in your [warm] heart where neither husband or child can creep in for me. And never suspect that you will louse your place in my affectio[ns]." However, she later discarded the safely "separate but equal" orientation and compared her affection for Gilman, her husband, to her feelings for Sarah Carter. In fact, she implied that one could replace the other:

> I could almost forget for a time that Gilman is absent if you would only be so kind as to step in. *I wish to see you so much. Why won't you come!* But now I think of it, I am almost sorry that I told you of Gilman's absence. Will you not imagine that I only think of you when he is away? You must not think so. 'Tis far from being true. I think of you every day & often. We often talk of you. . . . do . . . you believe me? I must tell you that I love & care for you, whether you believe or doubt for 'tis a releif to me to write it. And I hope to be able to regain your confidence in time.

While this letter could easily have been written by a middle-class woman, the relationship differed markedly from those studied by Smith-Rosenberg. The middle-class relationships coexisted peacefully alongside marital partnerships with little or no conflict. In the agrarian and working classes, scarce resources made demands on marriage that occasionally placed female friends in direct competition with husbands. Sarah Holmes Clark faced conflict with her husband over her commitment to a local friend:

> Mrs. Baker, my best friend in Madison, was very sick. I was with her two days & nights & when she was out of danger, I came home sick. & I have not been as well as I was before that event. Mr. Clark objected to my being with Mrs. B. but I would not refuse to go. We came to Madison about the same time, boarded at the same hotel the first year, made our baby clothes together, & our children were born about the same time & have been intimate

friends ever since. & I would not leave her when she was in so much trouble. But I do not intend to go to witness another such scene; 'tis too much for my nerves.

Her commitment to her friend won in this battle with her husband over competing loyalties, but not without consequences. Her nerves paid the price. Her actions appear to be subject to negotiation in future confrontations, and she may more readily yield her position. In this situation, friendship collided head-on with marriage rather than amiably coexisting. While friendship won in this instance, future outcomes appear more uncertain.[16]

The loneliness women suffered while separated from one another provided more evidence of their keen attachment. Sarah Trask, a shoe binder, recorded a June day full of visiting in her diary: "We had a grand time, comsidering M.E.R. was not there, for I don't injoy myself without her and I always miss her." Similarly for Addie Brown, separations tested her endurance. While working in New York City in 1861, Addie wrote about her wrenching departure from Hartford: "Rebecca, when I bid you good by it seem to me that my very heart broke. I have felt wretched ever since. Sometime I feel that I could not live one hour to another. My Darling Friend, I shall never be happy again unless I am near you, eather here on earth or in heaven. Since you have left me I want nothing. O Rebecca, why can't I be with you? Will I never have that pleasure? Don't tell me no, for I must." Four years later, after being together for a while, jobs once again separated Rebecca and Addie. Addie now lived back in Hartford, but Rebecca had moved away to teach school. Addie occasionally worked with Rebecca's younger sister, Henrietta Primus. Henrietta wrote to her sister about Addie's suitor and his impatience with Addie's fierce attachment to her love object. "Mr. Ti[ne]s has been down to see her to day, so that she is in very good spirits. He left word with Aunt Em that if she [cry]ed on the road with him up town that he would send her back home, for she [crys] a good part of her time about you."[17]

In spite of the intensity of emotion, perhaps because of it, the slightest inattention threatened some relationships. Correspondents and diarists experienced acute insecurity regarding the reciprocity of feelings and attachment. They acknowledged rules of behavior that accompanied friend status. Sarah Trask feared that she violated a tenet of friendship with her best friend:

My best friend was rather dull this evening, I wish I knew the cause, so I could cheer her up, then I think she would feel better. Fore one word from her when I ham dull, it cheer me up. That's why I think a word from me would cheer her. Perhaps I am mistaken, for she may think that I care not for her. Sometimes I think she has reasons to think so, for I do not treat people as I ought. But I hope my friends will forgive me, and I will try to do better in future.

Friends answered each other's pleas for attention with reassurance, reaffirming their love and commitment through words and action. Hephzibah, who described herself as plain, sincere, and straightforward, devalued her intelligence, at least in comparison to that of her friend, Sarah Carter:

> I often thought when with you that it was strange you could love me when your mind was traind to so much higher things than mine. And often wondered that you did not make a friend of some more capable of being a companion than I was.

Sarah responded by writing, thus reaffirming their friendship and reassuring her anxious friend. After her move to Georgia from Maine, Sarah Holmes Clark also pleaded with Sarah Carter not to forget her and to keep writing: "I fear you will cast me from your list. But I beg to be trusted & treasured a little longer. I cannot spare you. *I will not let* you go, so you may as well write me very soon. This with *very much love from* Sarah." She had a husband, but Sarah she could not spare. Her fear of being neglected came from feeling "dull," as she described herself, pointing to the importance of intelligence and spirit in friendship. Letter-writing provided but a tenuous means to sustain a friendship accustomed to being stoked by daily visits and a shared social world. In apologizing to Sarah for her neglect in not writing sooner, Sarah Holmes Clark wrote, "I do not possess the least disposition to allow you to forget me or to cease to love me. You may scold me, abuse me, tell me all the hard thoughts which you have formed of me during the past six months," but, Sarah implied, do not abandon me. In addition, she felt lonely. "I have some very dear & truly kind friends here, but they are not like old friends; *never can be*, I am not Sarah Holmes but Mrs. Clark to Ga. friends & there is a vast difference in these two, I assure you." Her distinction between new friends and those with a history remained central to her notion of true friendship.[18]

Addie's anxieties, like Rebecca's that she tried to address, also reflected an insecurity about their mutual commitment. At times, the anxiety seemed to arise from deeper conflict in the relationship. At other times, it appeared a consequence of occasionally desperate young love.

I miss you dearly, Beloved Friend. Now can you say it? You do not look upon me the same way. What is it, my Dearest, that make you feel thus? My heart is almost broke. I did not intend telling you my feeling[s] but I could not help it. . . . If I only know what I could do to win your affec back, I would willing do so.

Addie's reply to Rebecca indicated that Rebecca felt vulnerable to Addie's moods and was uncertain as to how to interpret them: "Sweat Sister, I have peruse your note again. It make the six time. I cannot perceive why you thought thus I was indefferent towards you that A.M. My Darling, I did not feel so, although I felt sad that morning." Addie eventually smoothed over the hurt feelings by going through the ritual of reassuring her beloved. While Addie attempted to fortify the relationship by addressing their mutual insecurities more often than white women did, the white women nonetheless also expressed great need for their friends to lavish their love and affection.[19]

However, the threat of conflict and dissolution lurked behind relationships between working women. With the intense highs and lows of the relationships, friction and misunderstanding occasionally erupted. The only visible breakup of friends that surfaced in the letters and diaries occurred between Sarah Carter and Marcella Holmes, Sarah Holmes Clark's younger sister. While Sarah and Marcella did not develop a romantic friendship, they corresponded with affection after Marcella moved to Berzelia, Georgia, in the late 1850s. At twenty-six, Marcella fancied herself independent, self-sufficient, and permanently single. She valued honesty, but apparently not tact. For example, in one letter in January, 1860, she wrote, "Miss Carter why don't you improve your bad writing? I am going to improve mine and advise you to do the same. You do not write well at all and I am surprised at you as well as at myself." Marcella provoked offense in Sarah when, in her unabashed style she boldly interrogated Sarah about her liaison with Dr. Jordon, a married man. Dr. Jordon and Sarah had been seen by "the people" talking in the store where Sarah worked. Marcella waited to raise some of these questions, "because I feared that I might hurt your feelings." Later she jettisoned her concern and plunged into the muck. "What has ruined your character in the town of Foxcroft? Every one that will answer me at all speaks against you." This news shocked Sarah, who demanded some evidence. Unfortunately Marcella made a practice of burning her letters once she answered them, so had to reconstruct the story from memory. "Miss C.'s associates are nearly all of an exceptionable kind, and it is the general impression that she is no better than she ought to be, that you walk the streets with Dr. Jordon at night." Marcella provided as much evidence as possible to the mortified Sarah but failed to overcome Sarah's indignation at her frankness and at the message she delivered. After this letter, Sarah found the Foxcroft residents "quiet" on the issue of her friendship with Dr. Jordon, perhaps raising questions in her mind as to the source of the gossip and the role of Marcella in circulating it.[20]

Marcella and Sarah exchanged only a few letters after that. Marcella attempted to make amends, but to no avail. She volunteered to go into business with Sarah, on the heels of advising her against setting up a millinery shop in the North. She endearingly inquired after Sarah's family and friends. After a six-month lapse, Marcella wrote, "I do not owe you a letter, at least I think not. Still you remain silent and I've come to the conclusion that I'll write anyhow." The attack on Fort Sumter and the unfolding of the Civil War intervened into the friendship irretrievably stamped with political differences as well as personal ones. Unaware or unconcerned with Sarah's abolitionist views, Marcella sealed her fate when she referred to Lincoln's recent presidential victory: "I did not think that the North would aspire to have a part negro to reign over them. I remember that mother used to say he was African decent." Marcella immediately followed this discrediting remark with an appeal to "write soon if you have not discarded me as a correspondent," a plea which appears to have gone unmet.[21]

Marcella Holmes's falling-out with Sarah Carter points to one of the differences between the friendships of middle-class white women and working women: their length. A notable characteristic of the romantic friendships that Smith-Rosenberg studied is their lifelong endurance, even in the context of lengthy, distant separations and heterosexual marriage. Hephzibah endorsed the importance of continuity in friendship over time and place when she wrote to Sarah Carter from Hallowell, Maine, in 1845: "What would be the use of all this intamacy and trustfullness when together if the first, short absense was to banish the recolection of the *dear one* and *all* the happy associations conected with them. But is it not to often so?" Confirming Hephzibah's observation, I was unable to locate evidence of lifelong friendship outside of family circles for working women, white or black. It is impossible to determine if friendships were shorter, that is, from ten to fifteen years (in part because of competition with marital relationships), or if they appear so because only fragmentary documentation has survived. That said, marriage, in part because of newly created geographic distance, drew women out of the female friendship loop, at least temporarily. Sarah Holmes Clark complained to Sarah Carter about not receiving a letter from her recently: "I had given up all hopes of ever hearing from you again and concluded that you was either dead or married."[22]

WORKING MEN'S FRIENDSHIPS

A corollary to the assumption of separate spheres for women is that all-male environments laid the foundations for male friendships. Some historians and sociologists argue that like their female counterparts, men had the opportunity to socialize free from distractions from women, which enabled them to develop intimate relationships with each other. In theory, gender segregation led to enormous emotional distances between men and women, dramatically inhibiting intimacy between them. Therefore, for deep emotional relationships, they turned to a homosocial world. While on the face of it, this perspective of separation and symmetry is compelling, one could reasonably argue that male culture, with its emphasis on competition, reduced the possibility for intimate friendship of the female variety.[23]

Yet some scholars argue that like their female counterparts, nineteenth-century men actively created opportunities to socialize independent of women. These situations enabled them to develop relationships with each other, some of them intimate. Historians and sociologists point to the all-male worlds of battlefields, the workplace, the western frontier, and fraternal societies as environments where men congregated together and discovered friendship and the treasures of same-gender intimacy. I would argue that the form of male bonding within the orders and lodges, with its valorization of that-which-was-not-female, would demarcate a place for activity, conversation, socializing, conducting business, camaraderie, but not for the type of intimacy so commonly displayed in friendships between women. Collectively, these studies indicate that indeed a world of male ritual flourished. But, the question remains, was there also a male world of love and intimacy?[24]

Historical evidence points to love between elite political and literary men as well as middle-class men. In his research on middle-class men, E. Anthony Rotundo finds that men in the nineteenth century formed friendships throughout their lives but established *intimate* relationships with men virtually only in the period between boyhood and manhood. Men's letters spoke of a physical component which may or may not have been explicitly sexual but at least included hugs, kisses, and sharing a bed. He asserts that during their youth men psychologically broke from their families and sought to establish themselves in the world, before they married or established a career. This was a time, according to Rotundo, that a young man passed "from the security and moral rectitude of women's sphere to the freedom and competitive rigor of men's sphere." When compared to white middle-class female relationships, Rotundo finds middle-class men's friendships similar in their social acceptability, daily content, and physical manifestations. The primary difference he observes is that the male relationships were bound by the life cycle; they did not continue into married life, as did their female equivalents.[25]

Thus, we come to the confirmation of ritual, love, and intimacy, at least in the middle and elite classes. The class character of these findings remains a question I want to address. The case of Brigham Nims and J. Foster Beal gives us a rare opportunity to delve into the intricacies of a friendship between working men. The larger challenge remains to interpret the meaning friendship and intimacy had in men's lives, the significance of such relationships for our contemporary understanding of separate spheres, and, given the broader context, the light they might cast on women's relationships of antebellum New England.

BRIGHAM AND FOSTER

In my search for source materials for this book, I had a much more difficult time unearthing evidence of friendship between working men than that between women (scattered evidence does exist; see for example, Figure 14). However, one case illuminates the possibilities and range of emotional expression open to men who worked at different kinds of manual labor. The correspondence between Brigham Nims and J. Foster Beal reveals a friendship that was both intimate and romantic.[26]

Although the two men grew up in the same county in rural New Hampshire, they did not meet until 1831, when Brigham was twenty and Foster was twenty-one. The earliest letter from Foster revealed a rowdy joyfulness in their relationship, with a decidedly masculine physical component:

Dear friend Sir B   Boston March 21st 1832

I received your letter by [G.] Tuffs which I read with the greatest pleasure. I rejoice to hear that you are in good health, and the rest of your friends. I want to see you very much, indeed to have a good box with you, which you

said you should like to have with me. I think if you are as fat as I be we
should puff and blow.

In contrast to elite men's romantic letters, the letter did not speak of
love. If we compare it to those between working women, we find it more
jovial, less romantic and flowery. Foster's letter assumed a mutual bond
and conveyed a sense of delight in the friendship. Foster's teasing ignored
Brigham's self-portrait as a man with whom others had difficulty getting
along. The physicality referenced in the letter—organized sport, ram-
bunctiousness, and physical competitiveness—reflected male expressions of affection (and sometimes attraction).[27]

A letter two years later expressed a similar teasing camaraderie.
Foster chided Brigham for his successes (becoming a schoolteacher) and
reminded him of his more humble origins (recently working in a box
factory). Although in jest, these comments' hostile edge revealed the
importance of the shared class background and the potential threat to
their relationship of the geographic and economic mobility of the early
nineteenth century. At the same time, Foster reminded Brigham of the
affectionate time they spent together and of his role in nursing Brigham
through an illness. Foster admonished him for neglecting to write:

Well Brig:

I suppose you have got to be a schooll masster, since you[r] was in Boston.
You need not be so, stuck up, (as J[a]ck Downing says), because you are
tu[c]ked down in the least post of Nelson. I have been there myself. I guess
you have forgot all about you being at Boston last Sept. when you was so
sick, and I took care of you, doctored you up, even tooke you in the bed with
myself; now you will not do as much, as, to write to me.

To share a bed in nineteenth-century Boston was not uncommon; with
the lack of space in most homes, visitors frequently shared beds with
their hosts. The striking tender image of Foster nursing Brigham contra-
dicts our twentieth-century stereotypes of nursing, historically a female
vocation. It also challenges a contemporary conception of the acceptable
boundaries of male behavior in the nineteenth century.[28]

Foster did not write to Brigham as a literary exercise, as did elite men
who cleverly coded their romance. As a box-factory hand and former
teacher, he frequently punctuated the letters with misspelled words and
grammatical errors. The letters focused not on work but on all matters
related to their friendship and community of shared acquaintances. They
contained a broad range of information and moods. Most letters in-

cluded some gossip—news of people, events, and greetings from others who knew Brigham. For example, Foster relayed a noteworthy event: "Wm Buckminster said there had been a weding to Old Father [Wonderell's]. Harriet was married. He and [Lucy] stood right up by the side of them, all the time—by the flash of [Gimblets]! If it didn't make his eyes weep, when he come to tie the nott."[29]

Foster comfortably divulged his confusion about his future and his soul-searching to Brigham. In one letter he pondered the precariousness of life and his wretchedness at his earthly material attachments:

> It is almost three years since we first formed an acquaintance. Time has rappidly passed on by and wrought changs that time nor eternity can replace. When I look[ed] around me, I see many of my fellow mortels deprived of health, many going down to an early gra[v]e and still I am blest with perfet health. Why is this distinction? Yet I hardly think of [Him], God that made me. My ungrateful heart clings to its mother [dirt] and there alone it seeks for happiness.

Foster clearly trusted Brigham to be his sympathetic philosophical sounding board.[30]

Some of Foster's passages resemble the letters exchanged between women who were intimates:

> Can not forget those happy hours [th]at we spent at G. Newcombs and the evening walks. But we are deprived of that priv[e]ledg now, we are separated for a time. We cannot tell how long perhaps before our eyes behold each other in this world.

In fact, this excerpt could have been written by a female hand. Compare its imagery to that in Hephzibah's letter to Sarah Carter in June, 1845: "I need not say how much I want to see you, I think of you often and the pleasant walks we had at twilight by that little *silver stream*." At the end of his letter, after signing his name, Foster composed a poem:

> O be on the Tenne[ac]e to night
> Look as far as your blue eyes can see
> Remember each star in your sight
> Will be gilding my cottage and me
> Take one from the many and think
> That Foster has singled it to
> Still bound by one lingering link
> To Boston, great City and you.

Its romantic simplicity connects the two men, separated by the demands of their work. Foster's poem situates their relationship within a cosmic context, dwarfing their geographic distance and maintaining their link to one another.[31]

However, no letters exist from Foster after 1834, and references to him in Brigham's letters disappear by 1840. Foster married Sarah Jane Day in 1838, and they had a son in 1839. Rotundo's explanation of the role of marriage disrupting male friendships seems appropriate here. While Brigham did not marry for another thirteen years, the obligations of marriage may well have overtaken Foster's emotional as well as recreational life.

Foster did not display discomfort with their relationship, nor did he express any need for secrecy regarding his declarations of affection. Brigham gathered and saved Foster's letters, indicating their value to him and suggesting that it was acceptable for men to reveal their feelings to one another and to write about them. From accounts in town histories, obituaries, and letters, it appears that Brigham's community respected him and did not treat him as a deviant. The example of Foster and Brigham's friendship suggests that unlike the twentieth century, manliness did not require the suppression of emotion.

FRIENDSHIPS BETWEEN WOMEN AND MEN

In the mid-nineteenth century, Thoreau wrote that friendship between those of the same sex was easier than those between men and women. In a middle-class world of separate spheres where men had little knowledge of women, this seems plausible. Arthur Schlesinger writes that courtship was considered "the only proper basis of companionship with the other sex," presumably for upstanding middle-class citizens. In the cultural milieu where working women and men mingled socially, a greater capacity for friendship existed. In the twentieth century, friendships between men and women are more possible among those who are young, single, and without domestic and child-care responsibilities. Most such friendships occur within couples, between male and female colleagues who share work, and where dramatic age differences exist, because these conditions mitigate sexual tension.[32]

In the social sphere of antebellum working people, visiting couples provided one forum for cross-gender contact. Some married couples befriended others, the marital context holding sexual tension in abeyance. For the most part, these were not intimate friendships, but nonetheless they were decidedly central to the nexus of community relations.

Farmer Nathan K. Abbott wrote in his diary about the visit of Mrs. Colby:

> Mrs. Colby of Hopkinton, wife of Capt. Moses B., formerly Elsy Abott, daughter of the late Mr. Moses Abbott of this town, made us a visit. Also a Franklin J. Emerson and wife and John E. Saltmarsh and wife. Mrs. Colby is an aunt of Mrs. Emerson and Mrs. Saltmarsh, who are sisters. Pleasant, but cold. Mrs. Colby has been married nearly 35 years; it was pleasant to see an old friend.

Nathan labeled Mrs. Colby an "old friend" in the carefully delineated context of her family relationships—identifying her husband, her father, and her two nieces. Other pertinent information further situated her— her lengthy marriage (thirty-five years, at a time when the hazards of life rarely allowed the luxury of shared old age) and her husband's title (though it is not clear if Captain Colby was a seaman or a soldier). These structural features of their relationship appear as important as the specific content of the relationship. Presumably, Nathan Abbott did not desire or seek intimacy with Mrs. Colby.[33]

Another common form of friendship between women and men emerged in circles of young people. It was difficult and novel for male-female relationships to be exclusive, intimate, and yet non-romantic unless they were between relatives. However, some men did have close women friends. Evidence of this type of relationship in my research comes more from women's diaries than from men's diaries or from letters. In one example, Sarah Trask wrote repeatedly about John, a friend of both her boyfriend Luther, who was away at sea, and herself. She recorded exchanges with John about many things, most pressingly, the status of her romantic involvement. He served as a touchstone that brought her closer to her beloved Luther, another lens through which to interpret Luther's feelings and actions. John was clearly Sarah's friend as well as Luther's; they often gathered in a group of other friends, male and female. In June, 1849, Sarah wrote in her diary, "J. said that he had promise to take care of me while L.W. is gone, so he must come a courting, he said. But he is a good friend to me, but now good night." Their mutual friendship with Luther and Sarah's status as "girlfriend" circumscribed their relationship. And yet, Luther was away, and John teased that his visits were to court Sarah, not to help her. She seemed to enjoy his flirting; and yet his testing of the boundaries of the relationship made her uncomfortable. She pushed the innuendos aside by placing John squarely in the category "friend," in effect denying the sexual

tension. For cross-gender friendship, the label friend assuaged sexual
tension whereas for female friendship, the label invited it.[34]

Another example of this type of relationship can be found in the
letters from James Holmes (older brother of Sarah Holmes Clark) to
Sarah Carter. James and Sarah had been family friends in Maine, and
they sustained a correspondence after James left to explore the Midwest.
In 1855, he wrote Sarah from Ohio, "I shall always—consider you as
one of my friends." And in effect regularly reasserting his status, he
signed virtually every letter, "Your friend, James." James's letters discussed common acquaintances, weather, religion, farm prices, and anti-
slavery politics. In fact, their relationship was sufficiently resilient that
James confided his concerns about his sister's political transformation
after moving South:

> I red a letter from Bro. Gilman Clark . . . principaly concerning the renewal
> of the slave trade of which he is an advocate. Sarah too seems to have become
> an advocate of slavery. Perhaps it is not strange that it is so, but it is strange
> to me, how the southerners can entertain such exalted ideas of what they call
> honor & yet be so contemptably mean as to be willing to get a living at the
> expense of the liberty, comfort & happiness of the negro race, because they
> have not the ability or power to defend themselves. I am not much of a
> fighting character but before I would submit to the renewal of the slave trade,
> I would help blow every advocate of such a scheme into the Gulf of Mexico.

Under the rubric of friendship, James discussed political ideas as well as
family antagonisms with one of his sister's closest friends. In another
example, Sarah's cousin, Henry Atwood, confided in her about his family
troubles and his six-month-and-twenty-day detention in an insane asylum, the "damned insanery" as he called it. And he signed his letter,
"Yours with friendship, Henry M. Atwood."[35]

At a later time in her life, friendship with men got Sarah Carter into
trouble with the community and at least one female friend. As discussed
above, reports concerning Sarah's relationship with Dr. Jordon filtered
down from Foxcroft, Maine, to Marcella Holmes in Georgia. It was
general knowledge, according to Marcella, that Sarah did not like Mrs.
Jordon, fueling the community's suspicions regarding this liaison. Dr.
Jordon was similarly seen accompanied by G. Lebroke's wife, marring
further his character and contagiously tarnishing his associates. At least
from the vantage point of Berzelia, Georgia, this friendship fell outside
the confines of acceptable male-female behavior. Marcella recommended
a remedy: leave town. Sarah saw herself as innocent, but in the eyes of

Marcella and her anonymous correspondents in Maine, she had transgressed the acceptable boundaries of male-female friendship, opening the door to a reinterpretation of her relationship as sexual and placing her reputation in jeopardy.

Another case that demonstrates the tensions potentially a part of male-female friendship involves the relationship between John Burleigh, brother to the famous abolitionist Charles Burleigh, and Ann Lilley. A former teacher of Ann's, John corresponded with her after she began teaching. After a while he stopped writing to her because of gossip that had been circulated about them by "an (*afraid she should be*) old maid," despite his assertion that their correspondence had been "from the purest motives." Their communities in general and this reputed "old maid" in particular, scrutinized their behavior. John responded to this pressure and ceased to write.[36]

The deepest and most complex friendships between men and women surfaced in letters between family members. At least in their childhood years, men shared households with women—their mothers and sisters. By examining brothers' relationships with their sisters, we are forced to rethink the gendered character of the home and men's capacity for intimate friendship. While not all brothers shared intimacy with their sisters, those who did found satisfaction and positive sanctions.[37]

Sibling relations ranged from formal/obligatory (where siblings had nothing in common except parents) to affable to intimate. The intimate type of friendship—supportive and purposely self-revealing—between brother and sister was not unusual. In 1820, Chloe Adams wrote to her brother James in Portland, Maine, responding to his suggestion to increase the level of honesty in their friendship:

> My dear brother,
>
>   I have retired alone to my chamber & taken my pen to answer your truly affectionate letter which was duly recieved. Altho it has caused some unpleasant anxious feelings . . . You wish me to write with as much 'freedom & plainness' as you did. I will if it is in my power.

In another example, Brigham Nims and his sister, Laura Nims, shared an understanding of each other. In one letter in May of 1834 from school, Laura wrote: "Dear Brother, I steal away a few moments to addss a friend." In other letters Laura expressed joy in seeing Brigham and hearing from him. Not surprisingly, the intimacy with Laura differed from that between Brigham and Foster. While she displayed similar comfort with Brigham and addressed him with great familiarity and directness, her letters to Brigham reported on her working conditions and her school activities rather than focusing on their relationship. She *demonstrated* her intimacy with him—through her trust and her expressed desire to be in his company—but she did not *speak* of it directly. One letter in particular reveals Brigham's trust in her; he closed with: "Foster stands laughing over my shoulder. Who can write? I am the same. Do not expose this. B. Nims." Especially before she married in 1845, Laura and her brother spent long hours together and at one point journeyed together to upstate New York to visit relatives.[38]

Separate spheres did not disassociate these two siblings, even in their adulthood. Laura may have had a host of women friends as well, bosom companions with whom she confided her deepest desires. However, she sustained a companionship with her brother; she worried about his religious salvation, and he confided secrets to her. They shared the profession of schoolteaching and both made their base at the Nims's homestead in Roxbury, New Hampshire. When Laura married at age thirty, Brigham toured the countryside inviting guests to come to the wedding, as was a custom at the time. More importantly, he helped bake her wedding cake and afterward carefully recorded the recipe in his diary.[39]

However, not all brothers and sisters were intimates. Relationships could be distant, emotionally as well as geographically. The Dame sisters, Permelia and Harriet, left a collection of letters written to their brother, George Washington Dame, revealing a formal and obligatory relationship. After the death of their mother, the sisters lived with their father who, because of ill health, could not provide for them. They wrote from their factory jobs in New Hampshire and Massachusetts to George, a schoolteacher in Prince Edward, Virginia, seeking his advice and financial support, and urging him to return North to visit. Mostly their letters and their prayers went unanswered. Even when George agreed to pay for Harriet's education, Permelia and Harriet found themselves hesitantly yet desperately awaiting his much-needed aid. They wanted George to adopt the role of patriarch, with its obligations and responsibilities (Harriet told him, "To me you have taken the place of a Father"), but he largely resisted, for reasons unarticulated. He provided neither emotional nor financial support.[40]

In a fundamentally more engaged fraternal-sororal relationship, Stephen Parker took pleasure in knowing about his sister Rhoda, seeing her, and teasing her, though he clearly did not know her well. The Parker children had been orphaned many years before the correspondence begins, and Rhoda in particular had been separated from the rest of the family since she was a young child. Stephen decided that Rhoda's residence, an hour's stagecoach ride away from North Andover, was unacceptably distant, and that they should overcome it by reactivating their family relationship. In one letter Stephen inquired, in a half-teasing, half-serious, older-brotherly way, about Rhoda's new beau, about whom another brother, Winthrop (who lived in New York), wanted to know more:

> By the way Sis—how do you & you "dancing school" beau get along? Are you not a going to let us *see* him this Winter? Would you be proud to introduce him to your friends? I told Winthrop about him just before he left town & he scolded me for not telling him of it before. Said he wanted to *see* him &c. Said I ought to have gone & seen him & if he was not a "*right one*" to set him afloat &c. But I told him our dear Sis was capable of *choosing for herself &c.* Now dear Sis, is not that truth? Time will show. In your next letter you will, I hope, tell us all about *this subject*—for it is a subject in which I feel a good deal interested . . . beleive me your ever afft *Brother Stephen.*

In his teasing playfulness, Stephen referred to himself as her friend. He also endorsed her capacity to judge character, though he reserved the right to assess her verdict. In a letter a month earlier, he had played upon her sense of obligation and affection as a sister and as an aunt to his children to try to bring her closer to him and his family: "Charley is growing finely. . . . We think he is the *finest* nephew you have. He weighed yesterday 15 #—can hold up his head & look about quite smart. Don't you want to see him?" Stephen and Rhoda related more as kin than as friends, and in that capacity were very important to each other. Their example helps map the range of behavior and feeling between brothers and sisters, and throws into relief the intimacy that sometimes did transpire, as between Brigham and Laura Nims.[41]

CLASS AND GENDER IMPLICATIONS

These working women and men actively sought intimate friendship. Their cultural ideal, they found it widely available and sympathetically understood in their environment. Women in particular strove to achieve friend relations. Rooted in mutual dependency, self-disclosure, and honesty, the friendships flourished as intimately and romantically as those of middle-class white women. For working women, friendship with women invited intimacy, even romance. True friendship validated a woman's character. But domestic networks and partners placed limits on working women's commitments to one another. At critical junctures in working women's lives, the friendships became more vulnerable to the demands of marriage and the family than did those between middle-class women. Smith-Rosenberg finds middle-class female friendship harmonious with marriage. In contrast, in these working women's friendships, competition occasionally surfaced between friends and partners, creating tension within heterosexual relationships as well as within the homosocial ones. In addition and not unrelated, the surviving evidence of working women's relationships is more fragmentary, suggesting perhaps that while the friendships lasted ten to fifteen years, they did not routinely span the adult life of the women, as they did in middle-class relationships.

The collection of Addie Brown's and Rebecca Primus's letters documents the extraordinary legacy of an African-American working-class friendship. The rare documents vividly attest to life in the free black community in the antebellum and postbellum North. We have few means for assessing how well the relationship represents those of other African-American working-class women at the time. To analyze this case study, we can say that Addie and Rebecca's friendship resembled white working women's relationships in their passion, in their longing for each other when apart, and in their commitment to one another. At the same time, they differed in at least one significant way. They had to confront another oppression in society—that of racism—although they rarely discussed it. They assumed that white skin—"oh that skin," as Addie said—would have made their lives easier in a host of ways. But judging from white working women's relationships, while white skin probably would have made life easier, it would not have guaranteed that they could remain together.

Research on nineteenth-century fraternal societies convincingly demonstrates that working-class men did construct a world of ritual. Other scholarship finds that middle-class and elite men shared love and compassion. Brigham's friendship with Foster suggests that a world of love between working men also existed. However, the two worlds—of ritual and love—did not necessarily overlap for men as they did for women. The Brigham-Foster friendship, although conceived in their work lives, existed apart from the framework of fraternal or trade organizations indicating that it did not require an exclusive, male-identified context in which to thrive. How many people participated in these worlds remains a question unanswered.

Brigham's and Foster's experience provides a window into a friendship between working men—the intimacy, the camaraderie, the physicality, the romance, and the sparring that it entailed. They found it acceptable to have strong feelings, to express them to each other, and to write about them. Manliness did not require the suppression of emotion (although it did demand stifling tears). Brigham Nims was not so different from his contemporaries in his work history, his family life, and his place within his community. Neither Brigham nor Foster gave any indication of feeling deviant. Their relationship fit comfortably within the matrix of their extended family lives. They did not overtly violate any societal taboos. If Brigham's and Foster's experience was any indication, expressions of feelings of fondness for and attachment to other men were irrelevant to the definition of working men's masculinity in antebellum New England.

How different was their friendship from relationships documented between middle-class and elite men? Rooted in shared employment and a common culture, Foster and Brigham developed a friendship that transcended the workplace. They spoke a less eloquent language; nevertheless, it was a language of caring and friendship. The friendship germinated and flourished while the two were single and in their early twenties but ended shortly after Foster married, rendering it similar to those transitional relationships of youth described by Rotundo. It also resembled the intense romantic friendships evident between working women.

In antebellum New England, friends expressed differing degrees of affection, with sexuality inescapably an undercurrent. The fear of homosexuality and consequent stigmas did not stifle the antebellum cultural consciousness, and therefore intimate friendship did not reflect negatively on masculinity or femininity—in fact, to the contrary. The friendship between Brigham and Foster did not undermine their manhood or their respectability in their community. Addie's friendship with Rebecca reaffirmed her honor and elevated her sense of herself. Hephzibah's relationship with Sarah Carter helped her rise above her daily circumstances and strive for self-improvement. Only after Freud and the transformation of economic and social relations did prescriptions for masculinity so rigidly constrict friendship and patterns of sexuality. This prompts the question as to why intimate friendships are so sexualized in the late twentieth century. Friendship is regularly viewed through a psychosexual lens. It is only from this vantage point that these romantic friendships appear daringly sexual.

Women also shared intimate friendships with men, although less commonly than with women. However, unless bounded by filial relations or marriage, the hint of a romantic dimension quickly rendered such friendships unacceptable (except perhaps, as courtship) or even dangerous (as in the example of Sarah Carter and Dr. Jordon). If male and female friends were not kin, neighbors and family members monitored their interactions, keeping them in check through gossip and community sanctions. While a cross-sex friendship between kin did not guarantee intimacy, it offered the option of divulging secrets and sharing a bond. The family provided one safe arena for friendship.

The dyadic friendships investigated in this chapter were not cloistered away from other social relations. Firmly embedded in social and domestic networks, they remained the building blocks of community life. The nineteenth-century culture did not force a mutually exclusive choice between intimate friendship and sociability. Friends' bonds entailed mutual economic aid as well as social obligations crucial to the well-being of the individual and the community.

CHAPTER FOUR

"Social Work"

Visiting and the Creation of Community

Farmer John Plummer Foster made a special trip from North Andover, Massachusetts, on Monday, December 21, 1857: "I went down to Boxford, and called at Edward Foster's, Caroline Batchelder's, Charles Spofford's, and Aaron Spofford's." After his morning sewing in April, 1845, Brigham Nims made a round of visits: "started for the P.O. about 9 o'clock. Called at Mr. Adams', Asa & Joshua, Lawrence's, Dr. Buckministr's, then to Wm. Nims'. Visited Laura . . . then I called at Uncle Rosewell's & Wright's, then home." The sheer volume of visitors filtering in and out of everyday routines astounds the twentieth-century reader. Looking at a diary can feel like reading a telephone book, calling roll for the community. For example, on that bustling Saturday in January, 1853, quoted at length in Chapter 1, Martha Barrett chronicled the visitors to her household: Pease Page, Cousin Hannah Grant, Sophia Roberts and little Mary, Parker Pillsbury, Lucy A. C., Uncle Thomas and Aunt Hetty Haskell, and James Wilkins. Nine people "dropped by" over the course of the day, and Martha went to visit three others. Occasionally, even diarists themselves perceived the volume as excessive. Such was the case for Sarah Root, a woman married to a forkmaker/blacksmith in Belchertown, Massachusetts, who took in boarders to make ends meet. One cold February day in 1862, she recorded in her diary: "Mr. Mrs. [A.] Owen. Suson Owen and company. Mary Smith company. All company, nothing but company. Who ever see so much company?" Visits—purposeful and systematic but informal and unplanned—provided occasions to exchange comfort, companionship, information, and moral evaluations, in addition to labor.[1]

Visits involved an individual or group going to another household. While there, visitors talked, occasionally worked, and sometimes ate food or drank tea. The many types of visiting ranged from pure social-izing to communal labor; visitors took afternoon tea, made informal Sunday visits, attended maple sugar parties and cider tastings, stayed for extended visits, offered assistance in giving birth, paid their respects to the family of the deceased, participated in quilting parties, and raised houses and barns. Visits lasted from a brief stopover, or a "call," to a leisurely afternoon, to a month-long stay. Visitors frequently stayed overnight. The difficulty of travel—particularly in winter, by foot, horse, stage, wagon, or train—created barriers to visiting but did not deter visitors who highly valued their contact with neighbors and kin. It was through visiting, in fact, that they created their communities.[2]

Visiting, as part of an elaborate system of exchange, reaffirmed group membership and incurred an expectation of reciprocity. It expanded the contacts of the private sphere, broadening and deepening the networks of social intercourse. Visiting maintained community life through a system of social and labor exchange. This interactive process—engaged in by both men and women—depended upon a premise of reciprocity which created demands and obligations amongst neighbors and kin. Unlike charitable or "friendly" visits, it assumed that visitor and host generally shared an equality of circumstance. The act of visiting honored the individuals visited as well as confirmed their inclusion in the community.[3]

Like the division of labor and friend relationships, the practice of visiting challenged the idea of separate spheres because both men and women visited, often in gender-integrated settings. Both men and women brought interests and skills to the social sphere, lavishing energy and time in performing its labors and partaking of its rewards.

Late-twentieth-century culture views visiting as a leisure activity. Antebellum New England culture did not separate leisure and work in the same way. As well-expressed in *Reminiscences of a New Hampshire Town*, neighborhood gatherings "had to be predicated upon a good honest excuse, since just gathering for pleasure would be a waste of time." While subjects visited as a form of entertainment, they also used visiting as an occasion for work. Work often intermeshed with leisure, and vice versa. During visits, subjects exchanged labor, critical services, and entertainment.[4]

The massive shifts in the market economy over the course of the nineteenth century transformed activity in the social realm. Industrial capitalism reorganized social life through the constraints it placed upon opportunities to visit and in the way it fundamentally reordered economic production. The production of textiles in particular was dramatically transformed from 1820 to 1865. In 1820, mothers and daughters still busily spun thread and wove cloth in the household. By 1865, the domestic economy rarely incorporated these activities. Also, as caretaking became professionalized in the expanding service sector over the course of the century, men and women performed fewer tasks such as attending births and caring for sick neighbors and friends. This transfer of activities diminished the place of labor in visiting exchanges, rendering them largely social in nature. In addition, the progressive specialization of production separated it from leisure, rendering the sociability of exchanged labor largely a relic of the nineteenth century.

How do these observations about visiting challenge the public/private framework? The dichotomy implies stark differences between the two realms and exaggerates their distance. The powerful images evoked by the terms *public* and *private* overshadow nuances that existed in practice. Visiting took place in the church, at schools, stores, town meetings, virtually everywhere people congregated. At the same time, a majority of visiting, at least that recorded in diaries, letters, and autobiographies, occurred in the home (either that of the diarist or that of the person named), in the "private sphere." But given the interactive dynamism of the visiting enterprise, to describe a visit as "private" simply because it often occurred in a household would distort the activity, its meaning, and its consequences.

Let us take the logic one step further. The use of the public/private dichotomy implies that private also means *not public*: not outside the household, not beyond the family, not involved in politics, not related to government. It suggests a turning inward, a self-absorption. But visiting, as this chapter will demonstrate, was not limited in any of these ways. Restructuring the dichotomy to include the social does not simply mean relabeling activities—it requires that we reconceptualize them. The boundaries between spheres were not absolute; they overlapped, constantly shifted, and were renegotiated by historical actors. Thus visiting must be understood as integral to alternative economies, as a welfare system executed without the state, as a conduit for exchanging ideas and opinions, and as a network for emotional and psychological support that linked individuals to one another.

Subjects engaged in a community network felt obligated to others and expected that good deeds and favors would be returned. Through the practice of visiting, Martha Barrett became part of the anti-slavery movement and the Reverend Noah Davis built a congregation for his church. Citizens did not act, think, or vote in a vacuum; they did so within the context of a dialogue, gauging reactions of neighbors and kin, rethinking their own activities and positions. Visiting was a composite of these activities. People discussed politics, religion, the weather, their neighbors' crops, and the evils of slavery. In the process, they circulated news, ideas, opinions. To characterize this ferment as "private" obscures the reality it plays in the process of crafting a community.

VISITING AS SOCIAL EXCHANGE

Diarists in this study rarely recorded the content of their interactions, but they religiously documented their visits and visitors, indicating their importance as events. Leonard Stockwell visited neighboring villages in western Massachusetts, telling stories and jokes. Talk focused on events and people, and as Horatio Chandler recorded, "upon religion." Eliza Adams wrote from Lowell, Massachusetts, of her Christmas celebration: "We are all out at the house in a most noisy mood; some talking, others sewing, all most busy in the enjoyments of the day. We have been very much excited on small pox, mad dogs, & reduction of wages."[5]

While visitors made routine stops, others practiced ritualized visiting for occasions such as greeting a newborn infant or paying respects to the family of a deceased. For example, seamstress Louisa Chapman logged the visitors during the sorrowful days in March, 1849, following her mother's death. Most diarists vigilantly recorded deaths; and some, taking their role as family or community historian quite seriously, also recorded causes of death. But unless the deceased was a close family member (and sometimes even then), diarists were most likely to record the social dimension (versus the personal/emotional one) of the death and its aftermath. For example, in keeping with the social focus, a female domestic servant commented on the size of the funeral she attended but not on her feelings about the deceased:

> Today is for the funerall. Arad is burried at eleven o'clock is to be burried with massonic honors had a verry large funerall. There was a great many of the friends here to supper.

Deaths were routine and frequent; funerals were events.[6]

Larger community gatherings—dances, parties, church services, town meetings, and fairs—stirred conversation and visiting. Communities planned events in advance (in contrast to routine visits) that included a wider range and larger number of people. The events varied seasonally, many scheduled in the evening (singing school, lyceum lectures, parties, and prayer meetings) and on weekends (church meetings, fairs). Although winter brought snow, simultaneously an impediment to travel and the means for sleighing, it also brought relief from long intense hours of farm work, freeing people to socialize. Singing school convened almost exclusively in December, January, and February. Neighborhood gatherings provided common ways of escaping farm chores and learning the latest gossip. The maple run in the spring provided the occasion for sugar parties. If one could find the time, one could go "berrying" with a group of friends in the summer or "chestnutting" in the autumn. And after the harvest, neighbors shucked corn at bees, peeled apples, and tasted cider.[7]

In antebellum New England, although women visited more than men, visiting was not an exclusively female enterprise. Both men and women called upon family members, neighbors and friends, often in gender-integrated environments. One hundred percent of the women and 86 percent of the men in this study recorded visiting activities in their diaries. Both men and women interrupted their day's labors to visit someone or to provide refreshment for an unexpected caller. Both traveled great distances to help raise a barn or quilt a bedcover or provide company for a lonely friend.[8]

However, the qualities of visiting differed for men and women. Female diarists recorded having guests over for tea dramatically more often than male diarists (54 percent as compared to 4 percent). Women mentioned receiving visitors in their own homes only slightly less often than they called on others (93 percent versus 100 percent), while the discrepancy between hosting and visiting was much greater for men (46 percent mentioned hosting, while 86 percent mentioned visiting). As these figures make clear, men acted as hosts significantly less often than women, or at least they reported hosting less frequently than women. It is important not to overstate this case, however, because men played active roles as both guests and hosts. Leonard Stockwell took great pride in hosting visitors: "He was decidedly a home man and liked to have everything comfortable and make those welcome who came to visit him."[9]

OBLIGATION AND RECIPROCITY

Visiting, as part of a system of exchange built on the principle of mutual obligations, bound neighbors and kin. Visiting incurred reciprocal obligations, not simply to individuals but also to the group. The community logged individual visits into a kind of community trust to be used as a resource in times of need. Participation in the system offered group membership and the status and honor it bestowed, aid in times of need, companionship (at least occasionally), and access to the news circuit. People sustained their community life through the practice of visiting. Community studies identify institutions, such as the church, the school, labor unions, and volunteer associations, as pillars of community life. While these are unquestionably structures that connect individuals to a larger society, I examine community practices at a more intimate level. Individual work, active engagement, and reaffirmation of ties with other individuals are required to set these larger institutions in motion. Human action made an organization an entity, a church a congregation, and abstinence from alcohol a movement.[10]

Between neighbors and kin, visiting obligations acted as a powerful motivating force. Mary Adams wrote home to her family from the textile mills in Nashua, New Hampshire, in 1835, reminding her sister of promised visits: "Saw Mrs. Dole last week. She wants you to come over very much to alter that cap & bonnet for a dish of tea, *you recollect.* Mrs. H. says she is almost out of patience waiting for your company to go over there for the tea." Relatives and friends felt the imperative to visit when they traveled in the vicinity of someone they knew. Not acting on this obligation potentially slighted someone. Textile worker Sarah Metcalf expressed this fear to her mother in 1844: "Uncle . . . wants James and I to make them a visit before I go home. What would he say if he knew we had been to Middleboro, and not come to see them?"[11]

Parna Gilbert, a seamstress and caretaker of the sick, used the language of obligation in her diary entry for September 19, 1852: "Coming home from meeting we called to Cousin M.'s. Their child is verry sick, but I hope its life may be spared. Cousin is alone now. I suppose I *must* go there tomorrow and stay a few days." In fact, she stayed a week, leaving the baby and mother "more comfortable." Addie Brown wrote to Rebecca Primus about her brother in New York City, who had requested that she come to visit him during his ill health. She ultimately declined because of her need to work for money. Addie regretfully reported her brother's admonition for not complying: "My

Brother don't write any more to me. I suppose he don't like it I did not come. I wish I had of gone as I was not to work." She gambled insecure paid labor in lieu of observing an obligation within her kin network, and she suffered disappointment in both realms.[12]

Although subjects did not plan most visits, they did arrange some in advance, especially those that involved arduous travel. And then, when a plan fell through, they felt dejected. Domestic worker Lizzie Good-enough's morale relied on sabbath visits in particular, perhaps because it was her only day off. She complained of loneliness when no one showed up to visit. "It is realy a long lonesome forenoon, only four of us here." Sarah Trask felt disappointed when her visiting plans were thwarted: "called at the shop to see M.E.R. She told me that she would come up and pass the evening with, but she did not come. I suppose she could not come. I was very much disapointed." Although Brigham Nims did not label his feelings, his declaration of the absence of visitors documented a melancholy holiday: "Thanksgiving. Staid at home. Had the headache. No one visited."[13]

At an extreme, failed visits brought anger, disappointment, and in the case of school teacher Ann Dixon, a joking threat of retribution:

Friend Ann,

I beg to know why you have not called on me? Didn't you know it was *very* "imparlite" not to call on your new neighbors? Here I've been prink't up for most tu weeks in my light caliker gown spectin callers every day and not a soul has made their pearance . . . I hope Ann you haint tuk a miff at nothin as some o the foulk I could name hav . . . I donne whut this ere warld is cummin tu or the habitants in it. There's no pendance to be placed on um. Why you jest part with sum on um the best freends in the warld at nite and when you meet um in the mornin they'll be jest your beeterest inemis. Now I've no simputhe with sich freendshups. I go in for the genwine creetur itself give me the freend that'ill stik tu you thru thik an thin and not be oggled about by every mischieffs maker that crosses there path—that's my doctrin.

Why Ann du you spose that I shud bleve one word if forty slandurus, tattlers an mischiffmakers shud cum and tell me that An Dixen was not the freend she peered, that she was wun thing to my face and anuther tu my bak? . . . but I'm ruther gettin off my trak my objec was in writin jist now— tu find out why yu hadn't called on me. I can't think its cuse your mad or any sich thing gess it mus be as how you hav'nt heered that your freend Luna had moved intu your neighburhud.

Presumably, Ann's good friend Erlunia adopted the pen name of "Luna." In her exceedingly illiterate letter, "Luna" conveyed her affront at Ann's neglect. Under the veneer of humor, she attempted to manipulate Ann's sense of obligation as a neighbor and as a friend. For whatever reasons, Erlunia had not seen Ann for a while and held her responsible. The letter was funny precisely because it exaggerated the ethics of social exchange, although it did not distort them. "Luna" thought herself entitled to a respectful welcome; it was incumbent upon Ann to welcome her properly. Visiting identified those visited as part of a community circle; conversely, those not visited remained outside. For example, in recording the festivities surrounding a surprise party for Abba, a male friend, Mary Mudge revealed the weight of the message conveyed by visiting as opposed to not visiting: "Martha Jane lives in the house with Abba and did not come in *because the girls do not visit her.*"[14]

Customs dictated not only whether or not to make a visit, but also how one behaved once there. If a host did not observe the local rules regarding hospitality, a visitor might feel insulted. William J. Brown, a freeborn black man who lived his entire life in Providence, Rhode Island, wrote about visiting expectations in a waterfront neighborhood:

> If a person went out to make a call or spend the evening and was not treated to something to drink, they would feel insulted. You might as well tell a man in plain words not to come again, for he surely would go off and spread it, how mean they were treated—not even so much as to ask them to have something to drink; and you would not again be troubled with their company.

Subjects also evaluated the duration of a visit in assessing whether the mutual obligations had been sufficiently met. Was the visit long enough? If not, as in the case of Sarah Carter (in the estimation of Sarah Holmes), the host could rebuke the visitor:

> You only complain however of being alone. Indeed I will not sympathize with you in word or though[t]. I will rejoice if possible over your feelings of loneliness for you should not have left Foxcroft so soon. So short was your visit here that I was not sure that you had been here at all this spring.

Three years later, Sarah Holmes (who by 1854 had become Sarah Holmes Clark) discussed the impact of *obligation* on how she spent her day.

> I was interupted by company yesterday. I had visitors all day, nearly, & this morning I devoted to visiting. I felt obliged to go as I am much indebted, owing to my long illness, and I fear that people will think me very unsociable if I do not i[m]prove the first opportunity.

Company interrupted her labors, but she owed it to her community to repay the attention she received while ill. Her neighbors successfully communicated a message to her: to be unsociable repudiated community commitments. Such behavior was unacceptable. Sarah observed the culture of Madison, Georgia, with the eye of an untrained but perceptive anthropologist. Teaching at a school where her husband was schoolmaster, she noted that Madison folks visited more than those in Foxcroft, Maine, where she grew up. And the southern, purely "ceremonious" calls, she found taxing:

> As I have said before, the ladies here visit as much as in a city & dress the same. When I am in school, my friends, particular friends, those with whom I visit sociably, come to see me at night & consequently we are seldom alone at night. & other call at 12 & 1 o'clock. You may be assured that I do not care to see or receive fashionable & ceremonious people at noon when I have been in school all the morning.

Clearly, Sarah Holmes Clark thought the women of Madison, Georgia, extreme. The cultural differences between North and South irritated her, although she did her best to accommodate the new visiting expectations.[15]

In spite of Sarah Holmes Clark's observation of regional differences, white working women in New England described their routines as bustling with social activity. Susan Brown Forbes acknowledged an unusual day in her schedule, "I staid at home for a wonder." A few subjects indicated it was possible to visit too much. Mary Mudge, a very active visitor, wrote, "Have been a good girl this week and not been away evenings." She also wrote that her boyfriend, Phillip, "don't approve of making calls 'till the work is done." Sarah Trask acknowledged that her mother similarly prioritized work over visiting: "My shoes are not done yet, I begin to think that I am lazy, and yet I try to do all I can. . . . Mother tells me that I run about too much to do anny work. I can't think so, but suppose I shall have to." These slight admonitions suggest that beyond an undefined but mutually agreed upon limit, women (men did not appear to share the same constraint) became gadabouts. Margaret, Mary, and Hannah Adams wrote to their parents in 1841 about their cousin: "We like our Cousin Eliza very much. She has a good deal of Adams' blood in her, very industrious, prudent & steady, not given to gad." However, while female diarists kept an ear to the message, the threat of sanctions did little to keep them at home.[16]

EMOTIONAL SUSTENANCE

Visits could provide essential emotional support to those who needed it. Sarah Trask described her mood change when visitors arrived:

> This day, I am not so cross. I have been at home today. Ironing and shoes have been my work, Lizzy came over and pass the afternoon. William came to tea. S. Trask came over from Danvers, came to go down to the Sons meeting with Joshua, so came up to tea. I was glad that he did, for I am always glad to see my friends. M.E.R. and L.A.B. called in the evening.

The companionship of her friends helped lift her out of the dark gloom in which she stewed while brooding about Luther, her boyfriend at sea. A visitor could help combat the occasionally oppressive loneliness of rural life. Soon after she married Stephen Parker and moved to North Andover, Massachusetts, from New Hampshire, Anne Parker wrote to her sister-in-law about being lonely. She had few friends and no nearby kin, except in-laws. Her husband, a farmer and shopkeeper, worked long hours at the store.

> One in a store has not much spare time for sisters, or wives either. At least I find it so. I cannot even get an half hour, these long lonesome evenings. You may be sure I do not fail to beg for it, and receive the encouraging reply, "I'll come up if I can," which always means "I can't come." I have a little kitten for company, but then she does not talk even as much as *you* do. And as to the matter of reading, I verily believe she is as ignorant of it, as the man in the moon.

Elizabeth Metcalf wrote to her mother-in-law about the importance of visiting her aunt, uncle, and cousin Edward after the death of their young daughter/sister:

> They are lonely, O, how lonely they must be without her. For in her and Eddard all their plans in life were connected. Aunt says that Edward appears like a man that has lost his wife. His health is quite poor, his limbs trouble him much. Aunt said she wished that I would spend the winter with her for she did not feel as if she could be alone so much as uncle and E. are at home but little except nights. I told her that I would spend some weeks with [them] this winter.[17]

Individuals recognized social contact as restorative and acted when possible to dispel isolation and loneliness. Pregnancy in the context of frequent moves kept Paulina Bascom Williams out of the social loop. Paulina, who described herself as "Evangela," was a missionary married to a poor itinerant minister. Between 1830 and 1833, her husband's ill health and search for a good job repeatedly disrupted her social world, as they moved from Parma, New York, to Orwell, West Haven, and then Tinmouth, Vermont. Compounding the situation, her status as mother-to-be in 1831 confined her to the household, kept her out of church, and provided little opportunity for her to meet people in each locale. Paulina found the West Haven community particularly reserved and unwelcoming and looked forward to the next move as something of a relief: "I have been confined at home & by that means am immeasurably unacquainted so that I have no favourite friends to leave & the loneliness of the place forbids local attachment."[18]

For some, a visit for its own sake was not satisfactory. Martha Barrett revealed that in order to combat her deep loneliness, she needed companionship based on mutual interests:

> Read awhile. Then closed my book and sat by the window. I was lonely, felt a strong yearning for society. How very few associates I have. Suppose it is my own fault, because I make such a recluse of myself, stay so much at home, but I find few girls who have the same thoughts as I have, or feel interested in the same subjects.

This example serves as a reminder that loneliness and isolation penetrated people's lives on many levels. At other times, Martha Barrett's life bustled with activity and swarms of people. Neighbors and casual acquaintances did not quell her desire for deeper, more intimate friendships.[19]

THE WORK OF VISITING

Despite their rewards and satisfactions, New England working people sometimes perceived visiting obligations as demanding labor. After leaving her New Hampshire schoolteaching job to become a farm wife in Connecticut, Mary Coult Jones (see Figure 15) recorded her struggle to make a place for herself in the new community: "Saturday have called on the neighbouring populace. Had a fine time and feel as if it was hard work." In his autobiography, the Reverend Noah Davis, a former slave who purchased his own freedom, wrote about a similar phenomenon in the South. He visited as part of his strategy to build the Saratoga Street African Baptist Church he founded in Baltimore, Maryland. "During this time we succeeded in getting a better place for the Sabbath school, and there was a larger attendance upon my preaching, which demanded

reading and study, and also *visiting*, and increased my daily labors."
Sarah Holmes Clark observed that "The ladies of Madison visit a 'great
deal.' I sometimes wish that they would not come to see me quite as
often as they do for if I pretend to pay all my visits in '*due season*,' I can
find time to do nothing else. Besides I consider it a task to make
ceremoneous calls." Parna Gilbert, a seamstress, caregiver to the sick,
and no stranger to work, recorded her exhausting week in September,
1851:

> Mother was absent until Wednesday. I washed Monday and had 8 men to
> dinner & three folks to supper and the same the next day. & Wednesday Mr.
> B. brought M. home & was here to dinner. & Thursday Phebe visitted here
> & yesterday we had eight to dinner and supper. & today Mr. Tower & wife
> have visitted here & thus the week has finily ended. My health has become
> much impaired by this week's labour.

With her mother/coworker away, Parna managed the responsibility of
preparing meals for boarders in addition to visitors. Cooking required
enormous amounts of time and energy, physically exhausting Parna by
the week's end.[20]

In analyzing twentieth-century Italian American communities, anthropologist Micaela di Leonardo has introduced the concept of *kin
work* to refer to "the conception, maintenance, and ritual celebration
of cross-household kin ties, including visits, letters, telephone calls,
presents, and cards to kin; the organization of holiday gatherings; the
creation and maintenance of quasi-kin relations;" and many other
activities. This concept of social activities as "work" can be usefully
expanded to include visiting activities within a community, not solely
those within a family. Community-building activities also required time,
intention, and skill; they were a kind of "social work," or work in the
social sphere. Social work included planning, visiting, maintaining connections and ties, caring for sick neighbors and extended family members, sponsoring functions in the church, monitoring the behavior of
wayward individuals, and for the recently converted, bringing others to
Christianity.[21]

Di Leonardo found kin work to be largely women's work. In her
study, Italian American women exclusively constructed ethnicity (through
food preparation and holiday celebrations) and maintained extended
family connections. Their centrality to these endeavors brought them
greater power and familial authority. The evidence in this chapter
suggests that as in di Leonardo's ethnic communities in the twentieth

century, New England women in the antebellum period were at the nucleus of a system of exchange. But men were not excluded from this world; they too engaged in the intricate construction of community life by participating in the social sphere.

Family ties had to be sustained by kin work, as did community ties. Biological relationships became kin networks only through dynamic deeds. In a letter to his younger sister Rhoda in 1841, Stephen Parker lamented his lack of contact with her during the years of their separation. While it is not clear what prompted his remorse, Stephen attempted to renew ties and regular visits that to him symbolized being a family:

> I have been expecting for a long-time to find time to give you a call, for I want to see you *very much*. It does seem a great while since I have seen you. And in fact *it is a great while*. And I hope, and intend it shall never be so long again. While we live so near each other—I have been thinking of it lately and really it is *too bad* we live in about one hours ride each other and yet do not see, or meet together oftener than *once or twice in a year*. This is certainly not right—and what is almost as bad we do not write each other *once, every* year hardly—in fact we hardly seem to be "brothers & sisters." Let us my dear sister be more like "children of one family," let us see each other as often as is posible.

To him, brothers and sisters became a family through visiting. While Stephen's subsequent visiting may not have been as constant as he planned, thereafter he sustained a regular correspondence with Rhoda.[22]

PARALLEL PROJECTS AND SHARED WORK

Work entered into the visiting scene in another way, through parallel projects. Many female diarists tried to arrange to do their work in a social context. In the example earlier in the chapter, Sarah Holmes Clark experienced visits that affirmed friendship or that incorporated work differently from those which she characterized as "ceremoneous." When visitors brought their work, she could work too. "There are many ladies who take their work, for southern ladies are very industirous, and spend a whole morning or evening with me. These are the visits that I prize." Visiting did not interrupt the work in her life, and work did not distract from visiting. She happily combined the activities. For some occupations, such as shoebinding or sewing, arranging to work with someone else alleviated the isolation endemic to domestic piecework. Sarah Trask customarily worked on shoes in a group of sister shoebinders: "At home today. Mrs. Claxton came in this afternoon with her work. Lizzy and

L.A.B. pass the afternoon with us." And on another day, "A.A.B. came in with her work and we had a grand time." Again, the social dimension transformed the work into an enjoyable activity. Seamstresses and shoebinders shared her practice. Mary Holbrook took shoes and sewing to other households on a regular basis. For example, "I went up to Mrs. Hines & bound shoes." "I went up to Uncle's & sewed." Marion Hopkins, a leather pieceworker, stitched wallets with her mother, her sister-in-law Phoebe, and her friend Sarah: "Mother & P. stitched wallets, p.m. Sarah came down to stitch & staid all night."[23]

Subjects relieved the isolation of their work through parallel projects. Domestic worker Lizzie Goodenough of Vermont recorded her shared project with fellow worker Mary Lynch: "we had two hundred & seventeen pieces in all to iron." While nothing could transform the task of ironing 217 items into joyful leisure, working with at least one other person lightened the psychological as well as the physical burden. The work became social rather than solitary. Given women's objections to the oppressive isolation of domestic labor, paid and unpaid, over the last two centuries, this transformation should not be underestimated. Subjects also shared other domestic chores, particularly the weekly laundry. A division of labor was facilitated in households with large staffs of domestic servants, such as in the household of Francis Cabot Lowell II where Lorenza Berbineau worked (see Figure 16).[24]

It was not uncommon on a farm for an employer to work alongside the hired help. Lizzie Goodenough wrote about knitting, washing, and baking with her employer, Mrs. Howe:

> This is another dull morning as we have not got much to do this forenoon except get boiled dinner. Have been knitting nearly all the time since I got the work done. We have had quite a knitting scircle this afternoon. Mrs. Howe. Celia. Sarah. Mellissa & myself have all been knitting.

The morning work passed dully, but the afternoon work in a "knitting scircle" of five became a pleasurable occasion.[25]

For male diarists, whose work was different, the sociability dimension is more difficult to analyze. Farm work often necessitated the participation of more than one person. This resulted in farmers having large families, neighbors helping each other, and/or farmers hiring extra hands. Farmers' daily diary entries enumerate endless lists of people. For example, John Plummer Foster wrote about a typical workday in 1852 that involved many people:

> We were weighing out hay for Dane Foster, diging up trees for Isaac Stevens, and Wm Wood, picking over apples for Mr. Balch, grafting trees for Joseph Carleton and myself, trading cows with Daniel Abbot, and hay with Mr. Howard &c, &c, &c.

How much of this resulted from a conscious attempt to make the labor social as opposed to efforts to lighten the physical burden is often impossible to tell. But either way, the diaries reveal that farmers consistently performed work in a social context.[26]

VISITING AND THE EXCHANGE OF LABOR

The emerging market economy and industrial organization of work transformed visiting as an exchange of labor as well as visiting as social exchange. Throughout the late nineteenth century, social activities became increasingly differentiated from economic ones. In the antebellum period, as in colonial New England, leisure and work were often intertwined. Today, we often think of them as mutually exclusive. This separation has been shaped by the evolution of a capitalist economy and an industrial organization of work. Urbanization also increased the need for interacting with strangers as opposed to acquaintances, friends, or relatives. In the early nineteenth century, many activities still combined economic and social dimensions. Examples below illustrate the exchange of labor through the diarists' accounts of caring for the sick, attending births, and participating in communal labor.[27]

CARING FOR THE SICK

Friends, relatives, and neighbors exchanged at least one essential service in the social realm: caring for the sick. Illnesses routinely shortened longevity and heightened infant mortality in the nineteenth century. Medicine remained more an experimental rather than a scientific practice. Illnesses such as cholera and scarlet fever periodically infested communities, took many lives, and spread rapidly, their causes unknown and their contagion misunderstood. Medicine often ineffectually treated patients, and disease frequently brought death. Becoming ill always foretold economic hardship in the form of lost wages or unattended farm chores.[28]

Regardless of the conditions, the sick needed to be tended and "watched." Subjects used the means available—home remedies, herbs, bleeding, water treatments, prayers, doctor visits if the illness was severe—to try to cure their patients. Sometimes nothing could be done, leaving bedside company and hot tea the only comforts. In this context, visiting became central to the treatment of the sick person.

Propriety dictated that at a minimum, neighbors and family must visit the sick to cheer them up. Addie Brown recorded: "Miss H. Freeman fell. Very bad. I must go and see her." In this instance, the obligation to visit resembled visiting in general, but the need intensified because of the immediacy of the injury. Few diarists recount their conversations with the ill; exactly what transpired during these visits we can only speculate. In one rare exception, Parna Gilbert offered a glimpse of a conversation, revealing her forthright but tactless bedside manner. She went to call on the neighboring Brown family (not that of Addie Brown) and found Mrs. Brown in bed with typhus:

> She said, "I am very sick." I told her I was sorry she was so sick. She replyed, "It is distressing." I asked how long she had been so. She said she was taken down very suddenly about a fortnight ago with Typhus fever. I said, "I am afraid you will never get up again." She said she thought it dreadful. I said, "I suppose you can look forward to a more blissful abode." She replied, "I wish I might."

Mrs. Brown asked Parna to pray for her and Parna found herself feeling "a peculiar sympathy" for the Brown children.[29]

Diarists did not consistently distinguish watchers from visitors in their diaries, although in practice, watchers, in contrast to the more limited role of visitors, performed any task that provided comfort for the patient. Watchers waited on the person, administered medicine, tried to make him or her comfortable, and as their job title implied, watched him or her. They watched to monitor the patient's breathing. They watched for a change in the patient's condition. Zeloda Barrett reported such an alert the night before her sister Samantha died: "The watcher awakened me & told me there was some alteration."[30]

Some women made caring for sick people, or nursing, their occupation. For example, Pollie Cathcart, who remained unmarried at fifty-one, cared for her mother as she grew old and approached death. After her mother died, Pollie became a community nurse rather than a family one. She cared for ill people and assisted in households with new babies, staying anywhere from one night to four months. In addition to the few female diarists who made nursing and watching their primary trade, numerous others were called upon to watch with the sick when circumstances necessitated it.[31]

The need to care for seriously ill patients demonstrated the particular importance of community responsibility for the sick. When patients had to be watched around the clock, community members rotated responsibility for watching them. In one extreme example, Samantha Barrett, a farmer, recorded the visitors and watchers at her side for the last twenty-one days of her life. Seventeen neighbors, friends, and kin watched her (in addition to a doctor) during that final three-week period.[32]

Clearly, caring for the sick was essential to individual households as well as the community. However, the degree to which that service was honored and valued by community and family members is a matter of debate. Susan Reverby finds this contradiction a central dilemma in American nursing. She claims that women have been ordered to care "in a society that refuses to value caring." As Reverby found in her research, extended families in this study routinely called single women away from their paid employment to care for the sick. Mary Parker wrote to her sister-in-law Rhoda:

> Beloved Sister . . . if your health will permit and Mrs. Lovjoy can spare you, we should like to have you come and see Lydia and stay a week or fortnight to set in the rooms to wate on her. You could bring sewing or any other work that would be conveniant to cary abroad. If you can come Stephen will go after you.

Pulling women from paid employment evidenced the importance of their skills to the family. Mary Giddings Coult said, "dismissed my school to go & take care of Cousin Lydia C." Similarly, schoolteacher Louisa Chapman wrote in 1849 that "owing to the sickness of my mother my school closes to-day." Another schoolteacher, Pamela Brown, wrote, "About eight o'clock this morning Cephus Wheeler called at Mr. Hall's and let us know that Mrs. Taylor's babe was dead. He wanted to go to help them today. As Mrs. Hall was gone I told him I would go and did not keep school today." Such a practice was common among millgirls as well as teachers; Mary Hall left her job as a weaver and returned to New Hampshire in response to one of her many calls to familial duty: "Heard from home to-day. Brother I. and sister J. sick and grandfather not able to walk or step. And father and mother wish me to come home." Harriet Severance refused to return to her domestic work for her Uncle Calvin because "I could not leave home till Meroa is better."[33]

Reverby declares that nursing was "a woman's duty, not her job," and that "no form of women's labor, paid or unpaid, protected her from [the] demand" of caring for sick relatives. However, evidence from diaries and letters of working women contradict that assertion. As alluded to above in Mary Parker's letter to Rhoda, when one occupational calling conflicted with another, paid work could supersede nursing obligations. Rhoda made a living as a combmaker's apprentice, and leaving her job could jeopardize it, if Mrs. Lovejoy, her employer, did not consent to a temporary absence. A similar conflict existed for Addie Brown, who decided, as did Rhoda, not to go take care of her sick brother. She needed her job, and she needed the money it would bring. Parna Gilbert placed the ultimate decision in the hands of the Almighty. "I went to assist Mr. Reed's people. Mr. R. being sick expected to stay until tomorrow, but a tailor came last night wishing me to go & work for him to day. I am expecting to go if it is the will of my heavenly father." In Parna's case, both occupations paid her. Yet in this instance, under the sanction of her "heavenly father," she went with the tailor. An important difference existed between those women who left their jobs to care for the sick and those who did not. Those who stayed with their paying jobs supported themselves; they could not rely on their families, even when they were embedded in an active kin network. They had deep attachments to their families and vice versa, but they had to earn their way in the world. Whatever altruism or obligation they may have felt was counterbalanced by the need to make a living.[34]

The need to work for pay was not the only way to excuse oneself from the duty to nurse. A farm woman, for example, had a job besides caretaking, even though it did not pay a salary, with responsibilities at home that could conflict with traveling elsewhere to care for someone else. Martha Ballard's turn-of-the-nineteenth-century midwifery business could flourish only when she had adult daughters to tend to household chores such as weaving, baking, and cleaning. In antebellum New England, obligations to the nuclear family could also override obligations to others. Mary Parker Hall wrote to her sister Rhoda Parker, who had taken ill, "I thought after I came home if I could only wash-bake-and-brew, and then fly back to you, I should have been glad. But am pleased to know that you have been *well* provided with help." Her commitment to "wash-bake-and-brew" for her nuclear family necessitated that she stay at home. Similarly, Abigail Baldwin steadily traipsed back and forth to the household of her sick mother; she returned home frequently to bake and tend to chores.[35]

Despite having limited resources, the married women in this study found themselves more financially secure than the single women, and their nuclear family obligations bound them more tightly. Even with these demands, women could and did negotiate their visiting and caretaking responsibilities. The Parker family demonstrated the premium placed on the caretaking enterprise; when Winthrop Parker requested that his sister Rhoda come to New York to take care of him and his wife and son, he offered her a *salary* commensurate with her current one as a domestic/combmaker's apprentice. Stephen Parker wrote to Rhoda about his conversation with Winthrop:

> Lucy to had nearly made herself sick in attending him & baby but was better. Baby quite well. They think of going to keeping house. & W. says, (to me), "cannot I presuade Rhoda to come & live with me?" "I will give her as much as she can make at West Newbury" &c. Wanted me to mention it to you & tell him what you thought of it. When you come up at Thanksgiving we will talk it all over.

Winthrop did not simply appeal to Rhoda's obligations as a family member. He respected her right to make her own decision about where to go. In this instance, Rhoda did not accept his offer. He also recognized her role as a wage earner and the monetary value of her caretaking services, and he offered to pay her accordingly. In another example, Harriet Severance's Uncle Calvin paid her $42 for her six-and-one-half-month care of his terminally ill wife and household. Harriet kept a careful account of Uncle Calvin's installment payments.[36]

The evidence suggests that families weighed the value of a woman's paycheck against the services she could provide as a family nurse. Women's wages, consistently less than half that of men, could not always match the value of the services. In the case of Rhoda, the Winthrop Parkers recognized that she depended on the wage for her well-being, and they offered to replace it. If a family or a single woman struggled to eke out an existence, giving up the wage was not an option. If the woman maintained her own livelihood, even though part of an active kin network, she could and often did opt to stay with her paid employment. However, in situations where kin networks shared economic resources, the women often left their paid employment to care for family members.

In light of her parents' recent death, Mary Giddings Coult exercised supreme sensitivity to the issues of family obligation as well as her need to support herself. Her Uncle L. Colby came to get her to stay with her aunt and Hatty. "I must try to do all I can for them. If I do perhaps when I am sick, some one will take pitty on a *poor lone orphan* and be as a Mother to me." Her fear of potential ill health and eventual death (whenever it might come—she contemplated it at least monthly) overrode her concerns about supporting herself. She determined that service to family members, a form of social insurance, better suited her needs in the long run. This decision did not trade autonomy for simple dependence; it enabled Mary to navigate the unpredictable seas faced by a young single woman with no parents to help her.[37]

It was not unusual to bring a sick individual to live with a family, although it was less common than sending a nurse elsewhere. Millworker Mary Metcalf discussed caring for her married sister: "I went out to Sarah's during my v[a]cation. Took care of her a while and brought her home with me. She has been sick but is gaining rapidly now. We shall try to keep her till after Chirstmas but William is lonesome now and wants his wife at home as soon as she is able to come." Schoolteacher Louisa Chapman recounted the deliberations that brought her grandmother to live with her and her brother in 1849, a few months after her widowed mother died:

> 9 May—At home. Mr. Merriam from Middleton called to see if we will take Grandmother. Her children will not have her. And we think we will not.
>
> May 10—At home. Concluded to take Grandmother.
>
> May 14—At home. Grandmother came to our house. She is feeble and partly helpless and will need a great deal of care and attention.

As Louisa's equivocation indicates, not everyone eagerly took on such a responsibility because the work demanded time, patience, and adequate resources. Like Louisa Chapman, Adelaide Crossman, a farm woman and seamstress, took in her ill grandmother for whom everyone else in the family refused responsibility. She found dealing with the elderly woman frustrating: "Got home. Found Uncle Milton's folks here. Grandmother mad. I am out of patience." Parna Gilbert and her parents used their home as a sick house, a hospice of sorts. They faithfully took in the infirm and cared for them. Parna recorded the ordeal of Mrs. Packard's arrival: "Oh what a change hath been wrought in one short week. Little did I think last Sabath that she who is now here was to be brought here, in all probability no more to go away until carried to her grave. But God only knows what trials we have yet to endure." Obviously not an easy patient, Mrs. Packard led to caretaking responsibilities that physically taxed Parna and her mother: "Mother is already nearly worn out from the fatigue of the past week having had the whole care of Mrs. P. which has been a dreadful task."[38]

More obviously than with pure socializing, caring for the sick could be physically difficult and emotionally trying. Every nurse and watcher risked catching contagious diseases. And one's social sphere typically contracted to a minute circle when an individual had primary caretaking responsibilities. Sarah Trask managed the loneliness of caring for the sick by bringing a companion with her to visit a friend who "had the cramp": "L.A.B. and I took our work and went down to set with her a little while, for I think it is rather lonley to set alone when anny one is sick." In addition to the isolation, women consistently complained about the difficulty of the work and its fatiguing qualities.[39]

The advice literature of the antebellum period described nursing as a consummate female task, helping women to fulfill their destiny. Motz finds it a female responsibility in middle-class families. While the historical literature identifies nursing as a woman's duty, evidence from my research shows that men cared for the sick as well. With their higher wages and greater political power, men who were teachers or factory workers were not called away to care for the sick. However, male farmers and artisans who had greater flexibility in work routines took time from work and cared for sick relatives and friends.[40]

The gender differences in caretaking activities began with the patient. Men's nursing focused almost exclusively on other men and boys—their fathers, male friends, and sons. J. Foster Beal, a box factory worker, chided Brigham Nims for not writing: "I guess you have forgot all about you being at Boston last Sept. when you was so sick, and I took care of you, doctored you up, even tooke you in the bed with myself." Farmer John Plummer Foster nursed his father, who lived and worked with him:

> Friday. Fair and cold. I was half sick with a cold, did nothing but the chores, Father was taken in the evening with a slight shock of the palsy.
> Saturday. Fair and cold. I helped take care of Father.

Each day thereafter John gave an account of the weather and the condition of his father's health. The prominence of his father's health in the diary provides a clear sense of its centrality to John's life. Occasionally his distress baldly erupted through his rote entries. "It is enough to make one's heart ache to be with him, and see him, when he has his spasms." Gradually, John began working again, but he remained deeply concerned about his father's care. His father died five months later.

Despite John's immeasurable emotional involvement, he characterized his attendance to his father's needs as "helping." He saw himself as an assistant rather than a primary care provider. John also mentioned staying home to care for his sick son: "Friday. Cloudy. I staid in the house most of the day, and took care of Horace, he was sick." Horatio Chandler, another farmer and a store clerk in New Hampshire also took care of his son: "Wednesday . . . stayd at home A.M. to take care sick little Geo—that my wife might finish working. Geo [no better.]" Ivory Hill, shoemaker, took care of his sick friend, Moses, and had responsibility as a liaison with Moses' family:

> Moses [T] sick taken last night. Threatned with fever.
> . . . Set up with Moses [T] last night
> . . . Moses very sick don't have much hopes of him. Been over to Deerfield twice to his father's.

It is not clear why his family did not send someone to help care for him or even to visit. The next day Moses died. The number of men caring for other men makes clear that nursing was not exclusively a female vocation.[41]

The widespread conformity to same-sex caregiving for men reflects a deep-rooted taboo about gender-appropriate touching and bodily modesty. The healing arts had long been a primarily female enterprise, and renewed nineteenth-century concerns about female chastity placed male-female physical intimacy in a particularly delicate situation. Conversely, women did care for non-kin men, but much less frequently than women cared for women.[42]

Married men cared for their ill wives, exercising their responsibility as married persons, the primary exception to same-sex nursing. Sarah Holmes Clark wrote to her friend about the fine nursing skills of her husband. Given her current state of health, she insisted she could not possibly venture to New England and leave his healing hands:

> Gilman has spoiled me since I have been sick so much. And I can not do without him for a nurse when my health is so poor. I depend on his as a child relies on its mother. I believe that no one could nurse me so well as he does, because no one loves me as well as he does. Gilman is the best husband in the world; if you do not believe it come & live with us & judge for yourself.

Sarah, in this instance, equated nursing skill with love, an equation that others did not make. However, in using the mother/child metaphor to describe her reliance on Gilman's care, she evokes the centrality of kin in caretaking obligations.[43]

In a second notable exception to the above gender rule of nursing, two former slaves, James Mars and William Grimes, wrote in their respective autobiographies of their employment and skill in taking care of the sick. James Mars wrote about the adult daughter of his former owner, Miss Munger, calling him to her bedside:

> As I had been accustomed to take care of the sick, she asked me to stop with her that night. I did so, and went to my work in the morning . . . She asked what I thought of her; I told her I feared she would never be any better. She then asked me to stay with her if she did not get any better, while she lived. I told her I would. A cousin of hers, a young lady, was there, and we took the care of her for four weeks.

James had a long-term acquaintance with this young woman, and she valued the skills and comfort he brought to her bedside. His skin color combined with his familiarity mitigated the taboo of male nurse to a female patient. In essence, race overrode gender concerns. Had James not been black, it is highly unlikely that he would have been asked or allowed to care for this sick woman. However, because of his status as a black man—once slave, now free but still not a full citizen—James did not pose a sexual threat. A job as a subordinate male did not challenge the status quo of gender relations and actually reinforced existing racial stratification.[44]

The gender of patients was not the only consideration that figured into the caretaking division of labor. As a rule, men stayed in their own households (most of the time), and women acted as a mobile caretaking force, sometimes traveling long distances to care for sick relatives and friends, often staying with them. That said, men had the onus of going to get the doctor, nurse, neighbor woman, or midwife. In the diaries, men frequently gave accounts of their role as messengers or procurers of a nurse. A cabinetmaker's apprentice, Edward Carpenter, recorded his search for a care provider in 1844 in central Massachusetts:

> When I went home to supper tonight Mrs. Wells, Mrs. Miles' mother, who has been staying there a few days, was in what they called a cramp fit. I went as quick as I could for Dr. Stone & found that he was not at home. I then came back & went up after Dr. Deane, he came down & gave her some laudnum which quited her. The fit was caused by a Cancer on her breast, which will probably break out in a few days & kill her.[45]

BIRTHING

The birth of a newborn infant launched a round of ritual visiting as well as a renewed exchange of essential services. Birthing practices transformed over the nineteenth century. In the sweep from the colonial period to the end of the nineteenth century two major changes transpired: (1) medicine professionalized, prompting, in particular, the replacement of female midwives by male doctors; and (2) birth transformed from an open affair that included many female friends and kin, a "social childbirth," to a restricted, private event, monitored by a male doctor, that included few if any women. In colonial America, birth was a woman-centered event, a ritual central to female culture. It was not unusual for women to have as many as ten friends attending the birth, assisting the midwife or simply cheering on the laboring woman. At eighty percent of the births recorded by Martha Ballard, between two and four women were listed as attending the birth. Nearby neighbors acted as birth attendants more often than kin. After the birth, the household sponsored a celebratory supper, with all the attendants participating. Relatively soon after the baby was born, the midwife left, and a nurse (sometimes called a "monthly" nurse) took over to help the mother, child, and household for approximately one week to one month while the mother recuperated. The new mother would gradually resume her regular responsibilities.[46]

By the late nineteenth century, a doctor typically presided over the lying-in of urban middle-class women, secluding the occasion and incorporating few, if any, female attendants. For working-class and rural women, birth practices continued to rely on women's networks. Male doctors did not dominate until hospitals became the site of birthings in the 1920s. According to Judith Walzer Leavitt, in her history of childbearing in America, women in the nineteenth century "went to considerable sacrifice to help their birthing relatives and friends; they interrupted their lives to travel long distances and frequently stayed months before and after delivery to do the household chores."[47]

Women in this study fall into the category Leavitt labels the "traditionalists"—those who had limited access to modern, urban medical "advances" and continued to rely on female-centered home birth, as in the colonial period. None of the subjects gave birth in a hospital. Leavitt maintains that traditionalists relied primarily on midwives. While this is plausible, no diarist or correspondent labeled her birth attendant a "midwife." Nonetheless, subjects assumed certain women had a birthing-related competency and skill, making their services actively sought. While virtually all the women who gave birth called on neighboring women, several called for a doctor and in one instance a nurse. When diarists recorded details of a birth they invariably mentioned other women. Some of the women could have been midwives, but the diaries did not designate them as such.[48]

Diarists, correspondents, and autobiographers rarely recorded information about birth practices. They did not reveal what women did, how they felt, the pain they endured, the joy they felt, the despair that must have overwhelmed them at times. Mary Coult Jones detailed the only elaborate account of the birth room. In 1856 she gave birth to an eight-and-one-half pound boy, named Edwin after her husband. "I am in my room. Friends are around me while from the adjoining room I hear a low & mournfull wail." Her mother-in-law came the day after the birth and stayed for eleven days. Her brother came for one month, beginning when the baby was two weeks old. (She had no sisters, and her parents were dead.) In addition, when the baby was five days old, Lydia Cowdery came to stay with the family, presumably to care for them and the baby. Numerous visitors filed in and out of the house.[49]

Women helped each other with postpartum care, and friends, neighbors, and relations came and welcomed the newborn. As with death, those who mentioned births discussed the social dimension—visiting—rather than personal emotions or physical details. Farmer and seasonal store clerk Horatio Chandler recorded the bustle that surrounded his household the day after his wife gave birth:

> Saturday. Fine day. Mrs. Partridge staid with my wife to day. I drove my cow to Farwell's . . . went after Lydia Cheney—got her to take care my wife. She is a good hand. Mrs. Hopkins, Scott and Mrs. Leonard been here this P.M.

One woman in Minnesota wrote to her sister in 1856, "Every day there were different helpers about. The ladies in the neighborhood took turns caring for me."[50]

Visiting that welcomed the child's arrival began almost as soon as the birth took place. For example, textile worker Mary Hall wrote on 14 May 1829: "Home. This morning Mrs. Cassen brought a little Son. O that it may be trained up in the ways of virtue. Called in to see her." She visited Mrs. Cassen on the very day she gave birth. She wanted to welcome the new child into the world and probably congratulate Mrs. Cassen for her hard work.

The gendered division of labor in the birth event was clear. As in the colonial period, women were the sole birth attendants unless they called a doctor. Visitors and nurses, virtually indistinguishable from each other in the diaries, included a mix of married and unmarried women. Women managed all activities inside the birthing room, and men executed those outside. The male doctor proved the exception to this rule. Men recorded births, and men who were closely associated with the mother served as messengers, purveyors of news, and seekers of help. Obtaining assistance for the pregnant woman was often routine, although, like birth itself, tinged with adventure. Store clerk Francis Bennett, Jr., of Gloucester, Massachusetts (see Figure 17), wrote about getting help for his mother when his seaman father was away at sea:

> About 2 o'clock this morning Mrs. Hadley waked me up and told me to go over to Uncle John's and tell him to go over after the doctor and up after Mrs. Larvey, as she was not very well. I went over and got Uncle John out and we went together. I got home to Uncle John's again about 3 o'clock and staid there for the rest of the night. About 11 o'clock this forenoon we had an addition to the family of a little girl. It weighed 6 1/2 lbs. This afternoon I hired a horse and buggy and went down after Mrs. Rust, the nurse.

It is interesting that Mrs. Hadley, who was the one giving instructions, called for a doctor *and* Mrs. Larvey, probably a midwife. John Plummer Foster wrote that he simply "went after the doctor for the baby, and rode round after help." At times, finding someone to help required tenacity, as is evident in Horatio Chandler's account of his wife's labor:

> My wife grew worse & by 11 O'clk found it necessary to send for a physician. I sent Marshall for Dunbar. He arrived about 1 O'clk and at 1/4 past 2 my wife was safely delivered of a fine boy, weighed 8 [lb.] At 6 I went to Mr. Fields to get a girl to take care my wife. She could not come. Then went to Mr. Luts for Mrs. [Coble] did not succeed. At 10 O'clk went for Mrs. Albee. She come for the night.

After the baby was born, Horatio Chandler needed the help of a female assistant. When his first effort to hire "a girl" failed, he persisted until he found someone to come and stay with his wife.[51]

Again, we see both men and women involved in what has been perceived to be solely a female activity. Men fetched women to attend the birth and provide postpartum care. Such services, while at the periphery of birthing, were nonetheless crucial to the well-being of the mother and baby. Men in this case became the intermediaries bringing women to assist other women in the most physically dangerous of female rites of passage.

Diarists' accounts of births varied in the amount of detail elaborated. They ranged from a resounding silence (failure even to record the birth of their own child) to an enthusiastic announcement extolling the virtues of the new little family member, particularly for male infants. But most diarists minimally acknowledged births. Samuel Shepard James's accounts of his children's births reflected the typical understated style of recording births: "Cold with snow, squally. Abby A. James born. P.M. Peeling bark," or "Orrin M. James' birth day." Diarists often did not record the weight or health of the baby. In this vein, Joseph Kimball wrote: "Wife put to bed with daughter." Although if something had gone dramatically wrong with the mother, diarists surely would have recorded it, Joseph did not bother noting details when his sister's child was stillborn: "Sophia confined, child dead."[52]

Subjects' celebration of male babies greatly exceeded that of female infants. Stephen Parker, the most ebullient father of a newborn son, wrote a letter conveying his joy: "Now don't you want to hear something about our little *red head*. Well he is *just the prettiest little fellow you ever saw*. Grows finely. Is, upon the whole a *very good baby*." He then discussed the condition of his wife. Seven years later he expressed his jubilation over the birth of another son in a letter to his sister and her husband:

> Dear Brother & Sister, I have the pleasure to inform you that our *third Son* was born Oct 29th, 1852 at 10 1/2 o'clock in the evening. He is a good looking little Lad, weighs *nine pounds*, and appears healthy. His mother is, I hope, doing well. He is just beginning to nurse a little. We should be happy to have you make his acquaintance. He has said nothing about his unkles & aunts yet, but will, probably soon be enquiring for them, as near as I could understand him, he wishes to be remembered to his little cousin in W. Newbury. He does not speak our language very fluently. But is quite a linguist. He is an out & out "*Free Soiler*," and an "independent Democrat." We think he has all the characterestics of a *Great Man*.

John Plummer Foster more subtly revealed his gender preferences. Several times he wrote, "Ann presented me a son," as if he had won a prize. When his fifth son (his seventh child) was born, he underlined the passage—highlighting the event in a way he treated no other, as if he could not believe his good fortune. In contrast, the day his daughter Sarah was born, he wrote: "I was choring round, carried mother Peabody home and brought her back again in the afternoon." He failed to mention the birth itself. The baby daughter arrived a nonentity. If behavior reflects values, then diarists expressed preferences for boys. Viviana

Zeliger explains the phenomenon in the nineteenth-century United States: because "the useful child" contributed to the domestic economy (through farm labor, piece work, factory wages, or scavenging and the like), families considered children economic assets. The prized child, the adoptable one in the nineteenth century, was an adolescent boy, who presumably could make the greatest contribution to the household economy. In the context of a sex/gender system that privileged men in countless ways, this preference becomes understandable, even if unacceptable.[53]

COMMUNAL LABOR

Communities purposely organized work activities, referred to as "bees," in advance and treated them as special events. Quilting parties joined the list of bees to pare apples, haul wood, shuck corn, and perform other chores that required many hands. Osterud finds that in rural upstate New York both men and women attended quilting parties (see Figure 18): "It was the presence of men that made a 'quiltin' into a social event rather than an occasion of shared labor." In character with other types of antebellum visiting, in this study, both women and men attended bees, which were shaped by both work and leisure. Typically around the time of a wedding, subjects organized an explosion of quilting activity as well as other tasks in preparing the household for a new member. Elizabeth Metcalf casually wrote her mother-in-law about the gender-mixed quilting group that busily prepared for an upcoming marriage:

> Well I went with Carrie that afternoon to help Lissie *quilt*, all of the young folks in the neighborhood were present. We had a very social time, Lissie thinks that they shall be married some time this winter.

References to quilting are sprinkled through the diaries.[54]

Women did not guard a quilting as their exclusive province, and therefore it did not function solely as a women's ritual. In 1845, Brigham Nims organized a gathering of quilters:

> 29—Sharped the stone tools. Then went to the stone lot by Seth Towns. Asked his wife & Mrs. Nye & [Mis.] Daniel Towns to quilt. Come home. Brot [Mis.] Towns home at noon. P.M. asked the young ladies to quilt to morrow. Carried Mrs. Clark home at night, then to [Mr.] Newcombs &c.
>
> 30—Work about home. Helped put in a quilt and worked it. P.M. E. & F. Buckminister, M. Stebbins, A. & M. Davis, E. & A. & L. Towns quilted. Filled the leach with ashes &c.

In 1829, Vestus Haley Parks, onetime gunpowder-mill worker and later an itinerant peddler of tin and rags, organized entertainment for a quilting:

> Sunday. Went to Freman Powerses to get him to come to play on his violin at the widow Phoebe Tuttles on Wednesday evening. Then went to meeting . . . went to Freman Powerses again to have him come Tuesday evening on account of the qwilting being one day sooner than I expected . . . Went to Dan Sperry's and had quite a dance. The girls went there from the widow Tuttle's after quilting.

Mary Holbrook, seamstress and shoebinder, wrote, "Lewis carried Maria & me down to sewing society at Benjamin Nichols. There was several present. The bed quilt was put up in a lottery at 12 1/2 cts a ticket. Harriet Nichols drew it." At a later date she told of thirty people who attended Mr. Bidwell's sewing society. Arthur Bennett, who worked at a Vermont sawmill, went to a quilting and had such a good time that afterward he remorsefully pledged to redeem himself:

> Work some till 4 o'clock then went to Mr. [?] King to a quilting party. Quite a large company. Ate sugar, sung, and talked nonsense till 10 o'clock. Came home with a determination not to go into a party of pleasure for three months to come.

Despite the festive details, the specific division of labor at the quilting parties remains obscured. The diaries and letters revealed that both men and women attended, but surviving documents do not say exactly who did what. Men organized quiltings, but how much did they sew? Regardless, the fact that men even attended these events challenges the notion that women's culture grew out of a separate female sphere where women did "women's work" to the exclusion of men. Men involved themselves in domestic activities, in a world that organized a division of labor by gender but did not religiously observe boundaries segregating men and women.[55]

A system of mutual aid and shared work existed for women on a scale more modest than that of the bees. As in the parallel projects described above, small groups of women would gather, teaching each other skills and helping with the demanding work load. One anonymous farm woman in Essex County taught her neighbor to knit. Zeloda Barrett wrote, "My friend Harriet basted me a frock." Mary Mudge and her friends devotedly helped one another with household chores, child care, and sewing. For example, "This eve we were all going up to

Rebecca's to sew for her but when we got there she wanted to go to the concert, so we (Marth & I) went into Sarah's. I should not have cared much about it had I not wanted to go to the concert so much myself. I worked for Sarah on a collar and Marth tended the baby." Betsey Babb helped Susan Brown pare apples. Several women mentioned others assisting them with making carpets and rugs. Adelaide Crossman's friend helped her sew rags. Pamela Brown's friend Marcia drew patterns for her; Mrs. Holcomb made herself the regular partner of her neighbor, Samantha Barrett, for many arduous as well as pleasurable tasks including salting their cows, making carpets, and husking corn. This was true for quilting also. Mary Holbrook recorded two weeks of regular visits by her friends Phebe and Maria, who helped her with her star bed quilt.[56]

Two types of organized work bees tended to be male-centered: raising barns or houses and slaughtering animals. The bees organized the community to share skills and labor power when performing labor-intensive jobs. Although it is not clear whether they attended, women recorded the raisings as did men. After a vicious storm demolished the new home of Abigail and Thomas Baldwin, neighbors gathered to raise another. "Ten or a dozen kind neighbors come to assist about the house." As with quilting, the division of labor was not made explicit. It is possible that women prepared food for those doing the carpentry. The fact that women recorded these events in their diaries (as they did other male-only events, such as town meetings—25 percent of the women logged town meetings in their diaries, as opposed to 57 percent of the men), makes it clear that they registered in the minds of both men and women.[57]

Participation in a barn- or house-raising incurred an obligation, as did routine visits. The contributor expected work-in-kind, or at a minimum, acknowledgment or appreciation. Cabinetmaker's apprentice Edward Carpenter expressed resentment for not being thanked after helping build a barn: "I went up to H. W. Clapp's this afternoon to the raising of a barn. & worked considerable hard & didn't get as much as 'thank you sir' for it." Parallel to visiting as social exchange, the exchange of labor built upon the expectation of reciprocity. The moral imperative behind the reciprocity of both kinds of visiting insured that community-building would be complex and multidimensional.[58]

Communal labor served two important purposes during the antebellum period: (1) the need for helping hands in the face of a labor-intensive project; and (2) the need for sociability. Work was intertwined with leisure. Occasions for work were simultaneously opportunities for visiting, talking, sharing news, catching up on family gossip, and reinforcing ties—in essence, reaffirming the interdependency of the community.

THE CHANGING STRUCTURE OF WORK

The structure of work fundamentally shaped visiting patterns. Cott suggests that the structure of work explains gender differences in social life. She relies on E. P. Thompson's distinction between preindustrial task-orientation and industrial time-discipline. By the mid-nineteenth century, factory schedules ordered men's work, while married women's work in the home remained task-oriented, observing the rhythms of everyday life. Cott claims that the organization of women's lives in the industrializing nineteenth century resembled the "premodern" work of both men and women in the eighteenth century: "unsystematized, inefficient, nonurgent." Separate spheres for men and women emerged, according to Cott, not simply because women did their work at home and men went elsewhere, but because women's work in the household, unlike men's work in the labor market, "seemed to elude rationalization and the cash nexus, and to integrate labor with life."[59]

Because of their work environments, farmers and artisans continued a task-orientation in the mid-nineteenth century more than factory workers did. A substantial percentage of diarists in this study worked in factories (21 percent) at some point during their diary-keeping. Some had to keep strict hours as clerks or apprentices under someone else's direction (12 percent). The other diarists worked in positions that were seasonal (e.g., teaching—29 percent), paid by the piece (e.g., shoebinding, leather pieceworking, itinerant sewing—21 percent), or self-employed (crafts—23 percent—and farming—39 percent). Because farmers, pieceworkers, and artisans worked autonomously, their working lives had a task-orientation, analogous to the work of women who were not employed for wages. Their time was not measured by an hourly wage and could be interrupted; they executed their work in a context where social activities integrated with economic ones. The industrial organization of work largely separated social and economic activities and reduced the amount of time available for visiting.[60]

Although factory schedules interfered with visiting, they did not prevent visiting altogether. Before the speed-up in the textile mills in the 1840s, workers commonly gabbed, read aloud to coworkers, and received calls on the shop floor from out-of-town visitors. Whenever the mills were shut down due to unstable demand for textiles or weather impediments (e.g., a frozen river meant no source of energy to run the factory), factory workers shifted instantaneously into a visiting mode. In addition, they regularly spent their evening hours fraternizing with coworkers and friends and attending community events.[61]

The demands of work excused both men and women from the chain of visiting obligations. Erlunia Smith commented on her job as a department-store clerk in Worcester, Massachusetts: "I have scarcely made a call upon any of my friends for the last six months untill within a week for which time I have been out of the shop." The schedule of her paid labor proved an impediment to visiting until she took a vacation. In contrast to women, when work imposed conflicting demands, married men could delegate the "social work" to their womenfolk. Anne Parker, wife of a farmer and storekeeper, accepted female responsibility for visiting. Acknowledging the division of labor between men and women regarding visiting duties, she wrote to inform her sister-in-law Rhoda Parker, an apprentice combmaker, that her brother-in-law, Winthrop, would be visiting Boston on business: "You know these business men say 'business before friends,' though they love their friends. So we 'ladies of leisure' must do the visiting for them." Her reference to Rhoda and herself as "ladies of leisure" sarcastically acknowledged the cultural discourse of middle-class femininity. Placing the phrase in quotation marks emphasized its inappropriateness as a description of the two women. At the same time, Anne accepted the responsibility delegated to her—visiting her husband's relatives. The labors that excused women from visiting obligations did not have to be paid. Caretaking responsibilities as the mother of young children or as the daughter of elderly or infirm parents circumscribed social life, confining one to a more domestic life.[62]

Antebellum New England was an extremely mobile society geographically. Residents moved to the frontier, to a new factory town, to any place that held the promise of a better way of life. Not surprisingly, relocating to take a job was one work dimension that made a huge difference in the regularity and continuity of social life. Many millworkers, teachers, and apprentices faced moving as a condition of employment. Charles Metcalf wrote a letter to his parents in 1843 discussing the advisability of sending his younger sister, Mary, to join him in Lowell to work in the textile mills:

> You must do as *you* think best about it. I should be glad to have her come but I wish her to know what to expect should she come. I wish not to discourage *her* or *you*. She would probably find some place to work if not

immediately. Soon but whether she would like it or not I don't know. In the 1st place she would find there's no place like *Home* every one here is wrapped up in self and looks out for N.1. She would find her patience taxed to the utmost. I was going to say, she would find few very few to care for her in her troubles except relations and none to sympathize like *parents*. There can be no *I can'ts* here. If she has fortitude, patience, and perseverance enough for th[e]se and wishes very much to come and you think it best *I say come* and we will do the best we can for her. She must leave home if she [lived sometime], and perhaps this is as good as any and the lesson though a hard one will be good [when learned.]

Likewise teachers regularly had to move, typically "boarding around"—living with the parents of their students—while teaching. Mariners even more radically absented themselves from their home community for extended periods of time. The diary of Charles Benson reveals the loneliness he experienced while at sea: "What a miserable life a sea fareing life is." As the ship steward and an African American man, he shunned contact, by choice and by design, with the large number of sailors on board:

> As to the men, I have hardly seen them. I suppose I shall find them the same as most all sailors these days, a pack of fault finding ignorant men. But it is all the same to me, for I have little to do with a sailor.

When the bark *Glide* left Salem harbor in April 1862 on its second voyage to East Africa, Charles began a diary intended as a protracted letter to his wife, Jenny (see Figure 19). Charles wrote of his homesickness and the loneliness endemic to his job: "I hope the time will come when I shall stay at home. A man that has a wife aught not go to sea, but all men don't fret as much about home as I do." After an eleven-month voyage to Arabia and East Africa, the *Glide* finally sailed back to Salem.[63]

Moving for work also dramatically affected the social lives of domestic workers. Because of their working conditions—living in the home of their employer, working long hours with few if any coworkers, remaining on-call day and night—domestic workers were isolated from their social networks and constrained in forming new ones. In Vermont, Lizzie Goodenough reflected on the isolation:

> It has been a long lonesome day to me. Oh how I wish the time would come when the [time] would seem pleasant to me. Something to think of besides working away from home and friends [just] for money. Long years have past since I had a Father's home to go to.

The diary entry also reflects the vulnerabilities of a young, single woman whose parents have died.[64]

CONCLUSION

This chapter began by investigating visiting rituals as a form of "social work." This formulation acknowledges both the need to actively maintain neighborly friendships and the labor—mental, physical, and emotional—that sustains them. The framework of the public, the private, and the social spheres allows us to reorient our perspective and see social activities as "work," the active weaving together of the fabric of society. Building on the writing of di Leonardo and others, we can expand our understanding of the "social work" of women beyond kin networks to look at the neighborhood, the village, and the town. Women and men within the social sphere dynamically mediated the various forces of society—tying the family to the community, neighbor to neighbor, the individual to the collectivity.

Furthermore, the practice of visiting reveals that between 1820 and 1865, laboring women were not confined to domestic space, as the label "private" suggests. They traveled to see distant neighbors and friends; they attended lectures; they organized church events, bees, and the like. The diaries, letters, and autobiographies demonstrate that women's networks reached out broadly and embraced people not related by blood. As in the colonial period, visiting linked households in an elaborate system of economic and social exchange. Work intertwined with sociability; both were fundamental to survival. Visiting provided essential services and labor to households and bound neighbors and kin.

The extensive gender integration of activities in the social realm refutes the belief that working people observed a culture of separate spheres. Men's involvement in the capitalist market did not render them inept at domestic affairs. Women's expansive everyday activities launched them into orbits far beyond the confines of the private sphere. Unlike middle-class women, working women did not control channels of communication within the family through exclusive access to visiting and correspondence. Juxtaposed to the social dimension, the private sphere seems small indeed, a shadow of working women's universe.[65]

The central role of visiting in the lives of working people raises some interesting questions about the value of "social work" and the status visitors derived from it. By dissipating the loneliness of others, comforting the bereaved, caring for the infirm, attending the births of future generations, engaging in the labor-intensive tasks of providing shelter and clothing, both men and women performed services that one century later would generate multibillion-dollar industries and keep federal and state governments scrambling. The industrializing organization of work over the course of the nineteenth century increasingly impinged upon working people's capacity for engaging in social exchange. However, diarists regularly moved in order to find employment, which profoundly disrupted local networks. They struggled to establish new ties and to maintain old ones through correspondence and visiting.

The question remains: did women and men derive a different kind of status in the social sphere than they did in the public or private, a status premised on their centrality to the communal enterprise and the provision of essential services? And if working women visited (slightly) more than working men in antebellum New England, but did so increasingly over the following hundred years, how did the value of their services change over time?

If visiting became increasingly feminized, as the literature suggests, did it, like other occupations, decline in its prestige and value? In this system of exchange, women, as "participant intermediaries," had the opportunity to exercise a certain kind of freedom and initiative as well as draw on important resources for the household. Through activity in the social sphere, were women able, as Osterud suggests, to redress gender hierarchy? While they did not direct all social activities, they indisputably acted at the heart of managing them. Their influence was not limited to individual households (private), nor was it public (affecting the state). It was social.

Figure 1. Martha Osborne Barrett dresses in costume
for a party of the Unity Club, a theatrical group
affiliated with the Unitarian Church in Peabody,
Massachusetts. Photograph, 1890. Courtesy of the
Peabody Historical Society, Peabody, Massachusetts.

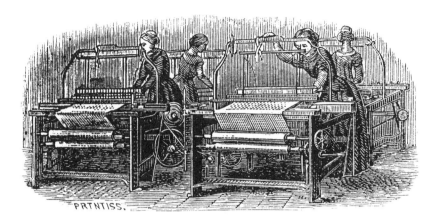

Figure 2. Four female weavers at their looms. Engraving from Sumner Pratt, Worcester, Massachusetts, Letterhead, 1860. Courtesy of the Museum of American Textile History, North Andover, Massachusetts.

Figure 3. Leonard Stockwell, a paper-mill worker and
farm laborer. Photograph. From *Leonard Stockwell
Memorial Volume*, ca. 1880. Courtesy of the American
Antiquarian Society, Worcester, Massachusetts.

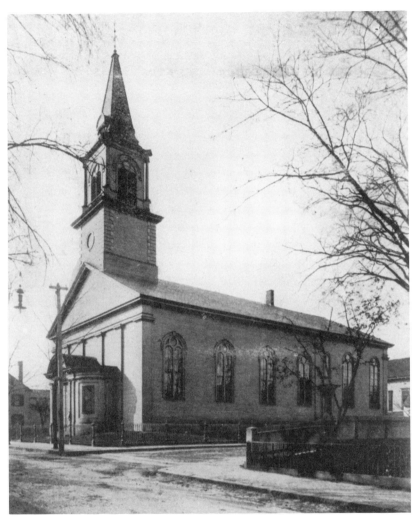

Figure 4. The Unitarian Church in Peabody, Massachusetts, which Martha Osborne Barrett attended for the second half of the nineteenth century. Photograph, 1906. Courtesy of the Peabody Historical Society, Peabody, Massachusetts.

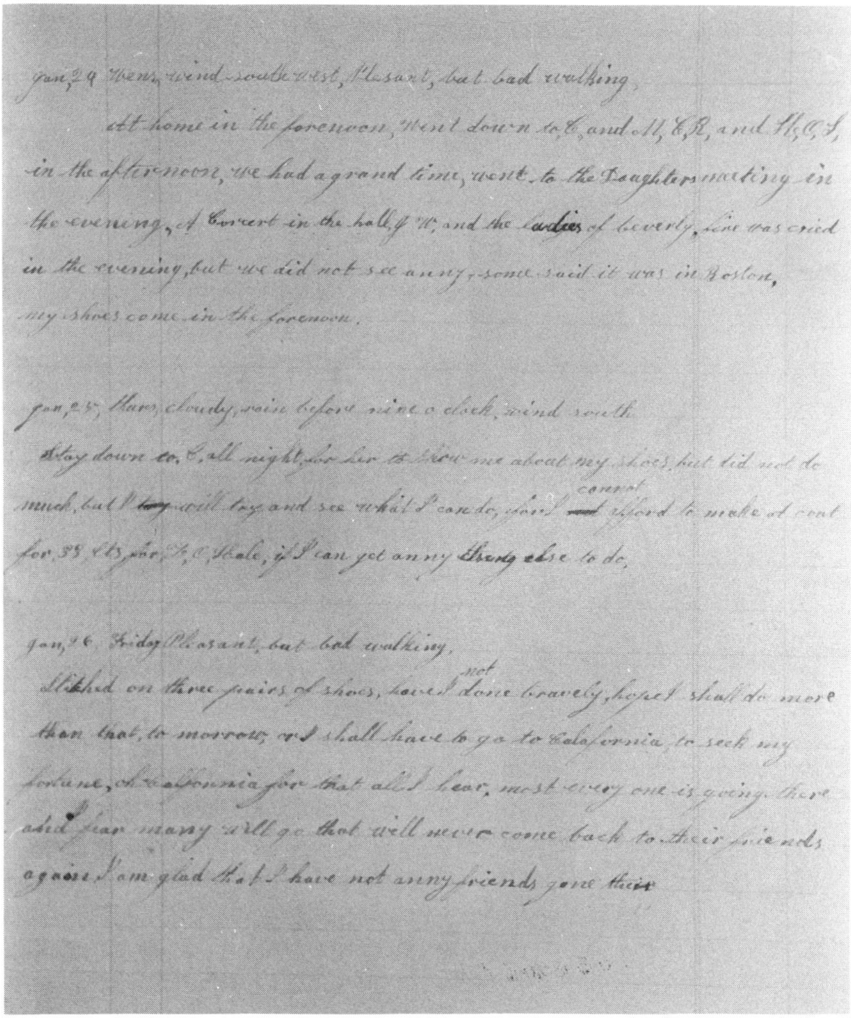

Jan, 24 Wens, wind south west, Pleasant, but bad walking,

At home in the forenoon, went down to C, and M, E, R, and H, C, F,
in the afternoon, we had a grand time, went to the Daughters meeting in
the evening, of Concert in the hall of W, and the Ladies of Beverly, fire was cried
in the evening, but we did not see anny, some said it was in Boston,
my shoes come in the forenoon.

Jan, 25, Thurs, cloudy, rain before nine o clock, wind south
Stay down to C, all night, she did to show me about my shoes, but did not do
                                                                    count
much, but I — will try and see what I can do, you — will afford to make at cent
for 38 cts, per, F, C, Seale, if I can get anny thing else to do,

Jan, 26, Friday Pleasant, but bad walking,
                                      not
I lined on three pairs of shoes, have done bravely, hope I shall do more
than that, to morrow, or I shall have to go to California, to seek my
fortune, of California for that all I hear, most every one is going there
and fear many will go that will never come back to their friends
again I am glad that I have not anny friends gone there

Figure 5. Handwritten page from the diary of Sarah Trask, shoebinder, January 24–26, 1849. Courtesy of Beverly Historical Society and Museum, Beverly, Massachusetts.

Figure 6. Image of an elegant woman pasted in Sarah Trask's Diary, 1851. The artist titles the engraving "A Lover's Signal." Sarah titles it "This is Sarah presented by C. H. Lewis." Beneath the image she recorded a poem: "For never can my soul forget / The loves of others years / Their memories fill my spirit yet / I've kept them green with tears." Courtesy of Beverly Historical Society and Museum, Beverly, Massachusetts.

Figure 7. Brigham Nims, box-factory worker, farmer, and teacher, poses for a silhouette, a popular form of representing one's likeness in antebellum New England. Courtesy of New Hampshire Historical Society, Concord.

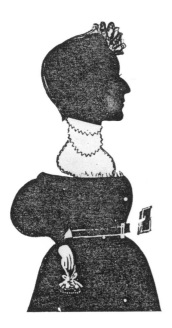

Figure 8. Laura Nims, sister of Brigham Nims, is made to look slightly ridiculous with the exaggerated features of her dress. Silhouette. Courtesy of New Hampshire Historical Society, Concord.

Figure 9. Holdridge Primus, father of Rebecca Primus, standing on sidewalk in front of Seyms & Co., Grocers, where he worked for forty-seven years. Main Street, Hartford, Connecticut. Trade card, ca. 1860. Courtesy of Connecticut Historical Society, Hartford.

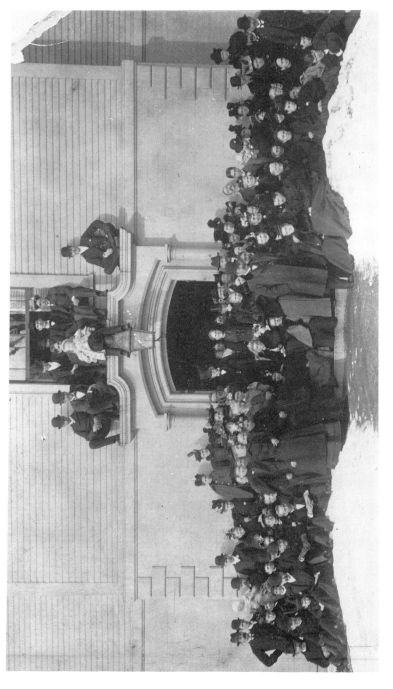

Figure 10. Chloe Fales Adams Metcalf on her hundredth birthday. Chloe is seated at the center of her family and friends. Photograph, 1897. Courtesy of Museum of American Textile History, North Andover, Massachusetts.

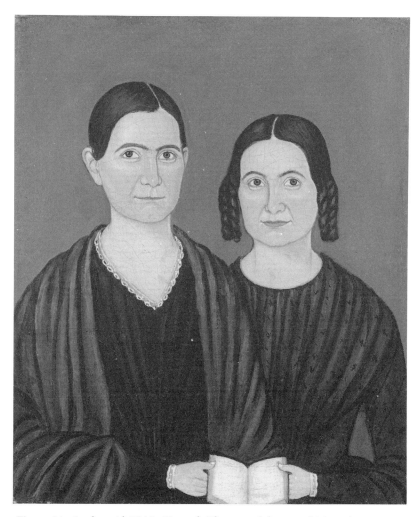

Figure 11. In the mid-1840s Hannah Thurston Adams and Mary Agnes Adams commissioned a portrait of themselves from an itinerant portrait painter. They stand proudly holding the account book from their tailoring business. Oil on canvas, artist unknown, ca. 1845. Photograph by Thomas Neill. Courtesy of Old Sturbridge Village, Sturbridge, Massachusetts.

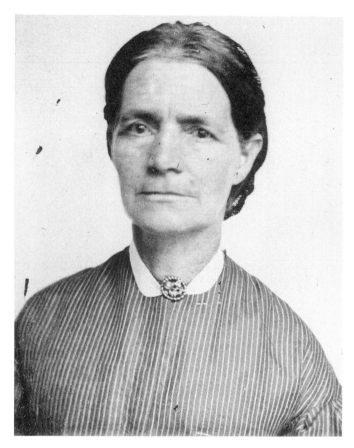

Figure 12. Eliza Adams, sister of Hannah and Mary Adams, worked as a textile operative and saved her money to buy a farm in western Massachusetts. As a single woman, she adopted and raised two daughters while also providing a home for other young orphans. Tintype, ca. late 1840s. Private collection.

Figure 13. Four anonymous working women link arms and directly confront the camera. Ambrotype, ca. 1860. Private collection.

Figure 14. Two anonymous friends affectionately pose for the camera. Note that the man on the left has his arm around the man on the right. Daguerreotype, ca. 1860s. Private collection.

Figure 15. After both parents died in an accident, Mary Giddings Coult Jones taught school for several years in New Hampshire. She married a farmer and moved to his home in Connecticut in 1853. Photograph, ca. 1860s. Courtesy of the Connecticut Historical Society, Hartford.

Figure 16. A staff of domestic workers. Tintype, ca. 1860–1880. Private collection.

Figure 17. Southwestern view of Gloucester, Massachusetts. Francis Bennett, Jr., grew up in this prosperous fishing town, where he worked as a clerk and began keeping his diary. Engraving, 1839. From *Historical Collections*, by John Warner Barber (Worcester, Mass.: Dorr, Howland & Co., 1839). Courtesy of the Society for the Preservation of New England Antiquities, Boston.

Figure 18. This quilting party in western Virginia, like those in New England, includes both men and women, along with animals and children of all ages. Engraving, 1854. From *Gleason's Pictorial Draw-Room Companion*, vol. 7 (October 21, 1854), p. 249. Courtesy of American Antiquarian Society, Worcester, Massachusetts.

Figure 19. Charles A. Benson served as the steward on the bark *Glide* on its maiden voyage to East Africa in 1861. On its next sojourn in 1862, he began keeping a diary to send back to his wife, Jenny. Oil painting by William Stubbs. Photograph by Mark Sexton. Courtesy of Peabody & Essex Museum/Peabody Museum Collection, Salem, Massachusetts.

Figure 20. The Reverend Peter Randolph, an ex-slave,
regularly preached to white audiences in the North.
Photograph, 1893. From *Slave Cabin to Pulpit: The
Autobiography of Rev. Peter Randolph; The Southern
Question Illustrated and Sketches of Slave Life*
(Boston: James H. Earle, 1893).

Figure 21. The Reverend Samuel Harrison was a shoemaker as well as a minister. He served as chaplain to the 54th Massachusetts, the first black regiment to fight in the Civil War. Daguerreotype, 1849. From *His Life Story as Told by Himself* (Pittsfield, Mass.: Eagle Publishing, 1899).

Figure 22. David Clapp worked as an apprentice printer
while he kept his diary in the early 1820s. He later became
a successful printer in Boston. Engraving, 1894. From
Memoir of David Clapp, by William B. Trask (Boston,
1894). Courtesy of American Antiquarian Society,
Worcester, Massachusetts.

Figure 23. Bethany Veney wrote her life story, recounting her life under slavery and her move to settle in New England. Engraving, 1889. From *Narrative of Bethany Veney, a Slave Woman* (Worcester, Mass., 1889).

Figure 24. Isaac Mason, an ex-slave, wrote his autobiography in the late nineteenth century. Photograph,
1893. From *Life of Isaac Mason as a Slave* (Worcester,
Mass., 1893).

Figure 25. Harriet A. Jacobs recorded her harrowing tale of life
under slavery, her heroic escape, and her struggle to make a living
in the North. Photograph, 1894. From her autobiography,
Incidents in the Life of a Slave Girl, Written by Herself, edited by
Jean Fagan Yellin (Cambridge, Mass.: Harvard University Press,
1987).

CHAPTER FIVE

"True Opinion Clear of Polish"

*Gossip, Reputation, and
the Community Jury*

Speculation about secrets—romance, marriage, the legal status of children, and other family skeletons—constituted a popular pastime in
antebellum New England. Like detectives, subjects would try to solve a
mystery based on the observable facts, the known history of the individual, and the degree to which they wanted to give the benefit of the doubt.
Eliza Adams attempted to assess the likelihood that a neighbor, Alphens's
wife, had an abortion:

> Alphens' wife has been up here with her mother all summer. Poor Alphens
> he has got so poor that he can't keep house so he sent his wife out to live on
> his father all winter. Her poor health was caused by gitting rid of a child as
> I suppose. Alphens did not feel able to maintain another one. You must not
> say any thing as I have only guessed it. She was very large when she came
> here and in a short time she slunk to her usual size. "*Perhaps it was the
> dropsy.*"

Dropsy, an extreme form of water retention, possibly explained the
temporary girth of Alphens's wife, although Eliza seemed skeptical. She
displayed sympathy for the economic condition of Alphens but judged
that his inadequacy as a breadwinner prompted his wife to abort her
pregnancy. Abortion was not illegal in 1857, but neither was it the most
socially sanctioned method of family limitation. Eliza hinted at her
disapproval of the abortion but placed greater emphasis on its secrecy,
the reasons for its necessity, and the lingering poor health of Alphens's
wife. Her demand for confidentiality demonstrated the sensitive nature

114

of the information but more important, its precarious reliability. Eliza knew that the unreliable information, difficult to retract, could be damaging. Her talk carefully bordered on the limits of acceptable speculation. Gossip incorporated news, speculation, and judgments, and subjects expected no less. They organized their lives with an understanding that talk about their behavior was part of the social environment.[1]

Gossip, or as Marcella Holmes put it, "true opinion clear of polish," could have consisted of simple information that included both good and bad tidings such as news of a sister's well-being or of a neighbor's death. Alternatively it could have been "talk to discredit" with potentially destructive repercussions. Most often, gossip was information tinged with judgment—explicit or assumed. The factual nature of the gossip was often suspect, because like all intelligence transmitted via many ears and tongues, the potential for distortion grew with time and travel— due to ignorance, the desire for sensation, or malice.[2]

Although contemporary dictionaries concur in defining gossip as "idle chatter," those who study it closely find it far from idle in its practice and in its individual and social consequences. For the purposes of this study, gossip refers to talk about people that reflects an "intense interest in the personal." In nineteenth-century New England, gossip relied upon the medium of the face-to-face contact that visiting afforded. Letters offered a less-preferred but nonetheless welcome substitute for exchanging information in person. Addie Brown wrote, "If I could see you I could tell you better than write it." Gossiping occurred in houses, pubs, and churches, and on street corners. It was central to community life because it was a primary means of circulating information and also because it regulated moral behavior.[3]

While working people's gossip focused largely on private matters, gossiping was necessarily social. Incorporating information, emotion, evaluation, and speculation, gossip constituted the mainstay of community discourse in antebellum New England. It provided a medium for monitoring as well as negotiating community opinion. In antebellum New England, the process of gossiping scrutinized information and determined factual correctness and appropriate behavior—in effect, it negotiated community opinion about people and about the acceptable parameters of behavior. People who gossiped potentially persuaded and influenced others and could, in effect, valorize or ostracize the subject of gossip.

How do we understand gossip within the public/private framework? Was gossip public because it was "accessible to all" and involved potentially an entire community? Or was it private because it was typically transmitted between two individuals, probably (though not necessarily) in the confines of a home? This chapter addresses the various roles of gossip in crafting antebellum communities. What were the acceptable parameters of gossip? Were there gender differences in who gossiped or who was gossiped about? What effect did gossip have on its subject, the "gossipee," as Ogden Nash would have it? This chapter examines the importance of reputation and the role of the community as a "jury" in formulating that reputation. Finally, it explores the implications for women of gossip's potential to influence reputations and events.[4]

Working people prized letters because of the important information they conveyed. In one example, Addie Brown relayed that she no longer corresponded with a male friend because he never said anything in his letters. She was not willing to waste three cents on a stamp for return correspondence that yielded so little news. Gossip, via letters and visits, was the primary medium for circulating news in the absence of television and telephones. In writing about the important role of "old maids" in antebellum communities, one millgirl raised the centrality of single women in circulating information: "In country towns where no weekly sheet [newspaper] is published, they are extremely useful in carrying the news," obviously an essential feature of community life.[5]

REPUTATION AND THE COMMUNITY JURY

Gossip acted as a mechanism for social control because working people cared about their reputations. Participation within a community necessitated a good reputation, which functioned as "social currency." A community jury, those concerned neighbors and friends who rarely convened but who always observed and evaluated behavior, exercised great influence in regard to reputation. The community could demand standards of behavior in conferring a good name and ensure accountability on the part of its members. Gossip could make or break a reputation. And because gossip necessarily involved relationships, it was subject to negotiation.[6]

A good name conferred status, guaranteed a certain modicum of attention, connoted group membership, and granted an individual the privilege of judging another. Peter Wilson notes that "the vulnerability of a good name stems from the fact that it is held and conferred by people other than the person who is said to possess it, and that it has no tangible substance, it consists entirely of words." Writing about the elaborate multifaceted network of women in colonial New England, Laurel Ulrich vividly articulates the importance of gossip within a neighborhood:

> Because this was a society which still depended primarily upon external rather than internal controls, many New Englanders responded not so much to guilt as to shame. The opinion of one's neighbor was everything. As Goody Bishop expressed it, a body might as well take an axe and knock one of her cows on the head as to take away her daughter's good name.

While the growing individualism of the nineteenth century diminished the importance of informal community sanctions, especially in large urban centers, antebellum religion continued to propagate the importance of reputation. Eliza Adams wrote to her sister about the previous Sunday's sermon that had attempted to fortify the congregation's concern for reputation: "Brother Beckwith preached his texts. A good name is better than precious ointment."[7]

Subjects in this study cared deeply what their neighbors and friends thought and said about them. Paulina Bascom Williams was a case in point. Paulina, a self-described evangelist, moved through Vermont in the 1830s with her child and her husband, a Congregationalist minister. The small itinerant family sought the right place to settle, and in the meantime suffered from the lack of a stable home. Exceedingly poor, Paulina constantly scrambled to make comfortable provisions, often in someone else's home when a village lacked a parsonage. In September, 1830, the Williams family stayed with Paulina's husband's brother and his family in Orwell, Vermont, a village of 1,598. From the moment they arrived, Paulina felt the community was insufficiently respectful. The final insult occurred when Sarah confronted her about her character:

> Tuesday returned to his brother's. Found things not very pleasant. Took in real lecture on *Economy*. The want of it in me being assigned as the sole cause of our poverty. A strange thing indeed that we should not get rich on less than $200 a year. To train me to the yoke, Sarah has taken the responsibility of overseer upon herself & exercises authority over me, becoming so important a station. She may find that those who are not accustomed to be servile in childhood are apt to be obstinate in youth. My character is dear to me & ought to be. I am commanded to follow those "things that are of a good report." 'Tis hard to try to do well & then be ill spoken of & have facts misrepresented & motives maligned.

She felt utterly wronged and turned to God, "him who judgeth righteously," for vindication. She asked him to give her a "prudent peaceful spirit" to cope with the situation. However, almost immediately she packed her bags and left for her uncle's house. In another example, the memorial volume about the life of Leonard Stockwell, a tenant farmer, boasted of his reputation for kindness, at least to his farm animals:

> Could he have had the means would undoubtedly have been one of the most successful farmers of his time and vicinity. He was kind and pleasant to all in his employ, a good word for all, even to the dumb cattle in his charge he was thoughtfull and kind. It was an oft repeated remark of those who knew him well that they should rather be his dumb cattle then many people's hired help, this remark indicates the respect of his neighbors as well as the feelings of deep consideration he had for everything under his care.

Subjects found a variety of recourses for restoring a damaged reputation: capitulation, waiting for the gossip to pass, revenge, social exoneration, moving out of the community (self-exile), and spurning the community jury.[8]

CRITERIA FOR A GOOD REPUTATION

In communities where people knew one another, people based their assessment of reputation on a host of activities: sexual conduct, the reputation of associates, fulfillment of neighboring responsibilities, choice of marital partner, upward mobility, church attendance, involvement in temperance activities, and race. In a race-stratified society, race played a major role in shaming. In nineteenth-century New England, while African Americans developed criteria of their own for respectability within their own communities, white culture judged African Americans and their behavior by prejudicial standards based on racist assumptions. Slavery flourished in the antebellum South and had been abolished in New England states only since the American Revolution. William J. Brown wrote about the role of interracial associations and reputation: "It was thought a disgrace to plead a colored man's cause, or aid in getting his rights as a citizen, or to teach their children in schools. The teachers themselves were ashamed to have it known that they taught colored schools." He gave the example of a Mr. Anthony, a white teacher in Providence, Rhode Island, who reprimanded one of his African American students for saying hello to him on the street. He punished the student for acknowledging their relationship and drawing attention to the fact that Mr. Anthony taught people of color.[9]

The basis for reputation varied by gender as well as race, but not as dramatically as the existence of the cult of true womanhood would suggest. Both white men's and white women's reputations rested on their sexual behavior, their relationships with members of the opposite sex, and fulfillment of their marital and familial obligations. Because of the fragility of sexual reputation, it was particularly difficult to restore once tarnished. And when challenged, women had fewer resources to restore their lost reputation.[10]

A woman's reputation depended on keeping "good company" (however her community defined it). In a letter filled with gossip, Erlunia Smith, a teacher, revealed how her mere association with Converse, a man suspected of fathering an illegitimate child, tainted her reputation:

> Oh Ann, that old creature has got a young one at last and they say it looks just like Converse. But then you know there would be enough to say so whether it did or not. Don't you think, Ann, that I heard by way of Dudley once and by way of Webster once that Converse was courting Miss Erlunia Smith? Now I think that is too bad for I never have given any one the least reason to connect my name with that of Converse. I have been very careful not to give any reason for I thought as he boarded with Evelina that unless I was very careful not to go with him that people would of course have something to say. So I always was on my guard and *never* called at Mr. Burleigh when I expected him to be there. And now I think to slander in this way is too horrid. But there is no help for it. I have only to stay and bear it patiently.

As an unmarried woman in her late twenties, Erlunia carefully monitored the appearance of her behavior. She learned of Converse's illegitimate child, although apparently gossip had already been circulating about Converse's relationship with "that old creature." She considered herself slandered because of Converse's poor reputation and his alleged association with her. Erlunia saw patience as her only recourse. Her appeal to her friend, Ann Lilley, regarding the injustice of the situation may have relieved some of her anxiety by virtue of simply venting, but it probably proved ineffectual in mitigating the news locally. To contest the implication in the social sphere would have drawn greater attention to Erlunia and perhaps damaged more than it would have repaired. Thus, she followed the strategy of waiting.[11]

Men were not exempt from the same considerations, particularly men with less power in the community, such as working-class men and men of color. William Grimes, an ex-slave living in Litchfield, Connecticut, employed a white girl to assist with the washing; his household took in laundry to make money. Two detractors registered a charge

against him with a grand juror, "for keeping a bad girl at my house.
. . . The girl was of a bad character; but I did not know it. She was
white. I sent her away as soon as I heard anything against her." In this
case, her employment depended upon her reputation, which in turn,
influenced Grimes, her employer. Grimes's reputation would have been
harmed if he had continued to be linked to her, because of her reputation
and probably because of her race.[12]

Subjects cast aspersions on men and women who made bad marital
decisions. Abigail Baldwin thought the future bleak for Alonzo Whitney
and Sarah Parker: "Married 7 o'clock p.m., wish them well, but the
prospects look dark." Addie Brown remarked on the decision by an
acquaintance to marry an uneducated woman: "Rebecca, I wish you
could take a view at Thomas' wife. Every body is surprise at his taste as
well as myself. I don't think she is educat[er]ed. She does not show it."[13]

Notably, subjects repeatedly assessed how well men and women met
their responsibilities as family members. "I heard Mr. P. S. has left his
wife and childdren," remarked Addie Brown. "He was here two or three
weeks ago and was up to father saloon. He was going out west and
didn't think he would ever come back." Abigail Baldwin wrote of a man
she judged harshly because of his inattention to his sick wife and to his
husbandly obligations:

> To Mr. Ford's. She is wasting in consumption with little care. A child ten
> years old is her nurse and housekeeper. Mother and child need pity. Their
> husband and father unkind. We that have the comforts of life should be very
> thankful.

Stephen Parker wrote to his sister about Samuel Davis's inability to
support his family and the consequences for his wife's respectability:

> Sam[l] Davis turns out to be a _poor husband_. Is married & has children. Has
> gone away to the upper part of the state—and I understand does not support
> his family without assistance. I pitty his wife—and think she would be quite
> respectable had she a good husband. Hope you—dear Sis—will see to it that
> you do get a "_shifty_" [i.e., not shiftless] husband.

Stephen found Sam Davis unworthy of respect because he did not live
up to his familial commitments. In turn, his wife's association with him
rendered her pitiable and unrespectable.[14]

A woman's fulfillment of her wifely obligations likewise figured
centrally in the community's assessment of her. Addie Brown voiced

concern about Rebecca's Aunt Emily Sands's treatment of her very ill husband:

> I feel worried. I suppose you will say I am always borrowing trouble. I will tell you what it is. I don't think Mr. Sands is long for this world. He has got a horrid cough yesterday. I send Sarah up to him for something for to eat. To day she found her father quite sick. Pray don't mention it. I don't think Aunt E. takes very good care of her husband.

Addie understood the gravity of her charge—such gossip endangered Aunt Emily. She cautioned Rebecca to keep quiet and anticipated Rebecca's warning that she was "borrowing trouble" to get involved in such accusations.[15]

The subjects recognized the limits of gossip in passing reliable information, in imposing standards of behavior, and in exercising influence over others. In a social system that relied on word-of-mouth dissemination of information, the potential for confusion or scrambled information increased with each new tongue it passed through. Stephen Parker attempted to reassure his sister about his health while implying that some women meddled intrusively and inappropriately: "I wish to *undo* what our good Old Maid Miss B. Chase. . . . I am sorry she has so alarmed you in regard to our healths. It is true Mary has had the mumps." Mary Adams tried to straighten out the misunderstanding caused by secondhand information that she herself had transmitted: "You must not be offended at her for what she said for I think it showed pleasure that you were not out of business. Perhaps she did not say exactly as I wrote as I did not hear but it came secondhanded."[16]

Community opinion created an audience larger than an individual's nuclear family but smaller than the polity. Gossip reflected engagement in a *social* world beyond an individual's household. As Robert N. Bellah has noted, "reputation by its very nature is indelibly social," an observation that holds especially true in small, bounded communities. Observing the rules of the community jury, anticipating its deliberations, and caring about its judgment and subsequent talk indicated a group attuned to social discourse. Subjects repeatedly demonstrated awareness of their watchful neighbors. For example, Mary Mudge reported after being sick with menstrual cramps: "They say Mrs. Haskell gave me quite a run yesturday, because I had not done Elisa Ann's blanket." And Parna Gilbert felt plagued by talk: "Never did I before spend a communion season with such unpleasant feelings concerning a difficulty which has been long existing with regard to singing, the unpleasantness some feel toward me on account of attending a party school, as it is called, last Tues. 29 at Mr. Welcome Gibson's."[17]

Recognizing the enormous weight of the community jury's opinions, a few subjects of gossip struggled unsuccessfully to minimize the effects. Leonard Stockwell illustrated the way in which a man could construct an account of his life which contradicted that of the community. His life was full of mishaps, disappointment, and failure. He discounted the negativity of others in order to maintain a positive self-image and a modicum of optimism about his future. In essence, he tried to minimize community opinion by dismissing his critics as perpetually negative and skeptical: "There are always relatives or friends who are quick to attach blame or shortsightedness to the adoption of any scheme or project which proves a failure, no matter how bright the promise or what good faith it is entered upon, or the circumstance that changes the aspect of things." Friends, relatives, and neighbors observed his limitations, some circumstantial and some personal, and judged him, he thought, too severely. His attempt to minimize what his community said about him demonstrated how deeply he cared about its disapproval.[18]

That some diarists strove to overcome their deeply felt accountability to their community supports the observation that their jury of peers assessed their private, social, and public lives, and that those judgments had a bearing on how subjects lived their lives. Shoebinder Sarah Trask felt the conflict deeply within herself. While she anxiously awaited the return of her sailor boyfriend, Luther Woodberry, she became the target of community ridicule. She stubbornly refused to accept the community's definition of the situation:

> No news for me, and I am disapointed. Now I shall not look for news, but for their return. And hope it will be soon. I don't care if I do get laugh at, for looking so soon, something seem to tell me that they will come soon. I rather hope and be disapointed, than have anny one tell me that they will not be here yet, for that's is provoking. I never believe them.

The taunting bothered her, but not enough to change her behavior. She desperately clung to her fantasy that the *Helen S. Page* (Luther's ship) would arrive soon, despite the sober reality that progressively seeped into her consciousness.

> I must say I was a little mad today. Mother said the Salem folks thought that L.W. better have gone to California. I don't, and other folks need not concern them selves, about him. I had much rather he would be were he is, than at California for then I should not expect to see him again and now I do if

nothing happens, . . . at anny rate whatever. I wish folks would not mention the barque H.S. Page to me, for every body knows better than me, when to expect them. Well I don't care for I shall look for them when I have a mind to, for I don't care if other folks don't look. I shall, I will. I can be disapointed I know, and it will not be the first time, I guess. But I am so ugly tonight, I am beyond control[?].

She turned her social torment inward, at great personal expense. She rejected the community's assessment of Luther's neglect of her. At the same time, she waged a protracted struggle to minimize its effects on her. She stubbornly continued her long-suffering waiting and subjected herself to ridicule, unable to rid herself of the socially ascribed stigma.[19]

The indomitable Sarah Holmes anticipated community talk when she applied to teach in Gardiner, Maine: "I have made aplication for a class in the high school at G. but don't know what the prospects is yet. I have no doubt but it will be food for some of the gosips if I do go there." She failed to explain what the gossips would be feeding on and claimed she did not care. She could say this in part because she had economic independence as a teacher and in part because she had a friend living in Gardiner: "I shall be much hapier to be where I have one friend to go to." Four years later Sarah Holmes advised Sarah Carter to harbor her secret from the townspeople in Foxcroft-Dover because she thrilled at the stir her mystery created:

If you chance to meet any one before you see me who talks of me, please don't tell that I am not going South. Let the wise people of F.-D. trouble themselves to guess. 'Twill do them good, much good. I like to see them vex themselves. I feel *strangely* independent, Sarah.

In 1853, two years later, from the distance of Georgia, Sarah wrote to her friend about the community jury she had left behind in Maine:

I presume that there are many people in F.-D. who *pretend* to grieve for me because I have "such a worthless husband" & would continue to do so even if they could know of all his kind care for me because they can not endure the thought that all of their predictions should prove unfounded. I care as little for their *sayings* as I did in times past. Such tales as I some times hear from them *only* seem to assure me that the gossips of my native town are unchanged. I would not make an effort to convince the people of F.-D. that Gilman was not the most cruel man in the whole world.

Sarah exhibited the self-confidence (tinged with a bit of defensiveness) of an independent being who could earn her way in the world. Despite flaunting her autonomy, she nonetheless felt the pull of community judgment. After moving to Georgia, Sarah Holmes Clark cautioned Sarah Carter, still back in Foxcroft, Maine, not to report on some aspects of her new life. For example, she asked Sarah not to divulge the fact that she taught school where her husband was the schoolmaster. "They do not know that I am teaching and if you please, you need not mention it." After all, she reasoned, she did not receive wages for her work. She also advised her against disclosing the new pro-slavery politics she had adopted since moving to Georgia:

> I see that my old friend Thurza is quite an abolitionist. She might entertain different views if she would come South and remain two years. She would soon forget I think, her sympathy for the poor negroes. They are the happiest class of people that I ever saw. But you need not tell this to Northern people."

In these complicated ways, Sarah Holmes Clark fought the crush of hometown opinions about her. The stretch of over one thousand miles between Foxcroft, Maine, and Madison, Georgia, undoubtedly fostered her autonomy. But regardless of the distance and her spunky defiance, she remained sensitive to townspeople's judgments and tried to control what information they received about her.[20]

NEGOTIATION AND COMMUNITY OPINION

As an expression of shared values and group membership, antebellum working New Englanders used gossip to delimit their communities. In gossip, diarists and correspondents communicated shared assumptions, by innuendo or indirect evaluation, of the community. They conveyed those assumptions in their blatant condemnations. In the process they designated who belonged and who did not, as well as what constituted appropriate behavior. For example, Arthur Bennett recorded his condemnation of the intemperate Otis Cox, which he thought accurately reflected the attitude of the entire community: "Went to the funeral of Otis Cox who died with a cancer on his neck occasioned by drinking *rum*. No tear were shed over his remains but was hurried to his grave as fast as convienance and decency would admit of. And in a very few days he will be forgotten." When evaluating the subject of gossip, diarists and correspondents *assumed* shared values about how to interpret behavior. The letter writer confidently expected the reader to exclaim, silently or aloud, "Isn't that terrible?!" and to then want to find out more. This process would begin subtle rearrangement of the place of that individual within the minds of the gossipers and within the social sphere.[21]

In antebellum New England, gossip assessed reputations; in effect it was "a technique for summarizing community opinions." In this sense gossip acted as a public opinion poll. In one case, a survey of local sentiments served to evaluate Mrs. Adams, who had applied for a nursing position. Erlunia wrote to her friend Ann:

> As for Mrs. Adams I have never seen the lady but from some enquiries, I learn that she is a very *nice* and ladylike woman but rather *slow*. I have made enquiries of several who know her but I cannot learn of any one that she has ever nursed. She has two children herself and Mrs. Marren, the lady that I board with, says she should not be at all affraid to trust herself to Mrs. Adam care were she needing a nurse. All speak very highly of her as a woman but no one seems to know whether she has ever been out nursing or not. There I have given you all the information I can.

Erlunia made "enquiries" about Mrs. Adams in order to assess community consensus about her. In essence, she polled and analyzed those assessments before reporting back to Ann.[22]

But neighbors and associates did not always share appraisals; they often contested one another's opinions. Gossiping enabled a group to examine the subtleties of a disputed issue, to hear alternative viewpoints, and to rethink the complexities of the issues at hand. Eliza Adams visited her brother in Darien, Georgia, in 1848, and wrote home to give people a flavor of life in the antebellum South. She devoted a large section of one letter to the impending marriage between Tom McGuire and Mary Parcel:

> A few doors farther, on the other side of the street lives two young men; one a bachelor & the other a widower, carpenters by trade, Amos Allen & Tom McGuire. Sally's sister Charlotte lived with McGuire as wife, till hearing he was courting another girl. She became jealous, discontented, & finally took poison & died. Now McGuire pays attention to Mary Parcel, up in the glen, ten miles off; they are engaged to be married soon. She is a blooming rosy girl of twenty, while he is a drinking, disipated man. John & I disagree; he thinks McGuire makes a bad bargain, & I think Mary will have the worst of it. While Hoffman says Tom won't make out much to take Mary Parcel, he further says it is a dreadful thing to take a wife from the ignorant girls brought up in the woods of Georgia.

Eliza outlined three contrasting perspectives that may never have converged. However, each opinion holder was convinced, and hoped to convince others, that he or she had correctly interpreted the situation. As the ethnographer, Eliza revealed that neither men nor women hedged their contributions in the negotiations of opinion regarding the match.[23]

Neighbors and kin had the power and responsibility to act as jurors as well as to submit to the jury's determinations of them. Some subjects saw fit to intervene in a situation involving someone with a tarnished reputation. This took the form of warning someone about to enter a shaky marriage or to make a questionable decision. It was also manifested in exercising independence of thought. In their role as jurors, subjects sometimes were empowered to counter a popular community verdict. Melissa Doloff, a schoolteacher in Vermont, wrote of Maria, a friend with whom she decided to continue a relationship despite the community jury's assessment:

> I have been over to see Maria this afternoon and had a very good time. I think she is a very good girl. She has been talked about a great deal and to be sure she has done wrong. But I think we ought not to throw her away for that. I think she is very sorry and has done no more than a great many have done only her sin was made plain to the world. While many who have done as bad if not worse, and have kept their sins hid are looked uppon with respect to those who would scorn to associate with her. She was a very lively girl and sometimes very [rud] which caused folks to make remarks about her that were very disrespectful. But I never believed them and shall not shun her society because she has sinned.

Melissa did not divulge Maria's sin because Melissa valued the fact of her transgression less than Maria's repentance. Melissa did not reject her—did not want to "throw her away"—and therefore intervened to override the community sanction against Maria. By acting contrary to the opinion of the community jury, she helped to bring Maria back into the community's pulsing network.[24]

Mary Mudge behaved similarly with her friend Sarah, who had a child *early* in her marriage. "Sarah Hutchinson has got a little son, I can hardly believe it. She has been married 6 mo and 2 weeks. It seems too bad." The next day she wrote, "Met Marth this morn. She could hardly believe what I told her." The following day, "Marth and I called up to see Sarah's baby. He is real fat, looks like Ben, but has Sarah's nose. He weighed 8 3/4 lbs. She says she did not expect so soon, but Peggy says he *looks old enough*." So Sarah's feeble suggestion did not convince Mary that the baby was born prematurely, but neither did it stop her from visiting. In contrast, Mary's beau, Philip Bryant (referred to as "B." in Mary's diary), "says he should not have thought we should have hurried. He would have waited and let her known we did not think she had behaved very pretty." But despite his suggestion, Mary continued to befriend Sarah and to help her with her baby on a regular basis. One week after the birth, Mary visited again, cooing about what a "little beauty" the baby was. She visited Sarah, helped care for the baby, sewed with her, and the like. However, Mary and Philip continued their courtship while maintaining their difference of opinion. Several months later Mary recorded that "B. spoke improperly to Sarah."[25]

These personal narratives document the many ways in which subjects attempted to confront or to avoid gossip and its consequences. Men had greater latitude and more resources at their disposal in this process, which meant they had more options. Sarah Trask would have been vindicated if the HS *Page* had returned when she said it would (despite the community skepticism) or if Luther had returned and married her, but when neither event occurred, she was left humiliated. Erlunia Smith felt she had "no help" when someone implicated her good name. The women who fared best were wage-earning women whose character or social status—as key members or as pariahs—enabled them to act independently. Mary Mudge and Marth made Sarah's life as a new mother much easier by delving into the business of newborn and mothercare. They acted despite the suggestion of premarital sex occasioned by the baby's early arrival. Those who acted in defiance of the community judgments participated in undermining an older system of social control. They acknowledged the stigma conferred by the community jury but shunned its verdict and sentence.[26]

GOSSIP AND SOCIAL CONFRONTATION

While gossip was indelibly social, subjects could shift it into the public realm through lawsuits, job loss, and expulsion from the community. Several examples well illustrate this point. In May, 1824, Sophia W. Bodwell of Methuen, Massachusetts, a village of 1,371 in 1820, discovered that her job was threatened. With her mother dead and her father given to intemperance, Sophia was the primary wage earner for her family. So why, after teaching in the Methuen public schools for nine years, cultivating dear young minds and taming wild ones, should her work be challenged? Benjamin Osgood, Esq., reputed to be the wealthiest man in Methuen, heard rumors regarding the chastity of Sophia Bodwell. Not a man to act rashly, Osgood commissioned his son to research the accusations. His son discreetly interviewed witnesses and gathered letters documenting stories about Bodwell's reputed fall from grace. After assessing the research, Osgood decided to send a letter to the school committee contesting Sophia Bodwell's virtue. The accusations grew in enormity with each consecutive charge:

> To the Committee of School District No. 8 in Methuen
>
> Gent.
>
> Being informed that you have employed Sophia W. Bodwell to teach the school in said District this summer I beg leave to remonstrate against her appointment because her character is bad & her conduct unworthy the imitation of your children. I do not wish to injure the character of Miss Bodwell but I conceive it improper to employ a person who is not lawfully [recomended] whose character is under such charges as hers now does concerning which I have made diligent inquiry & which I have no doubt that I can prove viz.
>
> About five years ago Sophia W. Bodwell was at Mr. Samuel Huse's on a visit with others & she left the company about one hour before the rest, & went home with Elisha Barker directly from her own residence in company with another young lady whom she told after they arrived at Mr. Barker's residence that she was a going into the chamber with said Barker & she must not tell of it.
>
> By what was heard that night it was suspected they conducted unlawfully.
>
> Sophia W. Bodwell has absolutely denied ever spending any time with Elisha Barker in private.
>
> She has been seen at unseasonable hours with a married man.
>
> She and a married man have manifested an unlawful attachment to each other.
>
> She has been suspected of having a child.
>
> The above statements have for a considerable length of time been currently circulated & believed. Judging from what I have heard, I have no reason to doubt the truth of them.

Osgood then disclosed his final rationale for writing the letter,

> The circulation of the statements above alluded to has been unjustly charged to my family. I consider it my imperative duty to have the subject investigated. To free my family from the aspersion that now rests on them and to fulfil the duty I owe them & society I pledge myself to prove them.
>
> Methuen, May 3, 1824
>
> Benj[a] Osgood[27]

Bodwell, probably frightened as well as outraged when news of the letter reached her, may have deliberated about how best to defend her character and her livelihood. The letter plundered her good name and jeopardized her job. Finding no easy recourse to such damning accusations, the embattled Bodwell sued Osgood for libel. The Essex County Court of Common Pleas found in favor of Osgood.

Undaunted, on the 20th of September, 1824, Bodwell filed an appeal of the case with the Supreme Judicial Court of Massachusetts. In her petition, she staunchly defended her character. She claimed she was "a virgin and chaste woman and a good, true, honest, just and faithfull citizen." In charging libel, she accused Osgood of knowingly and wickedly contriving to injure her good name "and to bring her into public scandall, infamy and disgrace." She maintained that she "was always reputed, esteemed and accepted by and amongst all her neighbors and other good and worthy citizens of this Commonwealth to whom she was in any wise known to be a person of good name, fame, and credit." She claimed Osgood purposely circulated false stories about her to her employer and her clergyman, the Reverend William Kimball, doing so out of envy of her happiness. In addition, he did not treat her in the manner she thought she deserved. One witness, Isaac Bodwell, told of a conversation he had had with Osgood, in which Osgood said that Sophia "had carried her nose up long enough." Sophia Bodwell's behavior affronted Benjamin Osgood's sense of propriety, given what he believed to be true about her. How dare a fallen woman feign respectability? She, in turn, felt rebuffed and outraged at the way he behaved. Among her grounds for suing Osgood was Osgood's refusal to treat her as a respected member of the community. But Osgood was not alone in harassing her about her reputation. Mrs. Caleb Swan, resident of Methuen, repeatedly slung epithets at Bodwell, accusing her of fornication and adultery, leading Bowdwell to also sue Caleb Swan, her husband, for slander.[28]

The *Bodwell v. Osgood* trial began in November, 1824, with Judge Samuel Putnam presiding. The twelve witnesses called for Osgood's defense testified that "the [Plaintiff's] general character was bad in regard to chastity." A stream of prominent citizens attested to their knowledge of Bodwell's reputation. In testifying about her character, J. Merrick of New Hampshire said that "it was not good—that these reports had circulated about her about three years last March." Mr. Currier, Esq., a selectman of Methuen, said "there were different opinions of her character—that many people think it is not good." The testimony for the defense repeatedly called her chastity into question. Witness after witness reported versions of the gossip, introduced into evidence as the accepted community opinion.

Bodwell's attorney presented her case by calling many upstanding citizens to "prove that she was of good character for chastity." The thirteen witnesses included selectmen, attorneys, military officers, and a clergyman. Witness after witness questioned the validity of the allegations. "They spoke of the reports which had been circulated—but did not think they had been generally believed and they gave the pl[aintiff] a good character for chastity."[29]

The judge advised the jury that in order to establish libel beyond a reasonable doubt, the plaintiff had to prove the defendant's *malice* beyond a reasonable doubt. This meant that Bodwell had to prove not only that her character was good and sound, but that Osgood had intentionally and maliciously damaged her good name. Osgood's defense needed only to prove that people perceived Bodwell to be a "fallen woman" in order to win. If Bodwell did have a "bad character," then Osgood's telling everyone she had a bad character was simply circulating news, not libel.

Sophia Bodwell won the case and public vindication. The jury decided in Bodwell's favor and awarded her $1,400 in damages, an enormous sum of money for someone who had been making less than $9 per month teaching. Osgood immediately moved for a new trial on the grounds that the damages were excessive. His motion was denied.[30]

This case raises the issue of the importance of gossip and reputation in the social fabric of antebellum New England. Gossip figured prominently in the case, from its inception in the community to its culmination in the jury trial before the Supreme Judicial Court. Osgood's original letter to the school committee, which shifted Bodwell's reputation from a social to a public issue, presented gossip as evidence of Bodwell's notoriety. Osgood's defense during the trial relied heavily on *what was supposedly known to be true* about Bodwell. He used phrases such as "what was heard," "it was suspected, "she has been suspected," "statements have . . . been curently circulated & believed." He based his judgment on secondhand reports and his informal poll of community opinion, in the context of the community standards of behavior. None of the witnesses gave firsthand evidence; rather, they relayed reports about Bodwell and estimated the length of time they had been circulating. Resolution through negotiation is a useful way to conceptualize the debates and proceedings. In this case, by challenging the believability of the reports, the witnesses collectively debated the community's assessment of Bodwell's reputation. Reputation was not a tangible thing but a fragile, constantly negotiated opinion. And what was reputation if not what people knew or thought to be true about a person?

Sarah Holmes Clark wrote of another case in Maine that involved a male schoolteacher. The community circulated rumors concerning Mr. Humphrey and his courting habits. However, allegations of sexual misconduct did not ruin his professional standing:

> Mr. Humphrey exists as usual. He is allowed to eat, drink, and sleep as usual but not to go to Mr. Brown's to see Celissia. Yet he does go there and not seldom, tho not so frequently as he did last summer. The people say that he is engaged to Celissia but I don't give credence to a word of the story. Celissia evidently loves him, and I have no doubt that he has said numerous loving words to her. 'Tis his habit & taste with those he thinks will bear soft speeches, I think, yes believe, but I have no thought that he intends either to marry or offer himself to Celissia. Humphrey loves the girls. There is truth in this assertion and if he was not a very diffident man he would be extremely foolish and is now where he becomes well acquainted. He has not a whole heart for one woman. But he is a good teacher still unchanged in his schoolroom.

Sarah related that even when purported by "the people" to be engaged to Celissia, Mr. Humphrey began to spend an inordinate amount of time with a new teacher from Bangor, Miss Chamberlain. The point remains that people knew of Mr. Humphrey's comings and goings. Celissia's family restricted his activities ("He is *allowed* to eat, drink and sleep as usual but not to go to Mr. Brown's to see Celissia"). But his flirtations did not diminish Sarah's perceptions of his ability to be a good teacher. This contrasts dramatically with Sophia Bodwell's case, whose alleged impropriety (admittedly more serious than that of Mr. Humphrey) was deemed by Osgood and others to make her an inappropriate teacher. Unproven allegations could damage a woman's reputation more easily than a man's.[31]

In a race-related case, former slave William Grimes took many townspeople in New Haven, Connecticut, to task for their insinuations regarding his character. He proudly boasted of his honesty:

> I have had to work hard; I have been often cheated, insulted, abused and injured; yet a black man, if he will be industrious and honest, can get along here as well as any one who is poor and in a situation to be imposed upon. I have been very unfortunate in life in this respect. Notwithstanding all my struggles, and sufferings, and injuries, I have been an honest man. There is no one who can come forward and say he knows anything against Grimes.

Nonetheless, for undisclosed reasons, town officials warned him out of town a few times. He fought to maintain his good name in the face of accusations.

> The enmity of some of my rivals in business, led them to make misrepresentations about town against my character, and one of them had some authority in town affairs. My conduct was good, and the strict laws of Connecticut could find nothing to punish; but the selectmen have power to warn any man out of town who has not gained a settlement, which is a difficult thing for a poor man.[32]

These cases illustrate how subjects zealously guarded their reputations. Gossip affected and regulated daily life in the social and sometimes public spheres. The moral behavior of schoolteachers was especially important to the community; as public figures teachers set examples for children, and they depended upon the community for their livelihood. A slandered schoolteacher in particular had to be on guard and to take action, for her job depended on it. Without a good reputation, Bodwell could not teach school. Bodwell was acutely sensitive to her community jury, but her battle to restore her good name required a formal public jury, not simply a social one. Robert Post likens the judicial process to a "status degradation ceremony" for the defendant and a "status rehabilitation ceremony" for the plaintiff. Bodwell's victory vindicated her in a way that negotiations in the social could not, and sanctioned Osgood, the source of the false gossip, reinforcing the community standards for the reliability of discourse. However, the differences in privilege and power cannot be overlooked. Osgood's sex, class, and race rendered him less vulnerable to the verdict of either jury—the social or the public.[33]

These examples of gossip gone awry also point to the power of race and gender in shaping the reputations of whites and African Americans. They lay bare the distinction between gossip used to coerce people to maintain moral standards *within* the community as opposed to purposely marginalizing them *from* the community. Gossip about Bodwell attempted to curb her sexual expression, relieve her of her job, and perhaps exile her from the community. In addition, even though Osgood targeted Bodwell, his message acted as a warning to other young women susceptible to their lusty impulses. In contrast, gossip about Grimes purposely warned him out of town. Gossip about African Americans sometimes aimed to push blacks out of the community, to deny them access to education, and to prevent them from crossing the color line.

GENDER AND POWER

This investigation of gossip, as with visiting, raises the question of power and the role of gender in wielding that power. Taking Steven Lukes's definition of power as the ability "to make a difference to the world," power can be described as the capacity to influence or affect other people's opinions or behavior. Its adaptability to interpret everyday life makes the definition appealing. Nancy Hartsock has examined power outside of the public realm and defined it as "ability, capacity, and competence" rather than simply dominance. When power is defined as such, gossip can be understood as "a powerful social instrument for any person who learns to manage it."[34]

Talk about others had the potential to equalize social relations and act as an avenue to exercise influence despite the constraints of women's subordinate position in society. This power was possible because gossip was about reputation, a necessary "social currency." Patricia Spacks says that gossip "incorporates the possibility that people utterly lacking in public power may affect the views of figures who make things happen in the public sphere." More importantly, I would argue, gossip provides a means of exercising power in the social sphere. When Laurel Ulrich discusses the "power of talk" in colonial New England, she says that community "news" importantly and effectively shaped the behavior of both men and women. She finds that women wielded power through gossip because "they could control reputation." "When women talked, men as well as other women listened." Older women in particular functioned as a crucial informal jury by deliberating about various people's fidelity and propriety. Mary Beth Norton finds women at the heart of defamation suits in seventeenth-century Maryland as well. Women made up a disproportionate number of litigants and witnesses in court cases involving defamation. Women used gossip and "defamation as weapon[s] to obtain redress for harm done to them." Women's standards were "more universal and uniform" in assessing the behavior of men and women, while men applied asymmetrical criteria. Norton notes that ultimately men controlled law and politics, so their standards won out in formal forums.[35]

In a twentieth-century Spanish village, Susan Harding claims gossip is an avenue for manipulating one thing women can affect—reputations. While she finds gossip a female avenue for exercising power, she notes that public power is ultimately not women's domain. According to

Harding, it is erroneous to conclude that women employ any substantial power, because men determine the structure and conditions of everyday life. I disagree; in conducting everyday life, it seems to me, both women and men shape its possibilities.[36]

Gossip took on a different meaning in the sex/gender context of the nineteenth century. Popular stereotypes in antebellum New England identified gossipers, like visitors, as female, the powerless in society who had nothing better to do, or who in spitefulness unleashed their tongues to their own advantage whenever possible. Like many clichés, this one contained a grain of truth but exaggerated the gendered nature of gossip. The evidence in this chapter shows that women gossiped in their letters and diaries much more than men. That said, however, both men and women gossiped, and both agonized over the status of their reputations. They gossiped not in spite, but as a fundamental part of everyday life. They talked about good news, the price of grain, the misfortunes of kin, their neighbors' marital choices, and everyone's reputations. The gender of the gossiper modified the meaning and the effects of that gossip. Gossip was a tool of influence, shaping events and behavior because working people cared about what their neighbors, relatives and friends said about them. And as Sarah Trask and Sarah Holmes Clark demonstrated, even when they ventured not to care, they grappled with what people said about them and how they were treated. Others more successfully minimized the effects of gossip in their lives, in a way that would have been virtually impossible one hundred years earlier. They had access to wage-earning jobs and a smattering of independence from the family and community that their predecessors did not enjoy.[37]

The gender differences reveal the operation of a double standard. Mr. Humphrey from Maine, who had multiple female liaisons, maintained his reputation as a good teacher despite his double-dealing. Ironically, concern for reputation constrained women more than men at the same time that it facilitated women's influence over others. While a man could have his reputation questioned on other grounds (such as his capability as a provider for his family), a fornication charge would usually tarnish his reputation less than it would a woman's. Reputation and chastity were not synonymous for a working man, but nor were they for a working woman. Working women's reputations were based on a broad range of issues: ability to care for the sick, marital choices and marital relations, and of course, "character with regard to chastity." There is no denying that sexual impropriety most endangered women's reputations; however, it was not the only issue to which the community jury attended.

Susan Dwyer Amussen argues that the contraction of women's roles in the family in early modern England narrowed the basis upon which their reputation was built until sexual conduct was the sole concern. We can conversely argue here that women's expanded economic roles *broadened* the criteria for their reputation, and simultaneously gave them more resources to shape their lives. The negative consequences for sexual improprieties, such as out-of-wedlock births and associations with questionable men, diminished as working women acted on their own standards of fairness and constructed a different set of criteria for good character.[38]

While we can only speculate, if Bodwell had lost her suit the consequences would have devastated her. In addition to paying litigation expenses, she most likely would have lost her job, her ability to find alternative employment, the likelihood of ever marrying, and most importantly, her standing in the community. In fact, Osgood lost the case, the family honor he sought to defend, and $1,400. However, he did not lose his capacity to earn a living, nor did he lose his family. While the decision by a jury of peers must have had consequences for Osgood, by virtue of his gender, race, and class he was not affected as severely as if he had been a working woman.

A racial double standard operated in a distinct way. Ex-slave and free-black autobiographers repeatedly told of dealings with white men and women, upstanding citizens in their communities, who swindled them out of money or balked at supposedly binding oral agreements. So when whites interacted with African Americans, male and female, they no longer felt bound by the conventions of respectful treatment they accorded their white neighbors.[39]

In antebellum working people's communities, gossip comprised a central feature of the social sphere, a critical means of communicating information. It created ties, affirmed membership in or out of a community, and clarified and negotiated acceptable behavior. Letters and diaries from antebellum New England richly describe the entanglements of working people in the lives of their neighbors and kin, those with whom they were not necessarily intimate but who comprised their community jury. Gossip provided a means for gathering information, examining facts, and evaluating their reliability, in effect negotiating community opinion and reaffirming a sense of the group and membership within it. In part, the intention behind gossip was to persuade. And because gossip was primarily about reputation, it had great potential to influence opinions and behavior. In the social sphere, women's talk found a resonant audience.[40] As with visiting, gossip placed women at the center of social discourse, the nexus of community life.

The power of talk was rooted in the social but held sway in the public and the private as well. While it did not lead nation-states, gossip undeniably influenced monumental as well as trivial decisions. The private sphere was not exempt from its influence either, as reputation had profound consequences in the decisions people made about their conduct and personal commitments. Gossip helped to construct the structures of everyday life while monitoring the activities within them and fashioning reputations.

CHAPTER SIX

"Getting Religion"

The Church as a Social Institution

Social ties were a means and an incentive for involvement in the church. In the letters, diaries, and autobiographies, the social character of conversion to Christianity, that it "hinged not on private prayer, arbitrary grace, or intellectual choice, but on purposive encounters between people," profoundly affected and inspired working people. Marcella Holmes queried Sarah Carter:

> Do you believe? Are you sure that religion does exist? I cannot understand about this change of heart. I know that I have changed very much since I left home—am better—more charitable—but I cannot see how one can get good all at once. Mr. Adams (Methodist preacher) says that he intends keeping up a night meeting 'till all that will go and listen are converted. *I fear that I shall be left behind.* There is not much peace for me as I am or ever have been, and if there is "a sweet peace" in religion I do wish to have it.

Marcella did not want to be ostracized, the only one not converted, but her feelings about religion were deeply ambivalent. That said, Marcella eventually fell for Mr. Adams and married him. We may assume that very likely some change of spiritual heart preceded or accompanied their engagement.[1]

While many activities defy categorization as simply public or private, involvement in the church, more than any other aspect of nineteenth-century working people's lives, points to the inadequacy of the public/private model. The church simultaneously represents a deeply personal, individual experience and a belief system; it facilitates powerful interpersonal bonds between individuals and families; and it acts as an institutional arbiter of community behavior. In addition, it inspires mutual aid as well as political activism. The difficulty in conceptualization stems from the fact that religion, the belief system, can be distinguished from the church, its institutional base, and can concurrently influence nations as well as individuals. While recognizing the potency of faith in people's lives, this chapter focuses on the church and working people's religious *practices*. It examines the power of individuals to influence one another, to shape an experience, and to craft and sustain a community.[2]

Organized religion offered people much more than spiritual salvation. Because it affected spiritual, emotional, educational, philosophical, and economic parts of people's lives, the church must be conceptualized as social, in addition to public and private. If we consider the church private, we miss the ways in which church involvement absorbed people into a social world. We fail to see the conversion process as a community endeavor, in which individuals pressured friends, neighbors, and kin to adopt religion, sparking a regional chain reaction of spiritual renewal. Framing the church as solely public conceals the intricate ways that socializing spread the gospel. If we recognize it as social, church activities and religiously inspired activism are thrown into relief, making it easier to discern their importance in mediating between individual concerns (private beliefs) and political life (public processes). The church advocated a particular ideology, and it also provided a ready-made community, mutual aid, entertainment, a base for organizing movements for political change, and an arena for socializing. These features collectively attracted working people to the church of antebellum New England.[3]

People, as much as ideas or beliefs, drew others—neighbors, relatives, work mates—into the church. Devout parishioners lured susceptible friends and kin into a realm of sociability, religiosity, and for some, political activism. The church provided an arena for cultural, political, and theological debate. It also served the community by performing integrative rituals associated with birth, death, marriage, and conversion to Christianity. It sponsored Sunday meetings, sabbath schools, singing schools, prayer meetings, conventions, and lectures. And especially in black communities (and a handful of predominantly white denominations, such as the Quakers), the church provided an essential organizing base and spiritual inspiration for social-reform activities. It offered economic aid, taught literacy, organized anti-slavery campaigns, harbored fugitive slaves, and acted "as the cultural womb of the black community."[4]

This chapter investigates several key aspects of the church as a *social* institution: attendance at Sunday services, people's role in the conversion process, sermons' entertainment value, church-visiting and sectarianism, and the empowerment of people, women and African Americans in particular, to exercise moral authority via "social work." As a realm of behavior, the social—through the vehicle of the church—provided a means for expanding women's venue and an opportunity for women to exercise autonomy and influence outside the private realm.

CHURCHGOING AS A SOCIAL PRACTICE

CHURCH ATTENDANCE

From the turn of the nineteenth century through the 1830s, religion in New England was dominated by widespread renewed religious enthusiasm known as the Second Great Awakening. Great awakenings occur in periods of social, cultural, and economic change; they revitalize religion and culture. In a time of tumultuous upheaval, religion addressed a profound desire for stability and certainty while the transforming practice of religion simultaneously acted as an agent of change. Rapid and profound changes in social and economic relations created deep anxiety, parting people from their familiar cultural and ancestral moorings.[5]

Unlike the First Great Awakening, with its great theological accomplishments, the Second Great Awakening produced an exponential increase in church participation and membership. The evangelizing and organizing of the Methodist and Baptist sects in particular spurred tremendous growth of church attendance in the first decades of the nineteenth century—hundreds of thousands of people joined churches. These dissenting religions, democratic in philosophy and observation, challenged the hierarchy and orthodoxy of Congregationalism. They exhibited a greater interest in the common person, preaching in the vernacular and making sermons accessible to all. They sought emotional resonance through exhortation rather than conviction through rational debate, and they regularly criticized the prevailing theological orthodoxy. The Second Great Awakening brought many into the folds of the church and, many argue, helped to build a national culture.[6]

Through church meetings, lectures, and revivals, religion touched the majority of diarists, correspondents, and autobiographers in this study. Some adopted the revivalist belief systems as their own pious philosophy and relied on its vocabulary as their instrument of understanding and communication. In a language that diverges from their other writings, newly converted subjects expressed their anxiety, concern, and love through allusions to scripture and biblical metaphors. Ninety-one percent of the diarists in this study mention going to meetings on Sunday. Of those, half regularly went at least once a week.[7]

A church often scheduled services three times on Sunday with intermissions between sessions, providing an opportunity for visits and meals. It was not unusual for a diarist to attend all three services. This frequent attendance can be interpreted as reflecting intense religiosity; however, it can also be understood as indicative of interest in the social dimension of the church. Sixteen-year-old George S. Whipple, who in his diary always referred to himself in the third person, recorded a primary incentive for attending church in 1838: "Singing meeting in the meeting house . . . some of the girls did not come. George S. Whipple and some others much *disapointed*." Similarly, ex-slave George Henry wrote, "I always used to like to attend meetings, but principally for the purpose of plagueing the girls." Sarah Trask recorded her deliberations about going to church one Sunday in 1849. She had not intended to go, but her friend "H.P.G. wanted to go so I went" to both afternoon and evening services. An analysis that attends to religion solely as a private faith would miss the motivations for going to church that were not strictly religious. An expansion of the theoretical frame to include the social sphere reveals that social factors as well as private religious ones promoted church-going.[8]

The act of attending church merited some respect. Eliza Adams told her sister Margaret about running into Mary Johnson and Mary Carr at church. "She was much surprised at seeing me & thought . . . that my zeal had greatly increased to bring me clear to Amoskeag to worship." The Marys' observation of Eliza's presence validated her sense of accomplishment and commitment. Their observation confirmed the depth of her faith, which she and they measured at least in part by her willingness to travel many miles to a service. The social context reinforced her Christianity. Being seen and respected by others validated Eliza's sense of her religious character. While it is impossible to comprehend the nature of working people's religion from their writings alone, my evidence reveals that workers and farmers derived comfort and respect-

ability, as well as camaraderie, from their participation in the church.
Charles Metcalf wrote to his mother about the chambermaid in his
Lowell, Massachusetts, boardinghouse. Her status as church member
prompted Charles to view her with high regard: "Miss Munson, a
maiden lady and sister to the Rev. Samuel Munson . . . lives here, and
does the chamber work. She is a fine lady, member of the church and
appears to be a devoted Christian. I love to talk with her on the subject
of religion."[9]

Subjects regularly assessed the turnout—the composition and size—
for Sunday services. Hannah Adams evaluated the congregation after
attending the Episcopal church one morning in 1854 and the Unitarian
in the afternoon. Reading from the text "Many are called but few are
chosen," one minister gave a sermon that was "a very good discourse—
well delivered. But the praying I will say nothing about, only it seemed
as if I was among the heathen [Gods]." Her sister Margaret fastidiously
assessed another service in terms of its tenor, size, content, and clientele:

> It was a very spirited meeting. The house was crowding to overflowing . . .
> Mr. & Mrs. Tillotson received me warmly. The house was quite full. Th[irt]y
> seemed to be the mass, no noted men or women being there. Mr. Tillotson
> preached well. The next Sunday I went to Mr. Bowles,' his seemed thin but
> of the better class.

Abigail Baldwin and Mary Orne Tucker, each married to ministers,
calculated crowd size after each week's service and recorded the number
of conversions where their husbands preached. Abigail reported on a
pre-communion meeting one Saturday afternoon in 1853: "Here we
have often met the professed people of God too speak of *His mercies
and our great sinfulness.* We are a feeble band, few in numbers and few
in graces. May God help us." In taking stock of the state of religion in
Parma, New York, while she and her family prepared to move, another
minister's wife, Paulina Bascom Williams, was at least as discouraged:

> My hope respecting the enlargement of Christ's kingdom in this place is
> constantly decreasing. There seems to be a general apathy spread over them.
> They have so long contended about the principles of masonry & anti-masonry
> that it seems as though the Holy spirit has been ground & taken its upward
> flight & left them to grope in darkness that may be felt.

Even when diarists did not attend services, they guiltily recorded their
reasons for not attending. They justified their absence by reference to ill
health, bad weather, want of proper clothing, and in the case of Parna

Gilbert, a sick horse. Sarah Beacham condemned her own behavior, even though her reasons for not attending services were benign: "Fears of snow kept me from meeting. Oh the lack of faith."[10]

Some diarists routinely recorded the substance of sermons, complete with reference to specific passages in the Bible. On June 21, 1829, Mary Hall reflected on the day's service: "Sabbath. Heard two interesting discourses by a clergyman whose name I do not know. The afternoon from 2nd Chron 12th. 2nd. Upon the danger of forming intimate acquaintances with the ungodly. May I long treasure it in my mind and prefit by the same." In keeping with the general lack of introspection in their writings, most diarists did not ruminate as elaborately about the sermons as Mary Hall.[11]

Most diarists failed to identify their status within a congregation, perhaps because they took it for granted. However, some antebellum believers revered church membership. It signified an extensive reciprocal commitment between the individual and the congregation and conferred community acceptance. Horatio Chandler, one of the more serious religious converts in this research, found comfort in the symbolic embrace of the church community. He carefully detailed the membership ritual in his diary:

> We were called upon and went forward in front of the pulpit & Priest Bickley read a confession of faith & the covenant. We gave our assent to it by bowing our heads. Then the numbers of the church all arose signifying their approbation to receive us into Christian fellowship & communion. After which, the solemn ordinance of the Lord's Supper were administered—in remembrance of Christ Death, & as a seal of that covenant which God has made with us in Christ. To seal unto us the pardon of our sins, and the assurance of everlasting life.

The amount of detail in this entry relative to almost all else in his diary reflects the importance he assigned to the ritual and the religious status it conferred.[12]

THE CHURCH AS THEATER

Regardless of how centrally, deeply, and intricately theology influenced their lives, subjects congregated at the church for reasons over and above religious beliefs. Church services provided entertainment in an environment lacking a variety of amusements. This interest in the social aspects was not religiously misguided; the church cultivated and encouraged it.

Narrowly conceiving of entertainment as profane, Christian churches attempted to force young people in particular to choose between frivolity and faith, as Barbara Loomis so aptly puts it. However, they found it necessary to establish alternative activities to fill the social void created by denial of the expanding and enticing array of worldly amusements. In some rural Vermont churches, reformers explicitly attempted to increase the church's role as a social institution and to promote sociability in order to counter the lure of an exciting urban life. The church sponsored regular activities such as revivals, fairs, and midweek prayer meetings, and church members hosted "religious parties" where they would invite only their Christian friends. Mary Orne Tucker wrote in her autobiography about her attempts in August, 1843, as an itinerant Methodist minister's wife, to create this culture:

> With the hope of doing some good to the young people of this place, who, I regret to say, spend much of their spare time in dancing, and other frivolous amusements, I had taken measures to form a society for improvement in literary exercises, such as writing compositions, reading, debating, etc. At our first meeting quite a number of young ladies and gentlemen were present, and all the preliminaries arranged for our future meetings. This society, which attracted considerable attention, was continued through the winter and succeeded beyond my expectations in diverting the attention of many young persons from amusements, sometimes of an objectionable character.

In effect, the evangelical religions created a competing subculture. Ironically, the evangelical religious culture took on dimensions of the culture it opposed, because its audience demanded entertainment—secular and religious—and because social activities were so intimately intertwined with religion.[13]

It was not unusual for a subject to attend church to observe a novelty—for example a "Quakeress" preacher or a black man at the pulpit. In his autobiography, ex-slave the Reverend Peter Randolph (see Figure 20) wrote, "In these times of which I speak it was not customary for a colored preacher to address a white congregation." When black ministers preached in white churches, they created a stir. Peter encountered blatant racism; people flung racist epithets and tried to prevent him from preaching because he was African American. He felt that when he did preach, however, he won people over. For example, at Monument Pond in Plymouth, Massachusetts, he gave the service when the regular minister did not show up. "The people there had never heard a colored preacher, and their curiosity was at a high pitch. Though I was somewhat of a novelty to them, they received my message, and the meeting was declared a success." On another occasion, it was clear to him that the large number of young white men in the audience had come to see a spectacle. "As I was getting along, in the midst of my sermon, I noticed quite a number of the white young men, who came looking for fun, leaving. As they did not see anybody jump up, or falling over the benches, they were doubtless disappointed and took their departure." C. Eric Lincoln and Lawrence H. Mamiya say that "the Black Church was the first theater in the black community. Like the Greek theater its functional goal was catharsis, but beyond the Greeks, the Black Church was in search of transcendence, not a mere emptying of the emotions, but an enduring fellowship with God in which the formal worship service provided the occasion for particular periods of intimacy."[14]

While it would be an egregious error to minimize the importance of religion as an ideology, subjects evaluated ministers' performances and politics (as opposed to purely spiritual messages), revealing that they felt drawn to the antebellum church in part as a diversion from everyday work routines. In a Yankee tradition of discourse and critique, parishioners criticized the Sunday services, commenting less on the content of sermons than on the minister's style and performance. Susan Forbes negatively evaluated Mr. Woodman's church in Lowell: "Was less pleased with the service than any other save the Catholic, that I have attended." Or, as Marcella Holmes wrote home from Georgia, "Winslow will tell you that good preaching is scarce about here." Hannah Adams wrote to her family in Maine about Reverend Hunting, who "fills my eye for a preacher. I shall go to his church. His house is filling up very fast." Sarah Metcalf compared local ministers in a letter to her mother:

> I have heard Mr. Blanchard preach once. I like him very much, though I like Mr. Hanks better. Mr. B. is a much prettier speaker than Mr. Hanks. I have been to meeting this forenoon. We had a beautiful sermon by Mr. Hanks on home & missions.

Her brother Charles preferred Mr. Hanks over all visting preachers, apparently because of his scintillating oratorical gifts:

> Mr. Hanks has not yet returned, and we have had almost as many preachers as sabbaths. Some were good and others were not more than midling. And perhaps that is one reason why I have been so drowsy. I do not think I should sleep much under Mr. H.'s preaching.

Martha Barrett set an exacting standard for the Unitarian church she attended in 1849: "Had a very *good* sermon, although not above mediocrity." Alfred Porter faced disappointment in seeing Reverend Fletcher's "tame sermon" in the morning service in 1854. Then Mr. Putnam's in the afternoon proved "quite midling." Diarists and correspondents searched for stimulation and excitement in church services, an expectation only sometimes fulfilled.[15]

Ministers and their church hierarchies did not overlook these issues. As Nathan Hatch points out, in a competitive religious marketplace "popularity rather than virtue was the clarion call of the movement" for spiritual awakening. The minister's ability to speak, to rouse emotion, and to translate theology into lay terms became the church's crucial link to a constituency. If the minister failed, the church failed. In the case of the Methodists, itinerant preachers struck a chord in multitudes, and the church prospered. As Hatch notes, "Whether Methodist, Baptist, Christian, Universalist, Millerite, or Mormon, these preachers had little else to fall back on if their presence and charisma were unconvincing." This meant that ministers had to know their audience, speak their language, sustain their interest, and cultivate their loyalty. When this combination succeeded, people flocked to a service, not hesitating to explain their rationale.[16]

The freedom to evaluate also stemmed from the new religious philosophy which dethroned the minister by elevating the individual's relationship with God. James Adams, Jr., an Episcopal clergyman, wrote to Joseph Metcalf, his brother-in-law, regarding whether or not a minister's character (as opposed to his performance) should be exempt from evaluation and gossip:

> As to the character of Dr. Payton it is not generally thought to be a caricature. On the contrary, many think (and I believe some of Dr. P.'s friends and members of his church are of the number) that it is certainly *not far* from correct. I know of no good reason why, if ministers of the gospel have faults, they should not be spoken of as we speak of the faults of other men. I doubt, myself, whether it would be beneficial, to consider the ministerial office so sacred that we could not condemn what is wrong in its members.

Acting on this license, Sarah Holmes Clark was not alone in basing her decision on whether to attend church on how she felt about the minister's performance. Sarah attended a new church in Madison, Georgia, after moving there from Foxcroft, Maine. She expressed no reservations about the racial customs of her new church but believed the minister was boring and unintelligent:

Yesterday I attended church for the first time since I left home, & listened a few very dull remarks from an old man who is of no account. I don't go to listen to him again I assure you. The people here only go to church in the morning & evening—the niggers hold there meetings in the churches in the afternoon, and unless the ministers are smarter then is the one who talked to us yesterday, I think that a half day is quite as long a time as I shall care to be preached to.[17]

Charles Metcalf discussed the conservative views on slavery of his sparky preacher, Mr. Hanks, and his response to the plea from adamant anti-slavery activists:

Some of his church are *Garrisonites* and they keep him in a [sirrole] all the time. There was a Garrison meeting here a short time since and he and Mr. Brewster, Protestant Methodist, refused to read the notice of the *Indignation* meeting, as Mr. H. calls it, which made them [wrathy]. And they took it up in the meeting and called them ministers of the Devil &c.

Taking the opposite position on the issue, Martha Barrett advanced her role as critic by evaluating her minister's gender and race politics in the context of her own passionately held convictions. On New Year's Eve, 1850, she attended a lyceum lecture by Mr. Braman, a regionally renowned Congregational minister, and dismissed his message about women's place: "Quite good. But I don't see so much to admire in him as many do. His subject was women. . . . He lauded woman highly but she must be in her sphere, and all that." On another occasion, she gladly listened to Mr. Appleton at the afternoon pulpit because she endorsed his abolitionist views:

I do not care to hear others preach, for very few ministers have his liberal sentiments. Or if they have, dare not preach them. Indeed, I could not consistently attend church where a pro-slavery clergyman performs. I cannot call it worships for can the worship of an oppression, or apologist for oppression, outrage and wrong, be acceptable to a liberty-loving God of purity and truth?[18]

SECTARIANISM? ON THE INDEPENDENCE
OF THOUGHT AND ACTION

The emphasis on entertainment in the pantheon of religious alternatives heightened interdenominational strife. Richard Rabinowitz writes that "the history of dogma has overemphasized conflicts among different schools of thought and undervalued the way each generation agreed upon the fundamental praxes of religion." Competition between churches reached a pitched battle in antebellum New England. The "sea of sectarian rivalries," as one Congregationalist missionary described it, stemmed from the democratization of religion and the growth of contesting doctrinal interpretations. Promoting the virtues of one denomination meant denouncing the fallacies of another. The rapid rise of the evangelical religions inspired fear and reaction in the hearts of many orthodox ministers, who viewed the change as ominous. The differences appalled the established churches, as orthodoxies went unobserved or overturned. The hundreds of thousands who flocked to the Baptist and Methodist churches rejected the prejudices of the orthodox clergy regarding belief systems, religious practices, and interpretations of the Bible, although many who stayed within the Congregational church accepted and adopted the evangelical innovations as their own. The clergy championed their biases; the religious rivalry whipped up a fervor and heightened morale.[19]

The evangelical sects competed for their constituencies, and their rivalry with one another surfaced in their rhetoric about each other as well as about the traditional Congregational practices. The Methodists battled with the Presbyterians, and all the evangelicals denounced Calvinism. For example, the Reverend Jeremiah Asher described the conflict in an African American congregation in Hartford, Connecticut, the Talcott Street Church, founded as a union church for Christians of all denominations. The spirit of tolerance foundered as sectarian prejudices surfaced and some members vented their enmity toward Baptists:

> When there was nothing else to contend about, the Baptists were accused of believing that they were better than other Christians, and none but themselves would ever reach heaven. Being tired of these unprofitable harangues, and also a believer in the Baptist doctrine, especially in the ordinance of baptism, and believed that immersion, and immersion of believers only, was scriptural baptism, I left, and attended the First Baptist Church."

Soon thereafter the Talcott Street Church became Presbyterian.[20]

The ministers and the women married to ministers in my research adopted doctrinal loyalties seemingly without reservation. Adopting organized religion's theological distinctions as his own, the Reverend Samuel Harrison (see Figure 21) wrote of his denominational proclivities: "I was born a Calvinist, I believe. If I was not, I was like Topsy, I 'growed so.' I was a great admirer of Rev. Albert Barnes of Philadelphia. I do not think I could make a Baptist or a Methodist or an Episcopalian." He then proceeded more ecumenically than some of his brethren, "and yet I believe there are followers of Christ among them all." One woman married to a minister, Mary Orne Tucker, described one Second Advent preacher as "bold, cunning, and unscrupulous." She reported that "he has created mischief which cannot be easily checked. The whole thing is a magnificent device of the devil to make dissensions in the Church of Christ." She expressed fury about doomsayers claiming to be Christians and foretelling the imminent end of the world. She described another minister preaching the second coming of Christ as "a remarkable specimen of egotistical ignorance." Emboldened by passionate conviction, she defended Christianity as she knew it and her husband's pulpit from a fanatical Millerite: "Whether my action in the case was regarded by some as unfeminine or not did not disturb me in the least; for I would not submit silently to the desecration of his pulpit." Sarah Metcalf Mann, a minister's wife and former textile worker, felt no more amenable to the evangelical methods of preaching:

> Benjamin and Susan went to Woonsocket to meeting found Perry Davis in the pulpit. Said he had been warned in a dream to go and preach to the people of Woonsocket. Took no text—and his object seemed to be to make a noise. Told all about the meetings at the Tabernacle—names and all. Such conduct it seems to me is very unlike the religion of Jesus Christ.

Some subjects adopted the denominational biases of ministers as their own. They found the new methods of preaching and observing faith antithetical to their beliefs and practices. Calvin Metcalf, decidedly not a fan of Universalism, bemoaned the state of religion in 1819. To him, a countryside afire with Universalism burnt an Eden into a heathen desert: "As to our local affairs, they proceed much as usual. Real religion, I fear, is rather declining among us while the enemies of truth are making great exertions to propagate error & delusion. The Universalists have of late become very zealous & active." From the more liberal point of view, the increase in evangelist revivals appeared equally threatening, if for different reasons. The *Universalist Watchman* in Vermont "asserted that 'intemperate preaching' had caused more deaths in the past year than 'intemperate drinking,' because it had driven weak, credulous people to lose all hope of salvation." The newer methods of preaching and their divergence from an older practice attracted thousands and distressed others.[21]

Like many others who held fast to denominational prejudices, Horatio Chandler could not allow himself to forgive those who made commitments to a church other than the Congregational church. He described his neighbors as if they had been besieged by the devil: "Mr. and Mrs. G. are members of the Methodist church. For pity & love towards these poor blind deluded creatures—that our Father in heaven should forgive them." He condemned the Reverend Putnam for his misbegotten beliefs: "Went to the school house to hear [J.] Putnam this eve'g. His preaching I believe is calculated to [deceive] and lead [precious] souls down to eternal death. I pray the *Lord* may deliver us all from the adversary of darkness." Similar sentiments led weaver Sarah Beacham to avoid the sabbath services in Ossipee, New Hampshire: "A Universalist preaches here to day. Do not believe their doctrin & so do not go to meeting. If their doctrin is true I think I [am] just as safe to stay at home." Simply believing in God was not sufficient. Diarists freely ascribed evil motives to those who chose the wrong path, i.e., the wrong denomination.[22]

The Christian evangelists felt their prejudices as ardently as the orthodox Calvinists. Joseph Lye, a shoemaker, decided to forgo services rather than listen to an orthodox service: "Staid at home this day rather to hear a Calvinistic preacher at the first parish." In fact, his antagonism toward Calvinism was so intense that he became involved in establishing a new church in Lynn, Massachusetts: "It is confidently hoped and believed by a few that a Society will be gathered in the course of a year in this town who will inculcate the doctrines of Liberal Christianity; and thus do away in some measure the pernicous effects of Calvinism." Similarly, Minerva Mayo wholeheartedly rejected the Calvinist prescription for relating to God. She encouraged Jerusha Clap to reach out beyond the strictures of orthodoxy in order to touch her savior directly: "Wherefore I beseech you not to put your trust in those who preach the doctrine of eternal damnable ruin but rather in him who is able to deliver you and who will have all men to be saved and come to the knowledge of the truth."[23]

In direct contradiction to the sectarian philosophies expressed by many subjects advocated by most clergy in this heyday of sectarianism, a significant number of subjects told of their ecumenical practice. They commonly attended churches of opposing denominations, even *on the same day*. Joseph Lye attended services for three different denominations on one day in 1817:

> Attended public worship. Heard Mr. Hooker preach from Heb. 4th 11. In the afternoon attended the Friends Meeting. Heard Friend Collins speak. In the evening heard in the Old meeting an uncharitable Hopkinsian Calvinistical sermon such an one as I never wish to hear again.

Many fledgling congregations were forced to share meeting houses. James L. Smith recounts in his autobiography the tensions in the African American community in Norwich, Connecticut, between Presbyterians and Methodists who shared a church:

> The agreement was that each denomination were to take their turns in leading the meetings. . . . The upper part of the church was used for the Sabbath school, and the basement for the preaching services. . . . The stove was moved to either part of the house, to suit their convenience. . . . The Methodists were very zealous, and generally conducted the services on the Sabbath that the Presbyterians rightfully claimed. This caused a strife among them. . . . The two societies never became reconciled to each other, and consequently there was a split in the church.

Many white denominations also shared meeting facilities. Recall that Sarah Holmes Clark described a situation in the South where whites and blacks shared a church. They carefully scheduled meetings to maintain segregation by color rather than denomination.[24]

Many native-born Americans particularly disdained the Roman Catholic church and the immigrants that flocked to its doors. One diarist reported, "Sunday at meeting stranger pr[eached] against Romanism." Julia Stevens wrote to her sister from the New York frontier. Lacking a meeting house nearby, she had to be content with a circuit preacher (probably Methodist) who visited every other week. Out in the wilderness, she struggled to accept her neighbors, many of whom were Catholic or Universalist: "It is a pleasant place where we now live but I cannot enjoy the principles of those around me. But I hope they may be renewed in the spirit of their minds and become the happy followers of Jesus." Yet despite the prejudices against Catholicism, the Catholic church was not exempt from serious and respectful consideration in Eliza Adams's rounds of "church visiting:"

> Christmas. I called accidentally into a Roman Catholic church and saw the great performance of high mass, so many manoeuvres, rising up, and sitting down, bowing, kneeling and making the holy cross. It made my eyes ache a week afterwards yet interested me to go again. So one sabbath I started alone no one being willing to go with me. Having reached the door, I halted thinking to be invited in as is usual in other churches. Here the custom is different so I had to stand and be [gazed] at, some looking inquisitive and others with disdain 'till a good looking Irishman nodding his head said 'cume into church.' I went in and seeing an empty seat close by the door I entered it and sat down. Presently one of the worshippers came into my seat appearing a little uneasy after fussing awhile he told me I had no home there but says

he wait awhile and we'll see stop 'till the singing is over. Finally I had the privilege or staying through the meeting.[25]

In the same spirit of religious curiosity, some diarists approached the church as a spectacle. The curiosity of both Francis Bennett, Jr., and Eliza Adams overcame any pre-existing religious affiliation. Acting like curious anthropologists, their practice transcended narrow doctrinal dictates while they examined the religious observances of another culture. Francis Bennett, Jr., went to the Bulfinch Street Church in Boston for services and then for a walk.

> Then went down to a Negro meeting house which is a little below where I board. Of all the screeching and yelling I ever heard, I *never heard* any beat those Negroes. One woman jumped right up and down screaming, 'glory, glory,' for as much as minutes.

His rapt surprise at the dramatic style of worship resulted from a combination of being unexposed to free black culture and unaccustomed to evangelistic, participatory services.[26]

Seeming to ignore the denominational battles altogether, approximately one-third of the diarists attended services at churches of two or more denominations (see Table 2). In a practice typical of diarists, Samuel Shepard James wrote about a mild November Sunday in 1840: "Very pleasant. A.M. I went to the meting at the Baptist meeting house, P.M. to the Orthodox." Albert Mason attended activities of several fundamentally different denominations—Methodist, Congregationalist, and Quaker. Other diarists attended seemingly inconsistent combinations of church services: several diarists attended Congregationalist and Freewill Baptist services; Brigham Nims visited Presbyterian, Quaker, and Methodist churches over the course of his diary. Attendance at a church did not signify membership, nor did it necessarily imply compatibility with the belief systems espoused from the pulpit. However, it indicated that many working women and men did not embrace sectarianism as the clergy advocated.[27]

How are we to understand this ecumenical behavior in a period of heated sectarianism? First, the social aspect of the church dominated the interests of working people. While religion itself played a large role in antebellum culture and intellectual life, working subjects recorded more about the social aspects of the church (for example, who preached, the quality of the minister's sermon, and who attended church) than they did about their religious beliefs. Once this is recognized, it is no

TABLE 2   CHURCH VISITING

Denomination	Diarists Attending Church		
	More Than One Church (N = 19)	*One Church* (N = 32)	*Total* (N = 51)
Methodist	15	2	17
Baptist/Freewill Baptist	11	5	16
Congregational	10	4	14
Quaker	6	2	8
Unitarian/Universalist	5	1	6
Episcopal	4	0	4
Presbyterian	3	0	3
Shaker	1	1	2
Catholic	1	0	1
Church of Christ	1	0	1
Unspecified	1	17	18
Total visited	58	32	90

surprise that concerns other than religious doctrine figured prominently in people's church-going practices. The church as a social institution, complete with community networks and entertaining activities, was as important as (if not more important than) religious ideology. Second, working people were less dogmatic and sectarian than the clergy or the middle class. Third, the minister of a church played a major role in attracting a congregation. Diarists held definite opinions about which ministers delivered the choice services and whether they were worth attending. A charismatic minister could interest people in religion and recruit them to his or her church. And finally, the church provided entertainment as religion underwent a democratic transition into a form of popular culture. Many subjects shunted sectarian messages aside and experimented with divergent faiths. By allowing the spectacle of worship rituals and ministering to lure them to a church, they willingly encountered new theological doctrine.[28]

MORAL AUTHORITY AND THE SOCIAL SPHERE

The moral authority religion invested in women and men had religious and secular repercussions. Empowered by their belief in the righteousness of God, they set about to their religious "social work"—converting others to Christianity, to abstinence, to abolitionism. The extension of religion through the New England hinterlands did not result simply from entreaties from the pulpit, it occurred through the encouragement, persistence, and at times coercion of women and men activating and operating their networks in the social sphere.

Undeniably, the tumultuous economic and cultural changes under way in antebellum New England shook the foundations and assumptions about life for both men and women. In spite of the insecurities it provoked, religion simultaneously evoked an image of a time when the family more fully controlled its individual members and the community ensured moral accountability. The church created spiritual and moral communities that sustained its members by providing mutual aid and a vocabulary for struggling to understand massive social and economic change. A turn to religion represented nostalgia for an idealized past and the promise of security. While economic dislocations created anxiety, religion offered eternal salvation as well as temporary redemption on earth. For people in general, the church offered a refuge from immorality and capitalist relations and promised a better, more stable world of "order, piety, and harmony."[29]

GETTING RELIGION AND PASSING IT ON[30]

A wave of religious reverberations flooded New England in the 1820s, 1830s, and 1840s, and pressure to join the Christian ranks contagiously intensified as the newly converted turned an anxious eye to unconverted friends and family. Permelia Dame urged her long-absent brother to turn to God: "I have found great peace in preying to Christ. My Dear Brother, do live in fear of the Lord, and prey that your sins may be forgiven." Eliza Adams wrote from the Lowell textile mills to her mother, discussing her care for a sick friend and her conflict with her overseer and also reporting the attempt by her friend, Miss Barns, to convert her:

> Miss Barns pressed me to go to her meeting one evening. At the close she got Dea. Bancroft to question me, they were tuff ones. The first was "If I had a saving hope in the blood of Christ! If I loved Christ?" The next question I forget. The next if I was a church member? & if I had recently experienced this hope? All of which I answered as well as I was able & shall leave you to guess how.

While she did not go through a conversion experience, the event obviously impressed Eliza, as did religion's impact on people, and the importance of choosing the right denomination in order to ensure salvation and the desired progress of religious development. The social pressure to conform swept even the skeptics.[31]

The ever-present fear of death catalyzed the conversion process. The prospect of dying with a sinful soul threatened eternal damnation. Preachers conjured fiery visions of the fate of unsaved souls in order to persuade people of the immediacy of their task. Death could come unexpectedly, at any moment. If an individual succumbed unprepared to meet God, she or he had failed. No further chance for salvation existed. Parna Gilbert reminded herself that she needed to be diligent: "Oh whence this stupidity when I am so frequently reminded of the uncertainty of life by the removal of friends." Domestic servant Harriet Severance, in the face of her sister's severe illness, wrote, "I feel like dedicating my life anew to God, live remembering *this* world is not my home." From her vantage point in Lowell, Massachusetts, Lavinia Merrill's fear of death loomed typically large. Her friend Harriet prompted concern for religion by proselytizing from her deathbed, the "makeshift pulpit":

> It was very hard to part with Harriet. I shall never forget the parting words although I did not realise that I never should see her again yet I never did. She told me to prepare to meet her and I promised her I would. I made up my mind that I would seek religion. I felt alone for there was not a pious girl in the mill. And I had no one to help me or that was with me much, but I had my Bible and my God and I felt determined that if I perished I would pray and perish only at the feet of Jesus. I did pray and I think that my prayers were answered.

She was convinced of the need for religion, for herself and Rhoda Parker (her friend and roommate's sister), to whom she was writing: "May I not hope that you have obtained a hope that you are a child of God. How can I bear to think otherwise?" Religion provided comfort to Lavinia, helping her her feel able to accept her lot in life and her mortality. She tried anxiously to share her new consciousness with Rhoda, setting the tide of influence in motion. One year later Lavinia wrote Rhoda about another deathbed scene—that of Mrs. Gilbert, her boardinghouse mistress. Again anxiety for her dear friend prompted her to write:

> She took me by the hand and many times bid me good-bye and entreated me to be faithful to my friends. And then I would weep for my unfaithfulness to you my beloved Rhoda. My love to you has not diminished a particle. Neither has my anxiety for your spiritual welfare lessoned in any degree but it has

increased. I feel deeply for you. I have often thought you was a more consistent Christian than I was, but if you do not feel that you have given your heart to the [Savour], and that he is precious to your soul, I entreat of you not to rest untill [w]ou build your hope on the rock of ages. What is there in this world world living for but to prepare for another and a better one.

Apparently Rhoda did not take in Christ as deeply as Lavinia thought appropriate. She urgently reminded Rhoda of omnipresent death. Rhoda was at risk, unless she purposely sought her savior:

> I do earnestly desire your salvation. I long to see you a decided Christian. Do you not feel that the [savour] is indeed precious to your soul. If you do not you are in a dangerous condition, every day exposed to death and no hope in Christ. Do not delay any longer.

The constant threat of death, and the incendiary doom of those not converted, impressed upon Christians and soon-to-be-Christians the immediacy of their task.[32]

Many diarists converted not at a revival but rather in the company of a friend. In a detailed account, Mary Metcalf wrote home to her mother about her friend's persistent attempts to convert her:

> I must introduce you to my chum who boards here and teaches school. Her name is Lizzy Brown. [Theodore]'s sister and a dear good girl is she. I shall always love her and have great reason to, for under God she, I hope and trust, was the means of my soul's conversion. Yes dear Mother, I trust your prayers and dear father's and brother's and all those who have offered up a prayer in my behalf, are answered. I have felt ever since I left the spot where I was born and have spent my childhood. Rather serious. I thought *now* was the time to obtain the *pearl of great price* if ever. But still I did not say "*now is the accepted time*," although I thought I did, and did not see why God did not answer my prayers. I kept putting it off untill tomorow or some convenient reason.

Symptomatic of the effort involved in achieving the conversion experience, she relayed her struggle to "get religion." She went to church several times and found the personal obstacles to taking God into her life extremely frustrating.

> The next Tuesday eve. I went to prayer meeting and I was made a subject of prayer, but all this while I thought I wanted religion, and did not know what the reason was I could not obtain it. The next Friday I had given up *all* idea of going to class meeting and *almost* of ever becomeing a Christian."

After lots more pressure from Lizzy Brown and the local preacher, and under the duress of multiple harangues and sleep deprivation, she finally experienced her conversion:

> She began to talk with me, and asked me if I would not make the resolution that I would not close my eyes in sleep until I had made my peace with God. It was hard but I did. And after spending 4 long hours in pleading for mercy I at last obtained it. But not untill I had given myself, soul, body and all, into the hands of the Lord and was willing he should do with me as seemed him good. The f[a]ct was after, in one sense I was willing. I was calcalating upon what feelings I should have and not untill I had said from my heart "Lord give me such feelings as will be most for thy glory," but just at that moment did I find peace in believing.

The conversion process demanded effort of those assisting in the conversion—the preacher and the believers—as well as of the person seeking salvation. The lure of immediate relief from anxiety and guilt created incentives to convert. The emergent evangelical religions "made salvation imminently accessible and immediately available."[33]

Addie Brown also experienced religion at the prompting of her beloved Rebecca, under the facilitation and skill of a churchwoman who diligently visited:

> I am now going to inform you of something that you long desire. That is this: I have found a *Friend*, this is *Jesus*. My beloved, you wish me happy New Year. It 'tis me; it has been happy week to me. Why did I put it of so long? I would not have spent so many unhapy hours I have spent. I had to seek for *salvations* before. O Rebecca, could I but see you for a hour I could tell you all . . . Dear Rebecca, I will tell I was determined to have a *change heart*. There is a pious young lady her; she visit the house two or three times. So one evening she was here to tea and she was going to prayer meetings so she ask me, would I like to go? So I told her "yes" and we went. I was delighted with the meeting, so I went agan. So she has been talking to me and thinking of you my *love*. It realy made me unhappy two week ago. I did not. What was the matter with myself? I was not sick in body - but in mind. I was determin then to get religion, for I do not know when the hour will come. Dear Rebecca, your prayer are answered. I hope I will have the strength to keep up to my duty. Dear Rebecca, give my love to Henrietta and tell her not to put it of any longer, for now is the exceptud time.

Rebecca had encouraged Addie previously, but unsuccessfully. The knowledge that Rebecca advocated, desired, and promoted a conversion encouraged Addie. When the "pious young lady" made a bid, Addie was ready. Once converted, Addie immediately became an evangelist herself; she, in turn, resolved to bring Rebecca's sister, Harriet, into the Christian circle.[34]

Women were not the only evangelists. Charles Metcalf attempted to ensure his sisters' study of the Bible. In a common theme of the nineteenth century, he linked the need for religion to the hazardousness of life, and expressed his anxiety about making sure revelation came before it was too late:

> I feel anxious that the girls should choose that good part which shall not be taken away from them . . . how [very] uncertain life is and the great thing to live for is to prepare to die, also the deep interest I felt for their salvation, it is my earnest desire, and daily prayer to God that they may be _saved_, and that we _all_ as a family may be useful, and faithful in the service of our maker, kept from the evil that is in the world, from temptation and sin, that our health may be preserved if agreeable to the Devine Will fill up our days with duty, and be prepared to _die_.

James Adams encouraged his daughter, Chloe Metcalf, to seek religion: "I seriously and feelingly invite you to submit. And give yourself and all your friends up to that God whose you are and whom you ought to serve for this is your reasonable service and then you will feel that every thing is [per =] pretty safe in the hand of an allwise God." In another example, an African American man, William J. Brown, born free in Rhode Island, sought salvation after a serious illness:

> I concluded that I had no time to lose, so I fully made up my mind that I would attend the meetings and make every effort that lay in my power to save my soul. I went in company with some boys to the meeting house, and there heard the pastor preach a discourse, after which the meeting was turned into a prayer and conference meeting; three or four pews were cleared for the anxious to be seated in, and the invitation was given, that all those who wanted to get religion to take those seats and the members would pray for them.

William later took his place in the anxious seats, but did not find immediate peace. After several days of being unable to eat and numerous conversations with the minister and the male brethren of the church, he still felt miserable. He wrote, "I had tried everything that I knew of and given up everything, and was willing to do anything I could to bring peace to my mind." Finally, after more soul-searching and praying, William experienced the euphoria of conversion.[35]

The influence of friends and kin could also sway individuals away

from God and religious observation. Martha Barrett documented her
mother's concerns in her diary.

> Yes I do love the Sabbath, though I do not consider it a being really any more
> *holy* than the other days of the week. My dear mother thinks my views are
> change by the influence *another's* opinions have upon me. I do not think
> [you], yet it may be so. I hope if there has been any change it is for the better.
> I have lost some of the principles that so long have been cherished in my
> bosom.

But in spite of her wavering, she held fast to beliefs too deep to be
reconsidered: "Oh! No, I can never give up my anti-slavery faith."[36]

Through this series of examples it becomes clear that what could
arguably be framed as an individual and private set of concerns—
whether or not to convert to Christianity—was in fact a very *social*
process. While the ultimate commitment rested with an individual, the
process by which those decisions were made was intensely social. Neighbors, friends, and relatives constantly intervened as exhorters, evangelists, advisers, facilitators, and preachers to influence the outcome of the
process. Far from being private, "getting religion" was situated in
multiple overlapping networks, firmly embedded in the social sphere.
Faith was private. Church-going and converting to Christianity had a
strong social dimension.

KEEPING RELIGION AND THE
LANGUAGE OF UNCERTAINTY

The struggle to "keep religion" involved considerable self-doubt and
often necessitated intervention by those same people who facilitated its
acquisition. The precursor to the conversion formula—self-condemna-
tion—questioned an individual's self-knowledge, self-confidence, and
commonsense understanding. For example, Parna Gilbert condemned
herself unmercifully: "What a dreadful sink of wickedness is my heart.
Must resign the idea of ever feeling the power of religion. Surely if I am
a child of God I could not live so stupid." Subjects laced their talk about
the conversion itself with uncertainty. For example, Sarah Metcalf wrote,
"*I think* I feel the importance of it, and *if I know my own feelings* it is
my heart's desire to become a *sincere* Christian." And once converted,
keeping religion, an equally fragile process, became a problem. This
tentativeness surfaced almost immediately after conversion. Many struggled to maintain their faith in God. Lavinia Merrill's sincere desire to

accept faith was plagued with self-doubt. She confided in Rhoda that she *thought* she had experienced religion several weeks earlier. Later she compared herself unfavorably to Rhoda's brother Stephen, in her mind a model Christian:

> I wish I was as devoted a Christian as your brother Stephen and I suppose I can be. God knows my heart and *I hope I have not been decieving myself.* I want to have my hope founded on a rock so that nothing can sweep it of.

She feared self-deception, and this uncertainty profoundly tempered her faith. Permelia Dame, like so many in the aftermath of a conversion, felt her newfound zealousness wane. She wrote to her recently converted brother, George, who had helped to support her and her sister after their parents died:

> I feel greatly rejoised, my dear Brother, to think that you have made a profession of religeon and have taken a decided stand on the Lord side. I do not enjoy my mind as well as *I think I did once.* And I hope it may be the Lord will that I may be more engaged in the course of the redeemer for when I do not enjoy religion, I do not enjoy any thing.

After the monumental cathartic event, Mary Metcalf expressed doubt about its impact: "I have not felt that joy that some have expressed, still I have been happy." Religion did not irrevocably lodge itself in each individual soul. It sometimes flitted away, even when the individual struggled to hold fast. It continued to require effort on the part of the individual and social work on the part of the church community to maintain the religious fervor.[37]

GENDER AND RELIGION

The historical literature finds a significant gender difference in who performs the social work of the church. Acting on a sense of responsibility developed from personal piety, women in particular attempted to convert their children, husbands, other relatives, neighbors, and friends. In numerous accounts of antebellum New England, revivalism and religion became sources of conflict between men and women. They clashed over religious beliefs and over the issues related to "a woman's relative power in the family, such as her right to go to a religious meeting without her husband's approval or her ability to bring him into church with her." In nineteenth-century culture, women came to be considered the moral authority within the family. "Women were God's vicegerents

in the home," wrote McLoughlin. "Not even the minister had such
spiritual authority over the young." Women constituted the majority of
church members and worked to convert their families. In 1830–31, in
Rochester, New York, the scene of numerous waves of revivals, "65
percent of male converts were related to prior members of their churches,"
a statistic that suggests that men often converted to Christianity under
the influence of female relatives. In Utica, New York, of the converts to
the Whitestown Presbyterian Church who had been preceded by relatives, 61 percent were preceded by solitary women. This striking gender
difference documented by other scholars did not emerge in the letters,
diaries, and autobiographies of this study. Men recorded attending
church as often as women (91 percent of male diarists, as compared to
93 percent of female diarists), and men and women were equally likely
to experience conversion.[38]

That said, religion held special promise to the working women in this
study; it offered influence and autonomy. The dissenting Christian
theology promoted a new ideal of the white middle-class woman—the
true woman, submissive to her husband, pious to an angelic extreme—
and simultaneously assuaged women's anxiety and uncertainty about
this emerging cultural standard. Despite the messages of subordination,
evangelical Christianity unquestionably empowered some women to act
in ways antithetical to socially prescribed behavior. In addition to their
social work among family and friends, women took their religious
message on missions to their neighborhoods and to foreign countries.
Numerous women conducted prayer campaigns to pray for the unconverted. Parna Gilbert spoke of her church's plan to form a committee to
visit people in order to keep the growing revival alive. A handful of
women ventured a more hazardous proposition; against all odds and
aggressive social opposition, they pursued the ministry. A small but
strong-minded cluster of women, black and white, became ministers.
As Marilyn Richardson has observed, "religious faith gave [African
American] women strength, courage, comfort, and above all, vision—a
vision that was at once creative, intellectual, and pragmatic." Often in
direct opposition to their fellow believers and their religious superiors,
women followed their calling from God to preach the gospel.[39]

Conversion to Christianity had a private dimension but simultaneously
had numerous social consequences. The evangelical revivals "transformed conversion from a private to a public and intensely social event."
"Getting religion" gave women in particular the courage to approach

others, draw them into the church, and preach to them in the social sphere. In getting and keeping religion, networks of relationships held individuals accountable to the church and God, and influenced the way they behaved.[40]

"SOCIAL WORK" AND SECULAR REFORM

"Getting religion" translated into secular activity as well, not the least of which was involvement in the host of reform movements of the antebellum period. Moral reform, temperance, and abolition emerged as three primary social movements deeply rooted in middle-class women's religiosity. In keeping with the democratic spirit of the antebellum period, voluntary associations, anti-slavery societies, and temperance societies—the organizational vehicles of these social movements—provided a means to mold public discourse as well as to modify political decisions. "The concept of voluntary reform societies," notes McLoughlin, "fitted perfectly into the republican ideals of a virtuous citizenry sacrificing itself for the greater good of the community. After 1830 they became effective agencies of social revolution." While inspired by religious beliefs, the organizations extended beyond church congregations and clashed with the church over the radicalism of their reforms.[41]

Largely middle class in composition, the moral reform societies attempted to institute stricter standards of morality. Fueled by renewed religious enthusiasm and confronted with a growing urban working-class population, particularly of young people seemingly cut loose from family ties and of recent Irish and German immigrants, the reform activists set about to eliminate vice such as prostitution, to promote motherhood, to facilitate self-improvement, and to provide charity for the "worthy" poor. In part, these societies concentrated on how to absorb growing "disorderly" populations—immigrant and native-born—into the orderly folds of society. Given their focus, it is no surprise that members of the working class, mechanics, and farmers would be underrepresented in their ranks. The moral reformers targeted working people, immigrants, and the poor for assistance; they did not recruit them into their organizations. Consistent with the working-class and farm character of this study, only one woman mentioned involvement in a moral reform association. A handful of women (five, or 18 percent) attended sewing societies or sewing circles, which were typically affiliated with churches for the purpose of providing clothing and bedding for the poor or raising money for the church.[42]

However, reflecting a broader class base of support, twelve diarists (21 percent) expressed interest in abolitionist activities and twenty (36 percent) in temperance (seven diarists expressed interest in both). Activism on the part of diarists reflects a pyramid structure indicative of rank and file members in general. At the bottom of the pyramid, most people who expressed abolitionist sympathies—in virtually equal numbers of men and women—recorded going to an anti-slavery lecture or discussing the controversial abolitionist ideas. On a higher level of the pyramid, a smaller number of people exhibited greater commitment. Only three diarists exhibited sustained dedication to the issues and to anti-slavery activism. After moving to Michigan from Vermont, Pamela Brown Dix and her new husband turned their house into a station on the Underground Railroad. Both Joseph Kimball and Martha Barrett belonged to anti-slavery societies, Joseph in the 1830s and Martha in the 1850s. As a member of the Essex County Anti-Slavery Society, Martha attended lectures, meetings, and conventions and socialized with some of the more famous activists (e.g., Parker Pillsbury). African American autobiographers were more deeply involved in abolitionist activism. In addition to exposing slavery and trying to transform public opinion about it through the ex-slave narrative, some of the autobiographers, for example, Harriet Jacobs and James L. Smith, traveled and lectured about their experiences in bondage, exposing themselves to further harassment and abuse. Others who were born free wrote and lectured about their opposition to slavery. The Reverend Samuel Harrison became a chaplain for the 54th Massachusetts Regiment, the first black unit to fight in the Civil War.[43]

Temperance excited the most support among diarists. Approximately one-third of the diarists engaged in some kind of temperance activity—going to a meeting or lecture, joining a temperance society (e.g., the Daughters or Sons of Temperance), or signing a pledge of abstinence. As with abolitionists, many diarists' commitment to abstinence rarely transcended concern—only five (25 percent) of the twenty who mentioned the temperance issue joined organizations or took a pledge. The campaign for temperance was closely tied to the rise of evangelical religions and was situated in the center of the conflicting cultures of class and gender. In society at large, Epstein notes, "the antagonism toward men and toward masculine values that had led evangelical women to associate femaleness with piety was now translated into the secular terms of temperance." Among the subjects of this study, temperance issues generated conflict, but not between men and women as the historical literature on the middle class finds. Joseph Kimball, a member of the Franklin Total Abstinence Society, lost a local contest over temperance. After attending a Rowley, Massachusetts, town meeting in 1833, he wrote, "Rum is all the go." This meant the pro-alcohol forces won the day. Town politics offered an accessible and comprehensible forum for waging these battles, regardless of how they fared in the household or in the nation's capital. In my research, equal numbers of men and women voiced temperance viewpoints and appeared to feel equally strongly about it. For example, very early in the temperance campaign, David Clapp wrote of his heartfelt feelings about the corrupting influence of alcohol: "Thus are the learned and the ignorant, the high and the low, the rich and the poor, the merchant and the mechanic, alike led astray by this foul destroyer—*Intemperance*." In 1841, Hannah Adams tried to appeal to her parents' sensibilities:

> I am something like the girl who wrote to her sweetheart, to keep what lay nearest her heart to say last. I have a great favor to ask of you & as you have never denied me, I will take courage to ask it. I want you Dear Father & Mother to become temperance folks. I will not ask you to sign the pledge until you wish to - but I ask you in the name of all your children to leave off taking alcohol in any form, for it is the gall of bitterness to us to see you when reason is dethroned & appetite made ruler. O govern your passions with absolute sway & grow wiser & better as life wears away. I will [choose] the day if you please for you to begin, let it [be] Thanksgiving day & we will celebrate it in all our future generations with a truly thankful heart.

In the spirit of converting others, empowered by their religious beliefs, women and men acted on the power of their moral authority to advocate abstinence. They extended themselves within the social realm, speaking out with confidence and conviction they might not otherwise exhibit. Religious beliefs empowered them with missionary zeal to mobilize others in the social sphere.[44]

The social movements and reform societies had a significant impact on public debate, and in the case of abolition and temperance eventually brought about sweeping new national legislation. The anti-slavery movement undeniably molded public opinion in the North, and it effectively pressured the federal government to discourage and eventually to dismantle slavery. After the Civil War, those same organized constituencies, in conjunction with others, lobbied Congress to pass the Fourteenth and Fifteenth Amendments to the U.S. Constitution, granting suffrage to

African American men. Temperance activism also influenced local governmental action (e.g., the blue laws) as well as individual attitudes and, at times, behavior. Later in the century, female activists founded the Women's Christian Temperance Union, whose campaign eventually resulted in Prohibition. As another organization institutionalized within the social sphere, the temperance campaign altered national policy.[45]

Even this cursory assessment of these reform activities prompts us to acknowledge the central way that organized activity in the social sphere mediated debate and legislation in the public sphere. While informal activities in the social sphere modulated everyday life, their institutionalized counterparts—social-movement organizations and volunteer associations—had the most effective and sustained impact on the public sphere.

Whatever else it provided, the church acted as an important social center in working-class and farm communities in antebellum New England. Diarists, correspondents, and autobiographers attended churches of differing denominations, churches that may have been in a pitched theological battle with one another. To the church visitor, the spirit of exploration and experimentation compelled an ecumenical practice over and above the exhortations of the sectarian preachers. Working women and men involved themselves in the church to seek entertainment as well as mutual aid and spiritual solace. Subjects criticized and evaluated ministers, who often served as the primary appeal of a particular church or denomination. Furthermore, the practice of religion connected people to one another, as the recently converted turned to their neighbors, families, and friends to convert them as well. Religion rarely struck working people in isolation. It entered into the cultural arena and into individual minds via a complex system of social intervention. Getting religion and passing it on involved the work of individuals committed to spread the gospel and empowered to act as agents of Christianity. And finally, religious empowerment propelled men and women into secular activism as well. In the social realm, people engaged in temperance and abolitionist activities, politicizing the issues and working hard to push them into the public eye. The social sphere acted as a mediating arena for the engagement of individuals with other people outside their households, shaping, influencing, and changing the community, and in several key battles of the nineteenth century, shifting public policy via their collective endeavors.

Conclusion

If we view the world through the eyes of a seamstress, Louisa Chapman, we see the practical resonance of the category of the social sphere. On the 16th of April, 1848, she recorded the commonsensical distinctions between the different kinds of prayer that had been enumerated earlier in the morning by her minister:

> The duty of *secret social* and *public.*
>
> How solemn is secret prayer. To retire alone, to hold converse with God. It should never be neglected thought when the time arrives we may not feel like performing the duty. Without this no one can maintain intercourse with God or make any advances in the Divine life. Social prayer is also a duty enjoyned upon all and espescially upon those who are heads of families. How many impressions may be made upon those who witness this service that will remain and may lead them to do likewise.
>
> If God will hear and answer the prayers of a few who call upon him what will he not do where a congregation address him in this solemn act.

Louisa made a distinction between an individual, a household group, and a communal entity. While her (and her minister's) conceptions of secret, social, and public do not precisely coincide with ours, the parallel terms and divisions suggest that such distinctions had meaning in everyday nineteenth-century life and are not simply academic abstractions.[1]

Feminists have been instrumental in revaluing women's work within the home and inferentially, the private sphere itself. Several pathbreaking studies in the past twenty years have examined housework, childcare, and mothering, which had previously been unacknowledged or undervalued. In this tradition, my research has similarly sought to re-center the study of society around the work of women, revealing the interrelationships of public and private.[2]

However, I also want to go beyond revaluing the private to reassessing the centrality of private activities in women's lives. On the basis of this investigation of antebellum working people's behavior, we find that private activities occupied a minor corner in women's universe of action. In the days of a culturally ascendant private sphere, working women did not lead private lives. Perhaps nineteenth-century culture defined more of what women did as private, but women themselves did not withdraw from community networks, nor did they focus progressively more intensely on the nuclear family in the approach to the Civil War. The practice of visiting, for example, refutes the portrait of women as quintessentially private. It reveals that between 1820 and 1865, working women did not exist in isolation, nor were they concerned solely with "particular interests," as the label "private" suggests. They traveled to see distant neighbors and friends; they attended lectures; they organized church events, and the like. My research demonstrates that women's exclusion from the public activities of government did not render them essentially "private." Women were involved extensively in crafting and sustaining communal institutions and in politicizing aspects of everyday life. In reviewing a vast anthropological literature, Sylvia Junko Yanagisako similarly points to the importance of women's integrative activities: "Inquiries into women's relationships with people outside their own domestic group refute the notion that it is invariably men who link mother-child units to larger institutional structures in society."[3]

Furthermore, men's dominance in the public sphere did not preclude women's involvement in local political discourses, school-committee decisions, the regulation of alcohol use, or the dismantling of the southern system of slavery. Nor did male privilege in the public sphere elevate men above domestic concerns or prevent involvement in family and social life. It has been a tendency of some scholars and multitudes of lay people to assume that public and private are interchangeable with men and women. When one interprets "private" as encompassing everything related to women and considers everything women do as private, the resulting theoretical system is self-perpetuating and tautological, obscuring the ways in which women may not be private and men may not be public. Anna Yeatman maintains that using the terms in this way undermines the feminist agenda. I concur. Such a dichotomy can be used for anti-feminist purposes, and it can also lead to simple misinterpretation. The association of *public* with *man* and *private* with *woman* comes to be seen as natural, inevitable, and for the good of society. Thus, politicians can make claims about the domestic role of women and assign the weight of history and natural law as evidence. For these reasons, one objective of this book has been to decouple the gender links. Activities, not gender, define what is public and what is private.[4]

Visiting and gossiping must be understood as integral to alternative economies, as part of a welfare system executed without the state, as a conduit for exchanging ideas and opinions, and as a system of emotional and psychological support that linked individuals to one another. Subjects who engaged in community networks felt obligated and indebted to others, and expected that good deeds would be returned, as would rejection and bad favor. Working people did not act, think, or vote within a vacuum; they did so within the context of a dialogue and a set of collective interactions, which is primarily what visiting and gossiping, i.e., the social realm, was about. People discussed politics, religion, the weather, their neighbors' crops, and the evils of slavery. In the process, they circulated news, ideas, and opinions. To characterize this teeming activity as "private" obscures the activities and the processes of community-building.

The social is both central and important in antebellum society, and it is also central and important in our conceptual understanding of that society. The social was important not simply because of the industry and pleasure it facilitated, but because it in turn influenced the public on the one hand, and the private on the other. As suggested in Chapter 1, if one separates the notion of the public from the political, then activity in any realm can be political and can create political space. Therefore, action within the social sphere can shift the locus of debate from the social to the public (as we saw in the trial for libel and the movements for temperance and abolition).

The social equally influenced the private. The parading of people in and out of households, making family business social business and creating social space out of a private home, effaced the physical barrier of the house and the arbitrary boundary constructed around the conjugal family. Visitors, gossipers, extended kin, and friends transformed household interactions into social relations. Their involvement in household functions meant that household members were not isolated, that child-rearing was not a solitary activity, and that family problems were not individual problems. The exchange of goods and services between homes created interdependence amongst kin and neighbors. This meant that women were not economically dependent solely on men; they called on neighbors and extended relations as well as their own labor to bring scarce resources to the household.[5]

The social was not simply a benevolent sphere, however, and its positive qualities must not be valorized at the expense of its complexity. The social realm was not solely a sphere of ethical action and solidarity; needless to say, people did not always have the interest of the common good at heart and often acted to further their own self-interests in the social sphere. People did not always give much consideration to the consequences of exclusion. The negative side of the social realm includes violence, racism, retribution, hierarchy, bigotry, and the like. As the autobiographies in particular show, conflict—in the form of gossip, argument, and social violence—pervaded community interaction. The principles of inclusion in a community are inextricably tied to the underlying practice of exclusion. In antebellum New England, white people expressed a *social* racism to maintain white privilege and exclude free blacks from getting an education, learning a trade, or even traveling as free persons. Whites expressed this racism not simply in private households but in the community through verbal harassment, physical threats, intimidation, and actual abuse.

Gender association of the spheres confined women and limited their activities, but when boundaries between spheres were blurred, women had more opportunities to thrive and exercise influence. The greater fluidity gave both women and men more opportunity for action in more varied arenas. Less differentiation also meant greater overlap in the social and work lives of men and women. In turn there was less rigid enforcement of gender prescriptions. Flexibility enabled unmarried women to head farm households. For example, Eliza Adams saved her earnings from the textile factory and needle work to buy a farm in 1857. She adopted two daughters to create a family and to work the farm. Zeloda Barrett lived with her parents and sister in the 1820s and 1830s, and had enormous responsibility for overseeing the farm and doing the farm work. Other unmarried women supported themselves through their labors, over the course of their lives. Such independence empowered Martha Barrett to express her strong abolitionist views and to write political as well as sentimental poetry. Addie Brown defiantly proclaimed her love and passion for her best friend, Rebecca Primus, declaring the primacy of their claims on one another over and above those of male suitors. Mary Orne Tucker felt no compunction about publicly denouncing ministers who subscribed to a theology different from hers. Mary

Coult Jones left her husband and three-year-old child for a month to travel with her mother-in-law from Connecticut to New Hampshire to visit relatives.

Gender roles in the social sphere were not as rigidly conceived or enforced as in the public or the private. The personal narratives provide numerous examples of men as well as women who transgressed prescribed gender boundaries. Brigham Nims, John Plummer Foster, and other men involved themselves in domestic life through housework and in the community through caring for the sick and going to church. They attended quilting parties, which historical mythology has shrouded as solely a women's ritual. They proved themselves to be nurturing, engaged in social life, and emotionally expressive. The social sphere gave men and women more freedom of expression and a greater range of activity than the prescriptions of the advice literature might otherwise indicate. This broader social sphere gave women the opportunity to exercise a certain kind of freedom and initiative that they did not find in the private and that the public denied them. In the social sphere—an intersection of cultural prescriptions, individually held attitudes, and collective behaviors—women spoke in front of audiences, earned a living, and traveled the countryside.

Regardless of the openness, a blurred private or a vital social was no substitute for access to the public, which continued to be essential in shaping possibilities for women and African Americans. Voting in local and national elections, participating in the construction of a legislative future, and exercising a political voice remained crucial to equality for white women and people of color. The importance they placed on access to the public sphere can be seen in the viciousness of the fights in the postbellum era over suffrage. In an environment of limited political spoils, the struggle for expanded citizenship pitted white women against black men. Both constituencies recognized that while the vote was not a sufficient condition for equality, it was a necessary precondition.[6]

In examining the collective mosaic of working people pieced in this book, I have found that working people practiced an American culture rooted in work and community, not constricted by middle-class prescriptions. Even in an industrializing environment, working people energetically reconstructed locally based networks of support for themselves. In antebellum New England, the social mediated between the public and private spheres. It linked the private sphere to a larger entity and grounded the public sphere in human relationships. Within this forum for human interaction, people performed social work, negotiated insti-

tutions, made politics, and spread religion. My task has been to illumi-
nate life in antebellum New England by demonstrating the ways that
everyday practices were socially constructed, and by suggesting a better
way to analyze those circumstances. The question remains as to whether
the concept of the social remains bound to antebellum New England or
is helpful in understanding late-twentieth-century society.

The historical account presented here differs greatly from histories
using middle-class sources. The subjects used a distinctive language to
talk about themselves and to address their friends and family. Working
women actively developed their own definition of what it meant to be a
decent and honorable woman. Men engaged in housework without
perceiving it as a threat to their masculinity. In a time of great sectarian
ferment, church-going Christians ignored the dictates of their ministers
and attended churches of varied denominations and opposing theologies.
Working people set in motion a vast network of exchange that flourished
in a cultural sea of middle-class individualism. This window onto the
nineteenth century has opened only because working people gave voice
to their existence and their concerns. It will remain open only as long
as we listen.

Sources of Evidence

Diaries, letters, and autobiographies provide a vantage point for viewing work, social life, culture and religion through the eyes of the "common" workers rather than middle-class observers. The personal narratives reveal what the subjects chose to write about their lives. Although I quote large sections of their writings verbatim, my choices of themes, documents, and quotations necessarily filter a picture that is colored by my interpretation as well. The writings of 56 diarists (28 women and 28 men), 19 autobiographers, and approximately 100 correspondents comprise the body of historical materials on which this book is based. Subjects, however ordinary, could not be considered representative of the New England working population as a whole. The collection of materials is not a random sample, although it includes the totality of documents I found to fit my criteria. I carefully scrutinized primary documents before selecting them for study, accepting all materials that passed my screening text. Led by my hypothesis that those less privileged in American history would experience and describe their lives distinctively, I searched for working people—those who were *not* privileged, that is, were not middle class, not large land owners, and not highly educated. The complicated economic milieu of the early nineteenth century necessitated a dialectical process for determining whether to include a subject in the study. The process alternately involved trying to determine class status, reading the diaries or letters, researching family background (via vital records, genealogies, and town histories when available), reading more of the diary, assessing language and the content of daily lives, and discovering what the subjects did for a living (not always immediately apparent). Ultimately, the final group of class-appropriate materials included approximately one-fourth of all the documents I examined.[1]

Betsey Clark is a case in point. Initially, I was thrilled when I discovered diaries of both a husband and wife at the New Hampshire Historical Society.

As I read Betsey Clark's diary, I quickly became absorbed in the rhythms of her life, which involved taking care of grandchildren, attending sewing circles, and monitoring the farm's activities. On June 6, 1855, she wrote in her diary, "I arose very early this morning and dipped 13 doz. of candles. How many different sorts of business we farmers' wives have to perform. We are comanded to be diligent in business." Although she referred to trips to the dressmaker and to the doctor, both signs of privilege, she also contributed to the farm's capacity to produce. At haying time two months later she recorded a corresponding increase in her own workload:

> Monday. O, dear, how fatigued I am. Mr. & Mrs. Fairbanks have just took the stage for Chester. Have had six men haying. It is nothing but cooking and eating. I find I have not the courage or strength to wait on a large family as in my younger days. I wish not to complain.

Her husband's diary was no less bound to work patterns on the farm. Nathaniel Clark's daily entries chronicled the weather, farm chores, travels of his wife, and the like. Then in a typically understated entry, he let slip he belonged to the board of the Derry Bank: "I have been to the Derry Court to day and excepted the charter for a new bank as I was one of the grantees. They have got in eight loads of hay." In fact, he was one of a group of twelve men who legally incorporated the bank in June, 1848. That the bank failed to remain solvent for even two years is not the key issue. For my purposes, the fact that Nathaniel owned sufficient resources to become a bank director, however temporarily, rendered him privileged. Prosperous individuals of the early nineteenth century frequently owned farms, so this was not surprising in and of itself. The 1850 census revealed that he owned $6,000 worth of real estate, well above the $1,890 valuation typical of New Hampshire farms in 1850, and high above the resource level acceptable for this study. Thus, I did not include him. Nathaniel Clark was far more privileged than other people in this study, and including him, with his array of resources, would have compromised the principles of selection.[2]

The more difficult question was how to think about Betsey. She was not just a woman working on a farm, but also a banker's wife. Should I include her in the study and not her husband? In rural areas, privileged or not, most women toiled as Betsey Clark did. While some had resources that provided greater options, those resources seldom alleviated the burdens of labor. Ultimately, I decided not to include her in the study because she could conceivably benefit from her husband's abundant property assets and social standing.

Virtually all of the historical data are written documents. This means that the evidence consists of words, not action—words about action, but words nonetheless. The documents discuss behavior more than feelings and emotions, although the activities they discuss are necessarily mediated by the language used by the diarist, correspondent, and autobiographer. I am sensitive to the subjects' use of language and attempt to interpret its meaning to the subject writing it. Indeed, throughout my research I have been consistently struck by the ways that subjects articulate their unique world views. And it is my fascination with their means of expressing themselves as well as the substance of what they say that prompts me to quote large passages verbatim. However, my focus is not exclusively on their language; it is also on the sensory reality that the words reflect.[3]

The historical subjects were both rural and urban dwellers. I do not systematically compare these two groups, in part because the two groups were not mutually exclusive. It was not unusual for a subject to live on a farm, move to Boston for a while, move back to the farm, migrate to Lowell looking for work, and on and on. Geographical comparison is difficult when the unit of analysis is the individual rather than a culture or group. The evidence in the documents also suggests that because of this intermingling and back-and-forth migration, an urban/rural dichotomy draws the contrast too starkly.

For three reasons, the geography of New England bounds this investigation. First, the region initially published a literature on domestic ideology in the United States, which became an important cultural message in the nineteenth century. Second, it launched the first phase of industrialization in the United States. And third, its archives offer a wealth of primary documents and published background information about the period.

TYPES OF EVIDENCE

LETTERS

When relying on unique written documents we must ask how common it was for men and women to be literate and how often they wrote letters. White, native-born, adult Yankees—both male and female—had a literacy rate of 98%. For native-born free blacks in New England the rate was closer to 92%.[4] While it is not possible to determine precisely how common it was for an individual to write letters, the overall volume of mail in the United States indicates the growing popularity of written communication.

The postal-service load increased greatly during the antebellum period, growing from 1.61 letters per capita in 1840 to 5.15 letters per capita in 1860. Ronald Zboray makes the argument that the high geographical mobility of people in the early nineteenth century acted as an incentive for people to become literate and to write letters: "Perhaps nothing more explains the high literacy rates of the antebellum United States than this need, felt by those separated from kin, friends and community, to write letters." Economic insecurity and new environs prompted nineteenth-century Americans to rely more than ever upon family and community support, with letters providing "the only link, short of the individual making long and expensive trips back home, between separated loved ones." Letters constituted the primary means of maintaining social networks after people moved from their communities.[5]

For historical purposes, correspondence offers the advantage of suggesting interaction between individuals. A relationship reconstructed through letters can reveal more about a person than a heartfelt outpouring in his or her diary. A letter that intends to describe a circumstance discloses more because a diary tersely records events, assuming rather than explaining contextual information. By its nature, correspondence places individuals in a larger social context.

The use of letters as historical evidence has prompted scholars to examine the conventions of letter-writing and their implications. Marilyn Ferris Motz, for example, studies letters (and diaries) written by women and men of various economic strata in Michigan between 1820 and 1920. She finds a distinction between masculine and feminine styles: the masculine-style letters "relied on a direct, matter-of-fact, unemotional tone," while the feminine-style letters used descriptive and persuasive language. But women wrote business letters in a masculine style, Motz notes, and young single men and fathers writing to their children often wrote in a feminine mode. She states that the context and purpose of the letter shaped its style more than gender.[6]

My subjects wrote letters in a manner very different from those studied by Motz. While the letters reflected a decided range in style, they could not be sorted on the basis of gender. Married men did not drop the responsibility of corresponding with family members, nor did they stop expressing their feelings in letters or writing about family matters. The differences of interpretation may result from the class differences of our historical materials or from regional cultural variation (the western frontier versus settled New England).[7]

This investigation relies on 20 collections of letters, involving approximately 100 correspondents. Most of the letters are drawn from collections of family papers in New England archives. A small subset of these has been edited and published in twentieth-century books and journals. The primary methodological drawbacks of these collections result from the fact that most letters are from one person to another, rather than back and forth. Therefore it becomes necessary to infer the characteristics of the letter recipient, based on how other people related to him or her in the letters. For example, the letters in the Rhoda Parker Smith Correspondence at the James Duncan Phillips Library are all written by family and friends *to* Rhoda Parker Smith. All I know concretely about Rhoda is that she worked in West Newbury, Massachusetts, as an apprentice combmaker and that she faithfully preserved a large cache of letters. While her own voice never surfaces, the correspondence reacts to her, responds to her questions, and makes assumptions about her character sufficiently to reveal the contours of her life, much as an image emerges in a brass rubbing. In the absence of abundant sources, murky imprints have to suffice.[8]

DIARIES

While we can understand letter-writing as an attempt to weave together a fraying social universe, what would motivate a busy, perpetually exhausted working person to keep a diary, a seemingly private document? Some diaries were written as letters—documentation of daily life to be circulated among distant dear ones. Many diaries of the early nineteenth century were "semi-public documents intended to be read by an audience"—sisters, mothers, friends. In this manner they provided a means for disseminating the news and conveying the texture of everyday life in an environment foreign to the community left behind. Theories of diary-keeping abound. Cott found for an earlier period that "busyness, level of uncertainty, desire for expression, religious conscience, sense of tradition, self-consciousness might each and all have pertained, in addition to literacy."

And Ulrich demonstrated in her artful interpretation of Martha Ballard's diary that the desire to keep a record of her work motivated Martha to write down her life events regularly and systematically.[9]

The content of the diaries themselves hold the biggest clue to motivation. The diarists prominently documented the weather, work performed, and people visited. In addition, they occasionally recorded their explicit motivations for keeping a diary, which entailed no small commitment. Religious ruminations prompted some people to begin their documentary journey. Several diarists cited a desire to improve penmanship and grammar. For example, Arthur Bennett wrote: "This day I have been to village and purchased this book for the purpose of keeping a journal of business, improvement and progress through life. And by keeping it I hope to improve my penmanship & composition." Providing evidence of her need for improvement, Sarah Trask opened her journal with: "May I improve in written before I get though this book." Edward J. Carpenter, a cabinetmaker's apprentice, wrote, "According to my Father's advice when I came here, which I have long neglected, I have concluded to commence a journal and write down every night what has occurred during the day worthy of note." Planting an inverse clue about their motivations for diary-keeping, diarists occasionally acknowledged that they had done nothing worthy of note on a particular day. For example, domestic worker and teacher Ann Julia Stoddard wrote: "I can't think of any thing to write so I guess there is nothing very important." The obverse implies that what she does write—about visiting, work, and keeping school—is important and worthy of recording.[10]

In this cluster of diaries, only one subject, Charles Benson, a ship's steward, explicitly used his diary as an extended letter, to be openly shared with someone else. His diary collected his heartfelt yearnings for his wife, Jenny, in Salem while he was away at sea. He addressed diary entries as love letters to Jenny. However, other diarists left clues that they did not intend their journals to be secret documents. Sarah Trask concluded her first diary volume with a note to her friends: "And if my friends should this book, read, pleas to excuse mistakes and written as they will find it bad." In contrast, a few of the more introspective diaries, primarily by women, professed a desire for secrecy. Mary Mudge exploded with anger when she discovered Jessee Attwill read her 1853 diary. "I got really vexed with him before he left for he got my last year's diary and read some of it after I told him I did not want him to. When he left I did not ask him to call again." Regardless of stated goals, the diaries recorded a life, reaffirmed accomplishments and the value of work, and, for a handful of people, provided a quiet space for self-reflection.[11]

Diaries have proven to be a fruitful source, particularly during the second wave of feminism, in the quest to find a lost history and recapture women's historical experience. The careful examination of women's diaries as sources for historical inquiry has sparked a debate about how to best characterize them and the reasons for their differences in content and style. Margo Culley observes that women's diaries, from the eighteenth to the late nineteenth century, shifted from chronicling community activities to documenting introspection, reflecting the "emergence of the self" and the contraction of the social sphere. In the eighteenth and early nineteenth centuries, women laconically recorded events, community life, family activities, daily routines, illnesses, births, and deaths. By the late nineteenth century women discussed themselves, their feelings, their internal struggles. Culley describes the change as a shift from serving as witnesses to acting as subjects. As the earlier diaries ignored emotions, so the later diaries lacked a sense of context or community: "Utterly absent . . . is the sense of self as part of a social fabric." To an extent, this inattention to social context reflects women's growing conception of themselves as somehow apart, separate, or marginal. It also demonstrates a transformation in the relationship of the individual to the community and the social sphere, which Culley attributes to the increasing individualism of the nineteenth century.[12]

Alternatively, Motz claims that the critical distinction in diary-keeping is not historical time, but the diarists' residence. The rural diarist, according to Motz, "does not synthesize; instead, he or she breaks down the experiences of a day into discrete, self-contained units, the rhythm of the text coming from the relation of these units to one another and to the whole." The diarist presupposes that the account of the day represents something known; the context does not need to be explained. In contrast Motz poses the literary diary (most of which are urban), which parallels the introspective diaries that Cully finds in the late nineteenth century. According to Motz, they "focus on the diarist as a unique individual and relate the writers' anxieties, concerns, and emotional reactions to events both personal and national. These diaries represent, in other words, an attempt to differentiate the self from society."[13]

Proposing a third perspective, Elizabeth Hampsten insists that diary-keeping style is a function of class. Hampsten studies diaries and letters sent and received by women in North Dakota in the late nineteenth century and finds the same terse style and record-keeping approach, but her interpretation rejects the importance of time or place. She argues that the style of writing reveals a static, transhistorical, working-women's existence. The standard format routinely records and repeats a non-changing order, reflecting working women's lives on the prairie or in the city. Extreme elation or sadness seldom punctuate the diaries, although these emotions inevitably sharpened daily life. Hampsten argues that women's writings signify the predominance of work in their lives. The stylistic consistency gives evidence of how tangential factors such as age, time, or place were to consciousness:

> Whether women were farming, teaching school, or keeping house in town, their occupation did not make much difference to their manner of writing. Nor did age, or conditions of health, their family situation, even the year. Only women's expectations of social position appear to be reflected strongly in their manner of writing.

I think all three factors—historical time, geographic location, and class—play a role.[14]

The diaries in this study largely fell in the combined early-nineteenth-century/ working-class/rural styles just described. A vast majority straightforwardly recorded the day's work and activities. The understated style pervaded the diaries of working people in antebellum New England, though they range from non-affective, fragmented accounts of the daily activities of the diarist and her or his community to somewhat more introspective documents. They largely

record community activities, although a few also include self-reflection embedded within a visible social sphere. No matter how self-absorbed some were,
unlike those diarists described by Culley and Motz they remain firmly ensconced
in the social world. Even the more introspective diaries are stamped by concerns
about daily life. While both types of diarists locate themselves within a social
context, most do not link themselves to a political environment (with the
exception of town politics). Presidential and congressional elections appear less
prominently than annual town meetings except during the Civil War. The diaries
I studied do not exhibit a visible change in style or content from 1820 to 1865.[15]

The vast majority of the diaries written in a terse manner reveal a way of
thinking about oneself and the world that is oriented to labor and to people.
The diary of farmer Samuel Shepard James illustrates the rote, unembellished
style. While this specific example is chronologically later than the study, the
style of the entry was consistent with his antebellum records. Samuel marked
in his diary the infamous day in 1901 when Leon Czolgosz assassinated President McKinley. As usual, he recorded the weather and his chores. Set off from
his other entry, he wrote, "William McKinley, President of the U.S. died this
morning 2:15 at Buffalo, New York." A comparison to a middle-class, educated
diarist illustrates a dramatically different way of recording the event. On the
same day, Robert Corning, a law student, wrote: "I am shocked into silence.
To think that within my lifetime three chief magistrates have fallen before the
bullets of assassins yet we are a democracy. The frightful virus of anarchism is
more virulent here than in Europe." I attribute this difference in expressive style
to class. However, it is important not to ascribe the characteristics of the
writing to the individuals themselves. The flatness of description (for example,
where one inserts an announcement of a relative's death in the midst of the
day's activities with affect implied but not mentioned) does not mean that
diarists experienced no grief or anger. Letters, as alternative sources, verify
this. Letters embellished feelings, created a context, interactively revealed character and emotion. Diaries of working people recorded people, events, and the
weather.[16]

Several diaries in this study point to the capabilities—in literary skills and
depth of emotion—of individuals who initially appear constricted in their range
of emotion. One diarist, Horatio Chandler, who mainly recorded his activities
farming and working as a clerk, transformed his diary-keeping style after he
traveled to Pennsylvania in the winter of 1840–41 and experienced a religious
conversion. At that point, the diary became a vehicle for exploring his visions
and devotion to God, and for quoting scripture. His euphoria and ardent self-
condemnation (for being a sinner) in the diary lasted several months, and then
he returned to the truncated style, as his life settled back to normal and his
enthusiasm for spiritual exploration receded. Parna Gilbert similarly displayed
an ebb and flow of self-reflection and emotional elaboration in her diary that
commenced as spiritual reflection became compelling and waned as everyday
life resumed its hold on her attention.

Another set of examples involves not religious revelations but rather diary-
keeping as note-taking for another, more elaborate document. In discovering
that Mary Chesnut kept a journal only to serve as her notes for her elaborate

novelistic creation of a "civil war diary" in the 1880s, C. Vann Woodward has permanently instilled skepticism in scholars regarding the authenticity of documents. That said, however, the diarists in this study do not appear to have such devious motives. Mary Coult Jones, a recently orphaned schoolteacher, kept a small pocket diary for 1851, and in the same year wrote elaborately in another larger, thicker journal. The large diary repeated most of the activities recounted in the small diary (but not all), while it embellished emotions and elaborated events. In effect, Mary Coult Jones kept the slim diary for brief record-keeping and the heftier one for soul-searching. David Clapp (see Figure 22) kept a typical young workingman's diary during his apprenticeship to a Boston printer in 1821–23, from age 14 to 17. In researching his family background, I found a printed journal, supposedly written by him but published posthumously. It covered most of the same period, but had I not known the authorship, I would never have associated the two. The handwritten diary revealed a rather shy, busy, matter-of-fact young boy. The entry for May 13, 1822, reads:

> I went to Mr. John Cottons [Sr.'s] in Boston to learn the printer's trade. Terms 2,50 per week for my board. $10 and the privilege of doing jobs for the first year. I board at Mr. Bartholomew's blacksmith & engine builder in water street.

In contrast, the published diary reveals a talkative, sometimes timid but nonetheless adventuresome author moving to Boston along with his older sister. It begins by describing that same momentous day:

> May 13th, 1822, I left my father's house for Boston, where I am to learn the printing business. It being Sunday night, I accompanied my oldest sister into the city where she is also learning a trade of her cousins. She went with and introduced me to Mr. & Mrs. Bartholomew, where I am to board. It being the first night I ever slept in Boston, and the whole family entire strangers to me, I was rather inclined to wakefulness through the night, though less disturbed than I anticipated. Mr. Bartholomew's family consists of himself and wife, two children, his wife's sister, maid, one apprentice and one boarder (a carpenter), besides myself. His occupation is blacksmith & engine builder.
>
> Monday morning I arose with the other workmen and repaired to the printing office of John Cotton Jr. my future master. The office is pleasantly situated at the corner of Franklin St. But the character of the inhabitants is what I am most fearful about. Anticipation about being despised on account of coming from the country, and my naturally reserved disposition and ignorance of the world being treated with ridicule and contempt, and other circumstances, are the reasons of my approaching the office with trembling heart and faltering steps.

The handwritten diary provides informative documentation of a major life transition, but nothing so revealing as the ruminations of the published one. In this case the audience of the document is very important. It is not clear why the journal was published, or whether it was David Clapp who embellished the writing, and if so, when he embellished it. By virtue of its elaboration, the published journal acknowledges the necessity of articulating the many previously unspoken assumptions about daily life in order to be accessible to a wide audience. The handwritten diary is much more representative of the corpus of materials this study examines, which assumes that the readers (if any) know the context and parochial references.[17]

AUTOBIOGRAPHIES

Autobiography has long been a popular American genre. Although autobiographers could hardly be considered representative of the general population, one could argue that the reason for the vast audience has been their insight into American minds, characters, and cultures. Authors' accounts of their own lives, thoughtfulness about major decisions, private epiphanies, and sensational secrets heretofore hidden from the public compel readers to read voraciously the insiders' perspectives on the lives of prostitutes, rich men, or adventurers in the wilderness. Autobiography, "the poor man's [sic] history," allows an individual to tell her or his own story and to record experiences that history might otherwise neglect, and grants a public stage for righting misconceptions or misunderstandings. As such, the collection of autobiographies opens an invaluable door to the past.[18]

In determining how to read autobiographies as personal yet public documents, we must uncover authors' motivations for writing their life story, their perceived audiences, and what they seek to tell us. Because the majority of autobiographies I use in this study are written by African Americans, these questions pertain here primarily to ex-slave and free-black narratives. The question of motivation is relatively easy to answer for freed and escaped slaves, who aimed to tell more than a story; these autobiographers intended to persuade their audience that the institution of slavery abused individuals, perverted human nature, and must be abolished (see Figures 23 and 24). In her remarkable *Incidents in the Life of a Slave Girl*, Harriet A. Jacobs forthrightly stated her motivations: "I do earnestly desire to arouse the women of the North to a realizing sense of the condition of two millions of women at the South, still in bondage, suffering what I suffered, and most of them far worse" (see Figure 25). The narratives focused on the dehumanizing effects of slavery on an entire people, often pointing to the detrimental effects on slaveholders as well as slaves. Some authors used the autobiography to explore their identity, the significance of life, the systematic injustice accorded African Americans, politics, and religious and moral questions—seeking, all in all, to validate themselves and their experience. The narratives cover the journey from slavery to freedom, the quest for literacy and human dignity. The extreme injustice of the institution and the seemingly random assignment of some people to its chains while others less deserving roamed free prompted many people to utter Job's cry: "Why me, Oh Lord?" The process of writing helped them contemplate this unanswerable question. In addition, several authors noted a motivation not to be underestimated—the desire to make a living.[19]

Freeborn blacks pursued similar goals. That is, they also sought political ends—abolishing slavery and exposing northern racism. Autobiography offered a venue for exonerating the wrongly accused. For example, William J. Brown's autobiography recounts numerous occasions when white people swindled him out of money and ends with an exacting account of building a church in Providence, Rhode Island. During the church-building, William was accused of embezzlement, and the church threatened to excommunicate him. The autobiography provided a medium through which he could present his own version of the unfolding events; in effect, it offered the opportunity to vindicate himself.

Second, according to Frances Smith Foster, the audience for slave and free black narratives was "literate, white, northern, religious, socially concerned, alien to the social context of slavery, yet not entirely without some of the same racial attitudes of slaveholders." White northern abolitionists played a central role in casting the rhetorical approach of the narratives because they knew the audience and knew too that the slave narrative had great potential as an organizing tool. They tried to convince black authors that "their skeptical public would believe nothing but documentable facts in a slave narrative." At the same time, the narratives morally exhorted northerners to action. The abolitionists utilized the slave narratives in their public education campaign to combat rampant and willful ignorance in the North about the conditions of slavery by distributing, selling, and speaking about this literature. In the process, abolitionists profoundly shaped the style of the slave narrative.[20]

Ex-slaves—fugitive and free—collaborated intentionally and inadvertently with the growing anti-slavery movement in the 1830s, 1840s, and 1850s, by writing of their lives in bondage. Some autobiographers became famous as their accounts gained widespread readership and they mounted the lecture platform to tell their stories. Others remained more obscure but left an indelible imprint on the historical record by publishing their lives. In an effort to prove their case and combat charges of fabricating the narratives, autobiographers published letters vouching for their character and attesting to the veracity of their story. They sought to "endow their stories with the appearance of authenticity." In addition, abolitionists conducted research to verify the facticity of names, incidents, dates, and general accounts. As John Sekora poses the dilemma, their authenticity has been established, but their authority remains in question.[21]

Third, the vast majority of the approximately 6,000 published autobiographies of former slaves understandably focused on slavery. They revealed the dehumanizing effects of slavery on an entire race of people. The narratives dethroned notions of "benevolent" slaveholders, exposed the experience of everyday life for slaves, and laid bare the moral inconsistencies of slaveholding in a nation purporting to advocate equality and promote Christian goodwill. This focus necessarily restricts their value for understanding everyday life in New England. However, I have identified a handful of autobiographies (14, by ex-slaves and free blacks) that detail a settled routine in the North in a way that allows their accounts to overlap in content with diaries and letters. They recount their authors' search for jobs, their treatment by neighbors, their quarrels, and some of their civic involvements. For these reasons—their attention to the particular as well as the global, their concern for community life as well as racism—the African American autobiographies are extremely valuable to this study.[22]

Few white working-class autobiographies were published in the nineteenth century, and their accounts of daily life were less abundant. But because I have numerous diaries and letters for white subjects, I minimally rely on white autobiographies.[23]

TOWN HISTORIES

To commemorate the U.S. centennial anniversary, many New England towns commissioned local histories in the late nineteenth century. The histories record the towns' evolution and divulge chatty tidbits of information about early settlers, incorporation, officeholders, local citizens, and their lore. They resemble early-nineteenth-century newspapers in tone and in their lack of discrimination between historic events, gossip, hearsay, and local news. The town histories have proved to be a rich source of information about laboring people. They are superior to county and state histories, which tend to focus largely on prominent citizens: presidents of banks, legislators, mayors, and the like. The town histories frequently tell about the common citizenry—where people lived, what they did for a living, what organizations the town hosted—and they sometimes include genealogies of local families. Authors of the town histories exhibit little distance from their subject. They do not attempt to hold in abeyance their prejudices or those of their times, and they often fail to distinguish between anecdote, myth, and "fact," leaving the accuracy of their accounts always open to question.

GENEALOGIES

A superb historical resource, genealogies map familial relationships over generations. Such relationships are critical to this study because I interpret a subject's social world differently depending, for example, on whether a visitor is a cousin or a school chum, or both. I use genealogies whenever available to chart the family tree of a subject.

Like the town histories, genealogies are not always accurate. They are often written by amateur genealogists who are interested in tracing family lineage (even many Mormon documents, world-renowned for their breadth and volume, are compiled largely by volunteers). The primary problem in using genealogies is their incompleteness, or, in too many cases, especially for African Americans, their nonexistence. They underrepresent people who move from their town of origin. In addition, genealogies trace women less reliably, in part because women change their last names upon marriage and in part because women have not been documented by genealogists with the same kind of rigor accorded to men.

1850 AND 1860 U.S. MANUSCRIPT CENSUSES

A substantial literature methodologically critiques the host of problems that plague U.S. census data. Although many flaws exist, the 1850 and 1860 U.S. Manuscript Censuses in particular have been a rich resource for this study because they list household members, their age, race, sex, the occupation of the head of household and sometimes other members, the dollar value of personal and property holdings, and the literacy status of the household. I have used these records to reconstruct the households of the subjects whenever possible.

The major problem with the census, in 1850 as in 1990, is that it is not comprehensive; it systematically underenumerates the poor and people of color. The 1850 census does not include 9% of the diarists in the study who I knew to be alive in 1850. Even when I knew someone's exact address, sometimes he or she did not appear in the census index or in the census itself. Again, this was more true of female subjects, and exponentially more so for African American subjects.[24]

PROBATE RECORDS

Wills can reveal how much property an individual owned at the time of death and who inherited it. However, many people did not leave wills, particularly if they had little or no property to leave behind, as was especially true of women. But probate records exist even for many people who died with no will and left property or children behind.

MEMORIALS

A memorial is a short biographical document written posthumously about an individual. I am using two memorials of an exceptional character: one of a domestic servant and the other about a farm laborer. These two examples are unusual because of what they reveal, because they were written about people of the laboring class, and because they have survived. As I discussed in Chapter 2, the memorial of Leonard Stockwell reveals an intimate perspective on his life, exhibiting a great deal of knowledge of and loyalty to Leonard. The other memorial, also written anonymously, is for "Betsey," a domestic servant who worked for over 60 years for an upper-middle-class family in Dorchester and Boston. The author, also probably a woman, was possibly related to Betsey's employers (a younger generation perhaps). The tone is patronizing, reflecting a sincere affection for Betsey but distanced by class position. Regardless of tone, the memorial presents a vivid picture of at least part of Betsey's life.

Diarist Information

ABBOTT, NATHAN K., 1799–1878 (diary 1832–1874). Never married. Farmer, teacher. Bow and Concord, N.H.

BALDWIN, ABIGAIL, 1797–1876 (diary 1853–1854). Married 1823. Minister's wife, farmer. Plymouth, Vt.

BARRETT, MARTHA OSBORNE, 1827–1905 (diary 1848–1879). Never married. Teacher, needleworker, machine-shop clerk. Peabody, Mass.

BARRETT, SAMANTHA, ca. 1780–1830 (diary 1815–1830). Never married. Weaver, farmer. New Hartford, Conn.

BARRETT, ZELODA, 1786–1836 (diary 1804–1831). Never married. Weaver, spinner, caretaker/nurse. New Hartford, Conn.

BEACHAM, SARAH, 1838–1909 (diary 1863–1903). Never married. Millworker, weaver. Ossipee, N.H.

BENNETT, A[RTHUR], ?–1846 (diary 1844–1846). Married 1834. Sawmill worker. Woodstock, Vt.

BENNETT, FRANCIS, JR., 1837–? (diary 1852–1854). Single. Grocery clerk. Gloucester, Mass.

BENSON, CHARLES A., 1830–1881 (diary 1862–1881). Married. Ship steward. Salem, Mass.

BERBINEAU, LORENZA (STEVENS), ca. 1806–1869 (diary 1851–1869). Married 1842. Domestic servant. Boston.

BROWN, PAMELA, 1816–? (diary 1835–1838). Single during diary period (married 1840). Teacher. Plymouth (Plymouth Notch), Vt.

BROWN, SALLY EXPERIENCE, 1807–? (diary 1832–1834). Single during diary period (married 1835). Domestic worker, teacher. Plymouth (Plymouth Notch), Vt.

CAMPBELL, JOHN, 1762–1832 (diary 1795–1832). Married 1787, widowed, remarried 1814. Farmer. Windham, N.H.

CARPENTER, EDWARD JENNER, 1825–1900 (diary 1844–1845). Single during diary period (married 1850). Cabinetmaker's apprentice. Greenfield, Mass.

CHANDLER, HORATIO NELSON, 1804–1873 (diary 1839–1842). Married 1836. Farmer, store clerk, carpenter. Chesterfield, N.H.

CHAPMAN, LOUISA ANN, 1814–1892 (diary 1848–1849). Single during diary period (married 1853). Teacher, seamstress. Ipswich, Mass.

CLAPP, DAVID, JR., 1806–1893 (diary 1820–1824). Single during diary period (married 1835). Printer's apprentice. Dorchester and Boston, Mass.

CLARK, DANIEL, 1768–1828 (diary 1789–1828). Married. Farmer, potter. Concord, N.H.

CROSSMAN, ADELAIDE (ISHAM), 1837–1892 (diary 1855–1867). Married 1855, widowed 1864, remarried 1866. Farmer, seamstress. South Sutton, Mass.

CROSSMAN, FERDINAND, 1834–1864 (diary 1855). Married 1855. Farmer, cotton-mill worker. South Sutton, Mass.

DOLOFF, MELISSA, 1839–? (diary 1858). Single, married. Teacher. Sutton, Vt.

FORBES, SUSAN E. PARSONS (BROWN), 1824–1910 (diary 1841–1908). Married 1859. Millworker, teacher, boardinghouse keeper. Epsom, N.H.

FOSTER, JOHN, 1840–1902 (diary 1856). Single during diary period (married 1866). Millworker. New Ipswich, N.H.

FOSTER, JOHN PLUMMER, 1817–1891 (diary 1848–1888). Married 1845. Farmer. North Andover, Mass.

GILBERT, PARNA, 1825–? (diary 1848–1853). Single during diary period (married 1853). Seamstress, domestic, nurse. Peru, Worthington, and Cummington, Mass.

GOODENOUGH, LIZZIE A. (WILSON), 1843–? (diary 1865–1875). Married 1869. Domestic servant, seamstress. Brattleboro, Vt.

GREEN, HARRIOTT (SMALLEY), 1805–1849 (diary 1844–1845). Married 1824. Farmer. Williamstown and Brandon, Vt.

HALL, MARY, 1806–? (diary 1821–1836). Single during diary period (married 1838). Weaver, book-folder. Lowell, Mass., and Concord, N.H.

HILL, IVORY B., 1833–? (diary 1857–1880). Married 1854. Shoemaker, farmer. West Northwood, N.H.

HOLBROOK, MARY GRACE, 1834–1913 (diary 1852–1854). Single, married. Seamstress, shoebinder, dressmaker. Oxford, Conn.

HOPKINS, MARION, 1832–? (diary 1851–1855). Single, married. Millworker, leather pieceworker. Sunapee, N.H.

JAMES, SAMUEL SHEPARD, 1820–1907 (diary 1839–1907). Married 1845. Farmer, teacher, surveyor. Northwood, N.H.

JONES, MARY GIDDINGS (COULT), 1830–1910 (diary 1851–1859). Married 1853. Teacher, seamstress. Barkhamsted, Conn.

KENT, JOHN H., ?–? (diary 1854). Blacksmith, hauler. Rowley, Mass.

KIMBALL, JOSEPH, 1798–1881 (diary 1838–1881). Married 1824, widowed 1855, remarried 1856. Carpenter, farmer. Boxford and Georgetown, Mass.

KIMBALL, WALTER LEWIS, 1825–1849 (diary 1846–1849). Never married. Carpenter (joiner). Georgetown, Mass.

LANE, JOSHUA, 1762–1829 (diary 1788–1829). Married 1788. Farmer, teacher, town surveyor. Sanbornton, N.H.

LYE, JOSEPH, 1792–1834 (diary 1817–1832). Never married. Shoemaker, laborer, fisherman. Lynn, Mass.

MASON, ALBERT, 1807–1890 (diary 1830–1889). Married. Farmer. Monroe, N.H.

MUDGE, MARY JANE, 1830–? (diary 1854). Single during diary period (married 1856). Teacher. Lynn, Mass.

NIMS, BRIGHAM, 1811–1893 (diary 1840–1888). Married 1853. Farmer, teacher, blacksmith, tailor. Roxbury, N.H.

PARKS, VESTUS HALEY, 1805–1889 (diary 1827–1829). Single during diary period (married 1831). Gunpowder-mill worker, peddler of tin and rags. Russell, Mass.

PORTER, ALFRED, 1826–1864 (diary 1854–1856). Never married. Shoemaker, farmer, mariner. Danvers, Mass.

ROBINSON, PERLEY CARR, 1801–? (diary 1849). Married. Farmer, tailor. Poplin, N.H.

ROOT, SARAH, 1820–? (diary 1859–1864). Married 1838. Boardinghouse keeper. Belchertown, Mass.

SANBORN, EZRA, 1820–1892 (diary 1861–1878). Married 1851. Farmer, shoemaker. Contoocook, N.H.

SEVERANCE, HARRIET ANNE, 1838–? (diary 1862–1866). Single. Domestic, nurse, hoop-skirt factory worker. Northampton and Leyden, Mass.

SMITH, DAVID T., 1803–? (diary 1832–1860). Married 1833. Carpenter, farmer. Rowley, Mass.

STODDARD, ANN JULIA, ?–? (diary 1866). Single. Teacher, domestic servant. Lyndon and Sutton (North Ridge), Vt.

TAFT, NANCY, 1809–1843 (diary 1838). Single. Teacher. Barre, Vt.

TILTON, POLLIE (CATHCART), 1805–? (diary 1839–1860). Single during diary period (married 1860). Domestic, nurse. Goshen and Williamsburg, Mass.

TRASK, SARAH, 1828–1892 (diary 1849–1851). Never married. Shoebinder. Beverly, Mass.

UNKNOWN AUTHOR, ?–? (diary 1859). Married. Farmer. Newburyport, Mass.

WEYMOUTH, JAMES S., 1819–1912 (diary 1850–1869). Married 1843. Farmer, teacher. Belmont, N.H.

WHIPPLE, GEORGE S., 1822–? (diary 1838). Single. Store clerk. Newburyport, Mass.

WILLIAMS, PAULINA (BASCOM), 1803–1843 (diary 1830–1833). Married 1827. Wife of itinerant minister. West Haven, Orwell, and Tinmouth, Vt.

Abbreviations

AAS	American Antiquarian Society. Worcester, Mass.
BHSM	Beverly Historical Society and Museum. Beverly, Mass.
BPL	Boston Public Library. Boston.
CHS	Connecticut Historical Society. Hartford.
CSL	Connecticut State Library. Hartford.
HSCC	Historical Society of Cheshire County. Keene, N.H.
JDPL	James Duncan Phillips Library. Peabody & Essex Museum, Salem, Mass.
LHS	Lynn Historical Society. Lynn, Mass.
MANHS	Manchester Historical Society. Manchester, N.H.
MATH	Museum of American Textile History. North Andover, Mass.
MHA	Manchester Historical Association. Manchester, N.H.
MHS	Massachusetts Historical Society. Boston.
NHHS	New Hampshire Historical Society. Concord.
NHSA	New Hampshire State Archives. Concord.
OSVL	Old Sturbridge Village Library. Sturbridge, Mass.
PC	Private collection.
PHS	Peabody Historical Society. Peabody, Mass.
PVMAL	Pocumtuck Valley Memorial Association Library. Deerfield, Mass.
SL	Schlesinger Library. Radcliffe College, Cambridge, Mass.
SSC	Sophia Smith Collection. Smith College Library, Northampton, Mass.
VHS	Vermont Historical Society. Montpelier.
WHS	Waterville Historical Society. Waterville, Me.

Notes

1. MAKING THE SOCIAL CENTRAL

1. Elizabeth H. Metcalf to Chloe Metcalf, Metcalf-Adams Family Letters, 22 October 1851. While some historians have found similar complexity in the early nineteenth century (e.g., Laurel Ulrich, *A Midwife's Tale*) and mid-nineteenth century (e.g., Christine Stansell, *City of Women*), the theoretical framing of the period does not reflect their findings.

2. Minerva Mayo Autobiography, 1 January 1820.

3. Property holdings discussed here are as reported in the 1850 manuscript census. I was able to identify the census records of all but 9% of the diarists I knew to be still alive and living in New England in 1850. See Appendix B.

The mean property valuation of $978 (the median is $800) is consistent with Thomas Dublin's computations in *Women at Work*, his study of the social origins of female textile operatives. Dublin found that the median property holdings of millhands' fathers in 1850 was $960, slightly less than the median of $998 owned by other male heads of households of similar ages in the towns and villages where the fathers lived (p. 35). As another point of comparison, the average farm in Massachusetts in 1850 was worth $3,296 and included 99 acres (DeBow, *Statistical View of the United States, Seventh Census, 1850*, p. 169).

The reliability of the federal census is a subject of great dispute. But census data, despite limitations and distortions, have proven valuable, along with town histories, vital records, genealogies, and probate records, in supplementing the base of evidence for this book. Censuses before 1850 did not record property holdings and did not enumerate the names of household members.

The "winds of circumstance" quotation is from the Leonard M. Stockwell Memorial, ca. 1880, p. 5.

4. Martha Osborne Barrett Diary, 25 August 1854, 8 January 1853.

5. I elaborate the problems with this formulation below, in the section of this chapter dealing with "Middle-Class Ideology and Separate Spheres."

6. Martha Osborne Barrett Diary, 8 January 1853; Doug McAdam, "Gender Implications of the Traditional Academic Conception of the Political," p. 61.

7. For example, Clarke E. Cochran, *Religion in Public and Private Life*; Jean Bethke Elshtain, *Public Man, Private Woman*; Jürgen Habermas, *The Structural Transformation of the Public Sphere*; Barrington Moore Jr., *Privacy*; Linda J. Nicholson, *Gender and History*; Carole Pateman, "Feminist Critiques of the Public/Private Dichotomy"; Hanna Fenichel Pitkin, "Justice: On Relating Private and Public"; Rayna R. Reiter, "Men and Women in the South of France: Public and Private Domains"; Michelle Zimbalist Rosaldo, "Woman, Culture and Society"; Mary P. Ryan, *Women in Public*; Richard Sennett, *The Fall of Public Man*; Dorothy Smith, "Women, the Family, and Corporate Capitalism"; Susan Okin, *Justice, Gender, and the Family*; Patricia Hill Collins, *Black Feminist Thought*; Bell Hooks, *Feminist Theory: From Margin to Center*; Nancy Fraser, "Rethinking the Public Sphere"; Joan Wallach Scott, *Gender and the Politics of History*; and Chris Weedon, *Feminist Practice and Poststructuralist Theory*.

8. Brigham Nims Diary, 30 April 1845. My thanks to Susan Ostrander for bringing the W. I. Thomas parallel to my attention. For example, Lizzie Good-enough wrote in her diary: "Mr. Howe has gone to town meeting today. It has been very still about the place. Not a man on the farm this afternoon" (7 March 1865). In contrast, the account in Sarah Beacham's diary does not specify what genders participated in the meeting: "Town meeting rages so that we don't work in the mills" (10 March 1863).

9. For a contemporary overview of these debates, see Jean L. Cohen and Andrew Arato, *Civil Society and Political Theory*. Some scholars have characterized behavior that does not fit neatly into either sphere as occurring in an "intermediate realm," a "third place," or a "free space." See, for example, Ray Oldenberg, *The Great Good Place: Cafes, Coffee Shops, Community Centers, Beauty Parlors, General Stores, Bars, Hangouts, and How They Get You Through the Day* (New York: Paragon House, 1989). In Oldenberg's romanticized vision, cafes, beauty parlors, and the like serve a central integrative function in society. Similarly, Harry C. Boyte and Sara M. Evans identify "free spaces" for conversation and political organizing (*Free Spaces: The Sources of Democratic Change in America*).

Other observers consider everyday social intercourse a marginal activity in society, relegated to an inconsequential realm between public and private. Alan Wolfe has criticized this perspective in his discussion of the decline of sociology. He says that with the ascendance of economics and political science, scholars increasingly assume that either the market or the state organizes social relations. In fact, an independent type of interaction transpires among people in groups and communities, outside the market or the state (*Whose Keeper? Social Science and Moral Obligation*, p. 20). Wolfe makes a distinction between the state, the market, and what he calls civil society or "the intimate sphere," the realm that includes family life. He optimistically assesses the capacity of civil society, which he sees as mediating between individualism and collectivism, between culture and the market, though he recognizes that civil society is not a premodern organic community and that it operates under principles of exclusion as well as inclusion: "Even when relations in civil society are based on reciprocity and altruism, they can satisfy obligations to immediate group members to the exclusion of obligations to strangers and hypothetical others" (p. 18).

10. A similar argument is made by Nancy F. Cott regarding women's sphere in the early republic and the preconditions for the women's rights movement. In *Bonds of Womanhood*, she claims that the separation of men from women cultivated a "unique sexual solidarity" that feminism built upon when organizing for social change (p. 201).

My use of the term *the social* contrasts sharply with Hannah Arendt's. Her basic referent for "society" is the salon of turn-of-the-nineteenth-century Germany. She views high society as corrupting and characterized by a menacing imperative to conform, extinguishing the distinctiveness and initiative which characterize the public: "Society expects from each of its members a certain kind of behavior, imposing innumerable and various rules, all of which tend to 'normalize' its members, to make them behave, to exclude spontaneous action or outstanding achievement" (*The Human Condition*, p. 40).

Arendt maintains that although the important separation between social and public sometimes blurs, the social must be shunted aside for public space to emerge. She sees the social as erasing individuality, the essence of which is necessary for the public to thrive. While she analytically distinguishes the social, she disdains the banal activities that constitute its center. In her privileging of political action, she argues that the concerns of everyday life—social equality and labor, "mindless, routinized, and repetitious"—should not preoccupy noble individuals or governments because they fail to elevate human beings above their animal origins.

Arendt sees the social encroaching upon and subsuming both the public and the private, ultimately to the detriment of both. For Arendt, the social embodies the economic in addition to other things, miring it in everyday life-maintenance activities that "are by definition opposed to freedom and the capacity for action" (Pitkin, "Justice," p. 334). Therefore, in her scheme, the social and the political work in direct opposition to one another. As Bhikhu Parekh puts it, for Arendt, "civic consciousness is not the basis but the product of political consciousness" (*Hannah Arendt and the Search for a New Political Philosophy*, p. 136).

11. Mary P. Ryan, *Cradle of the Middle Class*, p. 154. There are many competing conceptions of the private, as with civil society and the public. In a useful taxonomy, in "The Theory and Politics of the Public/Private Distinction," Jeff Weintraub looks at four general theoretical perspectives that define *private* variously as the market economy (liberal economic approaches), the household (Aristotle's conception), the family (Marxist feminism), or domesticity (Aries's approach).

12. I do not mean to imply that the state is not social in a larger sense, because it is. Again, there are many alternative conceptions of the state. For example, Weintraub (ibid.) points to the parallel definitions of public as government (liberal economic); political community (Aristotle); the economy (Marxist feminism); and sociability (Aries). For Fraser, a public is decidedly "not the state; it is rather the informally mobilized body of nongovernmental discursive

opinion that can serve as a counterweight to the state" (Fraser, "Rethinking the Public Sphere," p. 75). Rather than conceive of one overarching public, Fraser contends that "an egalitarian, multi-cultural society only makes sense if we suppose a plurality of public arenas in which groups with diverse values and rhetorics participate" (p. 69). Thus the public sphere is a place to negotiate cultural and political difference.

13. Paula Baker, "The Domestication of Politics," p. 622. Feminists have consistently made this point throughout the second wave of feminism. Baker's definition locates politics in attempts to change social structures, and as such falls between an extremely broad conception, such as that of Joan Scott, and a more traditional conception of politics. Scott defines politics as "the process by which plays of power and knowledge constitute identity and experience" (*Gender and the Politics of History*, p. 5). In contrast, McAdam defines politics as "something that takes place in public domains between officially recognized political actors" ("Gender Implications of the Traditional Academic Conception of the Political," p. 61). Activities can also be spiritualized or, as Fraser points out, personalized, familialized, economized, or none of the above (Fraser, "Rethinking the Public Sphere").

14. See Jane Mansbridge, *Beyond Adversary Democracy*, for a discussion of the political processes that occur outside formal political events.

15. Ostrander, "Feminism, Voluntarism, and the Welfare State," p. 34; Ryan, *Cradle of the Middle Class*.

16. There were sister organizations in other cities, but this particular example relates to the New York City chapter. Carroll Smith-Rosenberg, "Beauty, the Beast, and the Militant Woman: A Case Study in Sex Roles and Social Stress in Jacksonian America," in *Disorderly Conduct: Visions of Gender in Victorian America*, p. 110. For moral reform activities in upstate New York, see Mary P. Ryan, "The Power of Women's Networks: A Case Study of Female Moral Reform in Antebellum America." For further discussion of women's activism outside the home in defense of it, which has again become a pattern of the contemporary debate on the role of women in families and society, see especially research on moral reform, Smith-Rosenberg, "Beauty, the Beast and the Militant Woman"; on religious movements, Ryan, *Cradle of the Middle Class*; and on suffrage activities, Ellen Carol DuBois, *Feminism and Suffrage*.

17. Smith-Rosenberg, "Beauty, the Beast, and the Militant Woman," p. 117.

18. Leon F. Litwack, *Been in the Storm So Long: The Aftermath of Slavery*, p. 267. Leonard P. Curry, *The Free Black in Urban America, 1800–1850*, ch. 6. William J. Brown, *The Life of William J. Brown*, p. 126.

19. It is interesting that the British transition to capitalism did not involve the same process. *Families*, not individual workers, entered the textile factories. So while work and home separated, work and family did not, at least until later. See Neil J. Smelser, *Social Change in the Industrial Revolution*; U.S. Bureau of the Census, *Historical Statistics of the U.S., Colonial Times to 1970*. Nancy Cott uses the term "employments" in *Bonds of Womanhood*, her study of late-eighteenth- and early-nineteenth-century America. On millworkers manipulating their work environment, see Dublin, *Women at Work*.

20. Richard M. Bernard and Maris A. Vinovskis, "The Female School Teacher in Ante-Bellum Massachusetts," p. 333.

21. In the United States, women became the first industrial proletariat. Alice Kessler-Harris states that women constituted 65% of New England's industrial labor force in 1840. *Out to Work: A History of Wage-Earning Women in the United States*, p. 48. Thomas Dublin finds that in 1836 women constituted more than 85% of the work force in the Hamilton Company mills in Lowell, Massachusetts (*Women at Work*, p. 26). Dublin finds that textile mill operatives energetically approached their factory work and set limits on their family obligations. The corporate planners in Lowell instituted a scheme to ensure the virtue (i.e., virginity) of its factory workers and to reassure millgirls' families of their safety. Their explicit intent was to control the young women's behavior. They established a boardinghouse system in Lowell whereby most single workers lived in the company boardinghouses under the jurisdiction of a company-employed housekeeper. The boardinghouses had strict rules for boarders (for example, a 10 P.M. curfew and mandatory attendance at church on Sunday). The boardinghousekeepers, who were touted as "surrogate parents," enforced the rules. They reinforced this system of control by keeping company blacklists of those who "misbehaved" morally or politically. For a full discussion, see Dublin, *Women at Work*, ch. 5.

22. Curry writes that "only in Boston, of the nation's fifteen largest cities, were free blacks entitled to vote on equal terms throughout the first half of the nineteenth century" (*The Free Black in Urban America*, p. 88). Leon F. Litwack writes that by 1840, "only in Massachusetts, New Hampshire, Vermont, and Maine could Negroes vote on an equal basis with whites" (*North of Slavery: The Negro in the Free States, 1790–1860*, p. 75), but he points out that racist actions in New England attempted to keep black voters from the polls (p. 92). John Hope Franklin, "Quasi-Free," *Stanford Lawyer* (Spring/Summer 1989): 47. The Fugitive Slave Law basically allowed charges that an African American was an escaped slave even if no proof was available. According to Herbert Aptheker, African Americans were no longer guaranteed a trial by jury, confrontation with witnesses, or the assumption of innocence (*Abolitionism: A Revolutionary Movement*, p. 115). This situation left all blacks vulnerable to false identification, and many rightfully "feared that the provisions of the act would be used to cloak extensive kidnaping of free blacks" (Curry, *The Free Black in Urban America*, p. 229). For an example of the response to the act, see Leonard W. Levy, "Sims Case: The Fugitive Slave Law in Boston in 1851." Ellen Carol DuBois, ed., *Elizabeth Cady Stanton, Susan B. Anthony: Correspondence, Writings, Speeches*; Marylynn Salmon, *Women and the Law of Property in Early America*; Elizabeth Bowles Warbasse, *The Changing Legal Rights of Married Women, 1800–1861*.

23. Barbara Welter, "The Cult of True Womanhood: 1820–1860," p. 152; Mary P. Ryan, *The Empire of the Mother: American Writing about Domesticity, 1830–1860*; and Kathryn Kish Sklar, *Catharine Beecher: A Study in American Domesticity*.

24. Welter, "Cult of True Womanhood," p. 159. Cited in Lee Virginia

Chambers-Schiller, *Liberty, A Better Husband; Single Women in America: The Generations of 1780–1840*, p. 37. Ronald Preston Byars, *The Making of the Self-Made Man: The Development of Masculine Roles and Images in Antebellum America*, p. 197; E. Anthony Rotundo, "Romantic Friendship: Male Intimacy and Middle-Class Youth in the Northern United States, 1800–1900," p. 18; Byars, *The Making of the Self-Made Man*, pp. 36, 143–44; E. Anthony Rotundo, *American Manhood: Transformations in Masculinity from the Revolution to the Modern Era* (New York: Basic Books, 1993), p. 105.

25. Gerda Lerner, "The Lady and the Mill Girl: Changes in the Status of Women in the Age of Jackson, 1800–1840," pp. 192–93, 190–91.

26. Ryan, *Empire of Mother*.

27. Karen Halttunen, *Confidence Men and Painted Women: A Study of Middle-Class Culture in America, 1830–1870*, p. 59.

28. Carl N. Degler, *At Odds: Women and the Family in America from the Revolution to the Present*; Karen Sacks, "Engels Revisited: Women, the Organization of Production, and Private Property," in *Toward an Anthropology of Women*, ed. Rayna R. Reiter (New York: Monthly Review Press, 1975), pp. 211–34; Cott, *Bonds of Womanhood*; Halttunen, *Confidence Men and Painted Women*; and Smith-Rosenberg, *Disorderly Conduct*. Cott maintains that the distinct female culture provided fertile ground to nourish the early women's rights movement. Lise Vogel argues that this vein of feminist scholarship achieved hegemony in women's studies in the late 1970s through the 1980s, to the exclusion and retrospective erasure of competing perspectives that were informed by analytic categories such as class, racial difference, and exploitation ("Telling Tales: Historians of Our Own Lives").

29. John Mack Faragher, *Women and Men on the Overland Trail*; Nancy Grey Osterud, "'She Helped Me Hay It as Good as a Man': Relations among Women and Men in an Agricultural Community," pp. 89, 91–92.

30. C. Dallett Hemphill, "'There is No Society Otherwise': Men, Women, and Manners in Antebellum America," and Laura McCall, "Gender in Fiction: The Creations of Literary Men and Women," both papers presented at the Social Science History Association Meetings, New Orleans, Louisiana, October, 1991. Also see C. Dallett Hemphill, *Manners for Americans: Interaction Ritual and the Social Order, 1620–1860* (Ph.D. diss., Brandeis University, 1987). Ryan, *Cradle of the Middle Class*, p. 191.

31. Linda K. Kerber, Nancy F. Cott, Robert Gross, Lynn Hunt, Carroll Smith-Rosenberg, Christine M. Stansell, "Beyond Roles, Beyond Spheres: Thinking about Gender in the Early Republic," pp. 566, 565, 568.

32. For example, Mary Blewett found that when married women in the New England shoe industry had the option to stop working, they did: "In developing and living the dual model of working girl and homebound wife, working women actively helped to create a sense of proper gender relationships within the new economic system and redefined the ideology of early nineteenth-century domesticity in accordance with their own class experience" ("Women Shoeworkers and Domestic Ideology: Rural Outwork in Early Nineteenth Century Essex County"). In contrast, Mary Ryan in *Cradle of the Middle Class* questions the degree to which notions of true womanhood affected even middle-class white

women. In addition, the growing population of single white middle-class women developed a competing ideology of their own, the "Cult of Single Blessedness," according to Chambers-Schiller. This cultural ideal recommended that women expand their intellectual horizons, develop self-knowledge, cultivate their autonomy, and dedicate their lives to public service. Women's domestic role was rejected, in favor of independence and vocational accomplishment. *Liberty, a Better Husband*, pp. 206–7.

33. Hazel V. Carby, *Reconstructing Womanhood: The Emergence of the Afro-American Woman Novelist*, p. 30. Collins, *Black Feminist Thought*; Angela Y. Davis, *Women, Race, and Class*; Paula Giddings, *When and Where I Enter: The Impact of Black Women on Race and Sex in America*; and Bell Hooks, *Feminist Theory*.

34. Lerner, "The Lady and the Mill Girl," p. 191; Marjorie Ruzich Abel, "Profiles of Nineteenth Century Working Women"; Blewett, "Women Shoeworkers and Domestic Ideology"; Lise Vogel, "'Humorous Incidents and Sound Common Sense': More on the New England Mill Women," p. 282.

35. JoAnne Preston, "Millgirl Narratives: Representations of Class and Gender in Nineteenth-Century Lowell," p. 21; Adaline Shaw to Daniel Shaw, Esq., SSC, 28 May 1848.

36. First and foremost, for the workers as well as the factory owners, this image had to combat that of the English textile workers, who were universally seen as a downtrodden, oppressed group. *The Lowell Offering* was supported and partially financed by the factory owners, and its message must be read with that in mind. Preston, "Millgirl Narratives," p. 25. As Preston puts it (p. 28), "In their writings, the women created a view of themselves which defied the negative conception of the industrial worker and the restrictive ideology of the lady."

37. JoAnne Preston, "Female Aspiration and Male Ideology: School-Teaching in Nineteenth-Century New England."

38. Sarah Trask Diary, 3 April 1849, emphasis added. Martha Osborne Barrett Diary, July 1854. The poem was titled "Woman's Duties" (ibid., 4 December 1858). For further discussion of "old maids," see Preston, "Millgirl Narratives," and Chambers-Schiller, *Liberty, a Better Husband*.

39. Hannah T., Mary, and Margaret Adams to Mother, 23 March 1842, Adams Family Papers.

40. Historically, observers of society have consistently witnessed a division of labor based on gender. That said, the specific tasks performed by and deemed appropriate for men and women have varied by culture, historical period, and circumstance. Furthermore, scholars have cited times of labor shortage, such as planting or harvest, as moments when traditions could be abandoned. In her review of American household work practices over two centuries, Ruth Schwartz Cowan notes that both men and women sewed, but they sewed different items. If the fabric was leather, for instance, it became the man's task. While men supposedly performed chores that required great strength, women washed clothes and made soap, which demanded enormous physical stamina (*More Work for Mother: The Ironies of Household Technology from the Open Hearth to the Microwave*).

John Mack Faragher, in *Women and Men on the Overland Trail*, finds that midwestern farms in the mid-nineteenth century had a fairly rigid division of labor, with little overlap between men's and women's work. However, the situation he researches is one of extreme hardship, and given the need for maximum adaptability on the frontier, the rigid rules he describes regarding the division of labor are not adequately explained. In contrast, Osterud finds that while men and women were responsible for specific tasks in Nanticoke Valley, New York, the division of labor was flexible depending on a combination of choice and necessity ("'She Helped Me Hay It as Good as a Man,'" pp. 87–97).

41. Elizabeth Metcalf to Chloe Metcalf, 15 June 1857, Metcalf-Adams Family Letters (emphasis in original); Unknown Woman Diary (ms. #86), 30 May 1859; Horatio Chandler Diary, 22 June 1840; John Plummer Foster Diary, 10 January 1859. The machine must have been quite rudimentary. But new technologies have often marked turning points in the division of labor in the factory—why not in the household? Thereafter, in the Foster household washing on Monday seemed to be John's job. Brigham Nims Diary, 12 August 1853 and 29 August 1843.

42. Only a few men performed these chores routinely. The work continued to be largely women's work, which points the analysis to a gendered division of labor but not a strict culture of separate spheres.

43. Nancy Grey Osterud, *Bonds of Community: The Lives of Farm Women in Nineteenth-Century New York*.

2. "I NEVER FORGET WHAT I REMEMBER"

1. For assessment of current issues within historical sociology, see Andrew Abbott, "History and Sociology: The Lost Synthesis," and Charles Tilly, *Big Structures, Large Processes, Huge Comparisons*.

2. I begin this comparison with the hypothesis that the working people's practices differed from those of the middle class. I expect this was more true in the urban context than in the rural, where citizens of all ranks mingled with greater familiarity and shared culture. In small towns and villages of New England up through the 1840s, the vast majority of people were white, spoke English as their first language, belonged to Protestant churches, attended the same elementary schools, and assumed the rights and entitlements that accompanied U.S. citizenship. In these environments, middle-class people mingled more extensively with working men and women than in cities. For a discussion of this point for a slightly later period, see John Meyer, David Tyack, Joane Nagel and Audri Gordon, "Public Education as Nation-Building in America: Enrollments and Bureaucratization in the American States, 1870–1930."

3. DeBow, *Seventh Census, 1850*, pp. 2–77. Free blacks constituted a somewhat higher proportion of the population of some cities: 1.46% in Boston and 3.61% in Providence, Rhode Island. Curry, *The Free Black in Urban America*, p. 246.

4. Many scholars would comfortably describe my subjects as the "middling sort." For example, Cott makes the distinction between middle-class and upper-

middle-class women in her sample of diarists. About the subjects in the middle-class group she says: "Those women worked. While unmarried, they engaged in school teaching, domestic work, handicraft and industrial labor" (*Bonds of Womanhood*, p. 9). In my opinion, not differentiating between domestic workers and women who work in the household as wives of professional men is a grave mistake. For example, one of the diarists studied by Cott is Paulina Bascom Williams, whom Cott appears to include among her middle-class subjects. But Williams, though married to a minister, was anything but comfortably situated; she wrote about her lack of decent clothing and many hardships she and her family endured. On December 6, 1831, she reported on her arrival at a recently built parsonage: "We have no cow & are out of provisions of every kind, & now whether it is our duty to stay in such a place after such indignity without cause or provocation is a doubt that remains to be solved. Would the Saviour have tarried with disciples that treated him thus! I certainly need a great measure of grace that my mouth may not utter perverseness."

For a discussion of the inadequacies of these attempts to conceptualize class, see Michael B. Katz, "Social Class in North American Urban History." Marx's categories of working class and petit bourgeoisie seem too narrow and inflexible to describe the weavers and farmers of this study, and C. Wright Mills's "old middle class" insufficiently discriminates between those who had to labor by their own hands in order to make a living and those who did not. In his influential *Chants Democratic*, Sean Wilentz argues that definitions and categories of class are too economically deterministic, making them fixed, flat, insensitive to historical specificity, and lacking in explanatory power (p. 7). Wilentz therefore proposes that we study the emergence of the working class as a process, constructed through human relationships, "part of a human achievement in which men and women struggle to comprehend the social relations into which they were born (or entered involuntarily) and in which, by the collective exercise of power, they sustain or challenge those relations, in every phase of social life" (p. 10). But Wilentz's proposed method, despite its compelling logic, is difficult to replicate with my subjects. How does one understand the "human achievements" of a domestic worker who left to posterity nothing but a record of her daily activities? While her struggle to survive painfully surfaces and she may have clashed with her employer, she did not document her conflict with a "capitalist class." Nor did she engage in the "collective exercise of power." Where did this place her in the class structure? Where did she place herself? Ira Katznelson poses an alternative that does not require choosing between location in the class structure and self-definition as a member of a particular class ("Working-Class Formation: Constructing Cases and Comparisons," pp. 3–41). These issues reveal the difficulty of applying class categories to individuals as opposed to aggregates of people.

Another complication results from attempting to analytically place farmers, especially poor farmers who owned their own land. The fate of farmers was intertwined with that of workers, as evidenced in legislation (the lot of workers was most likely to improve when a coalition of the two groups supported a campaign) and individual consciousness (witness organizations such as the

"Committee of Farmers, Mechanics, and Other Working Men"). See Amy Bridges, "Becoming American: The Working Classes in the United States Before the Civil War," pp. 157–196.

5. I attempted to assess an individual's class status and available resources at the stage of his or her life as close as possible to the time of the diary-keeping or other writing. An example illustrates the importance of timing: David Clapp wrote his diary while he was a printer's apprentice in the 1820s. He later became a successful printer in Boston. His father owned three acres of land in Dorchester, which David inherited. By 1850, he owned $5,000 of property, enough to have excluded him from my study. But as a boy from the ages of fourteen to seventeen who was struggling to learn a trade and uncertain about his future, he fit my definition of a working person in the 1820s. I decided to include him in the study.

6. Laurel Thatcher Ulrich, *Good Wives: Image and Reality in the Lives of Women in Northern New England, 1650–1750*, p. 72. For a discussion of the changes in dress and the rancor they provoked, see Christine Stansell, *City of Women: Sex and Class in New York, 1789–1860*. Joan Acker forcefully argues that this is grounds for reconsidering the elements of a useful conception of class: "In order to strengthen the theoretical links between gender and class, the conceptualization of the social relations that underlie class divisions must be changed. One way to do this is to see class as rooted in relations of distribution (as well as in relations of production) that necessarily embed gender, both as ideology and material inequality" ("Class, Gender, and the Relations of Distribution," p. 496). She says that in this way state transfer payments and the shared resources of a family wage are taken into account, as well as an individual's wages. However, she says that "the primary aim of class analysis is not to define bounded categories into which people fit, but to comprehend class formation" (p. 496). While I respect her intent, my object here is to locate individuals within the class system.

7. A decade later Brigham's and Mary's fortunes dramatically diverged. Mary married Philip Bryant, a cordwainer, in 1856 and continued to teach school. The 1860 census lists Philip as owning $1,500 worth of personal property and real estate. In 1853 Brigham married Susan Selina Gould and by 1860 had two children. His economic fortunes skyrocketed, and by 1860 he owned $5,500 worth of property, which included a building on Main Street in Keene, New Hampshire.

8. By 1840, free black property holders had the right to vote in Massachusetts, Maine, New Hampshire, and Vermont. They could vote in Rhode Island after 1842. Connecticut at one time allowed free blacks to vote, then revoked the right but did not reinstate it until 1869. Leon Litwack, *North of Slavery*, pp. 75, 80, and 92. Prior to the Civil War, African Americans were admitted as jurors only in Massachusetts (and then beginning only in 1860) (p. 94). However, Massachusetts prohibited interracial marriage until 1843, as did Rhode Island (pp. 105–6).

Brown, *The Life of William J. Brown*: "I could readily see that the people were determined not to instruct colored people in any art" (p. 102); "I soon found it was on account of my color, for no colored men except barbers had trades, and that could hardly be called a trade. The white people seemed to be combined against giving us any thing to do which would elevate us to a free and independent position" (p. 103). Willard B. Gatewood is quick to point out that some blacks in the African-American community had more status than others (*Aristocrats of Color: The Black Elite, 1880–1920*). In a table of the class structure of African Americans in mid-nineteenth-century Boston, James Oliver Horton and Lois E. Horton identify the professional class as including doctors, lawyers, ministers, music teachers, and schoolteachers (*Black Bostonians: Family Life and Community Struggle in the Antebellum North*, p. 129). In terms of stratification within the black community, this classification might make sense, but in terms of the type of work and the income level relative to the white community, it does not. Charlotte Forten Grimke kept an elaborate journal off and on between 1854 and 1892. But because she came from an affluent and politically influential African-American family in Philadelphia, it would have been inappropriate for me to include her in this study. See Brenda Stevenson, ed., *The Journals of Charlotte Forten Grimke* (New York: Oxford University Press, 1988). James L. Smith, *Autobiography of James L. Smith*, p. 192.

9. This was not categorically true. Particularly with the onset of the Civil War, men and women became more involved in politics, battlefield body counts, the draft, and presidential politics. That said, their everyday lives remained relatively unchanged.

10. As Victoria Bonnell points out, historical sources need cross-examination to ensure accuracy and authenticity—particularly large concerns in a historical study such as this one where evidence is generated from the vantage point of individuals who had no reason to be neutral. For a wonderful methodological discussion of the light these biases can shed, see Virginia Bernhard, "Cotton Mather's 'Most Unhappy Wife': Reflections on the Uses of Historical Evidence."

11. Leonard Stockwell Memorial, pp. 29–30.

12. In the 1840s, New England states began passing Married Women's Property Act legislation. These acts enabled women to own property independently after marrying, to own the wages they earned, to sue, to contract, and to write wills. For detailed information, see Warbasse, *The Changing Legal Rights of Married Women*, and Salmon, *Women and the Law of Property in Early America*.

13. The will specified that Leonard's money should be put in a trust, paying only the interest to Leonard, and that after Leonard's death the principal should be distributed among his children, or brothers and sisters if he had no offspring. Will of Enoch Stockwell, no. 56270, Worcester County Probate Court Records, signed 28 November 1833.

14. Mills, *The Sociological Imagination*, p. 143. See the discussion about interpretation of women's life stories in Personal Narratives Group, "Origins," pp. 3–15.

15. Martha Osborne Barrett Diary, 1 February 1852.

16. Ibid., 22 October 1854. Martha's mother, Gertrude Barrett, is listed as the head of household in the 1850 census, owning $700 worth of real estate and personal property.

17. Ibid., 1 February 1852. Martha Osborne Barrett, volume of poetry, 1854 or 1855.

18. Martha Osborne Barrett, "Paper Read before the Ladies' Unitarian Association, PHS, 28 October 1892; "Order of Services on the Fiftieth Anniversary of the Dedication of the First Unitarian Church, Peabody, Mass.," PHS, 26 July 1876; obituary, *Salem News*, 16 October 1905.

19. Louisa Chapman Diary, 3 February 1848.

20. *Report of the School Committee of the Town of Danvers, 1848–49*, p. 23.

21. Sarah Trask Diary, 7 May 1849.

22. Joshua Trask, her brother, is listed as the head of household in the 1850 census, and as owning $800 worth of property. Neither Sarah nor her mother are listed as having independent resources.

23. Sarah Trask Diary, vol. 2, p. 54. For an excellent exploration of Sarah's diary and family history, see Mary H. Blewett, "'I am Doom to Disapointment': The Diaries of a Beverly, Massachusetts, Shoebinder, Sarah E. Trask, 1849–51."

24. Pollie Cathcart Tilton Diary, 11 July 1859.

25. Brigham Nims to Susan Selina Gould, Roxbury Town Records, NHSA, 1 August 1853, emphasis in the original.

26. Nims Obituary, June 5, 1893, Nims Family Association. It is important to keep in mind that his prominence was limited to a remote area of New Hampshire with a population of less than three hundred.

27. Brigham Nims to family, HSCC, 17 October 1832.

28. The South Boston Broadway Church was an Orthodox Congregational church. They were married by a female minister, Joy H. Fairchild. The 1840 census reveals Beal and family to be living in Groton, Massachusetts. Vital records do not reveal his whereabouts or his death. In 1848, Sarah Jane Beal married Charles S. Travers of Gardner, Massachusetts. In 1851, Sarah Jane Travers petitioned the court to transfer guardianship of her son to Abel Thurston of Fitchburg, due to feeble health. It is not clear why her new husband could not help care for him. Shortly thereafter Nathaniel Day became young Foster's new guardian; the court records no reason why Abel Thurston terminated his duties.

29. Addie Brown to Rebecca Primus, Primus Family Papers, 25 June 1861.

30. Ibid., 22 July 1861; March 1862.

31. Ibid., 30 August 1859.

32. Ibid., 16 November 1865.

33. Ibid., 24 May 1861.

34. Metcalf-Adams Family Papers: Charles Metcalf to Chloe Metcalf, 10 July 1844; Elizabeth Metcalf to Chloe Metcalf, 23 January 1848.

35. Ibid., Sarah Metcalf to Chloe Metcalf, 28 March 1844, 25 September 1846, 31 May 1849.

36. Ibid., Mary Metcalf to Chloe Metcalf, file III.19, n.d.

37. JoAnne Preston, "Learning a Trade in Industrializing New England: The Expedition of Hannah and Mary Adams to Nashua, New Hampshire, 1833–1834."

38. Adams Family Papers: Hannah Adams to Mother and Father, 14 November 1841; Hannah, Mary, and Margaret Adams to Mother, 23 n.m. 1842.

39. Ibid., Eliza Adams to Brothers and Sisters, 26 November 1860.

40. Anne Abbott Parker to Rhoda Parker, Rhoda Parker Smith Correspondence, 17 November 1842, emphasis in original.

41. Mary Chandler Lowell, *Old Foxcroft, Maine, Traditions and Memories*, p. 152.

42. Ibid.

43. Ibid., p. 180. Sarah Holmes Clark to Sarah Carter, Holmes Family Papers, 17 September 1855.

3. "UNBOSOM YOUR HEART"

1. Susan E. Parsons Brown Forbes Diary, 16 February 1841; Smith-Rosenberg, *Disorderly Conduct*; Cott, *Bonds of Womanhood*. Other studies have found similar evidence of intense romance in friendships between middle- and upper-class women and inklings of it in the working class. Louise Berkinow, *Among Women* (New York: Harmony, 1980); Chambers-Schiller, *Liberty, A Better Husband*; Lillian Faderman, *Surpassing the Love of Men: Romantic Friendship and Love between Women from the Renaissance to the Present*; Jean Strouse, *Alice James: A Biography* (Boston: Houghton Mifflin, 1980). And for working-class friendship and solidarity, see Thomas Dublin, *Women at Work*, n. 48, pp. 262–63. Dublin's study of New England millworkers demonstrates that women who left farms to work in the factories also lived largely in female worlds because of the gender segregation of textile factories and boardinghouses.

2. "Informal relationships are not social luxuries, as they are sometimes portrayed, but are quite central in the organization of social life" (Graham Allan, *Friendship: Developing a Sociological Perspective*, p. 54, in reference to Eugene Litwak, *Helping the Elderly* [New York: Guilford Press, 1985]).

3. E. Anthony Rotundo, "Romantic Friendship," p. 1. The nineteenth century witnessed an increase in the acceptance of romantic courtship as a basis for marriage in the middle class. The degree to which romantic courtship operated among working and poor people remains a historical question. Stacey J. Oliker, *Best Friends and Marriage*; Allan, *Friendship*, p. 80. In the contemporary world, these social ties vary by class, gender, and race, as they did in the nineteenth century, though often in different ways. Research on friendship points to a class distinction: working-class people (in contrast to middle-class) count kin as friends more than they do non-kin. Extending this principle, working-class people may more often "treat the home as the exclusive preserve of the family, and not to entertain non-kin in it" (Graham Allan, "Class Variation in Friendship Patterns," p. 391). In contrast, the middle class entertains extensively in the home; they transform it into a space for socializing. Working-class friendship tends to be more situation-specific, emerging particularly at the work place and in the neighborhood. Even the label of "friend" may be questionable: working-class men and women define a friend as someone with whom they mix socially, as opposed to the middle-class definition that infers conscious intention

to socialize. In a study of African American families on welfare, Carol B. Stack reports a privileging of kin relationships. The title of a blood relation is bestowed upon very special friends, an honorary acknowledgment that Stack refers to as "fictive kin." This status confers a host of privileges and responsibilities (*All Our Kin: Strategies for Survival in a Black Community*). This tradition of constructing and adopting fictive kin was forged by slaves who were separated from their biological relatives. See also Herbert G. Gutman, *The Black Family in Slavery and Freedom, 1750–1925*, and Jacqueline Jones, *Labor of Love, Labor of Sorrow: Black Women, Work, and the Family from Slavery to the Present.*

The gender differences are more striking. There has been a popular and scholarly assumption, particularly prior to the second wave of feminism, that men bonded together in solidarity. The women's movement and research such as that of Cott (*Bonds of Womanhood*) and Smith-Rosenberg (*Disorderly Conduct*) have debunked the stereotype of women as competitive, petty, and incapable of friendship. However, reinterpretation of men's relationship with one another is also a result of the second wave of feminism and the lesbian and gay rights movement. See, Joseph H. Pleck, "Man to Man: Is Brotherhood Possible?"; Lillian B. Rubin, *Just Friends: The Role of Friendship in our Lives*; and Drury Sherrod, "The Bonds of Men: Problems and Possibilities in Close Male Relationships." Although men and women have about the same number of friends, women are more self-disclosing and seek friends who share similar values and feelings, while men find friends who enjoy similar activities; men want companionship and commitment. Pleck and Rubin claim that men's expectations for emotional intimacy focus on women in contemporary society; men need women for emotional expression. Sherrod finds that men reveal more to their female friends than to their male friends. Paul H. Wright characterizes female friendships as "face-to-face," in contrast to the male "side-by-side" style. However, he notes that "the differences between women's and men's friendships diminish markedly as the strength and duration of the friendships increases" ("Men's Friendships, Women's Friendships and the Alleged Inferiority of the Latter," p. 19). Allan offers a sociological explanation rooted in his assumptions about gender:

> Males generally lead a more 'public' life than females. Their routine work and leisure activities bring them into contact with a relatively wide range of others and require them to develop cordial, though not necessarily very close, relationships with them. In contrast, women tend to occupy a more 'private' realm and have less opportunity or reason to develop extensive social networks. (Allan, *Friendship*, p. 68)

In the 1990s when a majority of women work in the paid labor force, this explanation sounds like a quaint stereotype. And by now it is clear that I pose Allan's assertions of publicity and privacy as questions rather than assumptions. Karen Walker's work-in-progress challenges these recent assessments of men's versus women's friendships. She finds that men and women answer global questions about friendship with stereotypes about men's and women's friendships. However, when probed about specific *behaviors*, men's friendships do not look very different from women's. "Men, Women, and Friendship: What They Say; What They Do," *Gender & Society*, forthcoming.

4. Cott, *Bonds of Womanhood*, p. 168.

5. Ibid., pp. 182–83, citing letters from Eliza Chaplin (Nelson) to Laura Lovell, JDPL, 27 July 1820, 24 June 1821. Smith-Rosenberg, "Female World of Love and Ritual," in *Disorderly Conduct*, p. 57. Smith-Rosenberg's research has sparked a debate about the degree to which women's affection for one another expressed the cultural romanticism dominant in the early nineteenth century, reflected a unique women's culture, or revealed a lesbian sexual practice. How are we to interpret the nineteenth-century sources? Marilyn Ferris Motz, for example, argues that "the language used by these women cannot therefore be taken as a transcription of the usual interaction of female kin living in proximity" (*True Sisterhood: Michigan Women and Their Kin, 1820–1920*, p. 79). In each other's absence, she argues, the letters *created* an intimacy and way of behaving that had not existed when women were together. Smith-Rosenberg recommends that rather than try to label the behavior normal or deviant, we should consider it a part of a sexual continuum ranging from homosexual to heterosexual. I agree with her rejection of discrete categories and suggest that we explore an alternative vocabulary of friendship that more adequately addresses its nature.

6. Primus Family Letters: Addie Brown to Rebecca Primus, 31 May 1861, 23 February 1862 (emphasis in original), March 1862. Addie compared her hunger to her love in several other letters as well.

7. Grace Aguilar, *Woman's Friendship: A Story of Domestic Life*, p. 41.

8. Addie Brown to Rebecca Primus, Primus Family Papers, 30 August 1859, emphasis in original.

9. Ibid., 16 February 1860, 16 November 1865, 19 November 1860.

10. Ibid., 23 February 1862.

11. Ibid., 5 March 1862; Charity Jackson, New York, to Rebecca Primus, Primus Family Papers, March 1862; Addie Brown to Rebecca Primus, March 1862.

12. Philip S. Foner and Ronald L. Lewis say that "waiting on tables in northern hotels, restaurants, and saloons represented one of those occupations employing conspicuously large numbers of blacks" (*The Black Worker to 1869*, vol. 1, p. 190). Addie Brown to Rebecca Primus, Primus Family Papers, 8 November 1865.

13. Lavinia Merrill to Rhoda Parker, Rhoda Parker Smith Correspondence, 14 May 1841. Hephzibah to Sarah Carter, Holmes Family Papers, 15 June 1846. Hephzibah never signed her last name to her letters, so we do not know it. Ibid., 5 March 1848. Erlunia Smith to Ann Lilley, Ann Lilley Dixon Correspondence, 31 May 1841. Erlunia appeared less successful in establishing this exchange, perhaps because her anxiety to establish trust also exposed her compelling desire for information for its own sake.

14. Erlunia Smith to Ann Lilley, Ann Lilley Dixon Correspondence, 31 May 1841, emphasis in original.

15. Hephzibah to Sarah Carter, Holmes Family Papers, 5 July 1846. Lavinia Merrill to Rhoda Parker, Rhoda Parker Smith Correspondence, 14 May 1841. Martha Osborne Barrett Diary, 26 December 1852, emphasis in original.

16. Sarah Holmes Clark to Sarah Carter, Holmes Family Papers, 30 August 1853 (emphasis in original), 4 May 1851, August 1856 (emphasis in original), 19 July 1855. For another source that complicates the dominant view of harmonious relations between friends and husbands, see Ellen K. Rothman, *Hands and Hearts: A History of Courtship in America*.

17. Sarah Trask Diary, 19 June 1849. Primus Family Papers: Addie Brown to Rebecca Primus, 3 November 1861; Henrietta Primus to Rebecca Primus, 15 November 1865.

18. Sarah Trask Diary, 27 April 1849. Holmes Family Papers: Hephzibah to Sarah Carter, 15 June 1846. Sarah Holmes Clark to Sarah Carter, 9 April 1852 (emphasis in original), August 1856 (emphasis in original).

19. Primus Family Papers: Addie Brown to Rebecca Primus, 12 January 1862, 11 September 1862.

20. Holmes Family Papers: Marcella Holmes to Sarah Carter, 25 January 1860, 18 March 1860, 12 April 1860.

21. Ibid., 5 March 1861.

22. Rothman amends this conclusion in the context of her own research on the middle class. She finds that marriage *disrupted* friendship, but it often later resumed (*Hands and Hearts: A History of Courtship in America*, nn. 29, 30, pp. 338–39). Holmes Family Papers: Hephzibah to Sarah Carter, January 1845 (emphasis in original); Sarah Holmes Clark to Sarah Carter, 12 October 1852.

23. John D'Emilio and Estelle B. Freedman, *Intimate Matters: A History of Sexuality in America*; Elizabeth H. Pleck and Joseph H. Pleck, *The American Man*.

24. Mary Ann Clawson, *Constructing Brotherhood: Class, Gender, and Fraternalism*; D'Emilio and Freedman, *Intimate Matters*; and Pleck and Pleck, *The American Man*. Parallel to the experience of women, men's distinct social world allowed them to develop their own culture and "encouraged manly intimacy and affection, a love between equals, which was often lacking in sentiments toward the other sex" (Pleck and Pleck, *The American Man*, p. 13). Scholars point to the men-only spaces which nurtured male culture in the colonial and antebellum periods: lodges, clubs, militia, fire departments, taverns, and voluntary associations. All of these institutions, however, generally encouraged verbal rather than written expressions of affection, producing little documentation of the interpersonal dimension of these relationships.

Mary Ann Clawson sees these all-male spaces in a somewhat different light. In her investigation of fraternal organizations such as the Masons and Odd Fellows in the nineteenth century, she argues that the rise of male organizations, fraternal orders in particular, met a specific need in a turbulent and uncertain nineteenth-century society. Clawson asserts that the fraternal orders functioned as a lifelong defense against threats to manhood. She demonstrates that artisanal manhood was under assault because of industrial capitalism, the rise of female values, and the cultural critique of masculinity. The effect of these sacred bastions of masculinity "was to promote solidarity among men, to reinforce men's separation from women, and thus to validate and facilitate the exercise of masculine power" ("Nineteenth-Century Women's Auxiliaries and Fraternal

Orders," p. 41). Mark Carnes similarly argues that "fraternal ritual provided solace and psychological guidance during young men's troubled passage to manhood in Victorian America" (*Secret Ritual and Manhood in Victorian America*, p. 14). Also see Ann Douglas, *The Feminization of American Culture*. I assume Clawson would concur that the fraternal organizations did not encourage romantic friendship, though the different nature of the available evidence—organizational records versus personal correspondence—makes conclusions impossible. Also, friendship, even fraternity, was not necessarily the primary reason for joining an organization.

25. John W. Crowley convincingly argues that nineteenth-century middle-class male culture was homosocial and had erotic undercurrents. The culture at large associated male friendships with childishness and powerlessness. However, it did not promote shame or scorn, and certainly did not provoke the virulent homophobia evident in the twentieth century ("Howells, Stoddard, and Male Homosocial Attachment in Victorian America," pp. 301–24). Richard Rabinowitz dissents, arguing that in the 1850s, "men, except for writers and clergymen, seemed relatively immune from this passion for mutuality" (*The Spiritual Self in Everyday Life: The Transformation of the Personal Religious Experience in Nineteenth-Century New England*, p. 209).

Jonathan Ned Katz argues that the mere existence of romantic letters between men, so casually kept, "suggests more lenient social attitudes toward male-male intimacy" than we would find today or expect to find in late eighteenth- or nineteenth-century society (*Gay American History: Lesbians and Gay Men in the U.S.A.*, p. 451). Other historians range in their assessment of the material from a conviction that the language reflects only a spiritual love to a skeptical ambivalence about the innocence of the erotic messages. See Jeffrey Richards, "'Passing the Love of Women': Manly Love and Victorian Society," and D'Emilio and Freedman, *Intimate Matters*. Donald Yacovone flatly rejects the suggestion that romantic language reflects a homoerotic culture, claiming that instead it flows from the age-old tradition of Christian love and brotherhood ("Abolitionists and the 'Language of Fraternal Love'").

There is great difficulty in studying same-sex relationships in a heterosexist and homophobic society because of tendencies to distort unself-conscious relations and read consummated sexual activity into passionate innuendos and because of an inability to put aside twentieth-century biases to sensitively interpret a culture lacking a Freudian obsession with sex. In addition, due to the evidential limitations of historical research, we cannot know "what really happened." For these reasons the notion of a sexual continuum put forth by Smith-Rosenberg and Katz is most useful in capturing historical nuance. It eschews mutually exclusive categories and acknowledges the fluidity of boundaries between sexual and gender identities.

Physical expressions of affection—embracing, sharing a bed—carried no real stigma for men in the nineteenth century and in fact were culturally supported, as confirmed by Martin Duberman's research. He argues that the degree of physical affection men comfortably expressed to other men changed over time, particularly from the early to the late nineteenth century ("'Writhing Bedfellows' in Antebellum South Carolina: Historical Interpretation and the Politics of

Evidence"). Rotundo, "Romantic Friendship," p. 13. The reason male intimacy was limited to the period between boyhood and manhood, Rotundo claims, is that men entered the competitive marketplace which affected their values and attitudes, making them more calculating and instrumental in dealing with other men. While in part this explanation is convincing, if taken to its logical conclusion, it would indicate that anyone involved in economic activity under capitalism was incapable of intimate relations. Granted, men's primary competitors in the nineteenth-century work world were other men, but not necessarily their close friends.

26. The correspondence that has survived contains only letters from J. Foster Beal to Brigham Nims, and none of those Brigham wrote to Foster. The Beal-Nims correspondence was the only collection I found in my search for letters between farmers, artisans, and working-class men who were not relatives. The dearth of documents can be interpreted several ways. One is that scarcity of such letters reflects the rarity of the friendship. Another is that working-class men had friendships, but not ones that survived prolonged absences. Yet another is that the biases inherent in preserving documents of non-elites would render "pedestrian" letters that might have existed not worth preserving, therefore leaving few today, except those between family members.

27. J. Foster Beal to Brigham Nims, Roxbury Town Records, NHSA, 21 March 1832.

28. Ibid., 17 December 1834.

29. Grammatical errors in middle-class letters were sometimes intentional, used as a form of endearment, a kind of baby talk that took a less literate form. However, grammar and spelling were not standardized in the early nineteenth century, as is evident in diaries and letters of the time. Ibid., 17 December 1834. It is interesting to note that a man's tears became fodder for gossip.

30. Ibid., 1 April 1834.

31. Ibid., 21 March 1832; Hephzibah to Sarah Carter, Holmes Family Papers, January 1845, emphasis in original; J. Foster Beal to Brigham Nims, Roxbury Town Records, NHSA, 21 March 1832.

32. Arthur Schlesinger, *Learning How to Behave: A Historical Study of American Etiquette Books*, p. 25; Allan, *Friendship*. Rothman documents the difficulty of the transition from separate spheres for middle-class men and women to coeducation and overlapping spheres in the early twentieth century (*Hands and Hearts*, esp. pp. 190–95).

33. Nathan K. Abbott Diary, 11 January 1856.

34. Sarah Trask Diary, 3 June 1849. In the wake of Luther's death in 1851, Sarah painfully recorded the "names of my friends." She proceeded to list sixteen people—eight men and eight women—as couples. She added her own name and that of Luther Woodberry to the bottom of the list. Ibid., 21 May 1851.

35. Holmes Family Papers: James Holmes to Sarah Carter, 25 August 1855, 29 November 1857. That said, however, when the Civil War began in 1861, James did not enlist in the Union army, although several of his Holmes cousins did. He married in 1862 and settled in Illinois to raise a family. Sarah Holmes Clark also wrote to Sarah Carter about her opinions regarding slaves: "They are the happiest class of people that I ever saw. But you need not tell this to

Northern people. I do not expect them to think as I do because they know nothing about it" (17 September 1855). Most of the time Sarah Holmes Clark ignored the fact that Sarah Carter's opinions differed from hers. At one point in 1856, however, she wrote, "Do you know my dear friend that I am very sorry that you are an abolitionist?" In the next sentence she changed the subject. Henry M. Atwood to Sarah Carter, Holmes Family Papers, 12 March 184[7].

36. John Burleigh to Ann Lilley, Ann Lilley Dixon Correspondence, 30 April 1841, emphasis in original. Despite his protestations of innocence, other parts of his letters were sexually suggestive. If he acted the way he wrote, the "old maid" would not have needed jealousy to prompt speculation about romance. This supports the observation that sexual tension was assumed to exist between men and women, except within a safely defined context. Motz finds that in the middle class correspondence between the sexes was only considered proper if the correspondents were related or courting (*True Sisterhood*, pp. 58–59).

37. Those families who preserved letters were more likely to be involved family members, concerned about one another's well-being, anchored in a sense of obligation. Annette Atkins argues persuasively that conceptions of separate spheres ignore the fact that men often had homes and families where women also lived ("Brothers, Sisters, and Shared Spheres: An Introduction to a Work in Progress," paper presented at the Pacific Coast Branch Meetings of the American Historical Association, San Francisco, 1988).

38. That said, it is interesting to note that twentieth-century research on friendship reveals an important class distinction in sibling relationships. Allan finds that it was highly unusual for middle-class respondents to have their closest relationship with a sibling. The working-class respondents' relationships that most closely resembled middle-class "best-friendship" were those between sib-lings, invariably between siblings of the same gender ("Class Variation in Friendship Patterns," p. 392). Chloe Adams to James Adams, Metcalf-Adams Family Letters, 2 August 1820. Laura Nims to Brigham Nims, Roxbury Town Records, NHSA, 21 May 1834. Laura began a letter to Brigham on 14 September 1834, "Why, Brigham, I want to know if you have gone to Boston." She was not inhibited about displaying her impatience or her anger to her older brother. Brigham Nims to Laura Nims, Roxbury Town Records, NHSA, 18 September 1839.

39. For details of customs in the middle class, see Rothman, *Hands and Hearts*. The recipe begins: "6 lbs Butter, 6 lbs Flour, 6 lbs Sugar, 4 1/2 lbs Currants, 3 lbs Raisins, 6 lbs or 4 1/2 dozen eggs with the spices. . . ." (Nims Diary, 22 August 1845).

40. Harriet Dame to George Dame, Dame Sister Letters, 26 November 183[5].

41. Stephen Parker to Rhoda Parker, Rhoda Parker Smith Correspondence, 23 February 1845 (emphasis in original), 25 January 1846 (emphasis in original).

4. "SOCIAL WORK"

1. John Plummer Foster Diary, 21 December 1857; Brigham Nims Diary, 10 April 1845. Other diarists who record strings of visitors include Nathan K.

Abbott, Thomas Coffin, Susan Brown Forbes, Lizzie Goodenough, Mary Hall, Albert Mason, Ann Stoddard, and Unknown Woman. This level of visiting was not apparent in the diaries of Ivory Hill, Joseph Kimball, and James Weymouth. They did not name their visitors or assign visits the status of events worthy of being recorded in their diaries. Sarah Root Diary, 27 February 1862.

2. Extensive community studies in sociology, anthropology, and history uncover the processes involved in the creation of community. These studies focus on individual and household ties to extended kin and community and situate social networks within the context of urbanization and industrialization. For an overview of community studies and the theoretical issues they raise, see Thomas Bender, *Community and Social Change in America*, and Maurice R. Stein, *The Eclipse of Community: An Interpretation of American Studies* (Princeton: Princeton University Press, 1960). For historical studies see Cott, *Bonds of Womanhood*; Alan Dawley, *Class and Community: The Industrial Revolution in Lynn*; Paul Faler, *The Coming of Industrial Order: Town and Factory Life in Rural Massachusetts, 1810–1860*; Michael Frisch, *Town into City: Springfield, Massachusetts, and the Meaning of Community, 1840–1880*; Smith-Rosenberg, *Disorderly Conduct*; Stansell, *City of Women*; Ulrich, *Good Wives*; Martha Vicinus, *Independent Women: Work and Community for Single Women, 1850–1920*; Virginia Yans-McLaughlin, *Family and Community: Italian Immigrants in Buffalo, 1880–1930*. For contemporary analyses see Elizabeth Bott, *Family and Social Network: Roles, Norms, and External Relationships in Ordinary Urban Families*; Claude S. Fischer, *To Dwell Among Friends: Personal Networks in Town and City*; Gerald D. Suttles, *The Social Construction of Communities* (Chicago: University of Chicago Press, 1972); Michael Young and Peter Wilmott, *Family and Kinship in East London*.

3. "It is through personal connections that society is structured and the individual integrated into society. Although modern nations have elaborate arrays of institutions and organizations, daily life proceeds through personal ties" (Fischer, *To Dwell Among Friends*, p. 3). Reciprocal visiting identified some relationships as less intimate than friendships. See Mark S. Granovetter, "The Strength of Weak Ties."

4. In her anthropological study of friendships in contemporary Norway, Marianne Gullestad's subjects say visiting necessarily precludes work. "The contradiction between visiting and handiwork is related to the idea they have of what it means to relax. . . . To relax means to do nothing useful; it is the opposite of work." This belief results in the popular contemporary prohibition of work while socializing. In effect, Gullestad's subjects rarely work together except when women care for children and men fix cars or do home repairs (*Kitchen-Table Society: A Case Study of the Family Life and Friendships of Young Working-Class Mothers in Urban Norway*, p. 163). Wallace P. Rhodes, comp., *Reminiscences of a New Hampshire Town: Belmont Centennial, 1869–1969*, p. 49. Horton and Horton, *Black Bostonians*. Marilyn Ferris Motz makes the distinction between formal and informal visiting for the middle class. She maintains that people served informal calls on kin while formal calls reinforced the distinction between family and friends in the degree of intimacy and familiarity (*True Sisterhood*, pp. 50–51). Laurel Thatcher Ulrich finds this intermin-

gling of communal labor and sociability in eighteenth-century New England ("Housewife and Gadder: Themes of Self-sufficiency and Community in Eighteenth-Century New England"). In her study of a late-nineteenth-century rural community, Osterud similarly finds great conviviality at gatherings for communal labor (*Bonds of Community*, esp. ch. 10).

5. Leonard M. Stockwell Memorial Volume, p. 37; Horatio Chandler Diary, March 1841; Eliza Adams to Friends at Home, Adams Family Papers, 25 December 1848.

6. Louisa Chapman Diary, 21–24 and 26 March 1849; Lizzie Goodenough Diary, 9 February 1865.

7. Young, unmarried men were the only ones to mention gathering to socialize outside of someone's home. For example, Francis Bennett frequented Proctor's store in Gloucester and the YMCA in Boston, and Edward Carpenter went to a local barbershop in Greenfield, Massachusetts, to play cards and party. Rhodes states that "perhaps the most important social event of the year was town meeting" (*Reminiscences of a New Hampshire Town*, p. 49). It was a male-only event that was as important socially as it was politically (p. 48). For an extensive compilation of New England cultural practices, see B. A. Botkin, ed., *A Treasury of New England Folklore: Stories, Ballads, and Traditions of the Yankee People*.

8. This contrasts with historical studies of other periods and regions. Laurel Ulrich provides a clue for decoding the diaries. For the year 1790, Ulrich maps the social world of Martha Ballard, a New England midwife, and compares it to that of Henry Sewall, the town clerk of Hallowell, Maine. She finds that Martha's diary mentioned approximately three times as many people as Henry's, and it reflected a balance of male and female worlds, while his universe was almost exclusively male (*A Midwife's Tale: The Life of Martha Ballard, Based on her Diary, 1785–1812*, pp. 92–93). This apparent difference in social worlds may reflect diary-keeping practices more than actual behavior. If so, it is an important register of a state of mind, a gendered world view.

In *Women and Men on the Overland Trail*, Faragher characterizes men's labor as social because it extended beyond the family and connected to "the larger social world. Woman's work, always cyclical, always looking inward, did not qualify; it was hidden by domestic draperies" (p. 65). Thus Faragher sees women as isolated, and unlike men, building their social relationships largely *within* their own families (p. 121).

Marilyn Ferris Motz also finds women deeply involved in social life, a life centered in the extended family. In studying diaries of midwestern women, she notes, in agreement with Faragher, an economic motivation for the difference between married men's and women's attachment to their kin. Because of married men's economic independence, they needed their kin less than women did. When husbands failed to provide support (due to divorce, economic hardship, desertion, death, or incompetence), women had to rely on their kin because few economic opportunities were open to them, and those that existed paid low wages. "The expectation of future need thus led women to exert great effort to maintain ties with their kin" (*True Sisterhood*, p. 80). The extended family served as insurance, collateral against financial ruin. Nancy Tomes discovers that elite Quaker women of late-eighteenth-century Philadelphia established a similar system of "social insurance" maintained through visiting. Religion shaped the boundaries of the community, and within those confines women relied heavily upon extended kin ("The Quaker Connection: Visiting Patterns among Women in the Philadelphia Society of Friends, 1750–1850").

In *Bonds of Community*, Osterud similarly emphasizes the importance of the extended family. In her investigation of upstate New York, she concludes that women prized kin relations more than men because kinship served as the primary basis for forming women's networks. In contrast, men's networks were much broader than women's, including neighbors and coworkers as well as kin. Women gained power from their networks because they were a forum for exchanging resources (labor, services, emotional support) and also because the alliances set limits on a husband's exercise of power.

Other studies that investigate community life observe that the gendered division of "social work" shifts over time. In a study of "The Country Visitor" in rural Wisconsin, Jane Marie Pederson finds that in 1890, men were more likely to be visitors than women. By 1914 this is no longer true; 53% of the visitors are women, and 58% by 1922. That said, however, women were more frequently visitors to family members ("The Country Visitor: Patterns of Hospitality in Rural Wisconsin, 1880–1925," p. 355). This general finding is corroborated in a study of the visiting patterns of Afro-Americans who moved north from Norfolk, Virginia, during the great migration. Earl Lewis finds that the immigrants returned to Norfolk to visit in order "to maintain key relationships, mend strained family ties, and rekindle old friendships without relinquishing the dream of better opportunities." In the sample of 840 visits cited in the Norfolk *Journal and Guide* in 1917, 1921, and 1925, women were twice as likely to be visitors as men ("Afro-American Adaptive Strategies: The Visiting Habits of Kith and Kin among Black Norfolkians during the First Great Migration"). In her anthropological study of friendships in contemporary Norway, Gullestad finds a clear division of labor between men and women. Women "both receive more visitors and go visiting more than men do" (*Kitchen-Table Society*, p. 153).

In her ethnography of African Americans on welfare living in a large U.S. city in the 1970s, Carol Stack explores how families manage to survive on the pittance of government allowance. She finds black women at the heart of domestic networks, those "organized, durable network[s] of kin and non-kin who interact daily, providing domestic needs of children and assuring their survival" (*All Our Kin*, p. 31). As key strategic actors, women created and engaged the networks essential to their survival in conditions of extreme poverty. Women swapped clothes, furniture, food, and children in order to redistribute scarce resources within the community. Men contributed to their female kin, but were at the periphery of the female networks.

These percentages are derived from a content analysis of *diaries* on topics discussed. A diarist need only mention the topic once in order to be counted. The question remains as to how much women and men visited together in mixed groups. In Chapter 3 on friendship, I mapped the debates about men's and women's homosocial versus heterosocial environments. To extend that discussion, Cott finds that while women relied "on female friendship for emotional expression and security," women's relationships (particularly those of elite women) did not exclude men. In fact, Cott claims men and women in the eighteenth century shared an "extensive social life" (*Bonds of Womanhood*, p. 173). Martha Ballard's portrait of eighteenth-century Hallowell, Maine, complicates this account. Ulrich finds that Martha's social gatherings mixed gender, age, and marital status without concern. At the same time, husbands and wives rarely made calls together, and young girls commonly accompanied women (*A Midwife's Tale*, pp. 144 and 93). While men's and women's production occasionally overlapped, they operated largely independently (p. 80). So Martha describes a peaceful social coexistence between the genders and economic autonomy, even independence.

Reflecting continuity with the eighteenth century, Osterud also uncovers extensive mingling of men and women in nineteenth-century rural society. In contrast to Cott and Smith-Rosenberg, Osterud discovers that women actively attempted to integrate men into their social activities. Women's "social work" bridged husbands and wives as well as households. As a result of the extensive resources they brought to a household, women achieved greater equality in their relationships with men (*Bonds of Community*, p. 247).

9. Leonard M. Stockwell Memorial Volume, p. 38. It is possible that men and women recorded visits differently. The observed differences could reflect diary-keeping practices rather than differences in social behavior.

10. Or "social 'insurance,'" as Tomes put it ("The Quaker Connection," p. 181). Ulrich refers to this as "the common fund of neighborliness that sustained families in illness" (*A Midwife's Tale*, p. 63). As Gullestad observes in the twentieth century, "Close friendships have constantly to be confirmed by sociability and visiting" (*Kitchen-Table Society*, p. 161). For an elaboration of this principle, see Arlie Russell Hochschild, *The Managed Heart: Commercialization of Human Feeling*.

11. Mary Adams to Adams Family, Adams Family Papers, 1 March 1835; Sarah Metcalf to Chloe Metcalf, Metcalf-Adams Family Letters, 28 March 1847.

12. Parna Gilbert Diary, 19 September 1852 (emphasis added); Addie Brown to Rebecca Primus, Primus Family Papers, 10 December 1865.

13. Lizzie Goodenough Diary, 19 February 1865; Sarah Trask Diary, 11 May 1849; Brigham Nims Diary, 27 November 1851.

14. Luna to Ann Lilley Dixon, Ann Lilley Dixon Correspondence, August [12], n.y.; Mary Mudge Diary, 14 June 1854 (emphasis added).

15. Brown, *The Life of William J. Brown*, p. 93; Sarah Holmes to Sarah Carter, Holmes Family Papers, 4 May 1851. It is interesting that subjects assessed letters in a way similar to visits. Questions consistently arose regarding reciprocity. How soon did the recipient answer? How long was the letter? How many did each person send? What was the news value of the letter? Ibid., 30 October 1854 (written as an addendum to the letter dated 29 October 1854), 19 July 1855. The distinctions she observed between urban and rural visiting did not emerge in this study.

16. Susan Brown Forbes Diary, 28 May 1846; Mary Mudge Diary, 23

November 1854, 17 June 1854; Sarah Trask Diary, 10 April 1849; Hannah, Mary, and Margaret Adams to Mother and Father, Adams Family Papers, 14 November 1841.

17. Sarah Trask Diary, 3 April 1849. The "sons meeting" refers to the Sons of Temperance; Sarah belonged to the Daughters of Temperance. Anne Abbott Parker to Rhoda Parker, Rhoda Parker Smith Correspondence, 17 November 1842 (emphasis in original); Elizabeth Metcalf to Chloe Metcalf, Metcalf-Adams Letters, 22 October 1851.

18. Paulina Bascom Williams Diary, 8 June 1832.

19. Martha Osborne Barrett Diary, 30 June 1850. This sentiment was rarely expressed in other diaries.

20. Mary Giddings Coult Diary, 14 May 1853. Reverend Noah Davis, *A Narrative of the Life of Rev. Noah Davis, a Colored Man*, p. 37 (emphasis added); Sarah Holmes Clark to Sarah Carter, Holmes Family Papers, 30 October 1854 (written as an addendum to the letter dated 29 October 1854; emphasis in original); Parna Gilbert Diary, 13 September 1851. It is interesting to note that it appears that only women complain of the labors of visiting and attendant fatigue, perhaps because they do more. Men visit somewhat less frequently, although farmers in particular list extra men working with them on the farm almost daily. Men have contact with people through work, some of which they must organize. Because of the greater isolation of domestic labor and piecework, women had to make a greater effort to structure in sociability.

21. Micaela di Leonardo, "The Female World of Cards and Holidays: Women, Families, and the Work of Kinship," p. 442. Other people have applied the basic principle of "emotion work" done by women to a variety of settings. The concept was developed by Arlie Hochschild in *The Managed Heart*. See also Marjorie L. DeVault, *Feeding the Family: The Social Organization of Caring as Gendered Work*. Cott found in the early republic that "the characteristic 'work' of unmarried women of the elite largely consisted in maintaining social contacts" (*Bonds of Womanhood*, p. 52). Also see Pamela M. Fishman, "Interaction: The Work Women Do," in *Women and Work: Problems and Perspectives*, ed. Rachel Kahn-Hut, Arlene Kaplan Daniels, and Richard Colvard (New York: Oxford University Press, 1982), pp. 170–80. For development of the theme of Christian conversion, see Chapter 6. As Arlene Kaplan Daniels notes in her analysis of contemporary "sociability work," this labor influences people, events, and their commitment to organizations, causes, and giving money ("Good Times and Good Works: The Place of Sociability in the Work of Women Volunteers"). Daniels defines sociability work as "the creation of an ambience by those who provide some kind of hospitality" (p. 363). Thus her focus is a subcategory of what I call "social work."

22. Stephen Parker to Rhoda Parker, Rhoda Parker Smith Correspondence, 9 August 1841, emphasis in the original.

23. Sarah Holmes Clark to Sarah Carter, Holmes Family Papers, 30 October 1854 (written as an addendum to the letter dated 29 October 1854); Sarah Trask Diary, 22 May 1849, 22 June 1849. Also see: Mary Holbrook Diary, 22 December 1852, 30 December 1852; Marion Hopkins Diary, 27 April 1851.

Sarah came "to stitch" at least weekly. It was not clear whether Marion always stitched with her.

24. Lizzie Goodenough Diary, 10 October 1865. See, for example, Cowan, *More Work for Mother*; Glenna Matthews, *"Just a Housewife": The Rise and Fall of Domesticity in America*; Karen V. Hansen, *Taking Back the Day: The Historical Recovery of Women's Household Work Experience*, M.A. thesis, University of California at Santa Barbara, 1979; Ann Oakley, *The Sociology of Housework* (New York: Pantheon, 1974); Lucy Salmon, *Domestic Service*; Susan Strasser, *Never Done: A History of American Housework*. See, for example, Abigail Baldwin Diary, 1853–1854; Marion Hopkins Diary, 1851–1855; Pollie Tilton Diary, 1 March 1858; and Ezra Sanborn Diary, 1861–1878. Ezra "washt" regularly in addition to dipping candles and making soap. His activities came to a screeching halt soon after his wife gave birth to a baby, but resumed when she became pregnant again.

25. Lizzie Goodenough Diary, 23 March 1865.

26. John Plummer Foster Diary, 25 April 1852. The New Hampshire Historical Society has a name index to the diary of Thomas Coffin, a more prosperous farmer. The length of the index conveys the astonishing number of people involved in the life of Thomas Coffin. Covering the years 1825 to 1835, the index is six and one-half legal-sized pages long, single-spaced, and includes numerous page numbers after each name. The blur of laborers and visitors was true for the female farmers as well. The female heads of farm households included Samantha Barrett and Eliza Adams.

27. Economic historians debate the degree to which farm families supported themselves without aid from other households in the early nineteenth century. Some argue that few families had adequate land, tools, or labor power to be self-sufficient. In other words, a household could not produce its own food and clothing without a system of exchanged goods and services that linked it to the larger community. Ulrich creatively reinterprets evidence for this argument by looking at the work of women at the turn of the nineteenth century. She maintains that the eighteenth century was "a world in which self-sufficiency was sustained by neighborliness, and vice versa" ("Housewife and Gadder," p. 23). As in anthropological studies of economic exchange, Ulrich finds women central to this economic interdependence by trading goods and services, facilitating labor transactions, and engaging in communal work. See also Rayna Reiter, "Men and Women in the South of France," pp. 252–82; Marilyn Strathern, *Women in-Between: Female Roles in a Male World, Mount Hagen, New Guinea*; and Annette B. Weiner, *Women of Value, Men of Renown: New Perspectives in Trobriand Exchange* (Austin: University of Texas Press, 1976). Antebellum New England working people similarly exchanged services and labor.

28. See, for example, Barbara Ehrenreich and Deirdre English, *For Her Own Good: 150 Years of the Experts' Advice to Women*; Charles E. Rosenberg, *The Cholera Years: The United States in 1832, 1849, and 1866*. While life expectancy remained relatively constant from 1800 to 1860 for native-born whites and free blacks in the North, epidemics of several diseases—tuberculosis, cholera, and smallpox—hit hard and intermittently made health seem more precarious in the

antebellum period. See Peter D. McClelland and Richard J. Zeckhauser, *Demographic Dimensions of the New Republic: American Interregional Migration, Vital Statistics, and Manumissions, 1800–1860*, and Maris A. Vinovskis, "Mortality Rates and Trends in Massachusetts Before 1860."

29. Addie Brown to Rebecca Primus, Primus Family Papers, 10 November 1865. Parna Gilbert Diary, 19 April 1850.

30. Zeloda Barrett wrote in Samantha Barrett's diary, 28 October 1830.

31. This list includes Zeloda Barrett, Parna Gilbert, Pollie Tilton, and other women when they are younger and single, but not quite to the same degree. Pollie Cathcart Tilton Diary, 1858. According to Susan M. Reverby, many antebellum nurses based their claim to the trade on their experience caring for family members. "The Duty or Right to Care? Nursing and Womanhood in Historical Perspective," p. 135. Harriet Severance spent extended periods with relatives caring for the sick and for the household. For example, when she went to Uncle Calvin's in Charlemont, Massachusetts, in September 1863, she worked there until Aunt Elvira died in November. She stayed on, caring for the farm household and her young cousin Lottie. Harriet Severance Diary, 1863–64.

32. Samantha Barrett Diary, October–November, 1830. Names include sisters Zeloda and Margaret, brother Calvin, Mrs. Hudah Spencer, Mrs. Tharn, Emeline, Celestia Butler, Mrs. Holcomb, Fannie Kellog, Mary Teele, Mrs. Gordon Henderson, Sophronia Dowd, Mrs. Mason, Susan Ensign, Mr. Northrop, Mr. Edward Woodruff, and Marilla Tyler. Interestingly, this list includes three men, two of whom are not related to her. Others diaries with shorter lists of watchers include Abigail Baldwin, Pollie Tilton, Harriet Severance, and Sarah Root.

33. Emily K. Abel and Margaret K. Nelson write, "Caregiving also is an essential activity. The social fabric relies on our ability to sustain life, nurture the weak, and respond to the needs of intimates" ("Circles of Care: An Introductory Essay," p. 4). Susan M. Reverby, *Ordered to Care: The Dilemma of American Nursing, 1850–1945*, p. 1; Mary Parker to Rhoda Parker, Rhoda Parker Smith Papers, 12 May, n.y.; Mary Giddings Coult Diary, 30 June 1851; Louisa Chapman Diary, 5 March 1849; Pamela Brown Diary, 10 February 1838, in *The Diaries of Sally and Pamela Brown, 1832–1838, Hyde Leslie, 1887, Plymouth Notch, Vermont*, ed. Blanche Brown Bryant and Gertrude Elaine Baker, p. 66; Mary Hall Diary, 27 May 1831. It was rare for women to quit work to care for a friend as opposed to kin. Harriet Severance Diary, 8 June 1864.

34. Reverby, "The Duty or Right to Care?" p. 134. Motz similarly emphasizes the role of kinship in executing these duties. She says that strangers (i.e., non-kin) were a distant second preference to caretakers related by blood. Female kin thus acted as the family gatekeepers, protecting the infirm "from the moral and physical pollution of strangers" (*True Sisterhood*, p. 106). She does not say where neighbors fit into this matrix but implies that by their non-kin status they were "strangers." Parna Gilbert Diary, 22 May 1851.

35. Mary P. Hall to Rhoda Parker, Rhoda Parker Smith Correspondence, 28 April, n.y. She did not return but offered words of advice.

36. Stephen Parker to Rhoda Parker, Rhoda Parker Smith Papers, 18 November 1844.

37. Mary Giddings Coult Diary, 6 August 1851, emphasis in original.

38. Mary Metcalf to Emmons Metcalf, Metcalf-Adams Family Letters, n.d., but after 1849; Louisa Chapman Diary, 9, 10, and 14 May 1849; Adelaide Crossman Diary, Crossman Family Diaries, 11 November 1855; Parna Gilbert Diary, 23 September 1849.

39. Sarah Trask Diary, 29 June 1849.

40. Motz, *True Sisterhood*, p. 98. In a rare exception to the literature, Osterud also finds men caring for sick kin later in the nineteenth century (*Bonds of Community*, pp. 247–48).

41. J. Foster Beal to Brigham Nims, Roxbury Town Papers, 17 December 1834; John Plummer Foster Diary, 7, 8, and 12 February 1851, 29 January 1858; Horatio Chandler Diary, 16 February 1842; Ivory Hill Diary, 1, 3, and 5 April 1857. Other men caring for men include Daniel Root caring for Michael Austria (Sarah Root Diary, 3 March 1861); Reverend Baldwin caring for Edson Sprague (Abigail Baldwin Diary, 29 August 1853); Joseph Kimball caring for his son Walter (Joseph Kimball Diary, 7 July 1848); and Ferdinand Crossman caring for his father (Ferdinand Crossman Diary, Crossman Family Diaries, February 1855). Charles A. Benson, a ship steward, regularly cared for men on the ship, administering herbal remedies and comfort (Charles A. Benson Diary, 1862 and 1864). In her autobiography, Mary Orne Tucker recounted the debilitating effects of "watching" on her husband, a Methodist minister. He cared for neighbors and family who were striken with typhus fever, "and the strain upon him proved so great that he well nigh broke down; and for the remainder of his year he was in so poor a state, physically and mentally, that his pulpit was supplied by others" (*Itinerant Preaching in the Early Days of Methodism*, p. 101).

42. E.g., Sarah Root Diary, 9 September 1862, and Pollie Tilton Diary.

43. Sarah Holmes Clark to Sarah Carter, Holmes Family Papers, August 1854. Sarah seems a bit defensive about Gilman. She doubted that Sarah Carter and others believed her.

44. Mars, *Life of James Mars*, p. 53. See also William Grimes, *Life of William Grimes, the Runaway Slave, Brought Down to the Present Time*. The other major exceptions were of course doctors and ministers. Professional license granted doctors access to women's bedsides, but not without resistance (see, for example, Ehrenreich and English, *For Her Own Good*). Ministers were also acceptable watchers, visitors, or nurses; indeed, they were expected to call on the sick, regardless of gender. Motz observes that women preferred female caretakers because bedside interaction provided an opportunity for intimacy and a "sense of security" (*True Sisterhood*, p. 106). These exceptions indicate that acceptability as a caretaker involved a combination of status in society (minister, doctor, woman, or black man) and relation to the patient.

45. Edward J. Carpenter Diary, 10 August 1844. The examples of men fetching women caretakers are too numerous to mention.

46. Ehrenreich and English, *For Her Own Good*; Judith Walzer Leavitt,

Brought to Bed: Childbearing in America, 1750–1950; Richard W. Wertz and Dorothy C. Wertz, *Lying-In: A History of Childbirth in America*. Doctors were called in extraordinary circumstances, but midwives managed routine births.

47. Leavitt, *Brought to Bed*, p. 93.

48. Leavitt says that all women, except the very poorest, relied on female, home-based networks: "Women held in common the desire for and achievement of this female cushion of security despite class or opportunity differences" (*Brought to Bed*, p. 83). The fact that births were rarely discussed by women is partly an artifact of the sample. Of those women who had time to keep diaries, most were young, unmarried, or at least without children.

49. Mary Coult Jones Diary, 2 March 1856.

50. Horatio Chandler Diary, 8 August 1840. Quoted in Leavitt, *Brought to Bed*, p. 94.

51. Mary Hall Diary, 14 May 1829; Francis Bennett, Jr., Diary, 15 July 1854; John Plummer Foster Diary, 30 August 1857; Horatio Chandler Diary, 7 August 1840.

52. Samuel Shepard James Diary, 1 June 1848, 19 March 1868; Joseph Kimball Diary, 29 September 1838, 2 February 1833.

53. The diaries of Joseph Kimball and David Smith display no enthusiasm for babies of either sex. Stephen Parker to Rhoda Parker, Rhoda Parker Smith Correspondence, 9 October 1845 (emphasis in original), 2 November 1852 (emphasis in original); John Plummer Foster Diary, 30 November 1858 (emphasis in original), 25 December 1852. See Viviana Zeliger, *Pricing the Priceless Child: The Changing Social Value of Children*. Zeliger points out that people in the twentieth century prefer to adopt an infant girl, emotionally priceless and not expected to contribute to household production.

54. For example, Albert Mason Diary, 22 October 1845; Vestus Haley Parks Diary, Parks Family Papers, 5 December 1827; Osterud, *Bonds of Community*, p. 231. Elizabeth Metcalf to Chloe Metcalf, Metcalf-Adams Family Papers, 22 October 1851. For example of casual references to quilting, see Abigail Baldwin Diary, 6 January 1854 and 21 July 1854; Pollie Tilton Diary, 10 September 1856.

55. Brigham Nims Diary, 29 and 30 April 1845; Vestus Haley Parks Diary, Parks Family Papers, 11 and 13 January 1829. "Freman Powers," undoubtedly an African American, entered into the life of Vestus Haley Parks in the way many white-black encounters took place—via entertainment. Mary Holbrook Diary, 26 January 1853. Susan Brown, a textile worker and schoolteacher during the 1840s, attended a quilting party at Daniel Locke's house. Susan Brown Forbes Diary, 1 May 1845; Mary Holbrook Diary, 9 February 1854; Arthur Bennett Diary, 22 March 1844. Other examples include parties. Ann Stoddard wrote, "Riley here and a number of others in evening. The boys made some molasses candy. It was very good indeed" (Diary, 2 January 1866). She later went with Riley to an apple-paring.

56. Zeloda Barrett Diary, 28 January 1820; Mary Mudge Diary, 11 May 1854; Adelaide Crossman Diary, Crossman Family Diaries, 7 April 1856. For other examples, see Samantha Barrett Diary, e.g., 10 June 1828; Pamela Brown

Diary, 26 March 1838; Susan Brown Forbes Diary, 28 November 1845; and Unknown Author, Diary of Newburyport farmer's wife, 16 March 1859. See also Abigail Baldwin and Harriet Severance diaries for informal quilting. Mary Holbrook Diary, 6 September 1854 through 21 September 1854.

57. See, for example, Nathan K. Abbott Diary, 12 June 1855, and John Plummer Foster Diary, 28 June 1852; Abigail Baldwin Diary, 1 November 1853.

58. Edward J. Carpenter Diary, 16 May 1844.

59. Edward P. Thompson, "Time, Work Discipline, and Industrial Capitalism"; Cott, *Bonds of Womanhood*, pp. 61, 62.

60. The percentages total more than 100 because one individual could have multiple employments over the course of her or his life. See Table 1.

61. Dublin details the dual processes of speedup and stretch-out. The textile factories assigned double the number of looms to each weaver, dramatically increasing productivity. They compensated with a slight increase in wages, which made some workers happy, others angry, and the corporation much more profitable (*Women at Work*, pp. 109–11).

62. Erlunia Smith to Ann Dixon, Ann Lilley Dixon Correspondence, 27 January n.y.; Anne Parker to Rhoda Parker, Rhoda Parker Smith Correspondence, 4 April 1844. See, for example, Pollie Tilton Diary, 1839–1860. I think this would be true for mothers as well, but because of their workload, fewer mothers kept diaries.

63. See, for example, Hal S. Barron, *Those Who Stayed Behind: Rural Society in Nineteenth-Century New England*, and Stephan Thernstrom, *Poverty and Progress: Social Mobility in a Nineteenth Century City*. Nothing could compare to the traumatic dislocation resulting from life as an underground fugitive, fearful of detection, capture, and return to slavery. See, for example, Harriet A. Jacobs, *Incidents in the Life of a Slave Girl*, and Moses Roper, *A Narrative of the Adventures and Escape of Moses Roper, from American Slavery*. However, even free blacks in the North felt endangered after the passage of the Fugitive Slave Act in 1850. Charles Metcalf to parents, Metcalf-Adams Family Papers, 5 April 1843 (emphasis in original); Charles A. Benson Diary, 13 May 1862. In describing fraternity among sailors at sea, Margaret S. Creighton writes of the raucous life and hazing rituals of white sailors that created solidarity in the forecastle. Her description suggests the reasons Charles may have found sailors a "pack" of "ignorant" men ("Fraternity in the American Forecastle, 1830–1870"). Creighton's article also elaborates the reasons that common sailors found solace and camaraderie with one another. Charles A. Benson Diary, 21 May 1862. Of seamen and mariners, Foner and Lewis say that "blacks represented a very important percentage of the workers in that dangerous, exploited, and underpaid occupation" (*The Black Worker*, p. 190). The most common occupations for African Americans in Massachusetts in 1860 were, in descending order: laborers, mariners, barbers, farm laborers, and servants. Only eight people were identified as stewards, one of whom was presumably Charles Benson (Foner and Lewis, *The Black Worker*, p. 133). This information is derived from the 1860 Massachusetts Census, which appears to exclude women, or greatly undercount them. Charles A. Benson Diary, 21 May 1862.

64. For an excellent discussion of the tensions between employers and domestics, see Stansell, *City of Women*, ch. 8. Intriguingly, confusion regarding social status emerged for those domestic workers who were maids for wealthy urban families. Lorenza Berbineau, a domestic who worked for Francis Cabot Lowell II of Boston, regularly recorded visitors to the household. Nowhere in her diary did she specify whether the visitors called on the Lowells or on her. Lorenza worked for the family for thirty-nine years, and in the absence of an independent social life, intensely identified with her employers. Despite the fact that the demarcation between the class of her employers, their friends, and herself was blurred in no way, from simply reading the diary it is virtually impossible to discern whether the visitors she records in her diary were guests of the Lowells or visitors of hers. Lorenza Berbineau Diary, Francis Cabot Lowell II Papers, 1851–1869.

An anonymous author wrote "The Story of Betsey," a memorial for a woman who was a domestic worker for a proper Boston family. She too attested to the overlapping social life: "All the friends of our family were her friends, and it was pleasant to see them meet her with a welcome which her modest yet beaming smile responded to." This did not reflect social equality for Betsey; it was Betsey's job to be pleasant (*The Story of Betsey*). See David M. Katzman, *Seven Days a Week: Women and Domestic Service in Industrializing America*. And the patronizing tone of the memorial communicates the message that she assigned the label of "friends" to acquaintances who exchanged pleasantries and who understood their respective places in the hierarchy of relations between employer and domestic servant. While the author observed Betsey's "modest yet beaming smile," we do not know how Betsey felt when she was smiling. For a contemporary account of domestic servants' relationships with their employers, see Judith Rollins, *Between Women: Domestics and Their Employers* (Philadelphia: Temple University Press, 1985).

Lizzie Goodenough, a "hired girl" as opposed to an urban domestic servant, similarly recorded visitors. However, the visitors to the households probably did represent greater equality of circumstance and more of a blending of social life than was true for Betsey or Lorenza Berbineau. Yet Lizzie clearly noted when visitors came just to see her. Addie Brown was another domestic worker who did not experience status confusion. In great detail she documented her relationship with her African American employers in New York City. While she called her employers "Mother" and "Father," she did not reciprocate Mother's espoused affection for her. Addie never lost sight of her need for the paycheck. She shared a social standing as African American with Mother and Father, despite their class differences. But the class distinctions stood as a barrier in their relationship. She socialized with the other hired help, the boarders, Mother, and Mother's guests, but she did not misinterpret the situation. Lizzie Goodenough Diary, 19 March 1865. Ann Stoddard Diary, 1866, is another example of this. In the transition from schoolteacher to domestic servant, her social world contracted dramatically.

65. Motz, *True Sisterhood*, p. 5.

5. "TRUE OPINION CLEAR OF POLISH"

1. Eliza Adams to The Family, Adams Family Papers, 19 September 1857. For comprehensive discussion of nineteenth-century birth-control methods, see D'Emilio and Freedman, *Intimate Matters*, and Linda Gordon, *Woman's Body, Woman's Right: A Social History of Birth Control in America*.

2. This phrase was used by Marcella Holmes when she asked Sarah Carter her opinion of Marcella's sister's new husband, whom Marcella had not yet met. Marcella Holmes to Sarah Carter, Holmes Family Papers, 5 March 1861; Robert Paine, "What is Gossip About? An Alternative Hypothesis," p. 279.

3. Patricia Meyer Spacks, *Gossip*, p. 34; Addie Brown to Rebecca Primus, Primus Family Papers, 16 December 1861.

4. Laurel Ulrich referred to neighbors as "an informal jury of one's peers" in colonial New England (*Good Wives*, p. 61).

5. Addie Brown to Rebecca Primus, Primus Family Papers, 11 September 1862; Harriot Curtis, "Aunt Letty; or, The Useful," cited in JoAnne Preston, "Millgirl Narratives," p. 24.

6. Spacks, *Gossip*, p. 31. The community jury occasionally did convene to adjudicate disputes. For example, James Mars, a black man born into slavery, claimed that his owner, Mr. Munger of Connecticut, promised him a cow when he was freed. When Mr. Munger retracted his promise, James Mars went on strike. They turned their dispute over to a community forum to help them resolve it:

> I finally said I would leave it to three men if they were men that I liked: if they were not, I would not. He said I might name the men; their judgment was to be final. The men were selected, the time and place specified. The day came, the parties met, and the men were on hand. Mr. Munger had his nephew for counsel; I plead my case myself. A number of the neighbors were present." (James Mars, *Life of James Mars*, p. 52)

The "arbitrators," as James labeled them, decided that James owed Mr. Munger $90—a decision against James Mars, but one by which he abided.

In another example, Parna Gilbert discussed the role of her church as an arbiter in a community dispute. She recorded that the "Bretheren and Sisters of our church which have long been at variance with each other but whose difficulties were presented before the church on Thursday and Saturday last in the presence of Mr. [Birby] of C.W. & Mr. B. & Clark of [?] for an investigation of the matter, and their attendance in trying to assist in settleing the difficulty if all warm in exercise of that love" (Diary, 23 December 1849).

Robert N. Bellah, "The Meaning of Reputation in American Society," p. 743. Anselm Strauss, in *Negotiations: Varieties, Contexts, Processes, and Social Order*, observes that negotiations "pertain to the ordering and articulation of an enormous variety of activities" (p. ix).

7. Peter J. Wilson, "Filcher of Good Names: An Enquiry into Anthropology and Gossip," p. 100; Laurel Ulrich, *Good Wives*, p. 96. D'Emilio and Freedman characterize this shift from communal control over behavior to individual control as the psychological shift from shame to guilt (*Intimate Matters*).

Contemporary psychologists now challenge the portrait of late-twentieth-century culture as free of shame. For a comprehensive review of this literature, see Robert Karen, "Shame." Eliza Adams to Margaret, Adams Family Papers, 21 October 1837.

8. Paulina Bascom Williams Diary, 3 September 1830 (emphasis in original); Leonard Stockwell Memorial Volume, p. 33.

9. Litwack, *North of Slavery*, p. 3. The various New England states abolished slavery at different times, some gradually with grandfather clauses, and others immediately. Brown, *The Life of William J. Brown*, p. 86.

10. Susan Dwyer Amussen's study of early modern England points to a similar phenomenon: "Sexual behavior was not the only component of reputation. Relationships within families were observed and evaluated" (*An Ordered Society: Gender and Class in Early Modern England*, p. 100). Spacks, *Gossip*, p. 32.

11. Erlunia Smith to Ann Lilley, Ann Lilley Dixon Correspondence, 23 May 1841.

12. William Grimes, *Life of William Grimes, the Runaway Slave, Brought Down to the Present Times*, pp. 111–12. We do not know the race of his detractors or the role of racism in the accusation. A young white girl washing laundry for a black family would probably have provoked talk about her chastity regardless of her sexual conduct, both because of interracial contact and because it was unusual for a white woman to work for a black family.

13. Abigail Baldwin Diary, 8 September 1853; Addie Brown to Rebecca Primus, Primus Family Papers, 1 January 1866.

14. Addie Brown to Rebecca Primus, Primus Family Papers, 16 December 1861; Abigail Baldwin Diary, 4 August 1853. Stephen and Anne Parker to Rhoda Parker, Rhoda Parker Smith Correspondence, 23 February 1845.

15. Addie Brown to Rebecca Primus, Primus Family Papers, 10 December 1865.

16. Wilson, "Filcher of Good Names," p. 101; Stephen Parker to Rhoda Parker, Rhoda Parker Smith Correspondence, 11 April 1848 (emphasis in original); Mary Adams to Adams Family, Adams Family Papers, 1 March 1835.

17. Bellah, "The Meaning of Reputation in American Society," p. 743; Mary Mudge Diary, 29 September 1854; Parna Gilbert Diary, 2 March 1851.

18. Leonard M. Stockwell Memorial, p. 20.

19. Sarah Trask Diary, 7 May 1849, 10 August 1849.

20. Sarah Holmes to Sarah Carter, Holmes Family Papers, 5 November 184[7], 12 December 1851 (emphasis in original). Sarah wrote this letter shortly before she married. Ibid., 2[3] April 1853, 19 July 1855, 30 August 1853.

21. Gossip about deviant behavior reminds group members of their commonalities and heightens their distance from the subject. Max Gluckman characterizes gossip as the "hallmark of membership" ("Gossip and Scandal," p. 313). Arthur Bennett Diary, 20 May 1844, emphasis in the original.

22. John F. Szwed, "Gossip, Drinking, and Social Control: Consensus and Communication in a Newfoundland Parish," p. 435. Erlunia Smith to Ann Lilley Dixon, Ann Lilley Dixon Correspondence, 4 February n.y.

23. Eliza Adams to Adams Family, Adams Family Papers, 5 February 1848.

24. Melissa Doloff Diary, 10 September 1858.

25. Mary Mudge Diary, 7, 8, 9 March 1854. Mary refers to Philip Bryant, her future husband, as "B." in her diary. Ibid., 20 June 1854.

26. For a discussion of these issues, see Ryan, "The Power of Women's Networks."

27. All quotations relating to the *Bodwell v. Osgood* case come from Box 61, no. 90 files of the Court of Common Pleas, 1824, at the Essex County Courthouse, unless otherwise noted. Judge Samuel Putnam, who heard the case in the Supreme Judicial Court, kept notes summarizing the case that included some verbatim testimony. Osgood's letter to the committee of school district no. 8 in Methuen, May 3, 1824, was entered as evidence.

28. This point is not elaborated in the case records. It possibly relates to the circumstances of Osgood's daughter, who was at one time a teacher in the same school as Bodwell. She had not been reappointed to the 1824 summer session when Bodwell had been hired to teach. Mrs. Caleb Swan had no legal standing as a married woman in 1824, which is why Bodwell sued Mr. Swan for Mrs. Swan's behavior. Octavius Pickering, "Sophia W. Bodwell *versus* Caleb Swan *et ux.*"

29. Although the court records list two female witnesses to be remunerated for testifying, neither was mentioned in the judge's case notes. The midwife, Mrs. Jones, whom Osgood represented as being present at the birth of Bodwell's illegitimate child, was not called as a witness. The marginalization of women in civil legal disputes contrasts sharply with the colonial period, when women acted as primary witnesses, their wisdom called upon as an essential civic service.

30. Wage data is not available for the school district in Methuen in 1824. However, the *Massachusetts Secretary of the Commonwealth Abstract of Returns from the School Committees of Several Towns* reports that in 1833–34, Methuen paid its summer-school teachers $9 per month (less than half of wages for winter-session school—summer-school teachers were almost exclusively women, and winter teachers were mostly men at this time). JoAnne Preston, "Women's Aspirations and the Feminization of School Teaching in Nineteenth-Century New England," lecture given at Schlesinger Library, Radcliffe College, April 1992. Because wages generally rose over the course of the century, I assume that teachers made less in 1824 than they did ten years later. While Sophia Bodwell's settlement was large, it was considerably less than the $5,000 for which she had sued. The judge advised the jury on how to assess those damages:

> Upon the subject of damages (if the jury should find it necessary to consider that question) I remarked that the Pl[aintif]fs was not to come into court to acquire a character—but to vindicate her character which had been already acquired, from unjust aspersions—That if the Def[endan]t had proved that her Character was of little or no value—they would give little Damages.

Pickering, "Sophia W. Bodwell *versus* Benjamin Osgood."

31. Sarah Holmes to Sarah Carter, Holmes Family Papers, 13 October 1851.

32. Grimes, *Life of William Grimes*, pp. 119, 118. Grimes does not say specifically what those accusations were.

33. That said, the bravest of the female diarists to counter community

opinion, Mary Mudge, Sarah Holmes, and Melissa Doloff, were all schoolteach-ers. Robert C. Post, "The Social Foundations of Defamation Law: Reputation and the Constitution." Within such ceremonies, remuneration had less meaning than the decision regarding character because the dispute was about honor and dignity, which have no clear monetary value.

34. Steven Lukes, ed., *Power*, p. 5. Nancy C. M. Hartsock, *Money, Sex, and Power: Toward a Feminist Historical Materialism*, p. 225. Robert Paine, "What is Gossip About?" p. 283.

35. Spacks, *Gossip*, p. 6–7; Ulrich, *Good Wives*, pp. 220, 57; Mary Beth Norton, "Gender and Defamation in Seventeenth-Century Maryland," p. 22.

36. Susan Harding, "Women and Words in a Spanish Village," p. 303. Because they are subordinate in society, "women must defend and advance themselves with whatever everyday verbal skills, such as squabbling, finesse, and gossip, they may develop" (p. 295). Although forbidden to do so in the village she studies, women gossip. Like Gluckman, Harding sees the importance of gossip in maintaining village cohesion; talk effectively integrates village households. But unlike Gluckman, Harding assigns a unique role to women. Spanish men, who supposedly only talk and never gossip, create hierarchy, distance, and separation between households: "Their inclination is toward isolation and self-sufficiency. If it is the role of men to build and keep up the figurative fences, it is the role of women to climb them from time to time" (p. 301). Despite the taboo, women spread their news, good and bad, bringing village inhabitants closer to one another via information.

37. For a review of some of the stereotypes, see Ralph L. Rosnow and Gary Alan Fine, *Rumor and Gossip: The Social Psychology of Hearsay* (New York: Elsevier, 1976), ch. 6. In his study of a contemporary synagogue, Samuel C. Heilman finds gossip utilized by both men and women. In addition to gossip's role in the social construction of community reality, he characterizes it as a type of wealth whose value is determined by supply and demand for information. The more scarce the information, the more valuable it is, and the more it enhances its owner's status. However, there are limits to the wealth; if people overzealously indulge, they become gossipmongers, gossip gluttons. In the synagogue Heilman studies, secretive gossip—gossip that is shared only among a few—is used by the male leadership to maintain their prestige and power: "They use it to hold on to their power and to peddle influence, often at the expense of their rivals' reputations" (*Synagogue Life: A Study in Symbolic Interaction*, pp. 164 and 179).

38. That said, however, there are examples from the nineteenth century of reputations tainted and careers endangered because of adultery (e.g., Henry Ward Beecher), as well as examples of reputations and careers unaffected (e.g., Mabel Loomis Todd and Austin Dickinson). Amussen says the bases shifted differently over time for men and women. Women's reputations become based on increasingly narrow criteria, while men's reputations were more broadly based, including social and economic criteria (*An Ordered Society*, p. 103). One important difference between my research and Amussen's, other than time and place, is that I rely largely on what working people discuss in ordinary, everyday circumstances. She investigates situations that have passed a threshold, prompt-

ing the target of gossip to take public, i.e., legal, action against the perpetrator. Thus, court records reveal what is *most* insulting to an individual, and they do not necessarily reflect the range of criteria for a good character.

39. Numerous examples exist in the North as well as the South. For examples in the North, see Brown, *The Life of William J. Brown*; Mars, *Life of James Mars*; James L. Smith, *Autobiography of James L. Smith*; Jacobs, *Incidents in the Life of a Slave Girl*.

40. Wilson, "Filcher of Good Names," p. 99.

6. "GETTING RELIGION"

1. Paul E. Johnson, *A Shopkeeper's Millennium: Society and Revivals in Rochester, New York, 1815–1837*, p. 98. Marcella Holmes to Sarah Carter, Holmes Family Papers, 25 May 1860 (emphasis added). Marcella's brother was not so easily persuaded. He voiced his criticisms of Christian practice to Sarah (James Holmes to Sarah Carter, Holmes Family Papers, 21 November 1858), and did not similarly experience pressure from the group:

> I should think better of Christian denominations if they were willing to accord the sincerity they claim for themselves to those who dissent to their views yet act quite as consistently. . . . I have given it much thought and have examined the subject pretty thoroughly and I think impartially and cannot come to the conclusion that you probably have. And I am sorry to say that I have too often heard facts apparently wilfully perverted from the pulpit.

2. Some think it private, others public. Elizabeth Schussler Fiorenza conceives of it as a "middle-ground" in a continuum between public and private (*In Memory of Her: A Feminist Theological Reconstruction of Christian Origins*). Clarke E. Cochran argues it is both private and public (*Religion in Public and Private Life*). My discussion pertains almost exclusively to Protestant religions in New England.

3. Most scholars agree that the antebellum increase in religious enthusiasm stemmed from the rise of capitalism and the emergence of the middle class. Johnson, *A Shopkeeper's Millennium*; Donald G. Mathews, "The Second Great Awakening as an Organizing Process, 1780–1830: An Hypothesis"; Ryan, *Cradle of the Middle Class*; and Smith-Rosenberg, "The Cross and the Pedestal: Women, Anti-Ritualism, and the Emergence of the American Bourgeoisie." According to Charles Sellers, Christianity provided a kulturkampf, the battleground between land and market cultures, the cultural medium through which people managed and understood the intensification of capitalism in the nineteenth century (*The Market Revolution: Jacksonian America, 1815–1846*, p. 31). Religion was also a weapon brandished in both class and gender battles. Middle-class employers used religion to discipline their workers, while the urban poor used their faith as an instrument in their struggles with the middle class. At the same time, women employed morality against the godless proclivities of men. Sociologists have long studied the multiple dimensions of religious life. Beginning with Max Weber's *The Protestant Ethic and the Spirit of Capitalism*, this tradition continues today with books such as Gerhard Lenski, *The Religious*

Factor: A Sociological Study of Religion's Impact on Politics, Economics, and Family Life (Westport, Conn.: Greenwood Press, 1977). See also Nancy F. Cott, "Young Women in the Second Great Awakening in New England."

4. C. Eric Lincoln and Lawrence H. Mamiya, "The Religious Dimension: Toward a Sociology of Black Churches," p. 8. See also, Litwack, *North of Slavery*, p. 188. "The Negro church was far more than simply a religious institution. The church was 'school, his forum, his political arena, his social club, his art gallery, his conservatory of music. It was lyceum and gymnasium as well as *sanctum sanctorum*'" (George A. Levesque, *Black Boston: Negro Life in Garrison's Boston, 1800–1860*, pp. 266–67, quoting from *The Liberator*, 9 January 1852). As with white parishioners, most African Americans "appeared to maintain religious affiliations, at least for social, if not for spiritual, reasons" (Litwack, *North of Slavery*, p. 191). Obviously, religious beliefs played a major role in the black community as well.

5. William G. McLoughlin, *Revivals, Awakenings, and Reform: An Essay on Religion and Social Change in America, 1607–1977*. Paula Aymer argues that the awakenings also offered opportunities to the African-American community (*The Second Great Awakening: An Opportunity for Blacks in America*, M.A. thesis, Northeastern University, 1983). Although revivals occurred before and after, the Second Great Awakening was a period of numerous revivals and conversions. Revivals built upon pre-existing religious and organizational frameworks and a predisposition to religious beliefs.

6. Methodism became the largest denomination in 1844, when it reached a membership of one million. Ironically, 1844 was also the year that the Methodist church split—North versus South—over the issue of slavery. This split lasted almost one hundred years (Edwin Scott Gaustad, *A Religious History of America*, p. 188). American religion underwent a revolution in the antebellum period. The number of denominations proliferated and competing interpretations of the Bible multiplied. "This was a religious environment that brought into question traditional authorities and exalted the right of the people to think for themselves. The result, quite simply, was a bewildering world of clashing opinion" (Nathan O. Hatch, *The Democratization of American Christianity*, p. 81). In this milieu, religion promised stability but was largely unable to deliver. The spiraling number of world views could confuse as easily as it could enlighten. However, religion could offer a vision of the future, a path through the sea of change, some concepts and vocabulary with which to frame and understand the reorganization of antebellum economic and social life.

The dissenting religions offered immediate salvation through conversion, rather than predestination or a requirement for extended study of the scripture. The radical belief systems "empowered ordinary people by taking their deepest spiritual impulses at face value rather than subjecting them to the scrutiny of orthodox doctrine and the frowns of respectable clergymen" (Hatch, *Democratization of American Christianity*, p. 10). They did not require or encourage their clergy to be formally educated in theology, and for this reason opened the doors to uneducated whites and African Americans who would otherwise have been denied their calling. Unlike the Congregationalists, the dissenting religions spurned education and condemned attention to the arts and literature. This revolt against the dominant culture stemmed from several factors: (1) their rejection of elite religion as it had been practiced; (2) the impulse to democratize; and (3) the worry that "theology, philosophy, art, and science might lure the faithful from salvation" (T. Scott Miyakawa, *Protestants and Pioneers: Individualism and Conformity on the American Frontier* [Chicago: University of Chicago Press, 1964], p. 161). Evangelists adamantly condemned worldly amusements, including dancing, reading novels, going to the theater, and drinking. Reading fiction for entertainment became a target of virulent attacks from the pulpit.

A dispute exists about whether a national culture has ever existed in the United States. See, for example, Ronald J. Zboray, *A Fictive People: Antebellum Economic Development and the American Reading Public.*

7. In almost all cases, the shift in language was short-lived. Subjects returned to their previous ways of speaking and dropped their obsession with the religious condition of their friends. Only two diarists referred to their conversion to Christianity in their diaries. The other conversion accounts come from correspondents and autobiographers.

8. George S. Whipple Diary, 15 May 1838; George Henry, *Life of George Henry, Together with a Brief History of the Colored People in America*, p. 41; Sarah Trask Diary, 27 May 1849. Church did not live up to its spiritual promise for her. Then when she arrived at home, she found her mother in bed with the headache. In the same entry, she wrote, "I guess for the future I will stay at home, for there is no peace for me, all ways something to worry me."

9. Eliza Adams to Margaret Adams, Adams Family Papers, 21 October 1837; Charles A. Metcalf to Mrs. Joseph A. Metcalf, Metcalf-Adams Papers, 2 June 1844.

10. Hannah Adams to Edmund Adams, Adams Family Papers, 13 February 1854; Margaret Adams to Hannah Adams, 11 June n.y.; Abigail Baldwin Diary, 15 September 1853. In part, Abigail's and Mary's husbands' jobs depended on their ability to draw people into the church's folds, which in turn translated into money (alms/subscriptions). Paulina Bascom Williams Diary, 6 June 1830. Paulina was a Congregationalist but other Christian denominations shared her critique of freemasonry. "Many antebellum denominations from Presbyterians to Freewill Baptists condemned Freemasonry as heretical, in part because its universalist sentiments denied the uniqueness of Christian revelation and in part because it reeked of magic" (Jon Butler, *Awash in a Sea of Faith: Christianizing the American People*, p. 235). Paulina, Bascom Williams stayed home from services because she did not have proper shoes. Also, she was pregnant and did not have clothes that fit (Paulina Bascom Williams Diary, 14 October 1831). Addie Brown at various times lacked winter shoes or a winter hat, and one time she felt the flowers on her hat were too bright so she did not go to services (Addie Brown to Rebecca Primus, Primus Family Papers, 14 November 1861). Sarah Beacham Diary, 27 December 1863.

11. Mary Hall Diary, 21 June 1829. I excluded diaries from the study that focused solely on religious revelations.

12. Horatio Chandler Diary, 28 March 1841.

13. Barbara Loomis, *Piety and Play: Young Women's Leisure in an Era of*

Evangelical Religion, 1790–1840; Barron, *Those Who Stayed Behind*, p. 44. For a British example of this phenomenon, see Barbara Taylor, *Eve and the New Jerusalem: Socialism and Feminism in the Nineteenth Century* (New York: Pantheon, 1983). Tucker, *Itinerant Preaching*, pp. 109–10.

14. Mary Holbrook Diary, 12 February 1853. In her diary, Sarah Root records black men preaching at a church in Belchertown, Massachusetts, in 1859 and 1860. Peter Randolph, *From Slave Cabin to Pulpit: The Autobiography of Rev. Peter Randolph; The Southern Question Illustrated and Sketches of Slave Life*, p. 45. In the face of the widespread adoption of Christianity by African Americans, many whites in the North continued to exhibit ambivalence or even hostility. William J. Brown wrote in his autobiography about white treatment of black people in Providence, Rhode Island: "It was a common thing for colored people to be disturbed on the street, especially on the Sabbath" (*The Life of William J. Brown*, p. 126).

At the time of the American Revolution, African Americans in the North worshiped in predominantly white congregations. However, soon thereafter, northerners' prejudice against integrated services grew. Neither Christian faith nor anti-slavery sentiments overrode bigotry for most white northerners. Some churches segregated free blacks into separate pews, others exiled black worshipers to a balcony. In his autobiography, the Reverend Jeremiah Asher described segregated pews at the First Baptist Church in Hartford, Connecticut:

> There were situated at that time, in the gallery of the meeting house, two large pews, capable of holding some twenty persons. The pews, situated at the corner of the galleries, were separated from the other seats by partitions, about three feet high, between the minister and his colored hearers, which concealed them mainly from the view of the congregation and minister." (*An Autobiography*, pp. 35–36)

This segregation eventually prompted Jeremiah to move to the Union Church on Talcott Street in Hartford, Connecticut, established by the African American community.

Even Quakers, early and consistent abolitionists, admonished blacks not to sit in pews with white abolitionist Quakers. Sarah Mapps Douglass wrote about the treatment of her mother at a Quaker meeting, where a Friend told her "that the colored people sat up stairs 'as F[rien]ds do not like to sit by thy color'" (Dorothy Sterling, ed., *We Are Your Sisters: Black Women in the Nineteenth Century*, p. 131). It was this kind of hypocrisy that inspired the "come-outer" movement among abolitionists in the 1830s and 1840s. The radical wing of the anti-slavery movement encouraged principled Christians to leave their church if it did not declare itself staunchly against slavery and race prejudice.

Free blacks in the North established independent churches as "asylum from white prejudice" (Levesque, *Black Boston*, p. 266). The black leaders Absalom Jones and Richard Allen of Philadelphia organized two of the first independent churches for blacks in the North. Others, including the Methodists and Baptists, followed suit, particularly between 1790 and 1810 (Hatch, *The Democratization of American Christianity*, pp. 107–8). The first black churches in New England included First African Baptist Church of Boston in 1805, the nonsectarian

African Union Meeting House in Providence in 1820, and the Colored Union Church in Newport, Rhode Island, in 1824 (Edward D. Smith, *Climbing Jacob's Ladder: The Rise of Black Churches in Eastern American Cities, 1740–1877*, pp. 44–57). These churches provided a safe environment for African Americans to observe their cultural traditions and develop their own interpretation of the gospel. Randolph, *From Slave Cabin to Pulpit*, pp. 48, 54. Mary Orne Tucker brings up another example of a black man ministering in a white congregation. Her "evaluation" of Reverend Marrs is quite telling. On October 20, 1842, she notes that "Mr. Tucker is aided in the work by a colored man named MARRS, who is in many respects quite a remarkable person. He is gifted with a strong native genius, a good acquaintance of human nature, a readiness of delivery, and a happy faculty of illustrating his discourses with curious comparisons and quaint figures of speech. A good education would make him quite a prodigy; but he is unlearned, and sometimes too boisterous for good effect. He draws large audiences, and is attracting very general attention" (Tucker, *Itinerant Preaching*, p. 103). He was an oddity, someone "too boisterous for good effect" in a white church. Nonetheless, many white people came to see him, and he undoubtedly had a large following in the African-American community. Examples pop up in diaries as well. Joseph Kimball wrote, "Sunday at meeting white Negro pr." (31 August 1845), "Mr. Lang, a collerd man lectored in the baptist" (19 April 1846), and "black man pr. in the evening" (20 January 1850). Other black ministers also document the curiosity-seekers who come to see them preach (Lincoln and Mamiya, "The Religious Dimension," p. 6).

15. Daniel Calhoun, *The Intelligence of a People*; Susan Brown Forbes Diary, 12 March 1843; Marcella Holmes to Sarah Carter, Holmes Family Papers, 25 May 1860; Hannah Adams to Mary Adams, Adams Family Papers, 30 December 1858; Sarah Metcalf to Chloe Metcalf, Metcalf-Adams Family Letters, 25 December 1842; Charles A. Metcalf to Mrs. Joseph A. Metcalf, 2 June 1844. The theme of sleep in church rose repeatedly as a problem. Mary Orne Tucker told a story of an occurrence in her Universalist church in Charlestown, New Hampshire: "The bold preacher suddenly delivered with considerable emphasis that passage, 'Awake, thou that sleepest.' This aroused a sleepy old Frenchman, who, overcome by the fatigues of the week and the warmth of the day, sat nodding in his pew. He supposing the remark directed particularly at himself, jumped up in great anger, exclaiming, 'What you mean, sar? Can't I take von leetel nap in mine own pew without von insult, sar? I leaves dis house, sar, an' I comes here no more, sar!' and out marched the irate Frenchman, shaking his cane violently and stamping upon the floor. Such scenes were not uncommon" (*Itinerant Preaching*, pp. 26–27). Martha Osborne Barrett Diary, 19 August 1849; Alfred Porter Diary, 16 April 1854.

16. Hatch, *The Democratization of American Christianity*, p. 135; "Methodist itinerant preaching deliberately used theatricality to promote conversion," Butler, *Awash in a Sea of Faith*, p. 238. There are many parallels between the theater and the church, which I do not have the space to develop. Suffice it to say that the techniques of a minister, not unlike those of an actor, strove through gesture, voice, staging, and evocative imagery to spellbind the audience and move them to a transcendent understanding of greater truths. For a discussion

of these issues in the theater, see Antonin Artaud, *The Theater and Its Double*, translated by Mary Caroline Richards (New York: Grove Press, 1958). Hatch, *Democratization of American Christianity*, p. 134.

17. James Adams, Jr., to Joseph Addison Metcalf, Metcalf-Adams Family Letters, 14 May 1838; Sarah Holmes Clark to Sarah Carter, Holmes Family Papers, 18 January 1853.

18. Charles Metcalf to Parents, Metcalf-Adams Family Letters, 27 April 1844; Martha Osborne Barrett Diary, 31 December 1849, 30 June 1850.

19. Rabinowitz, *The Spiritual Self in Everyday Life*, p. xxvi. Church affiliation varied by race, class, and geographical location. African Americans were disproportionately drawn to the Methodist and Baptist faiths, the first denominations to establish independent black churches, as were the poor and working classes (Smith, *Climbing Jacob's Ladder*). In contrast, professionals and those of the upper classes disproportionately attended the Congregational, Episcopal, and Unitarian churches. White farmers were less likely to be church members than merchants or master craftsmen (Randolph A. Roth, *The Democratic Dilemma: Religion, Reform, and the Social Order in the Connecticut River Valley of Vermont, 1791–1850*, p. 95). These affiliations were not absolute. The culture of the countryside—cooperative, parochial, fatalistic, somewhat mystical, and superstitious—found the earthy emotionalism of the evangelical Baptist and Methodist churches appealing. But this, too, varied by region; in some areas, being a farmer meant being a Congregationalist. In contrast, the urban environment—which cultivated a belief in the role of the individual in one's own salvation and the moral culpability of the individual—found the rationality of Unitarianism and Universalism more compatible with people's conceptions of themselves and the competitive, cosmopolitan, and activist aspects of the new market. As Sydney E. Ahlstrom writes, urban life "tended both to stimulate evangelism and to expose the existence of a common tradition" (*A Religious History of the American People*, p. 470). According to Litwack, this was also true in the black community (*North of Slavery*, pp. 195–96).

20. Asher, *An Autobiography*, pp. 24–25.

21. Reverend Samuel Harrison, *His Life Story*, pp. 13–14. The Reverend Noah Davis tells of a similar distinction made in the South by free blacks. When he first went to Baltimore to establish a church, the Reverend Davis encountered the less generous biases of local people regarding their brand of theology. "I found that everybody loved to go with the multitude, and it was truly up-hill work with me. I found some who are called Anti-Mission, or Old School Baptists, who, when I called upon them, would ask of what faith I was,—and when I would reply, that I belonged to what I understood to be the Regular Baptists, they would answer, 'Then you are not of our faith,' &c." (*A Narrative of the Life of Rev. Noah Davis*, p. 33). Tucker, *Itinerant Preaching*, pp. 105–6, 102, 129. The elaborate detail regarding sectarianism seems unique to the autobiographies. In contrast, diarists reveal everyday religious practices and opinions but don't proselytize in the same way. In part this stems from the purposes for which each kind of document was written. Sarah Metcalf Mann to Chloe Metcalf, Metcalf-Adams Family Letters, 18 February 1850; Calvin

Metcalf to James Adams, 26 February 1819; Roth, *The Democratic Dilemma*, p. 190.

22. Horatio Chandler Diary, 2 April 1841, 27 October 1841; Sarah Beacham Diary, 7 June 1863.

23. Joseph Lye Diary, 22 March 1818, 17 February 1822; Minerva Mayo Autobiography, letter from Minerva to Jerusha Clap, 2 September 1820.

24. Ahlstrom referred to the early nineteenth century as a "sectarian heyday" (*A Religious History*, ch. 29). Joseph Lye Diary, 28 December 1817. He did not attend Calvinist services—those he exhorted against—but many others. Smith, *Autobiography of James L. Smith*, pp. 190–91. White diarists also mention sharing a meeting house. For example, Harriet Severance discusses how Methodists, Baptists, and Congregationalists shared a meeting house with the Unitarians. The Unitarian services were the only ones Harriet would skip (Harriet Severance Diary, e.g., 6 September 1863).

25. Joseph Kimball Diary, 27 October 1844; Julia P. Stevens to Rhoda Parker, Rhoda Parker Smith Correspondence, 26 September 1848; Eliza Adams to Uncle John, Adams Family Papers, 27 February 1842. Unlike Protestants, Catholics did not condone the practice of church visiting. The cultures clashed as Eliza waited to be invited into the church, and the Irishman did not know how to receive her.

26. Francis Bennett, Jr., Diary, 3 September 1854, emphasis in original.

27. Samuel Shepard James Diary, 29 November 1840. Diarists who recorded visiting both Congregational and Freewill Baptist meetings include Nathan Abbott, Ivory Hill, and Samuel Shepard James. Others attended Congregational and Baptist meetings: Lorenza Berbineau, Horatio Chandler, Susan Forbes, Joseph Kimball, and Harriet Severance. Male and female subjects did not differ in their church-visiting patterns. Some recorded going to meetings but did not specify at which church.

28. Hatch, *Democratization of American Christianity*, p. 9.

29. Roth, *The Democratic Dilemma*, p. 83. This absolutely contradicted the experience of the new religious marketplace. But the appeal of religion included the evocative images of life as it should be on earth and the promises of afterlife. See also Cott, "Young Women in the Second Great Awakening in New England."

30. Consumer language in the acquisition of religion is very striking, in contrast to colonial conversions. Religion was to be obtained, acquired. This consumptive terminology fit completely with the concept of a "religious marketplace."

31. Permelia Dame to George Dame, Dame Sisters Letters, 4 January 1832; Eliza Adams to Elizabeth Adams, Adams Family Papers, 1 May 1842.

32. Parna Gilbert Diary, 23 September 1848. Virginia Lieson Brereton also found death to be a stimulus for middle-class women's conversions (*From Sin to Salvation: Stories of Women's Conversions, 1800 to the Present*, p. 6). Harriet Severance Diary, 1 May 1864 (emphasis in original). Ryan coined the phrase, *Cradle of the Middle Class*, p. 87. Lavinia Merrill to Rhoda Parker, Rhoda Parker Smith Correspondence, 19 August 1840, 14 May 1841. Interestingly, the incidence of death was no greater in the antebellum period than it had been

earlier. Several waves of epidemics swept through New England—not enough to change the death rate but sufficient to alter perceptions concerning the threat of death.

33. Some individuals did decide to seek religion as individuals. In her life of great hardship, Nancy Prince, at the age of 20, turned to religion to lighten the burden of trying to support her mother and brothers and sisters (*A Narrative of the Life and Travels of Mrs. Nancy Prince*, p. 17):

> I resolved, in my mind, to seek an interest in my Savior, and put my trust in Him; and never shall I forget the place or time when God spake to my troubled conscience. Justified by faith I found peace with God, the forgiveness of sin through Jesus Christ my Lord. After living sixteen years without hope, and without a guide, May 6th, 1819, the Rev. Thomas Paul, baptized myself, and seven others, in obedience to the great command.
>
> > We, on him our anchor cast—
> > Poor and needy, lean on him,
> > He will bring us through at last.

However, the autobiographical accounts may convey a more individualistic message because they focus on the self, often to the exclusion of the social context. Mary Metcalf to Chloe Metcalf, Metcalf-Adams Family Letters, 24 May 1846 (emphasis in original). It is interesting to note the way the process juxtaposed passivity to extreme effort. Passivity was the hallmark of Calvinist religious experience, and fervent effort was the embodiment of dissenting religious conversions. The simultaneous contradictory impulses were probably unique to the historical moment of transition between the two. Winthrop Parker wrote to his sister Rhoda Parker (21 September 1839): "Cast your sins at the foot of the cross. Christ is able to give you a new heart. You must not exspect you can save your own soul for of *our selves we can do nothing* all that is neces[i]ry is to have faith in the promises of God that whosoever will come to him through Jesus Christ confessing their sins he will pardon" (emphasis added). This contradiction also surfaces in the published conversion narratives of middle class women. "These Protestants believed that prospective converts must labor constantly to prepare their hearts to receive the 'operations of the spirit.' In short, conversion required of the convert both enormous effort and also the cessation of all struggle" (Brereton, *From Sin to Salvation*, p. 5). Philip Greven notes that Arminian religions have a different conception of free will in the conversion process: people find "salvation by the performance of religious duties, of good works, and by virtuous behavior" (*The Protestant Temperament: Patterns of Child-Rearing, Religious Experience, and the Self in Early America*, p. 87). Hatch, *Democratization of American Christianity*, p. 172.

34. Addie Brown to Rebecca Primus, Primus Family Papers, January 1860.

35. Charles A. Metcalf to Parents, Metcalf-Adams Family Letters, 27 April 1844 (emphasis in original); James Adams to Chloe Metcalf, 15 September 1822; Brown, *The Life of William J. Brown*, pp. 136, 141.

36. Martha Osborne Barrett Diary, 18 August 1849, emphasis in original.

37. Greven discusses the hopelessness and despair that preceded rebirths in early America: "Not until individuals could bring themselves, or be brought by God, to reject their very selves as worthless, sinful, and justly damned creatures,

could they ever hope to be born again" (*The Protestant Temperament*, p. 75). He later states, "The breaking of the sinner's will was the decisive culmination of the process of conversion" (p. 92). Parna Gilbert Diary, 26 September 1848. Barbara Leslie Epstein finds the gendering of the conversion experience was a primary feature distinguishing religion in the nineteenth century from that in the eighteenth. In the eighteenth century, men and women experienced conversions similarly. In the nineteenth century, men's accounts of conversion veered dramatically away from women's. Men focused on a specific act of sin whereas women condemned their sinful being (*The Politics of Domesticity: Women, Evangelism, and Temperance in Nineteenth-Century America*, p. 47). Among these subjects, the gender differences were not so absolute. Some men condemned their souls as well as their sins.

Epstein's explanation for the difference revolves around men's increased worldly involvement in trade and commerce. She finds women attempted to resurrect those values that capitalism was destroying, through the venue of Christianity. Evangelism endorsed cooperation, altruism, generosity, love, self-sacrifice, emotionality—those qualities the market was eroding (pp. 62–63). Sarah Metcalf to Chloe Metcalf, Metcalf-Adams Family Letters, 14 December 1847 (emphasis added, except for *sincere*, which is underlined in the original). Brereton claims that for middle-class women it was "bad form" to express certainty. While it indeed may be a convention of the conversion formula, so much of the language of working women is saturated with insecurity and self-questioning that I cannot help but think the process of conversion and the group pressure deeply unsettled subjects' confidence in themselves. The differences could reflect class origins. Lavinia Merrill to Rhoda Parker, Rhoda Parker Smith Correspondence, 19 August 1840 (emphasis added). Permelia Dame to George Dame, Dame Sisters Letters, 14 n.m. 1834 (emphasis added); Mary C. Metcalf to Chloe Metcalf, Metcalf-Adams Family Letters, 24 May 1846. Interestingly, for others who experienced religion, its transience did not become an issue. It came, it went, and was not mentioned again. For many subjects (e.g., Horatio Chandler, Addie Brown, and Parna Gilbert) the conversion prompted an effusive deluge of concerns about spirituality which gradually receded. The diary-keeping then returned to the pre-conversion form. We must assume that the zeal in everyday life also abated. However, when the converted subjects decided to hold fast to their beliefs, anxiety and uncertainty riddled their personal reflections.

38. Epstein, *The Politics of Domesticity*, p. 48. Some studies reveal that church attendance varied dramatically by gender. For example, in upstate New York, women dominated church membership and disproportionately converted to evangelical Christianity during the Second Great Awakening, across all denominations and geographic locations. Johnson, *A Shopkeeper's Millennium*, p. 108; Martha Tomhave Blauvelt, "Women and Revivalism," p. 1. The one exception was the Mormon faith. McLoughlin, *Revivals, Awakenings, and Reform*, p. 121. See also Ann Douglass, *The Feminization of American Culture*; Johnson, *A Shopkeeper's Millennium*, p. 108; Ryan, *Cradle of the Middle Class*, p. 81. Cott gives evidence of the predominance of female converts in the New England region, in "Young Women in the Second Great Awakening in New England," p. 15. However, working women were more likely to write in their

diaries about church services and religious philosophy than men were. Forty-six percent of the women diarists in my sample recorded at least the service content, as compared to 17% of the men. And 36% of the female diarists discussed their religious philosophy, as compared to 10% of the male diarists.

39. See, for example, Smith-Rosenberg, "The Cross and the Pedestal," in *Disorderly Conduct*, p. 154. She clearly delineates the contradictory messages of Christianity. In this book I do not explore the ways religion encouraged women to submit to authority, to be silent, to lower self-esteem, and the like. The example of Paulina Bascom Williams (Diary, 6 December 1831) illustrates the power of these contradictions for a woman who struggled between her piety, her conviction, and the place to which the beliefs relegated her. When she and her family moved into a new parsonage, she had nothing but complaints about it:

> We have no cow & are out of provisions of every kind, & now whether it is our duty to stay in such a place after such indignity without cause or provocation is a doubt that remains to be solved. Would the Saviour have tarried with disciples that threated him thus! I certainly need a great measure of grace that my mouth may not utter perverseness.

Note that in spite of her "humility," she compared herself to Jesus in considering the inadequate circumstances and the ungrateful people with and for whom she worked. Marilyn Richardson, *Black Women and Religion: A Bibliography*, p. xv. For a discussion of the role of contemporary African American women in the church, see Cheryl Townsend Gilkes, "'Together in Harness': Women's Traditions in the Sanctified Church," and the narratives of female ministers, such as Almond H. Davis, ed., *The Female Preacher, or Memoir of Salome Lincoln*; Rebecca Jackson, *Gifts of Power: The Writings of Rebecca Jackson, Black Visionary, Shaker Eldress*; Jarena Lee, *Religious Experience and Journal of Mrs. Jarena Lee, Giving an Account of Her Call to Preach the Gospel*; and Nancy Towle, *Vicissitudes Illustrated, in the Experience of Nancy Towle, in Europe and America*.

40. Johnson, *A Shopkeeper's Millennium*, p. 97.

41. McLoughlin, *Revivals, Awakenings, and Reform*, p. 113. Alexis de Tocqueville also discusses voluntarism at length in *Democracy in America*.

42. See, for example, Ryan, *Cradle of the Middle Class*. In the 1830s and 1840s in particular, the explosion of organizations included maternal associations, Bible societies, missionary societies, anti-slavery societies, and female moral reform associations. The women's rights movement also grew out of the antebellum period. A self-selected group of women who were active in the anti-slavery crusade attended the Seneca Falls convention in 1848, which, like the moral reform societies, was largely a middle-class phenomenon. Mary Orne Tucker, the wife of a Methodist minister, joined and became president of a female moral reform society in Massachusetts. The number of women involved in collective sewing endeavors was much greater. This figure reflects only those who were a part of formal organizations.

43. As important as the principles were, in secular reform as in spiritual, the social dimension played an important role. Martha Barrett, one of the two white

anti-slavery activists, said after attending the Anti-Slavery Society convention in Boston in 1851, "Enjoyed it very much indeed. Not only the addresses, but meeting so many friends" (Diary, 4 June 1851). Seven years later and still involved, she made plans to go to the Essex County Anti-Slavery Society quarterly meeting. "Am anticipating much pleasure, not only from listening to the speaking, but also in meeting some esteemed friends" (15 December 1858). Only two subjects—Sarah Holmes Clark and Marcella Holmes—expressed pro-slavery opinions. Both of them moved to Georgia in the 1850s. This period was not covered by Pamela Brown Dix's diary, unfortunately. See preface to the published diaries, Blanche Brown Bryant and Gertrude Elaine Baker, eds., *The Diaries of Sally and Pamela Brown, 1832–1838, Hyde Leslie, 1887, Plymouth Notch, Vermont*, p. 4. Many ex-slaves wrote their narratives out of an expressed desire to end slavery. Free blacks in the North could not deny their connection to brothers and sisters in chains in the South the way that whites could.

Ex-slaves and women faced hostile opposition to their prominent place in the public eye and to their expression of radical opinions. Black and white abolitionists were called names, confronted physical threats, and lost their jobs or homes. James L. Smith wrote, "Brickbats and rotten eggs were very common in those days; an anti-slavery lecturer was often showered by them. Slavery at this time had a great many friends" (*Autobiography of James L. Smith*, p. 185). On one lecture circuit through Connecticut and Massachusetts, James L. Smith and his traveling companion, Dr. Osgood, found their horse mutilated by pro-slavery locals. But former slaves and free blacks in the North also faced possible kidnapping and deportation to the South, where they could be sold or returned to their former owners (especially after Congress passed the Fugitive Slave Law in 1850).

White abolitionists encountered animosity as well, the outspoken women in particular. Agent for the Massachusetts Anti-Slavery Society Abigail Kelley braved character assassination, barrages of rotten fruits and vegetables, and occasional physical threats because of her outspokenness. Abolitionists themselves were deeply divided on "the woman question." The national American Anti-Slavery Society split over the rights of women within the organization in 1840. See Dorothy Sterling, *Ahead of Her Time: Abby Kelley and the Politics of Antislavery*.

That said, many people supported the activism of women for a moral cause, and others "excused" activist women. Melissa Doloff wrote in her diary about seeing Julia Ward Howe lecture in 1858:

> She spoke very well indeed. Some think it very much out of place for a lady to be a public speaker, and I think myself that it is rather out of their sphere. But if they think it their duty to be a public speaker, I think there is no impropriety in it. This lady seemed to be very sincere in her remarks and very earnest that the poor slave should be liberated. (Diary, 9 September 1858)

44. In his diary entry of 5 December 1840, Horatio Chandler carefully recorded the Temperance Society Pledge that he had recently taken:

> Beleiving that the evils resulting to our community from the use of intoxicating drinks, are more pervading and intense than those flowing from any other of the dark sources

of misery which vice opens upon us—beleiving it to be our duty, by the obligations which rest upon us in our different capacities of patriots, philanthropists, and Christians, to use our best endeavours to eradicate those evils—& beleiving, also, that the best mode of effecting this great object is the exercise of a *moral influence* in an organized form:—therefore, we the undersigned, do agree that we will not use any intoxicating liquors, as a beverage, nor traffic in them; that we will not provide them as an article of entertainment, as for persons in our employment; & that in all suitable ways, we will discountenance their use throughout the community.

Epstein, *The Politics of Domesticity*, p. 89. Joseph Kimball Diary, 4 March 1833. Abigail Baldwin recorded another lost battle in 1853 in Plymouth, Vermont: "Freeman's meeting, great excitement, rum or no rum. Mr. Joselyn chosen as representative, a particular friend of Mr. Alcohol, arch enemy of sobriety" (Diary, 4 September 1853). David Clapp, *Journal of David Clapp*, p. 22. Hannah Adams to Father and Mother, Adams Family Papers, 14 November 1841. She signed the letter, "your dutiful daughter, H. T. Adams."

45. Toward the middle and end of the nineteenth century, as the flood of immigrants swelled, the temperance issue only superficially veiled anti-immigrant prejudice. Francis Bennett commented on the havoc wreaked by a mob in Gloucester, Massachusetts, that vandalized a store selling rum that was kept by an Irishman (Diary, 4 May 1852).

CONCLUSION

1. Louisa Chapman Diary, 16 April 1848, emphasis added.

2. Nancy Chodorow, *The Reproduction of Mothering*; Ann Oakley, *The Sociology of Housework*; Sara Ruddick, *Maternal Thinking*; and Susan Strasser, *Never Done: A History of American Housework*, to name a few. Some feminists also hold public life in great esteem and assert that "consciousness and personality are apt to develop most fully through a stance of civic responsibility and an orientation to the collective whole" (Rosaldo, "The Use and Abuse of Anthropology," p. 398). Others more forcefully assert the importance of the public as the seat of all power, where men make important decisions. See, for example, Ryan, *Cradle of the Middle Class*; Stansell, *City of Women*; DuBois, *Feminism and Suffrage*.

3. However, historians have successfully documented women's involvement in the public sphere over time, which until the past twenty years had been systematically buried and forgotten. "Women's involvements in exchange transactions, in informal women's communities, and in urban kin networks are now interpreted as having significance for extra-domestic arrangements rather than as mere extensions of women's domestic orientation" (Sylvia Junko Yanagisako, "Family and Household: The Analysis of Domestic Groups," p. 191).

4. Anna Yeatman, "Gender and the Differentiation of Social Life into Public and Private Domains," p. 43. She criticizes feminists such as Michelle Rosaldo, and, by inference, Linda Imray and Audrey Middleton for analytically conflating the terms when they are attempting to distinguish gender differentiation from public/domestic differentiation. Imray and Middleton, "Public and Private: Marking the Boundaries."

5. Both Osterud in *Bonds of Community* and Motz in *True Sisterhood* emphasize the importance of kin networks in particular as safety nets for women in the case of death of, desertion by, or mistreatment by their breadwinners.

6. DuBois, *Feminism and Suffrage*.

APPENDIX A

1. All, that is, until the group of diaries reached a critical mass. Men's diaries were more abundant and easier to locate. Several years into the project, I stopped looking for more men's diaries and intensified my search for women's diaries in order to match their numbers. Charles Stephenson notes that such a hypothesis has yet to be fully explored in the American context, although it can be taken for granted in the British one ("A Gathering of Strangers? Mobility, Social Structure, and Political Participation in the Formation of Nineteenth-Century American Workingclass Culture," p. 35).

2. Betsey Clark Diary, 6 June 1855, 6 August 1855; Nathaniel Clark Diary, 20 July 1848; DeBow, *Statistical View of the United States, 7th Census*, p. 169. I leave it to future studies to determine the most appropriate cutoff point in determining the class status of farmers. For the time being, I want to conservatively cluster those farmers, artisans, and unskilled laborers whose options were limited, and who were more similar to the majority of the population of antebellum New England.

3. I acknowledge the importance of more explicitly analyzing the language itself, but that project would lead to an entirely different book. I hope that someone else will undertake such a project, now that I have brought these sources to light.

4. DeBow, *Statistical View of the United States, Seventh Census*, calculated from pp. lxi and 2–77. Preservation is another potential source of bias—some people's papers are saved and others not. The scarcity of documents makes the research more challenging but not impossible.

5. Ronald J. Zboray, "The Letter and the Fiction Reading Public in Antebellum America," pp. 28, 29.

6. Motz, *True Sisterhood*, p. 55. That said, however, when she generalizes about the content of women's versus men's letters she finds that men mostly discussed political and economic issues, while women discussed community and familial matters, emotions, and opinions of other people. She also maintains that once men married they relied on their wives to continue correspondence with their own mothers, sisters, and brothers, except when writing about business.

7. Zboray has similarly found letters between middle-class men, married and single, to transcend sexual stereotypes and to be "rich in complex, emotional expressions" ("The Letter and the Fiction Reading Public in Antebellum America," pp. 33–34, n. 11). One problem of Motz's research, as Zboray points out, is that she disproportionately uses sources from the *late* nineteenth century without discussing the dramatic cultural shift over the century and the impact it must have had on letter-writing conventions. Thus, her analysis becomes less useful in examining early-nineteenth-century sources. Also, as Osterud points

out, she did not read correspondence between men and women (*Bonds of Community*, p. 7).

8. For example, see Thomas Dublin, ed., *Farm to Factory: Women's Letters, 1830–1860*. See also issues of *Vermont History* and *Historical New Hampshire*. For an excellent collection of African-American letters, see Dorothy Sterling, ed., *We Are Your Sisters*. Another critical source of letters written by African Americans includes those written to newspapers and to organizations, such as the American Colonization Society and the numerous anti-slavery societies around the country. Carter Godwin Woodson, *The Mind of the Negro as Reflected in Letters Written During the Crisis, 1800–1860*. Letters written for publication in newspapers such as William Lloyd Garrison's *The Liberator* or Frederick Douglass's *North Star* assume a public audience and focus on politics much more than on relationships and family issues. Therefore, for my purposes these letters were informative but not useful for reconstructing everyday life.

9. Margo Culley, *A Day at a Time: The Diary Literature of American Women from 1764 to the Present*, p. 3. The diary that most clearly fits this format is that of Charles Benson, who wrote his diary as a series of letters to his wife while he was away at sea. Subjects regularly circulated letters within a household and among neighbors. Cott, *Bonds of Womanhood*, p. 16; Ulrich, *A Midwife's Tale*.

10. A[rthur] Bennett Diary, 18 March 1844; Sarah Trask Diary, in cover of journal, 1849; Edward Jenner Carpenter Diary, 1 March 1844; Ann Julia Stoddard Diary, 10 July 1866.

11. Charles Benson Diary; Sarah Trask Diary, 14 August 1849; Mary Mudge Diary, 1 March 1854.

12. Culley, *A Day at a Time*, pp. 7, 3. Although her explanation differs, Culley's characterization of late-eighteenth- and early-nineteenth-century diaries almost identically matches that of Motz's rural dwellers and Hampsten's working-class women. These diaries, which Motz refers to as the literary diaries, "focus on the diarist as a unique individual and relate the writer's anxieties, concerns, and emotional reactions to events both personal and national. These diaries represent, in other words, an attempt to differentiate the self from society" (Marilyn Ferris Motz, "Folk Expression of Time and Place: 19th-Century Midwestern Rural Diaries," p. 132).

13. Motz, ibid., pp. 140, 132.

14. Elizabeth Hampsten, *Read This Only to Yourself: The Private Writings of Midwestern Women, 1880–1910*, p. 27. She contrasts this to men, who have exhibited sensitivity to regional location. Only class and upward mobility shaped women's language. Women of leisure "remove[d] themselves farther from the experience they describe[d]" (p. 27). Hampsten asserts that the language women used reveals their class status better than education or income, in contrast to what was true for men. And working-class language reflects the quagmire of everyday work life.

15. The only real exception involves those diaries wholly consumed with religious reflection. They often began with a religious conversion and continued to use the journal as a forum for spiritual exploration. In these cases, the social drops away; and for that reason I have excluded them from this study.

16. The contrast between these two diarists was the focus of an unsigned article, "Two Men, Two New Hampshire Towns, Two Sets of Diaries," *New Hampshire Historical Society Newsletter* 23:4 (July/August, 1985): 1–2.

17. C. Vann Woodward, ed., *Mary Chesnut's Civil War* (New Haven, Conn.: Yale University Press, 1981), p. xvi; David Clapp Journal, 13 May 1822; Clapp, *Journal of David Clapp*, p. 1.

18. Raymond Carver, *Where I'm Calling From: New and Selected Stories* (New York: Atlantic Monthly Press, 1988), p. 380. Female authors account for only 12% of all slave narratives published (Estelle C. Jelinek, *The Tradition of Women's Autobiography: From Antiquity to the Present*, p. 7). Charles T. Davis and Henry Louis Gates, Jr., eds., *The Slave's Narrative*.

19. Frances Smith Foster, *Witnessing Slavery: The Development of Antebellum Slave Narratives*; Jacobs, *Incidents in the Life of a Slave Girl*, p. 1. Sympathetic treatment of select white people combined with a criticism of the institution of slavery repeatedly emerge as themes in many slave narratives. See, for example, in *Narrative of the Life of Frederick Douglass, An American Slave*, the first of Douglass's three autobiographies, how he describes the change in his new mistress's behavior once she discovers the power of owning someone. In the beginning she considerately treats Douglass like a human being, but once corrupted, she makes him a target of her wrath. "She at first lacked the depravity indispensable to shutting me up in mental darkness. It was at least necessary for her to have some training in the exercise of irresponsible power, to make her equal to the task of treating me as though I were a brute" (p. 39). This account showed how slavery could turn a "pious, warm, and tender-hearted woman" (p. 39) into an insensitive, exploitative, sadistic monster. The theme of institutional corruption was no doubt more amenable to a northern audience than a sentiment which asserted the natural depravity of white people. Foster, *Witnessing Slavery*, p. 6. Also see Joanne M. Braxton, *Black Women Writing Autobiography: A Tradition within a Tradition*, p. 27. For example, Harriet E. Wilson, *Our Nig; or, Sketches from the Life of a Free Black, In a Two-Story White House, North. Showing that Slavery's Shadows Fall Even There.*

20. Foster, *Witnessing Slavery*, p. 74. William L. Andrews, *To Tell a Free Story: The First Century of Afro-American Autobiography, 1760–1865*, p. 6. Stephen Butterfield writes, "The slave narrator had little choice but to adapt the literary forms and traditions of white American culture" (*Black Autobiography in America*, p. 47). "Because they summarize what white abolitionist sponsors sought in the antislavery texts they would publish, they indicate the institutional conditions under which many of the narratives were composed" (John Sekora, "Black Message / White Envelope: Genre, Authenticity, and Authority in the Antebellum Slave Narrative," p. 495).

21. Andrews, *To Tell a Free Story*, p. 2. In his provocative essay "Black Message / White Envelope" (p. 484), John Sekora asks: Whose voice do the autobiographies represent? He argues that the antebellum slave narratives are not part of the autobiographical tradition because they are not about the self (the critical feature of autobiography, as Sekora sees it). The black self must be denied in slave narratives, being replaced by a white voice (p. 510). In her study of black women's autobiographies, Joanne M. Braxton views the genre as

evolving: "As a group, these autobiographies reflect a shift from the preoccupation with survival found in the slave narratives to a need for self-expression and self-identification" (*Black Women Writing Autobiography*, p. 10). Other writers and historians claim the slave narrative as the first form of a distinctive African American literature, despite the conditions under which it was produced. In this study, four of the autobiographies were written during the antebellum period by former slaves and two by freeborn African Americans. The remaining seven were written after the Civil War. The slave narratives discuss daily life in a stable free community less than do the autobiographies of free blacks or the narratives written later in the century.

22. Foster, *Witnessing Slavery*. Publication tends to emphasize the sensational or colorful events in an individual's life, while minimizing the routine and mundane. This makes autobiography fundamentally different from letters and diaries. It anticipates and seeks a large audience.

23. I draw on the published autobiographies of two white millgirls, a farmer, and a woman married to an itinerant Methodist minister. Harriet H. Robinson, *Loom and Spindle; Or, Life Among the Early Mill Girls with a Sketch of "The Lowell Offering" and Some of Its Contributors*; Lucy Larcom, *A New England Girlhood: Outlined from Memory*; Asa Sheldon, *Yankee Drover: Being the Unpretending Life of ASA SHELDON, Farmer, Trader, and Working Man, 1788–1870*; and Mary Orne Tucker, *Itinerant Preaching*. In addition, Minerva Mayo, a young woman living in Orange, Massachusetts, wrote a short document that she labeled an autobiography but did not write for publication. Her retrospective is only a few pages long. It then drops its initial focus and becomes a copy book, mostly containing letters.

24. See, for example, John W. Adams and Alice Bee Kasakoff, "Estimates of Census Underenumeration Based on Genealogies"; Margo J. Anderson, *The American Census: A Social History*; Peter R. Knights, "Potholes in the Road of Improvement? Estimating Census Underenumeration by Longitudinal Tracing: U.S. Censuses"; Donald H. Parkerson, "Comments on the Underenumeration of the U.S. Census, 1850–1880."

Selected Bibliography

UNPUBLISHED PRIMARY SOURCES

Abbott, Nathan K. Diary, 1834–1874. NHHS.
Adams Family Papers. Correspondence, 1834–1861. PC.
Baldwin, Abigail. Diary (misc. file 51), 1853–54. VHS.
Barrett, Martha Osborne. Diary, 1848–1879. JDPL.
Barrett, Samantha. Diary, 1815–1830. CHS.
Barrett, Zeloda. Diary, 1804–1831. CHS.
Beacham, Sarah. Diary, 1863–1903. NHHS.
Bennett, A[rthur]. Diary, 1844–1846. AAS.
Bennett, Francis, Jr. Diary, 1852–1854. AAS.
Benson, Charles A. Diary, 1862–1881. JDPL.
Berbineau, Lorenza Stevens. Diary in Francis Cabot Lowell II Papers, 1851–1869. MHS.
Brown Family Papers. Correspondence, 1762–1965. AAS.
Campbell, John. Diary, 1795–1832. NHHS.
Carpenter, Edward J. Diary, 1852–1854. AAS.
Chandler, Horatio Nelson. Diary, 1839–1842. NHHS.
Chapman, Louisa Ann. Diary, 1848–1849. JDPL.
Clapp, David, Jr. Diary, 1820–1823. AAS.
Clark, Betsey. Diary, 1855–1885. NHHS.
Clark, Daniel. Diary, 1789–1828. NHHS.
Clark, Nathaniel, Jr. Diary, 1848–1858. NHHS.
Coult, Mary Giddings. Diary, 1851–1854. NHHS.
Crossman, Adelaide Isham. Diary in Crossman Family Diaries, 1855–1867. AAS.
Crossman, Ferdinand. Diary in Crossman Family Diaries, 1855. AAS.
Dame Sisters Letters. 1830–1850. NHHS.

Dixon, Ann Lilley. Correspondence, 1841–1863. AAS.

Doloff, Melissa. Diary (msc. 175), 1858. VHS.

Forbes, Susan E. Parsons Brown. Diary, 1841–1908. AAS.

Foster, John. Diary, 1856. NHHS.

Foster, John Plummer. Diary, 1848–1888. JDPL.

Gilbert, Parna. Diary, 1848–1853. PVMAL.

Goodenough, Lizzie A. Diary, 1865–1875. AAS.

Green, Harriott Smalley. Diary (*B G821), 1844–1845. VHS.

Hall, Mary. Diary, 1821–1836. NHHS.

Hill, Ivory B. Diary, 1857. NHHS.

Holbrook, Mary Grace. Diary, 1852–1854. CSL.

Holmes Family Papers. Correspondence, 1840–1860. MHS.

Hopkins, Marion. Diary, 1851–1855. NHHS.

James, Samuel Shepard. Diary, 1839–1907. NHHS.

Jones, Mary Giddings Coult. Diary, 1855–1859. CHS.

Kent, John H. Diary, 1854. JDPL.

Kimball, Joseph. Diary, 1832–1881. JDPL.

Kimball, Walter Lewis. Diary, 1846–1849. JDPL.

Lane, Joshua. Diary, 1788–1829. NHHS.

Lewis, Hannah. Correspondence, 1811–1816. OSVL.

Lye, Joseph. Diary, 1817–1832. LHS.

Mason, Albert. Diary, 1833–1889. NHHS.

Mayo, Minerva. Autobiography, 1820–1822. OSVL.

Metcalf-Adams Family Letters. 1796–1866. MATH.

Mudge, Mary Jane. Diary, 1854. SL.

Nims, Brigham. Diary, 1840–1888. NHHS.

———. Correspondence. Roxbury Town Records, NHSA.

———. Correspondence. HSCC.

Parker Smith, Rhoda. Correspondence in Rhoda Parker Smith Papers, 1824–1854. JDPL.

Parks, Vestus Haley. Diary in Parks Family Papers, 1827–1829. AAS.

Porter, Alfred. Diary, 1854–1856. JDPL.

Primus Family Papers. Correspondence, 1859–1868. CHS.

Robinson, Perley Carr. Diary, 1849. NHHS.

Root, Sarah. Diary, 1859–1864. BPL.

Sanborn, Ezra. Diary, 1861–1878. NHHS.

Severance, Harriet Anne. Diary, 1862–1866. SL.

Shaw, Adaline. Correspondence, 1848. SSC.

Smith, David T. Diary, 1832–1860. JDPL.

Stockwell, Leonard M. Memorial, ca. 1880. AAS.

Stoddard, Ann Julia. Diary, 1866. SL.

"Story of Betsey." Memorial, ca. 1870. PC.

Taft, Nancy. Diary (msc. 3), 1838. VHS.

Tilton, Pollie Cathcart. Diary, 1839–1860. PVMAL.

Trask, Sarah. Diary, 1849–1851. BHSM.

Unknown Author. Diary (mss. #86), 1859. JDPL.

Weymouth, James S. Diary, 1850–1869. NHHS.

Whipple, George S. Diary, 1838. AAS.
Williams, Paulina Bascom. Diary (mss. 28 #91), 1830–1833. VHS.
Woolson Letters. 1829–1840. MHA.

PUBLISHED PRIMARY SOURCES

Aguilar, Grace. *Woman's Friendship: A Story of Domestic Life*. New York: D. Appleton & Co., 1850.

Asher, Rev. Jeremiah. *An Autobiography, with Details of a Visit to England and Some Account of the History of the Meeting Street Baptist Church, Providence, R.I., and of the Shiloh Baptist Church, Philadelphia, Pa.* Philadelphia, 1862.

Brown, Pamela, and Sally Brown. *The Diary of Sally and Pamela Brown*. In *The Diaries of Sally and Pamela Brown, 1832–1838; Hyde Leslie, 1887, Plymouth Notch, Vermont*, edited by Blanche Brown Bryant and Gertrude Elaine Baker, 7–94. Springfield, Vt.: William L. Bryant Foundation, 1979.

Brown, William J. *The Life of William J. Brown, of Providence, R.I., with Personal Recollections of Incidents in Rhode Island*. 1883; rpt. Freeport, N.Y.: Books For Libraries Press, 1971.

Clapp, David. *Journal of David Clapp*. Boston, [1904].

Curtis, Harriot. "Aunt Letty; or, The Useful." *The Lowell Offering*, ser. II, vol. 3 (1842–43).

Davis, Almond H., ed. *The Female Preacher; or, Memoir of Salome Lincoln*. 1843; rpt. New York: Arno Press, 1972.

Davis, Rev. Noah. *A Narrative of the Life of Rev. Noah Davis, a Colored Man*. Baltimore, Md.: John F. Weishampel, Jr., 1859.

DeBow, J. D. B., Superintendent of the United States Census. *Statistical View of the United States: Compendium of the Seventh Census, 1850*. Washington: Beverley Tucker, Senate Printer, 1854.

Douglass, Frederick. *Narrative of the Life of Frederick Douglass, An American Slave*. 1845; rpt. Garden City, N.Y.: Anchor, 1973.

Dublin, Thomas, ed. *Farm to Factory: Women's Letters, 1830–1860*. New York: Columbia University Press, 1981.

Grimes, William. *Life of William Grimes, the Runaway Slave, Brought Down to the Present Time*. 1855; rpt. in *Five Black Lives: The Autobiographies of Venture Smith, James Mars, William Grimes, The Rev. G.W. Offley, and James L. Smith*, edited by Arna Bontemps, 59–128. Middletown: Wesleyan University Press, 1971.

Harrison, Rev. Samuel. *His Life Story*. Pittsfield, Mass.: Eagle Publishing, 1899.

Henry, George. *Life of George Henry, Together with a Brief History of the Colored People in America*. 1894; rpt. Freeport, N.Y.: Books for Libraries Press, 1971.

Jackson, Rebecca. *Gifts of Power: The Writings of Rebecca Jackson, Black Visionary, Shaker Eldress*, edited by Jean McMahon Humez. Amherst: University of Massachusetts Press, 1981.

Jacobs, Harriet A. *Incidents in the Life of a Slave Girl*. 1861; rpt. edited by Jean Fagan Yellin. Cambridge: Harvard University Press, 1987.

Larcom, Lucy. *A New England Girlhood: Outlined from Memory*. Boston: Houghton Mifflin, 1889.

Lee, Jarena. *Religious Experience and Journal of Mrs. Jarena Lee, Giving an Account of Her Call to Preach the Gospel*. 1836; rpt. in *Sisters of the Spirit: Three Black Women's Autobiographies of the Nineteenth Century*, edited by William J. Andrews, 25–48. Bloomington: Indiana University Press, 1986.

Lowell, Mary Chandler. *Old Foxcroft, Maine, Traditions and Memories*. Concord, N.H.: Rumford Press, 1935.

Mars, James. *Life of James Mars, a Slave Born and Sold in Connecticut*. 1864; rpt. in *Five Black Lives: The Autobiographies of Venture Smith, James Mars, William Grimes, The Rev. G.W. Offley, and James L. Smith*, edited by Arna Bontemps, 35–58. Middletown, Conn.: Wesleyan University Press, 1971.

Mason, Isaac. *Life of Isaac Mason as a Slave*. 1893; rpt. Miami, Fla.: Mnemosyne Publishing, 1969.

Pickering, Octavius. "Sophia W. Bodwell *versus* Caleb Swan *et ux*" and "Sophia W. Bodwell *versus* Benjamin Osgood." In *Reports of Cases Argued and Determined in the Supreme Judicial Court of Massachusetts*, vol. 3, 404–8, 408–15. Boston: Charles C. Little and James Brown, 1848.

Prince, Mrs. Nancy. *A Narrative of the Life and Travels of Mrs. Nancy Prince*. 1853; rpt. in *Collected Black Women's Narratives*. New York: Oxford University Press, 1988.

Randolph, Peter. *From Slave Cabin to Pulpit: The Autobiography of Rev. Peter Randolph; The Southern Question Illustrated and Sketches of Slave Life*. Boston: James H. Earle, 1893.

Report of the School Committee of the Town of Danvers, 1848–1849. Danvers, Mass.: G. R. Carlton, Courier Press, 1849.

Rhodes, Wallace P., comp. *Reminiscences of a New Hampshire Town: Belmont Centennial, 1869–1969*. Concord, N.H.: Capital Offset, 1969.

Robinson, Harriet H. *Loom & Spindle; or, Life Among the Early Mill Girls with a Sketch of "The Lowell Offering" and Some of Its Contributors*. 1898; rpt. Kailua, Hawaii: Press Pacifica, 1976.

Roper, Moses. *A Narrative of the Adventures and Escape of Moses Roper, from American Slavery*. 1838; rpt. Philadelphia: Historic Publications, 1969.

Sheldon, Asa. *Yankee Drover: Being the Unpretending Life of Asa Sheldon, Farmer, Trader, and Working Man, 1788–1870*. 1862; rpt. Hanover, N.H.: University Press of New England, 1988.

Smith, James L. *Autobiography of James L. Smith, Including, Also, Reminiscences of Slave Life, Recollections of the War, Education of Freedmen, Causes of the Exodus, etc.* 1881; rpt. in *Five Black Lives: the Autobiographies of Venture Smith, James Mars, William Grimes, The Rev. G.W. Offley, and James L. Smith*, edited by Arna Bontemps, 139–240. Middletown, Conn.: Wesleyan University Press, 1971.

Thompson, John. *Life of John Thompson, a Fugitive Slave*. Worcester, Mass., 1856.

Towle, Nancy. *Vicissitudes Illustrated, in the Experience of Nancy Towle, in Europe and America*. Portsmouth, N.H., 1833.

Tucker, Mary Orne. *Itinerant Preaching in the Early Days of Methodism.* 1872; rpt. in *Women in American Protestant Religion, 1800–1930,* edited by Carolyn De Swarte Gifford, 1–160. New York: Garland Publishing, 1987.

Veney, Bethany. *Narrative of Bethany Veney, a Slave Woman.* 1889; rpt. New York: Oxford University Press, 1988.

Wilson, Harriet E. *Our Nig; or, Sketches from the Life of a Free Black, In a Two-Story White House, North. Showing That Slavery's Shadows Fall Even There.* 1859; rpt. New York: Vintage, 1983.

Woodson, Carter Godwin. *The Mind of the Negro as Reflected in Letters Written During the Crisis, 1800–1860.* New York: Russell and Russell, 1969.

SECONDARY SOURCES

Abbott, Andrew. "History and Sociology: The Lost Synthesis." *Social Science History* 15, no. 2 (Summer 1991): 201–38.

Abel, Emily K., and Margaret K. Nelson. "Circles of Care: An Introductory Essay." In *Circles of Care: Work and Identity in Women's Lives,* edited by Emily K. Abel and Margaret K. Nelson, 4–34. Albany: State University of New York Press, 1990.

Abel, Marjorie Ruzich. "Profiles of Nineteenth Century Working Women." *Historical Journal of Massachusetts* 14, no. 1 (January 1986): 43–52.

Acker, Joan. "Class, Gender, and the Relations of Distribution." *Signs* 13, no. 3 (1988): 473–97.

Adams, John W., and Alice Bee Kasakoff. "Estimates of Census Underenumeration Based on Genealogies." *Social Science History* 15, no. 4 (Winter 1991): 527–43.

Ahlstrom, Sydney E. *A Religious History of the American People.* New Haven, Conn.: Yale University Press, 1972.

Allan, Graham. "Class Variation in Friendship Patterns." *British Journal of Sociology* 28, no. 3 (September 1977): 389–93.

———. *Friendship: Developing a Sociological Perspective.* Boulder, Colo.: Westview Press, 1989.

Amussen, Susan Dwyer. *An Ordered Society: Gender and Class in Early Modern England.* New York: Basil Blackwell, 1988.

Anderson, Margo J. *The American Census: A Social History.* New Haven, Conn.: Yale University Press, 1988.

Andrews, William L. *To Tell a Free Story: The First Century of Afro-American Autobiography, 1760–1865.* Urbana: University of Illinois Press, 1988.

Aptheker, Herbert. *Abolitionism: A Revolutionary Movement.* Boston: Twayne, 1989.

Arendt, Hannah. *The Human Condition.* Chicago: University of Chicago Press, 1958.

———. *On Revolution.* Harrisonburg, Va.: R. R. Donnelley and Sons, 1965.

Aymer, Paula. *The Second Great Awakening: An Opportunity for Blacks in America.* M.A. thesis, Northeastern University, 1983.

Baker, Paula. "The Domestication of Politics: Women and American Political

Society, 1780–1920." *American Historical Review* 89, no. 3 (1984): 620–47.

Baron, Ava. "Questions of Gender: Deskilling and Demasculinization in the U.S. Printing Industry, 1830–1915." *Gender and History* 1 (1989): 178–99.

Barron, Hal S. *Those Who Stayed Behind: Rural Society in Nineteenth-Century New England*. New York: Cambridge University Press, 1984.

Bellah, Robert N. "The Meaning of Reputation in American Society." *California Law Review* 74, no. 3 (May 1986): 743–51.

Bender, Thomas. *Community and Social Change in America*. Baltimore: Johns Hopkins University Press, 1978.

Benn, Stanley I., and Gerald Gaus. "The Liberal Conception of the Public and the Private." In *Public and Private in Social Life*, edited by Stanley I. Benn and Gerald Gaus, 31–66. New York: St. Martin's Press, 1983.

Berg, Barbara J. *The Remembered Gate: Origins of American Feminism, The Woman and the City, 1800–1860*. New York: Oxford University Press, 1978.

Bernard, Richard M., and Maris A. Vinovskis. "The Female School Teacher in Ante-Bellum Massachusetts." *Journal of Social History* 10, no. 3 (March 1977): 332–45.

Bernhard, Virginia. "Cotton Mather's 'Most Unhappy Wife': Reflections on the Uses of Historical Evidence." *New England Quarterly* 60, no. 3 (September 1987): 341–62.

Blauvelt, Martha Tomhave. "Women and Revivalism." In *The Nineteenth Century, A Documentary History*, vol. 1 of *Women and Religion in America*, edited by Rosemary Radford Ruether and Rosemary Skinner Keller, 1–45. New York: Harper and Row, 1981.

Blewett, Mary H. "'I am Doom to Disapointment': The Diaries of a Beverly, Massachusetts, Shoebinder, Sarah E. Trask, 1849–1851." *Essex Institute Historical Collections*, July 1981, 192–212.

———. *Men, Women, and Work: Class, Gender, and Protest in the New England Shoe Industry, 1780–1910*. Urbana: University of Illinois Press, 1988.

———. "Women Shoeworkers and Domestic Ideology: Rural Outwork in Early Nineteenth-Century Essex County." *New England Quarterly* 60 (1987): 403–28.

Bonnell, Victoria. "The Uses of Theory, Concepts and Comparison in Historical Sociology." *Comparative Studies in Society and History* 22 (1980): 156–73.

Botkin, Benjamin Albert, ed. *A Treasury of New England Folklore: Stories, Ballads, and Traditions of the Yankee People*. New York: Crown, 1947.

Bott, Elizabeth. *Family and Social Network: Roles, Norms, and External Relationships in Ordinary Urban Families*. New York: Free Press, 1971.

Boyte, Harry C., and Sara M. Evans. *Free Spaces: The Sources of Democratic Change in America*. New York: Harper and Row, 1986.

Braxton, Joanne M. *Black Women Writing Autobiography: A Tradition within a Tradition*. Philadelphia: Temple University Press, 1989.

Brereton, Virginia Lieson. *From Sin to Salvation: Stories of Women's Conversions, 1800 to the Present*. Bloomington: Indiana University Press, 1991.

Bridges, Amy. "Becoming American: The Working Classes in the United States Before the Civil War." In *Working-Class Formation: Nineteenth-Century*

Patterns in Western Europe and the United States, edited by Ira Katznelson and Aristide Zolberg, 157–96. Princeton: Princeton University Press, 1986.

Butler, Jon. *Awash in a Sea of Faith: Christianizing the American People*. Cambridge: Harvard University Press, 1992.

Butterfield, Stephen. *Black Autobiography in America*. Amherst: University of Massachusetts Press, 1974.

Byars, Ronald Preston. *The Making of the Self-Made Man: The Development of Masculine Roles and Images in Ante-bellum America*. Ph.D. diss., Michigan State University, 1979.

Calhoun, Daniel. *The Intelligence of a People*. Princeton: Princeton University Press, 1973.

Carby, Hazel V. *Reconstructing Womanhood: The Emergence of the Afro-American Woman Novelist*. New York: Oxford University Press, 1987.

Carnes, Mark. *Secret Ritual and Manhood in Victorian America*. New Haven, Conn.: Yale University Press, 1989.

Chambers-Schiller, Lee Virginia. *Liberty, A Better Husband; Single Women in America: The Generations of 1780–1840*. New Haven, Conn.: Yale University Press, 1984.

Chodorow, Nancy. *The Reproduction of Mothering*. Berkeley and Los Angeles: University of California Press, 1978.

Clawson, Mary Ann. *Constructing Brotherhood: Class, Gender, and Fraternalism*. Princeton: Princeton University Press, 1989.

———. "Nineteenth-Century Women's Auxiliaries and Fraternal Orders." *Signs* 12, no. 1 (Autumn 1986): 40–61.

Cochran, Clarke E. *Religion in Public and Private Life*. New York: Routledge, 1990.

Cohen, Jean L. *Class and Civil Society: The Limits of Marxian Critical Theory*. Amherst: University of Massachusetts Press, 1982.

Cohen, Jean L., and Andrew Arato. *Civil Society and Political Theory*. Cambridge: MIT Press, 1992.

Collins, Patricia Hill. *Black Feminist Thought*. Boston: Unwin Hyman, 1990.

Cott, Nancy F. *Bonds of Womanhood*. New Haven, Conn.: Yale University Press, 1977.

———. "Young Women in the Second Great Awakening in New England." *Feminist Studies* 3, nos. 1/2 (Fall 1975): 15–29.

Cowan, Ruth Schwartz. *More Work for Mother: The Ironies of Household Technology from the Open Hearth to the Microwave*. New York: Basic, 1983.

Creighton, Margaret S. "Fraternity in the American Forecastle, 1830–1870." *New England Quarterly* 63, no. 4 (1990): 531–57.

Crowley, John W. "Howells, Stoddard, and Male Homosocial Attachment in Victorian America." In *The Making of Masculinities: The New Men's Studies*, edited by Harry Brod, 301–24. Boston: Allen & Unwin, 1987.

Culley, Margo. *A Day at a Time: The Diary Literature of American Women from 1764 to the Present*. New York: Feminist Press, 1985.

Curry, Leonard P. *The Free Black in Urban America, 1800–1850: The Shadow of the Dream*. Chicago: University of Chicago Press, 1981.

Daniels, Arlene Kaplan. "Good Times and Good Works: The Place of Sociability in the Work of Women Volunteers." *Social Problems* 32, no. 4 (April 1985): 363–74.

Davis, Angela Y. *Women, Race & Class.* New York: Vintage, 1983.

Davis, Charles T., and Henry Louis Gates, Jr., eds. *The Slave's Narrative.* New York: Oxford University Press, 1985.

Dawley, Alan. *Class and Community: The Industrial Revolution in Lynn.* Cambridge: Harvard University Press, 1976.

Degler, Carl N. *At Odds: Women and the Family in America from the Revolution to the Present.* New York: Oxford University Press, 1980.

D'Emilio, John, and Estelle B. Freedman. *Intimate Matters: A History of Sexuality in America.* New York: Harper and Row, 1988.

DeVault, Marjorie L. *Feeding the Family: The Social Organization of Caring as Gendered Work.* Chicago: University of Chicago Press, 1991.

Di Leonardo, Micaela. "The Female World of Cards and Holidays: Women, Families, and the Work of Kinship." *Signs* 12, no. 3 (Spring 1987): 440–53.

Douglas, Ann. *The Feminization of American Culture.* New York: Avon, 1977.

Duberman, Martin. "'Writhing Bedfellows' in Antebellum South Carolina: Historical Interpretation and the Politics of Evidence." In *Hidden From History: Reclaiming the Gay and Lesbian Past,* edited by Martin Duberman, Martha Vicinus, and George Chauncey, Jr., 153–68. New York: Penguin, 1989.

Dublin, Thomas. *Women at Work: The Transformation of Work and Community in Lowell, Massachusetts, 1826–1860.* New York: Columbia University Press, 1979.

DuBois, Ellen Carol. *Feminism and Suffrage.* Ithaca: Cornell University Press, 1978.

————, ed. *Elizabeth Cady Stanton, Susan B. Anthony, Correspondence, Writings, Speeches.* New York: Schocken, 1981.

Ehrenreich, Barbara, and Deirdre English. *For Her Own Good: 150 Years of the Experts' Advice to Women.* Garden City, N.Y.: Anchor, 1979.

Elshtain, Jean Bethke. *Public Man, Private Woman.* Princeton: Princeton University Press, 1981.

Epstein, Barbara Leslie. *The Politics of Domesticity: Women, Evangelism, and Temperance in Nineteenth-Century America.* Middletown, Conn.: Wesleyan University Press, 1981.

Faderman, Lillian. *Surpassing the Love of Men: Romantic Friendship and Love between Women from the Renaissance to the Present.* New York: William Morrow, 1981.

Faler, Paul. *The Coming of Industrial Order: Town and Factory Life in Rural Massachusetts, 1810–1860.* New York: Cambridge University Press, 1983.

Faragher, John Mack. *Women and Men on the Overland Trail.* New Haven, Conn.: Yale University Press, 1979.

Fiorenza, Elizabeth Schussler. *In Memory of Her: A Feminist Theological Reconstruction of Christian Origins.* New York: Crossroad, 1983.

Fischer, Claude S. *To Dwell Among Friends: Personal Networks in Town and City.* Chicago: University of Chicago Press, 1982.

Foner, Philip S., and Ronald L. Lewis. *The Black Worker to 1869*, vol. 1. Philadelphia: Temple University Press, 1978.

Foster, Frances Smith. *Witnessing Slavery: The Development of Ante-bellum Slave Narratives*. Westport, Conn.: Greenwood Press, 1979.

Fraser, Nancy. "Rethinking the Public Sphere: A Contribution to the Critique of Actually Existing Democracy." *Social Text* 25/26 (1990): 56–80.

———. *Unruly Practices: Power, Discourse and Gender in Contemporary Social Theory*. Minneapolis: University of Minnesota Press, 1989.

———. "What's Critical About Critical Theory? The Case of Habermas and Gender." *New German Critique* 35 (Spring/Summer 1985): 97–131.

Frisch, Michael. *Town into City: Springfield, Massachusetts, and the Meaning of Community, 1840–1880*. Cambridge: Harvard University Press, 1972.

Gamarnikow, Eva, and June Purvis. Introduction to *The Public and the Private*, edited by Eva Gamarnikow, David H. J. Morgan, June Purvis, and Daphne Taylorson, 1–6. London: Heinemann, 1983.

Gatewood, Willard B. *Aristocrats of Color: The Black Elite, 1880–1920*. Bloomington: Indiana University Press, 1990.

Gaustad, Edwin Scott. *A Religious History of America*. New York: Harper and Row, 1966.

Giddings, Paula. *When and Where I Enter: The Impact of Black Women on Race and Sex in America*. New York: Bantam Books, 1985.

Gilkes, Cheryl Townsend. "'Together in Harness': Women's Traditions in the Sanctified Church." *Signs* 10, no. 4 (Summer 1985): 678–99.

Gluckman, Max. "Gossip and Scandal." *Current Anthropology* 4, no. 3 (June 1963): 307–16.

Gordon, Linda. *Woman's Body, Woman's Right: A Social History of Birth Control in America*. New York: Penguin, 1976.

Granovetter, Mark S. "The Strength of Weak Ties." *American Journal of Sociology* 78, no. 6 (May 1973): 1360–80.

Greven, Philip. *The Protestant Temperament: Patterns of Child-Rearing, Religious Experience, and the Self in Early America*. New York: Knopf, 1977.

Gullestad, Marianne. *Kitchen-Table Society: A Case Study of the Family Life and Friendships of Young Working-Class Mothers in Urban Norway*. Oslo: Universitetsforlaget, 1984.

Gutman, Herbert G. *The Black Family in Slavery and Freedom, 1750–1925*. New York: Vintage Books, 1977.

Habermas, Jürgen. "The Public Sphere." In *Rethinking Popular Culture: Contemporary Perspectives on Cultural Studies*, edited by Chandra Mukerji and Michael Schudson, 398–404. Berkeley and Los Angeles: University of California Press, 1991.

———. *The Structural Transformation of the Public Sphere: An Inquiry into a Category of Bourgeois Society*. Translated by Thomas Burger and Frederick Lawrence. Cambridge: MIT Press, 1989.

Halttunen, Karen. *Confidence Men and Painted Women: A Study of Middle-Class Culture in America, 1830–1870*. New Haven, Conn.: Yale University Press, 1982.

Hampsten, Elizabeth. *Read This Only to Yourself: The Private Writings of Midwestern Women, 1880–1910.* Bloomington: Indiana University Press, 1982.

Hansen, Karen V. "'Helped Put In a Quilt': Men's Work and Male Intimacy in Nineteenth-Century New England." *Gender & Society* 3, no. 3 (September 1989): 334–54.

Harding, Susan. "Women and Words in a Spanish Village." In *Toward an Anthropology of Women*, edited by Rayna Reiter, 283–308. New York: Monthly Review Press, 1975.

Hartsock, Nancy C. M. *Money, Sex, and Power: Toward a Feminist Historical Materialism.* Boston: Northeastern University Press, 1983.

Hatch, Nathan O. *The Democratization of American Christianity.* New Haven, Conn.: Yale University Press, 1989.

Heilman, Samuel C. *Synagogue Life: A Study in Symbolic Interaction.* Chicago: University of Chicago Press, 1973.

Hemphill, C. Dallett. *Manners for Americans: Interaction Ritual and the Social Order, 1620–1860.* Ph.D. diss., Brandeis University, 1987.

Hochschild, Arlie Russell. *The Managed Heart: Commercialization of Human Feeling.* Berkeley and Los Angeles: University of California Press, 1983.

Hooks, Bell. *Feminist Theory: From Margin to Center.* Boston: South End Press, 1984.

Horton, James Oliver, and Lois E. Horton. *Black Bostonians: Family Life and Community Struggle in the Antebellum North.* New York: Holmes and Meier, 1979.

Imray, Linda, and Audrey Middleton. "Public and Private: Marking the Boundaries." In *The Public and the Private*, edited by Eva Gamarnikow, David H. J. Morgan, June Purvis, and Daphne Taylorson, 12–27. London: Heinemann, 1983.

Jelinek, Estelle. *The Tradition of Women's Autobiography: From Antiquity to the Present.* Boston: Twayne Publishers, 1986.

Johnson, Paul E. *A Shopkeeper's Millennium: Society and Revivals in Rochester, New York, 1815–1837.* New York: Hill and Wang, 1978.

Jones, Jacqueline. *Labor of Love, Labor of Sorrow: Black Women, Work, and the Family, From Slavery to the Present.* New York: Vintage, 1986.

Karen, Robert. "Shame." *Atlantic Monthly*, February 1992, 40–70.

Katz, Jonathan Ned. *Gay American History: Lesbians and Gay Men in the U.S.A.* New York: Harper and Row, 1976.

———. "The Invention of Heterosexuality." *Socialist Review* 20 (1990): 7–34.

Katz, Michael B. "Social Class in North American Urban History." *Journal of Interdisciplinary History* 11, no. 4 (Spring 1981): 579–605.

Katzman, David M. *Seven Days a Week: Women and Domestic Service in Industrializing America.* New York: Oxford University Press, 1978.

Katznelson, Ira. "Working-Class Formation: Constructing Cases and Comparisons." In *Working-Class Formation: Nineteenth-Century Patterns in Western Europe and the United States*, edited by Ira Katznelson and Aristide Zolberg, 3–41. Princeton: Princeton University Press, 1986.

Kerber, Linda K., Nancy F. Cott, Robert Gross, Lynn Hunt, Carroll Smith-

Rosenberg, and Christine M. Stansell. "Beyond Roles, Beyond Spheres: Thinking about Gender in the Early Republic." *William and Mary Quarterly* 46 (July 1989): 565–85.

Kessler-Harris, Alice. *Out to Work: A History of Wage-Earning Women in the United States.* New York: Oxford University Press, 1982.

Knights, Peter R. "Potholes in the Road of Improvement? Estimating Census Underenumeration by Longitudinal Tracing: U.S. Censuses." *Social Science History* 15, no. 4 (Winter 1991): 517–26.

Lapansky, Emma Jones. " 'Since They Got Those Separate Churches': Afro-Americans and Racism in Jacksonian Philadelphia." *American Quarterly* 32, no. 1 (Spring 1980): 54–78.

Leavitt, Judith Walzer. *Brought to Bed: Childbearing in America, 1750–1950.* New York: Oxford University Press, 1986.

Lerner, Gerda. "The Lady and the Mill Girl: Changes in the Status of Women in the Age of Jackson, 1800–1840." In *A Heritage of Her Own: Toward a New Social History of American Women,* edited by Nancy F. Cott and Elizabeth H. Pleck, 182–96. New York: Simon and Schuster, 1979.

Levesque, George A. *Black Boston: Negro Life in Garrison's Boston, 1800–1860.* Binghamton: State University of New York Press, 1976.

Levy, Leonard W. "Sims Case: The Fugitive Slave Law in Boston in 1851." *Journal of Negro History* 35, no. 1 (1950): 39–74.

Lewis, Earl. "Afro-American Adaptive Strategies: The Visiting Habits of Kith and Kin among Black Norfolkians during the First Great Migration." In *Perspectives on the Family: History, Class, and Feminism,* edited by Christopher Carlson, 68–78. Belmont, Calif.: Wadsworth, 1990.

Lincoln, C. Eric, and Lawrence H. Mamiya. "The Religious Dimension: Toward a Sociology of Black Churches." In *The Black Church in the African-American Experience,* edited by C. Eric Lincoln and Lawrence H. Mamiya, 1–19. Durham, N.C.: Duke University Press, 1990.

Litwack, Leon F. *Been in the Storm So Long: The Aftermath of Slavery.* New York: Vintage, 1979.

———. *North of Slavery: The Negro in the Free States, 1790–1860.* Chicago: University of Chicago Press, 1961.

Loomis, Barbara. *Piety and Play: Young Women's Leisure in an Era of Evangelical Religion, 1790–1840.* Ph.D. diss., University of California, Berkeley, 1988.

Lukes, Steven, ed. *Power.* Oxford: Basil Blackwell, 1986.

Lystra, Karen. *Searching the Heart: Women, Men, and Romantic Love in Nineteenth-Century America.* New York: Oxford University Press, 1989.

McAdam, Doug. "Gender Implications of the Traditional Academic Conception of the Political." In *Changing Our Minds: Feminist Transformations of Knowledge,* edited by Susan Hardy Aiken, Karen Anderson, Myra Dinnerstein, Judy Nolte Lensink, and Patricia MacCorquodale, 59–76. Albany: State University of New York Press, 1988.

McClelland, Peter D., and Richard J. Zeckhauser. *Demographic Dimensions of the New Republic: American Interregional Migration, Vital Statistics, and Manumissions, 1800–1860.* New York: Cambridge University Press, 1982.

McLoughlin, William G. *Revivals, Awakenings, and Reform: An Essay on Religion and Social Change in America, 1607–1977.* Chicago: University of Chicago Press, 1978.

Mansbridge, Jane. *Beyond Adversary Democracy.* New York: Basic, 1980.

Markus, Maria. "The 'Anti-Feminism' of Hannah Arendt." *Thesis Eleven* 17 (1987): 76–87.

Martin, Robert K. "Knights-Errant and Gothic Seducers: The Representation of Male Friendship in Mid-Nineteenth-Century America." In *Hidden From History: Reclaiming the Gay and Lesbian Past,* edited by Martin Duberman, Martha Vicinus, and George Chauncey, Jr., 169–82. New York: Penguin, 1989.

Mathews, Donald G. "The Second Great Awakening as an Organizing Process, 1780–1830: An Hypothesis." *American Quarterly* 21, no. 1 (Spring 1969): 23–43.

Matthews, Glenna. *"Just a Housewife": The Rise and Fall of Domesticity in America.* New York: Oxford University Press, 1987.

Meyer, John, David Tyack, Joane Nagel, and Audri Gordon. "Public Education as Nation-Building in America: Enrollments and Bureaucratization in the American States, 1870–1930." *American Journal of Sociology* 85, no. 3 (November 1979): 591–613.

Mills, C. Wright. *The Sociological Imagination.* New York: Oxford University Press, 1959.

Mintz, Stephen, and Susan Kellogg. *Domestic Revolutions: A Social History of American Family Life.* New York: The Free Press, 1988.

Miyakawa, T. Scott. *Protestants and Pioneers: Individualism and Conformity on the American Frontier.* Chicago: University of Chicago Press, 1964.

Moore, Barrington, Jr. *Privacy.* Armonk, N.Y.: M. E. Sharpe, 1984.

Motz, Marilyn Ferris. "Folk Expression of Time and Place: 19th-Century Midwestern Rural Diaries." *Journal of American Folklore* 100, no. 396 (April–June 1987): 131–47.

———. *True Sisterhood: Michigan Women and Their Kin, 1820–1920.* Albany: State University of New York Press, 1983.

Nicholson, Linda J. *Gender and History: The Limits of Social Theory in the Age of the Family.* New York: Columbia University Press, 1986.

Norton, Mary Beth. "Gender and Defamation in Seventeenth-Century Maryland." *William and Mary Quarterly* 44, no. 1 (January 1987): 3–39.

Oakley, Ann. *The Sociology of Housework.* New York: Pantheon, 1974.

Okin, Susan. *Justice, Gender, and the Family.* New York: Basic, 1989.

Oliker, Stacey J. *Best Friends and Marriage.* Berkeley and Los Angeles: University of California Press, 1989.

Osterud, Nancy Grey. *Bonds of Community: The Lives of Farm Women in Nineteenth-Century New York.* Ithaca: Cornell University Press, 1991.

———. "'She Helped Me Hay It as Good as a Man': Relations among Women and Men in an Agricultural Community." In *"To Toil the Livelong Day": America's Women at Work, 1780–1980,* edited by Carol Groneman and Mary Beth Norton, 87–97. Ithaca: Cornell University Press, 1987.

Ostrander, Susan. "Feminism, Voluntarism, and the Welfare State: Toward a

Feminist Sociological Theory of Social Welfare." *The American Sociologist*, Spring 1989, 29–41.

Paine, Robert. "What is Gossip About? An Alternative Hypothesis." *Man* 2, no. 2 (June 1967): 278–85.

Parekh, Bhikhu. *Hannah Arendt and the Search for a New Political Philosophy*. Atlantic Highlands, N.J.: Humanities Press, 1981.

Parkerson, Donald H. "Comments on the Underenumeration of the U.S. Census, 1850–1880." *Social Science History* 15, no. 4 (Winter 1991): 509–15.

Pateman, Carole. "Feminist Critiques of the Public/Private Dichotomy." In *Public and Private in Social Life*, edited by Stanley I. Benn and Gerald Gaus, 281–305. New York: St. Martin's Press, 1983.

Pederson, Jane Marie. "The Country Visitor: Patterns of Hospitality in Rural Wisconsin, 1880–1925." *Agricultural History* 58, no. 3 (July 1984): 347–64.

Peiss, Kathy. *Cheap Amusements: Working Women and Leisure in Turn-of-the-Century New York*. Philadelphia: Temple University Press, 1986.

Personal Narratives Group. "Origins." In *Interpreting Women's Lives: Feminist Theory and Personal Narratives*, edited by Personal Narratives Group, 3–15. Bloomington: Indiana University Press, 1989.

Pitkin, Hanna Fenichel. "Justice: On Relating Private and Public." *Political Theory* 9, no. 3 (August 1981): 327–52.

Pleck, Elizabeth H., and Joseph H. Pleck, eds. *The American Man*. Englewood Cliffs, N.J.: Prentice-Hall, 1980.

Pleck, Joseph H. "Man to Man: Is Brotherhood Possible?" In *Old Family / New Family*, edited by Nona Glazer-Malbin, 229–44. New York: Van Nostrand, 1975.

Post, Robert C. "The Social Foundations of Defamation Law: Reputation and the Constitution." *California Law Review* 74, no. 3 (May 1986): 691–742.

Preston, JoAnne. "Female Aspiration and Male Ideology: School-Teaching in Nineteenth-Century New England." In *Current Issues in Women's History*, edited by Arina Angerman, Geerte Binnema, Annemieke Keunen, Vefie Poels, and Jacqueline Zirkzee, 171–82. London: Routledge, 1989.

———. "Learning a Trade in Industrializing New England: The Expedition of Hannah and Mary Adams to Nashua, New Hampshire, 1833–1834." *Historical New Hampshire* 39 (Spring–Summer 1984): 24–44.

———. "Millgirl Narratives: Representations of Class and Gender in Nineteenth-Century Lowell." *Life Stories / Recits de vie* 3 (1987): 21–30.

———. "Women's Aspirations and the Feminization of School Teaching in Nineteenth-Century New England." Lecture given at Schlesinger Library. Radcliffe College, April 1992.

Rabinowitz, Richard. *The Spiritual Self in Everyday Life: The Transformation of the Personal Religious Experience in Nineteenth-Century New England*. Boston: Northeastern University Press, 1989.

Rapp, Rayna. "Family and Class in Contemporary America: Notes Toward an Understanding of Ideology." *Science and Society* 42, no. 3 (Fall 1978): 278–300.

Reiter, Rayna R. "Men and Women in the South of France: Public and Private

Domains." In *Toward an Anthropology of Women*, edited by Rayna R. Reiter, 252–82. New York: Monthly Review Press, 1975.

Reverby, Susan M. "The Duty or Right to Care? Nursing and Womanhood in Historical Perspective." In *Circles of Care: Work and Identity in Women's Lives*, edited by Emily K. Abel and Margaret K. Nelson, 132–49. Albany: State University of New York Press, 1990.

———. *Ordered to Care: The Dilemma of American Nursing, 1850–1945*. New York: Cambridge University Press, 1987.

Richards, Jeffrey. "'Passing the Love of Women': Manly Love and Victorian Society." In *Manliness and Morality: Middle-Class Masculinity in Britain and America, 1800–1940*, edited by J. A. Mangan and James Walvin, 92–122. New York: St. Martin's Press, 1987.

Richardson, Marilyn. *Black Women and Religion: A Bibliography*. Boston: G. K. Hall, 1980.

Rosaldo, Michelle. "The Use and Abuse of Anthropology: Reflections on Feminism and Cross-cultural Understanding." *Signs* 5, no. 3 (Spring 1980): 389–417.

———. "Woman, Culture, and Society: A Theoretical Overview." In *Woman, Culture, and Society*, edited by Michelle Rosaldo and Louise Lamphere, 17–42. Stanford, Calif.: Stanford University Press, 1974.

Rosenberg, Charles E. *The Cholera Years: The United States in 1832, 1849, and 1866*. Chicago: University of Chicago Press, 1962.

Rosenzweig, Roy. *Eight Hours for What We Will: Workers and Leisure in an Industrial City, 1870–1920*. New York: Cambridge University Press, 1983.

Roth, Randolph A. *The Democratic Dilemma: Religion, Reform, and the Social Order in the Connecticut River Valley of Vermont, 1791–1850*. New York: Cambridge University Press, 1987.

Rothman, Ellen K. *Hands and Hearts: A History of Courtship in America*. Cambridge: Harvard University Press, 1987.

Rotundo, E. Anthony. *American Manhood: Transformations in Masculinity from the Revolution to the Modern Era*. New York: Basic Books, 1993.

———. "Romantic Friendship: Male Intimacy and Middle-Class Youth in the Northern United States, 1800–1900." *Journal of Social History* 23, no. 1 (Fall 1989): 1–25.

Rubin, Lillian B. *Just Friends: The Role of Friendship in our Lives*. New York: Harper and Row, 1985.

Ruddick, Sara. *Maternal Thinking*. Boston: Beacon Press, 1989.

Ryan, Mary P. *Cradle of the Middle Class: The Family in Oneida County, New York, 1790–1865*. New York: Cambridge University Press, 1981.

———. *The Empire of the Mother: American Writing about Domesticity, 1830–1860*. New York: Harrington Park Press, 1985.

———. "The Power of Women's Networks: A Case Study of Female Moral Reform in Antebellum America." *Feminist Studies* 5, no. 1 (Spring 1979): 66–85.

———. *Women in Public: Between Banners and Ballots, 1825–1880*. Baltimore: Johns Hopkins University Press, 1990.

Salmon, Lucy. *Domestic Service*. New York: Macmillan, 1911.

Salmon, Marylynn. *Women and the Law of Property in Early America.* Chapel Hill: University of North Carolina Press, 1986.

Schlesinger, Arthur. *Learning How to Behave: A Historical Study of American Etiquette Books.* New York: Macmillan, 1946.

Scott, Joan Wallach. *Gender and the Politics of History.* New York: Columbia University Press, 1988.

Scott, Joan, and Louise Tilly. "Women's Work and the Family in Nineteenth-Century Europe." *Comparative Studies in Society and History* 17, no. 1 (January 1975): 36–64.

Sekora, John. "Black Message / White Envelope: Genre, Authenticity, and Authority in the Antebellum Slave Narrative." *Callaloo* 10, no. 3 (Summer 1987): 482–515.

Sellers, Charles. *The Market Revolution: Jacksonian America, 1815–1846.* New York: Oxford University Press, 1991.

Sennett, Richard. *The Fall of Public Man.* New York: Vintage, 1977.

Sherrod, Drury. "The Bonds of Men: Problems and Possibilities in Close Male Relationships." In *The Making of Masculinities: The New Men's Studies,* edited by Harry Brod, 213–39. Boston: Allen & Unwin, 1987.

Sklar, Kathryn Kish. *Catharine Beecher: A Study in American Domesticity.* New York: W. W. Norton, 1973.

Smelser, Neil J. *Social Change in the Industrial Revolution.* Chicago: University of Chicago Press, 1959.

Smith, Dorothy. "Women, the Family, and Corporate Capitalism." *Berkeley Journal of Sociology* 20 (1975): 55–91.

Smith, Edward D. *Climbing Jacob's Ladder: The Rise of Black Churches in Eastern American Cities, 1740–1877.* Washington, D.C.: Smithsonian Institution Press, 1988.

Smith-Rosenberg, Carroll. *Disorderly Conduct: Visions of Gender in Victorian America.* New York: Oxford University Press, 1986.

Spacks, Patricia Meyer. *Gossip.* Chicago: University of Chicago Press, 1985.

Stack, Carol B. *All Our Kin: Strategies for Survival in a Black Community.* New York: Harper and Row, 1974.

Stansell, Christine. *City of Women: Sex and Class in New York, 1789–1860.* New York: Knopf, 1986.

Stephenson, Charles. "A Gathering of Strangers? Mobility, Social Structure, and Political Participation in the Formation of Nineteenth-Century American Workingclass Culture." In *American Workingclass Culture: Explorations in American Labor and Social History,* edited by Milton Cantor, 31–60. Westport, Conn.: Greenwood Press, 1979.

Sterling, Dorothy. *Ahead of Her Time: Abby Kelley and the Politics of Antislavery.* New York: W. W. Norton, 1991.

———, ed. *We Are Your Sisters: Black Women in the Nineteenth Century.* New York: W. W. Norton, 1984.

Stevenson, Brenda, ed. *The Journals of Charlotte Forten Grimke.* New York: Oxford University Press, 1988.

Strasser, Susan. *Never Done: A History of American Housework.* New York: Pantheon, 1982.

Strathern, Marilyn. *Women In-Between: Female Roles in a Male World, Mount Hagen, New Guinea.* London: Seminar, 1972.

Strauss, Anselm. *Negotiations: Varieties, Contexts, Processes, and Social Order.* San Francisco: Jossey-Bass, 1978.

Szwed, John F. "Gossip, Drinking, and Social Control: Consensus and Communication in a Newfoundland Parish." *Ethnology 5*, no. 4 (October 1966): 434–41.

Thernstrom, Stephan. *Poverty and Progress: Social Mobility in a Nineteenth Century City.* Cambridge: Harvard University Press, 1964.

Thompson, Edward P. "Time, Work Discipline, and Industrial Capitalism." *Past and Present 38* (1967): 56–97.

Tilly, Charles. *Big Structures, Large Processes, Huge Comparisons.* New York: Russell Sage Foundation, 1984.

Tocqueville, Alexis de. *Democracy in America.* Edited by J. P. Mayer. Translated by George Lawrence. Garden City, N.Y.: Anchor, 1969.

Tomes, Nancy. "The Quaker Connection: Visiting Patterns Among Women in the Philadelphia Society of Friends, 1750–1850." In *Friends and Neighbors: Group Life in America's First Plural Society,* edited by Michael Zuckerman, 174–95. Philadelphia: Temple University Press, 1982.

Ulrich, Laurel Thatcher. *Good Wives: Image and Reality in the Lives of Women in Northern New England, 1650–1750.* New York: Oxford University Press, 1980.

———. "Housewife and Gadder: Themes of Self-sufficiency and Community in Eighteenth Century New England." In *"To Toil the Livelong Day": America's Women at Work, 1780–1980,* edited by Carol Groneman and Mary Beth Norton, 21–34. Ithaca: Cornell University Press, 1987.

———. *A Midwife's Tale: The Life of Martha Ballard, Based on Her Diary, 1785–1812.* New York: Knopf, 1990.

U.S. Bureau of the Census. *Historical Statistics of the U.S., Colonial Times to 1970.* Washington, D.C.: Bureau of the Census, 1975.

Vicinus, Martha. *Independent Women: Work and Community for Single Women, 1850–1920.* Chicago: Chicago University Press, 1985.

Vinovskis, Maris A. "Mortality Rates and Trends in Massachusetts Before 1860." *Journal of Economic History 32* (March 1972): 195–201.

Vogel, Lise. "'Humorous Incidents and the Sound Common Sense': More on the New England Mill Women." *Labor History 19,* no. 2 (Spring 1978): 280–86.

———. "Telling Tales: Historians of Our Own Lives." *Journal of Women's History 2,* no. 3 (Winter 1991): 89–101.

Walker, Karen. "Men, Women, and Friendship: What They Say; What They Do." *Gender & Society,* forthcoming.

Warbasse, Elizabeth Bowles. *The Changing Legal Rights of Married Women, 1800–1861.* New York: Garland Publishing, 1987.

Weedon, Chris. *Feminist Practice and Poststructuralist Theory.* New York: Basil Blackwell, 1987.

Weintraub, Jeff. "The Theory and Politics of the Public/Private Distinction." In *Public and Private in Thought and Practice: Perspectives on a Grand Di-*

chotomy, edited by Jeff Weintraub and Krishan Kumar, 1–33. Chicago: University of Chicago Press, forthcoming.

Welter, Barbara. "The Cult of True Womanhood: 1820–1860." *American Quarterly* 18, no. 2 (Summer 1966): 151–74.

Wertz, Richard W., and Dorothy C. Wertz. *Lying-In: A History of Childbirth in America*. New York: Free Press, 1977.

White, David O. "Addie Brown's Hartford." *Connecticut Historical Society Bulletin* 41, no. 2 (April 1976): 57–64A.

Wilentz, Sean. *Chants Democratic: New York City and the Rise of the American Working Class, 1788–1850*. New York: Oxford University Press, 1984.

Wilson, Peter J. "Filcher of Good Names: An Enquiry into Anthropology and Gossip." *Man* 9, no. 1 (March 1974): 93–102.

Wolfe, Alan. *Whose Keeper? Social Science and Moral Obligation*. Berkeley and Los Angeles: University of California Press, 1989.

Wolin, Sheldon. "Hannah Arendt: Democracy and the Political." *Salmagundi* 60 (Spring–Summer 1983): 3–19.

Woodward, C. Vann, ed. *Mary Chesnut's Civil War*. New Haven, Conn.: Yale University Press, 1981.

Wright, Paul H. "Men's Friendships, Women's Friendships, and the Alleged Inferiority of the Latter." *Sex Roles* 8, no. 1 (January 1982): 1–20.

Yacovone, Donald. "Abolitionists and the 'Language of Fraternal Love.'" In *Meanings for Manhood: Constructions of Masculinity in Victorian America*, edited by Mark C. Carnes and Clyde Griffen, 85–95. Chicago: University of Chicago Press, 1990.

Yanagisako, Sylvia Junko. "Family and Household: The Analysis of Domestic Groups." *Annual Review of Anthropology* 8 (1979): 161–205.

Yans-McLaughlin, Virginia. *Family and Community: Italian Immigrants in Buffalo, 1880–1930*. Urbana: University of Illinois Press, 1977.

Yeatman, Anna. "Gender and the Differentiation of Social Life into Public and Domestic Domains." *Social Analysis* 15 (August 1984): 32–49.

Young, Michael, and Peter Wilmott. *Family and Kinship in East London*. New York: Penguin, 1962.

Zaretsky, Eli. *Capitalism, the Family, and Personal Life*. New York: Harper and Row, 1976.

Zboray, Ronald J. *A Fictive People: Antebellum Economic Development and the American Reading Public*. New York: Oxford University Press, 1992.

———. "The Letter and the Fiction-Reading Public in Antebellum America." *Journal of American Culture* 10, no. 1 (Spring 1987): 27–34.

Zeliger, Viviana. *Pricing the Priceless Child: The Changing Social Value of Children*. New York: Basic, 1985.

Zonderman, David A. *Aspirations and Anxieties: New England Workers and the Mechanized Factory System, 1815–1850*. New York: Oxford University Press, 1992.

Index

Compositor: Terry Robinson & Co., Inc.
Text: 10/13 Sabon
Display: Sabon
Printer: Malloy Lithographing, Inc.
Binder: John H. Dekker & Sons